Lecture Notes in Computer Science 16679

The series Lecture Notes in Computer Science (LNCS), including its subseries Lecture Notes in Artificial Intelligence (LNAI) and Lecture Notes in Bioinformatics (LNBI), has established itself as a medium for the publication of new developments in computer science and information technology research, teaching, and education.

LNCS enjoys close cooperation with the computer science R & D community, the series counts many renowned academics among its volume editors and paper authors, and collaborates with prestigious societies. Its mission is to serve this international community by providing an invaluable service, mainly focused on the publication of conference and workshop proceedings and postproceedings. LNCS commenced publication in 1973.

Jesica de Armas · Eduardo Lalla Ruiz
Editors

Logistics and Maritime Systems

14th International Conference, LOGMS 2026
Held in Conjunction with EUROMar 2026
Barcelona, Spain, July 7–10, 2026
Proceedings

Springer

Editors
Jesica de Armas
Universitat Pompeu Fabra
Barcelona, Spain

Eduardo Lalla Ruiz
University of Twente
Enschede, The Netherlands

ISSN 0302-9743 ISSN 1611-3349 (electronic)
Lecture Notes in Computer Science
ISBN 978-3-032-30794-1 ISBN 978-3-032-30795-8 (eBook)
https://doi.org/10.1007/978-3-032-30795-8

This Springer imprint is published by the registered company Springer Nature Switzerland AG
The registered company address is: Gewerbestrasse 11, 6330 Cham, Switzerland

Preface

This volume contains the proceedings of the 14th International Conference on Logistics and Maritime Systems (LOGMS 2026), jointly organized with the EUROMar Conference on Maritime Optimization and Logistics (EUROMar 2026). The event took place from July 7 to July 10, 2026, at the Universitat Pompeu Fabra, Campus de la Ciutadella, in Barcelona, Spain.

Under the overarching theme of "Networks, Energy and Intelligence: Designing the Next Generation of Maritime Logistics", the conference served as a premier platform for establishing international networks among researchers and practitioners. Since its inception in 2005, the LOGMS conference series has continually brought together maritime logistics and systems experts to share innovative research methodologies, present groundbreaking results, and explore future development directions in port operations, sustainable shipping, and advanced maritime digitalization. The EUROMar series of conferences organized by the EURO Working Group on Maritime and Port Logistics is dedicated to fostering collaboration and advancing research in maritime and port logistics across Europe and beyond. The joint organization of LOGMS and EUROMar reflects a shared commitment to bridging communities and strengthening the international research network in this field.

The high quality of the scientific program was ensured through a rigorous evaluation process. Every submission underwent a strict single-blind peer-review process, with each paper carefully evaluated by at least two independent expert reviewers. For this edition, we received a total of 35 short paper submissions. Following the thorough review phase, 25 papers were accepted for presentation and publication in this volume, reflecting a highly competitive and scientifically rigorous selection process.

We extend our deepest gratitude to all the authors who contributed their latest research to the conference. Their insightful presentations, thought-provoking questions, and inspiring comments significantly contributed to the progression of scientific advances in the field. We also wish to express our sincere appreciation to the members of the Steering and Program Committees, whose dedication and hard work were instrumental in the success of LOGMS and EUROMar 2026.

May 2026

Jésica de Armas
Eduardo Lalla-Ruiz

Organization

General Chair

Jésica de Armas	Universitat Pompeu Fabra, Spain

Program Committee Chairs

Sara Hatami	Universitat Politècnica de Catalunya, Spain
Eduardo Lalla-Ruiz	University of Twente, Netherlands
Jessica Rodríguez Pereira	Universitat Politècnica de Catalunya, Spain
Jingjing Yu	Universitat Pompeu Fabra, Spain

Steering Committee

Roar Adland	Simpson Spence Young, UK
Panagiotis Angeloudis	Imperial College London, UK
Hyerim Bae	Pusan National University, South Korea
Michael Bell	University of Sydney, Australia
Christian Bierwirth	Martin Luther University Halle-Wittenberg, Germany
Chew Ek Peng	National University of Singapore, Singapore
Rommert Dekker	Erasmus University Rotterdam, Netherlands
Leonard Heilig	University of Hamburg, Germany
Haiying Jia	Norwegian School of Economics, Norway
Kap Hwan Kim	Zhejiang University, China
Erhan Kozan	Queensland University of Technology, Australia
Paul Tae-Woo Lee	Zhejiang University, China
Chengji Liang	Shanghai Maritime University, China
Xuan Qiu	Hong Kong University of Science and Technology, China
Fan Wang	Sun Yat-sen University, China
Zhou Yanjie	Zhengzhou University, China

Program Committee

Rocio Alfaro Pozo	Universitat Politècnica de Catalunya, Spain
Majsa Ammouriova	German Jordanian University, Jordan
Sean Arisian	La Trobe University, Australia
Kai Brüssau	University of Hamburg, Germany
Philip Cammin	University of Hamburg, Germany
Pedro Jesus Copado Mendez	Universitat Politècnica de Catalunya, Spain
Sofia Estelles-Miguel	Universitat Politècnica de València, Spain
Christopher Expósito Izquierdo	Universidad de La Laguna, Spain
Asefe Forghani	Cranfield University, UK
Eliana María González Neira	Pontificia Universidad Javeriana, Colombia
Marc Juanpera	Universitat Politècnica de Catalunya, Spain
Mehdi A. Kamran	German University of Technology in Oman, Oman
Julio César Londoño	Universidad del Valle, Colombia
Manuel Mateo-Doll	Universitat Politècnica de Catalunya, Spain
Belén Melián Batista	Universidad de La Laguna, Spain
J. Marcos Moreno Vega	Universidad de La Laguna, Spain
Paz Perez-Gonzalez	University of Seville, Spain
Antonin Ponsich	Universitat Politècnica de Catalunya, Spain
Lorena S. Reyes Rubiano	RWTH Aachen University, Germany
Alberto Santini	Universitat Pompeu Fabra, Spain
Carla Talens	University of Seville, Spain
Mehdi Toloo	University of Surrey, UK
Thalis Zis	Cyprus University of Technology, Cyprus

EUROMar Committee

Eduardo Lalla-Ruiz	University of Twente, Netherlands
Dario Pacino	Technical University of Denmark, Denmark
Rosa González Ramírez	Universidad de Los Andes, Chile
Frederik Schulte	Delft University of Technology, Netherlands
Çağatay Iris	University of Liverpool, UK

Contents

Port Operations and Terminal Optimization

Bi-level Simulation-Optimisation Strategies for Solving the Berth Allocation Problem in Non-container Ports

Joseph Collins(✉) and Alexandru-Ciprian Zăvoianu

School of Computing, Engineering and Technology, Robert Gordon University, Aberdeen, Scotland, UK
{j.collins1,c.zavoianu}@rgu.ac.uk

Abstract. Traditional Berth Allocation Problem (BAP) research predominantly addresses high-throughput container terminals, often overlooking the complex constraints inherent in non-container ports. This paper proposes a bi-level simulation-optimisation framework designed to automate scheduling in these highly constrained environments. The best-performing of two bi-level solvers employs a $(\mu + \lambda)$ Evolution Strategy (ES) on the upper level to manage berth and temporal shift relaxations, while the lower level utilises a CP-SAT solver to ensure deterministic feasibility across a nodal graph of the port's topology. The methodology incorporates high-fidelity constraints, including minute-by-minute tidal depth verification and non-overlapping waterway transits. Using the Port of Aberdeen as a case study, the bi-level solvers were evaluated against eight real-world scenarios of increasing complexity. Results indicate that bi-level approaches consistently identifies near-global optima where purely stochastic baselines fail. The findings demonstrate that the proposed architecture provides a scalable and robust solution for complex maritime logistics, balancing operational efficiency with absolute safety requirements.

Keywords: Berth Allocation Problem · Bi-level optimisation · Non-container ports · CP-SAT solver · Tide-dependent constraints

1 Introduction and Motivation

In the domain of maritime logistics, the Berth Allocation Problem (BAP) [2] has traditionally focused on high-throughput container terminals where the primary objective is the efficient movement of standardised container units [3]. However, many non-container ports across the globe operate under significantly different environments where lower throughput is offset by high-complexity physical and environmental constraints. In these settings, the lack of dedicated BAP research forces port authorities to rely heavily on manual planning, which cannot quickly check alternative plans and is prone to inefficiencies regarding vessel interactions.

J. de Armas and E. Lalla Ruiz (Eds.): LOGMS 2026, LNCS 16679, pp. 3–14, 2027.
https://doi.org/10.1007/978-3-032-30795-8_1

Given the NP-hard nature of the BAP [7], developing an automated solver for non-container settings requires a framework capable of navigating (very) large solution spaces while adhering to a strict set of heterogeneous constraints. Domain experts have indicated that for a solver to be practically viable, it must prioritise absolute feasibility and safety over theoretical optimality. Specifically, any proposed solution must account for multi-stage vessel requests – including arrival, internal movements, berthing and departure – while respecting the predefined order of operations. Furthermore, the solver must integrate static physical dimensions of pertinent vessels and berths with dynamic environmental variables, such as time-varying tide levels and draught requirements.

As a case study, in the present work we focus on the Port of Aberdeen (PoA) – the UK's largest trust port. Its geographic position in the North-East of Scotland, makes it a critical hub for the global energy industry in the North Sea, with a higher vessel throughput than other UK non-container ports. Furthermore, after nine hundred years of being situated in the centre of Aberdeen, in 2023, the PoA completed a £420 million expansion that resulted in the construction of an additional harbour containing large deep-water berths capable of accommodating offshore platforms, cruise ships and other large vessels. For the first time, the PoA is split across two harbours, having two harbour control towers. Daily berthing plans must now account for vessel traffic between the harbours, causing increased traffic and delays in the entrance waterways. These plans are time consuming to create, and are inflexible to handling increases in requests. In light of these reasons, the PoA is an excellent choice for validating our approach to solving BAPs as an effective computational solver would enable staff to improve operational performance by significantly reducing the time to (re-)create a berthing plan while simultaneously ensuring a better exploration of berthing options.

The remainder of this paper is organised as follows: Section 2 describes our formalisation of the BAP for non-container ports (i.e., the BAP-NCP). Section 3 describes our novel bi-level approach to solving the problem. Section 4 presents the deatils of the real-world case study. In Sect. 5 we present the setup and results of our numerical experiments alongside their interpretation. Finally, Sect. 6 contains conclusions and gives an outlook on future work.

2 Problem Description and Formalisation

The main challenge of the standard Berth Allocation Problem is to assign (incoming) vessels to specific mooring locations (i.e., berths) along a quay and determine their associated service times in such a way that minimises waiting and handling intervals in order to maximise overall port throughput. In non-container ports, berth servicing levels are fairly heterogenous (e.g., fueling might only be available at some specific berths, heavy cranes and direct link to rail at others) so internal harbour movements required to fully service a vessel also need to be factored in. Furthermore, given the higher likelihood of specialised servicing requirements/contractually-linked onshore supply chains, vessels are far more likely to also have "preferred berthing locations" within a non-container port. Lastly, non-container ports are more likely to be historical in nature and therefore have geographically-constrained layouts.

Each of our BAP-NCPs scenarios is defined by a list of vessel (movement) requests that must be carried out in the planning horizon. Each entry in the requests list contains detail regarding the vessel (name, length, breadth, draught), the type of request (*arrival*, intra-port *movement*/berth change, *sailing* out), preferred berth, and the preferred earliest start time. If the vessel is currently in Port (likely in the case of intra-port movements and sailings), the current berth is also specified.

In its simplest interpretation, the BAP-NCP can be seen as a permutation-based scheduling problem: the goal is to find the best possible ordering (not: R^*) for the vessel requests. The underlying assumption for this interpretation is that requests will be processed in the specified order, but the actual resolution for each request r_k depends on the state of the port when the individual request is initiated. Thus, if previously processed requests $r_1 \ldots r_{k-1}$ are blocking a critical waterway or berth, the actual start time of r_k will be delayed accordingly. If the incurred delays result in not being able to process a request in the specified planning horizon the entire proposed ordering (i.e., schedule) is not valid. Otherwise, a penalty will be applied to each delayed request, resulting in an overall weighted delay penalty for an arbitrary schedule R given by:

$$P_{sch}(R) = \sum_{i=1}^{|R|}(V_i \cdot \Delta t_i \cdot W_i) \tag{1}$$

where: V_i is the volume (tonnage) of the vessel from position i in the (ordered) request list, Δt_i is the delay in minutes from the preferred start time, W_i is the operational weight with $W_i = 2$ for sailings and $W_i = 1$ otherwise. It is worth noting that weighting by tonnage and prioritising sailings (i.e., creating space in the port) can be seen as proxies for revenue generation and client satisfaction.

If two vessels request the same berth for the entire planning horizon, the purely permutation-based version of the BAP-NCP will not have a valid solution. To mitigate this, we allow the relaxation of original vessel requests based on a differentiation between preferred berth types. Thus, we distinguish between *true wildcards* (where, based on the original request, any valid berth can be assigned), *relaxed wildcards* (where there is a preferred berth in the original movement request but any valid berth can be assigned upon the relaxation of the request) and *fixed berths* (where the preferred berth from the original movement request must be used). An arbitrary ordering R, incurs a weighted penalty for every relaxed wildcard:

$$P_{rlx}(R) = \sum_{i=1}^{|R|}(\alpha_i + (\beta_i \cdot d_i(o, r))) \tag{2}$$

where: α_i is a constant penalty for the act of relaxing the fixed request in position i in the movement request list R, β_i is a scaling coefficient for geographical deviation and $d_i(o, r)$ is the topological distance (sailing time derived) between the originally preferred berth o and the assigned berth after relaxation r. For requests that have not been relaxed $\alpha = \beta = 0$.

Finally, our BAP-NCP can be defined as finding an ordering of vessel movement requests R^* that minimises P_{tot} - the overall scheduling and relaxation penalty, i.e.:

$$P_{tot}(R) = p_{sch}(R) + p_{rlx}(R) \tag{3}$$

3 Proposed Methodology

3.1 The Baseline

Our baseline strategy is inspired to a large extent from the classic (human-based) way of handling vessel (movement) requests: priorities are established (based on intrinsic port operation heuristics and/or staff experience) and requests are subsequently processed in decreasing order of their priority. If a vessel can't be assigned to its preferred berth, it will wait for it to become available. If the latter does not happen, the vessel will be directed towards the nearest berth from a predetermined *Valid Berth Set* (V)[1]. This approach prioritises ordering/scheduling (Eq. 1) with relaxation (Eq. 2) used as a measure of last resort.

In order to emulate this, we have opted to couple a random search heuristic (not: **RND**) with a purpose-built lightweight discrete event simulator [6] that traces the movements of vessels using a spatial-temporal graph-based representation of the port. This graph based representation allows the system to track the position of any vessel during the planning horizon across key nodes of interest (e.g., berths, waterways/channels), while realistic transit times between all node pairs are based on historical Automatic Identification System (AIS) data of port movements coupled with Dijkstra's algorithm [4] for rare routing combinations. The advantage is that it allows for fast simulations at different levels of temporal detail, while also offering the ability to quickly model different port setups.

3.2 Job Shop Scheduling Model and CP-SAT Solver

The primary scheduling part of the BAP-NCP lends itself very well to modelling (being reformulated) as a classic *Job-Shop Problem* (JSP) [1] where each node within the port's navigational infrastructure is modelled as a *machine* with a predefined unit capacity. Each vessel request (i.e., job) is decomposed into a sequence of dependent tasks across these machines. The processing time for each task is derived using historical data and Dijkstra's algorithm as in the baseline approach.

In order to solve the JSP, we apply Google OR-Tools' CP-SAT solver [9] that uses a constraint programming (CP) approach to solve combinatorial optimisation problems. In our case, CP-SAT enforces the following deterministic constraints aimed to ensure the physical and operational viability of the schedule:

---

[1] For each vessel request i, the associated valid berth set V_i contains only those berths whose physical constraints (length, depth, and specialised equipment) meet or exceed the requirements of the requesting vessel.

Precedence Constraints: Every vessel follows a strictly ordered chain of operations: *arrival* → (intra-port) *movements* → *sailing*. Any additional intra-port movements between berths must maintain this chronological sequence, where the start time of task n is $\geq$ the completion time of task $n-1$.

Tide Constraints: A vessels transit is only permitted if the water depth at a node (accounting for tidal variations) exceeds the vessel's draught plus a user-defined safety margin. *Nodes with insufficient depth are pre-filtered during the Valid Berth Set (V_i) generation.*

Resource Disjunction (No-Overlap): Nodes are treated as non-shareable resources (i.e., unit capacity = 1). With the exception of the designated anchorage area (i.e., unit capacity = ∞), no two vessels may occupy the same node simultaneously.

Temporal Lower Bounds: A request's actual start time is constrained by the value specified in the preferred earliest start time field. The solver may delay the operation associated with a request to resolve conflicts but cannot move it earlier than the pre-defined time.

3.3 Iterative Bi-level Approach

In its basic form, the CP-SAT solver cannot produce solutions for scenarios where vessels compete for the same shared resource (e.g., same fixed berth for the entire planning horizon). The approach we adopt is to embed the scheduling-focused CP-SAT in a bi-level optimisation approach [5] in which it is coupled with a higher-level heuristic that is responsible for the relaxation policy.

Our first heuristic approach is iterative in nature (not: **ITR**) and only targets berth relaxation. The procedure first assigns a random berth from the valid berth set (V_i) for every request i that has a *true wildcard* berth. It then runs CP-SAT to calculate the final (scheduling) solution. If a solution cannot be found, an increasing number of *fixed* berths are considered for relaxation. Firstly, single individual *fixed* berths are independently switched to a *relaxed wildcard.* In ITR, a relaxed wildcard is always assigned to the valid berth that is closest (lowest β) to the original preferred wildcard before running CP-SAT. If none of the runs with a single *relaxed wildcard* returns a valid schedule, ITR will proceed to relax two *fixed* berths at the same time. The procedure continues to increase the number of simultaneously relaxed berths until CP-SAT produces a valid schedule and the only requirement to eventually achieve this is that the port has sufficient empty berths to satisfy the vessel request list in the considered planning horizon.

While it is possible to design a single level wildcard-aware global optimiser with OR-Tools, the likely presence of concurrent wildcards within BAP-NCP formulations can easily make even medium-scale instances computationally intractable. In our real-world case study, a chain of requests for the same vessel of the form "*arrival* to *true wildcard 1* → (intra-port) *movement* to *true wildcard 2* → (intra-port) *movement* to *fixed*" can entail more than $35 \cdot 35 = 1225$ combinations between the two wildcards if the requested services are widely available and the port is relatively empty, resulting in large valid berth sets for both wildcards. A metaheuristic-based (global) search avoids this, allowing our approach to scale efficiently for larger global ports and a higher number of requests.

3.4 Evolutionary Bi-level Approach

Our second (meta) heuristic approach comes in the form of a $(\mu + \lambda)$ Evolution Strategy [10] (not: **EVO**) that aims to relax both berth and temporal lower bound constraints. The reason for the latter is historical practice: in certain situations, discussions can be initiated to pull forward the earliest start time of a request within a limited time interval. In order to produce human-competitive results across a variety of planning scenarios, the automated solver must have the option to integrate such types of time-wise relaxations.

Chromosomes (i.e., solution candidates) in our ES implementation use a triplet of three consecutive genes (b_i, l_i, t_i) to encode choices/modifiers associated with each original vessel request i. Therefore, the size of the ES encoding is $3|R|$ where R is the original list of vessel (movement) requests. Each encoding triplet contains:

A Berth Gene (b_i): An integer index representing the specific choice from the valid berth set V_i. By restricting the gene's domain to V_i, the ES avoids evaluating physically impossible solutions, significantly reducing the effective search space. It also avoids the need for a repair operator.

A Lock Gene (l_i): A boolean {True, False} that denotes whether the specific request is eligible for berth mutation (i.e., relaxation). If l_i = True, the ES is prohibited from altering the Berth Gene, effectively treating the request as a fixed constraint while still allowing for temporal shifts.

A Temporal Relaxation Gene (t_i): A real value $\in [0, 1]$ representing a shift earlier than the original desired start time.

The overall ES for BAP-NCP presented in Algorithm 1 follows the standard $(\mu + \lambda)$ elitist approach with two domain adaptations worth highlighting, apart from the mandatory problem-specific fitness assignment on Line 9. The first one concerns initialisation (Lines 2 to 5), where the initial population is seeded with the original requests list R and stochastic (mutation-based) variants of R that aim to ensure a wide spread over the search space.

As with most ES approaches, the key part is the Mutation operator (Lines 4 and 18) as it is linked to our chosen encoding triplet. Our mutation process is governed by three independent stochastic trials based on pre-defined probability parameters: Pr_b, Pr_l, and Pr_t. After generating three uniformly distributed random values $r_b, r_l, r_t \in [0, 1]$, the mutation logic relaxes constraints as follows:

1. **Berth Change:** If $r_b < Pr_b$ and $l_i = False$, a new berth is selected for request i via uniform random sampling from the *valid berth set* V_i.
2. **Berth Unlock:** If $r_l < Pr_l$ and $(l_i = True)$, l_i will be toggled to $False$, making request i eligible for future berth changes.

Algorithm 1. $(\mu + \lambda)$ Evolution Strategy for BAP-NCP

Input: number of parents μ, number of offspring λ, requests list R, generations g
$Pop \leftarrow \{R\}$
for λ times **do** ▷ build initial population
    $Pop \leftarrow Pop \cup \{\text{Mutate}(\text{Copy}(R))\}$
end for
$Best \leftarrow \emptyset$
repeat
    for each individual $Ind_i \in Pop$ **do**
        $Ind_i.fitness \leftarrow \text{CP-SAT}(Ind_i)+P_{rlx}(Ind_i)$
        if $Best = \emptyset$ **or** $Ind_i.fitness > Best.fitness$ **then**
            $Best \leftarrow Ind_i$
        end if
    end for
    $Elites \leftarrow$ the μ individuals in Pop with best fitness ▷ Truncation Selection
    $Pop \leftarrow Elites$
    for each individual $E_j \in Elites$ **do**
        for $\frac{\lambda}{\mu}$ times **do**
            $Pop \leftarrow Pop \cup \{\text{Mutate}(\text{Copy}(E_j))\}$
        end for
    end for
    $g \leftarrow g - 1$
until $g = 0$
return $Best$

3. **Temporal Shift:** If $r_t < Pr_t$, a random magnitude δ is added to or subtracted from the current *temporal relaxation gene* (t_i).

To maintain the relaxation within a user pre-defined temporal shift window $[0, T_{max}]$, wihere T_{max} corresponds to the gene setting $t_i = 1$, we implemented a *reflective boundary condition* on t_i mutations. In the first step, the base mutation is computed as:

$$t_i = t_i + (\delta \times sgn) \tag{4}$$

where $\delta \in [0, 0.5]$ is a uniformly distributed random magnitude and $sgn \in \{-1, 1\}$ is a random sign multiplier. In the second step, to ensure the shift remains within the normalised domain $[0, 1]$, we apply:

$$\Delta t_i = \begin{cases} 2.0 - t_i & \text{if } t_i > 1.0 \\ -t_i & \text{if } t_i < 0.0 \end{cases} \tag{5}$$

4 Case Study Scenarios

The Port of Aberdeen made their harbour layout, the berthing facilities, berth physical properties, tidal data and safety-related operating procedures available for our research. Furthermore, port personnel provided the historical AIS data that underpin the realistic movement time and routing assumptions our models operate with. We used this information to create the nodal map of the port shown in Fig. 1 which is used by the solvers when requiring critical scheduling information (e.g., berth facilities, water levels, routing times, waterway capacity).

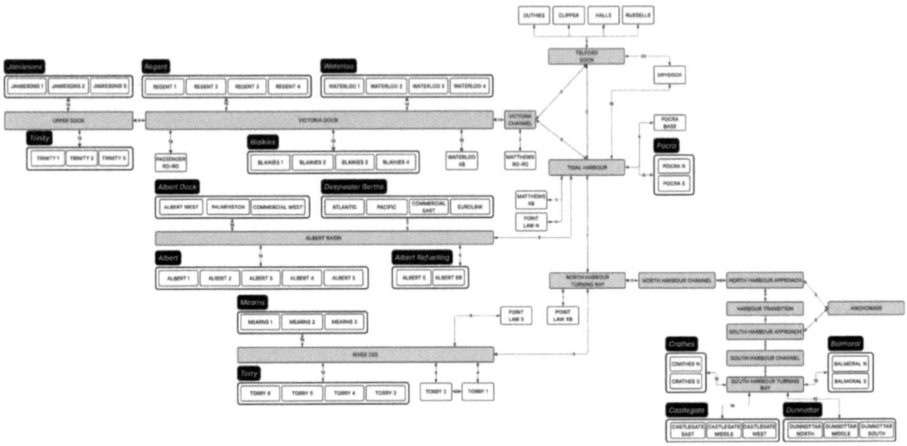

Fig. 1. The Nodal Graph of the Port of Aberdeen

To validate and stress test the solver we created eight scenarios that aim to replicate those that port staff solve regularly. These scenarios range from simple planning with no conflicts, to high traffic standard days, and operationally complex storm haven situations where up to eight additional vessels of varying sizes have to be accommodated:

Scenario 1 (Baseline): Three vessels arrive, perform an internal movement and depart. This establishes a baseline schedule with no conflicts, checking the solver's basic functionality.

Scenario 2 (Drydock/Berth Conflict): There is a forced berth overlap between vessels of different size. It assesses if a solver can successfully reallocate a vessel when its primary choice is not available and if a solver is able to prioritise larger vessels as per Eq. 1.

Scenario 3 (Escort Logic): A test of the solver's ability to maintain safe separation distances between a large vessel and their support craft. Suitable berthing nearby should be found for the smaller vessel. This tests a solver's ability to manage temporal and berth conflicts.

Scenario 4 (Standard Day): A mix of transits and shared berths designed to test all hard constraints. In addition, one vessel wishes to arrive at low tide, but must wait for high tide to satisfy depth requirements. This assesses a solver's tidal routing capability, and the user defined critera that a vessel should not be penalised for tide delays.

Scenario 5 (Escort Bottleneck): A high-stakes version of Scenario 3, where four vessels compete for the same specialised infrastructure, testing the priority weighting logic in the objective function.

Scenario 6 (Wildcard Arrivals): Eight vessels arrive in a relatively tight interval with no requested berths. This assesses the capability of the solver to assign suitable berths in a way that does not cause blockages, while also minimising delays.

Scenario 7 & 8 (Stress Tests): Combining Scenario 4 and Scenario 6, Scenario 7 is limited to arrivals and sailings. Scenario 8 adds the full complexity of *internal movements*. These scenarios allow stress testing the port by simulating higher than standard traffic caused by an upcoming storm.

We summarise in Table 1 the key features of our 8 test scenarios, including $|R|$ – the total number of vessel (movement) requests. Across all scenarios we used a planning horizon of 24 h, a high time-scale precision of 1 min (PoA human-designed schedules use 15 min) and a tide-level update rate of 1 h. In particular, we used tidal data from the 5th December 2024. Across all numerical experiments and solvers, we use the same penalty parameterisation that is largely informed by PoA practice. Thus, in Eq. 2, we have set $\alpha_i = 0$ and $\beta_i = 20$ with the topological distances between *o*riginal and *r*elaxed berths $d_i(o, r)$ normalised between 1 (closest possible) and 100 (furthest possible) using an exponential scale. Furthermore in Eq. 1, Δt_i is quantised in 15 min intervals (42 min delay $\Rightarrow \Delta t_i = 3$) and the vessel volume is divided by 1000.

Table 1. Experimental Scenarios for the Port of Aberdeen Case Study

ID	Scenario	Traffic	$\|R\|$	Primary Constraint/Conflict
1	Baseline	Low	7	No conflicts
2	Drydock/Berth Conflict	Low	7	Two vessels allocated to same berth
3	Escort Logic	Low	8	Smaller vessel follows large vessel closely
4	Standard Day	Medium	11	Mixed transit, same berths and forced delays
5	Escort Bottleneck	Medium	12	Four vessels selecting same berths
6	Wildcard Arrivals	High	8	Eight true wildcard arrivals
7	Stress Test - External	High	17	Standard day with true wildcard arrivals
8	Stress Test - Full	High	19	As 7, with extra internal movements

5 Numerical Experiments and Results

When comparing the three solvers (i.e., RND, ITR and EVO) across the 8 scenarios we used a budget of 1000 solution candidates (i.e., scheduling attempts). Given the stochastic nature of each solver, we made 30 independent repeats for each experiment. The EVO solver uses a parameterisation of $\mu = 5$ and $\lambda = 20$ and $T_{max} = 1h$ aimed at ensuring a relevant number of generations (i.e., 40) within the somewhat limited evaluations budget. The summary of results is presented in Table 2. The observed difference between the (average) best results of EVO and ITR for scenarios 3 and 5 is confirmed as statistically significant (one-tailed Mann-Whitney U test [8] calculated at 5% significance). However, it is worth mentioning that ITR was the only solver that achieved a 30/30 (i.e., 100%) success rate across all experiments EVO achieved only a 93.3% (28/30) success ratio on Scenario 5, while RND achieved only 56.7% on Scenario 5 (17/30) and 80% on Scenario 3 (24/30).

Table 2. $P_{tot}(R)$ average performance of RND, ITR, EVO and the associate average iteration/attempt no. when the best solutions were found. Best results are highlighted.

ID	Best Solution			Attempt No.		
	RND	*ITR*	*EVO*	*RND*	*ITR*	*EVO*
1	**0.00**	**0.00**	**0.00**	23	1	**0.4**
2	27.12	**26.55**	**26.55**	482	**4**	167
3	130.59	44.76	**5.97**	284	**22**	194
4	8.13	**0.00**	**0.00**	367	1	**0.87**
5	265.00	80.00	**65.14**	407	**163**	630
6	86.10	**0.00**	**0.00**	377	**1**	1.5
7	99.33	**0.00**	**0.00**	427	6	**2.0**
8	206.7	**0.00**	**0.00**	473	9	**6.4**
ALL	102.87	18.91	12.20	355	25.87	125.27

The experimental results indicate a clear progression in solver capability, from a basic stochastic search to a robust bi-level evolutionary architecture. Thus, the RND baseline solver can identify acceptable schedules in low-complexity environments (scenarios 1,2) and accommodate limited temporal conflicts (scenario 4). It does not scale well when faced with complexity (high traffic and wildcards) as shown in Scenarios 6–8 or increased levels of temporal conflict (scenarios 3 and 5). The basic top-level heuristic of ITR is able to address the operational requirement for berth flexibility (i.e., relaxation). This translates to perfect ITR performance on scenarios with high-complexity (6–8) and limited temporal conflict (4). With respect to RND, ITR also shows improved performance when temporal conflicts are increased (scenarios 3 and 5). The extra flexibility of EVO to also relax the temporal lower bound constraint by at most $T_{max} = 1$ h/request results in further increased performance on scenarios 3 and 5 and the best overall performance across our 8-scenario benchmark. This performance appears to be associated with an increased exploration of the search space for on scenarios with strong conflicts (i.e., 2, 3 and 5).

6 Conclusions and Future Work

This research has introduced novel bi-level approaches for the Berth Allocation Problem in non-container ports. By decoupling high-level (meta)heuristic exploration (especially a global approach like Evolution Strategies) from low-level deterministic constraint satisfaction (CP-SAT), we have developed solvers capable of navigating an NP-hard search space while respecting the rigid physical and environmental constraints of a modern trust port.

The application of an evolutionary bi-level approach to the Port of Aberdeen case study confirms its practical utility. The solver successfully managed the transition between dual-harbour topologies, resolved complex wildcard arrival scenarios and temporal conflicts that typically necessitate intensive manual planning. Very good performances across the 8-scenario benchmark set suggest that bi-level approaches offer a viable path toward the digital transformation of PoA port control operations. Overall, this work provides ports with a tool that, while prioritising safety and feasibility, ensures that efficient automated scheduling becomes accessible and reliable in the face of increasing maritime traffic.

Future work will focus on stress-testing the solver with time-constrained heterogeneous task types and more complex scenarios. By introducing berth-specific constraints for in-demand specialised operations – such as bunkering, mechanical repairs, or fresh-water replenishment – the present modelling and optimisation strategy can be extended to reflect the resource-constrained nature of modern multi-service port facilities.

References

1. Applegate, D., Cook, W.: A computational study of the job-shop scheduling problem. ORSA J. Comput. **3**(2), 149–156 (1991)
2. Bierwirth, C., Meisel, F.: A survey of berth allocation and quay crane scheduling problems in container terminals. Eur. J. Oper. Res. **202**, 1–15 (2010)
3. Carlo, H.J., Vis, I.F., Roodbergen, K.J.: Storage yard operations in container terminals: literature overview, trends, and research directions. Eur. J. Oper. Res. **235**(2), 412–430 (2014)
4. Dijkstra, E.W.: A note on two problems in connexion with graphs. Numer. Math. **1**(1), 269–271 (1959)
5. Lassoued, R., Elloumi, A.: A bi-level optimization model for solving the berth and quay cranes allocation problems in port terminal. In: 2021 International Conference on Decision Aid Sciences and Application (DASA), pp. 1095–1100. IEEE (2021)
6. Legato, P., Mazza, R.M.: Berth planning and resources optimisation at a container terminal via discrete event simulation. Eur. J. Oper. Res. **133**(3), 537–547 (2001)
7. Lim, A.: The berth allocation problem with specific quay cranes. Naval Res. Logist. (NRL) **45**(1), 89–104 (1998)
8. Mann, H.B., Whitney, D.R.: On a test of whether one of two random variables is stochastically larger than the other. Ann. Math. Stat. 50–60 (1947)

9. Perron, L., Didier, F.: Cp-sat solver (v9.12) (2025). https://developers.google.com/optimization, google Optimization Tools (OR-Tools)
10. Rechenberg, I.: The evolution strategy. a mathematical model of darwinian evolution. In: Synergetics—From Microscopic to Macroscopic Order: Proceedings of the International Symposium on Synergetics at Berlin, 4–8 July 1983, pp. 122–132. Springer, Heidelberg (1984). https://doi.org/10.1007/978-3-642-69540-7_13

A Reinforcement Learning Approach for the Dynamic Berth Allocation Problem

Carlos March Moya[1(✉)], Frederik Schulte[1], Kevin Tierney[2], and Neil Yorke-Smith[1]

[1] Delft University of Technology, Delft, The Netherlands
{c.marchmoya,f.schulte,n.yorke-smith}@tudelft.nl
[2] Department of Business Decisions and Analytics, University of Vienna, Vienna, Austria
kevin.tierney@univie.ac.at

Abstract. Efficiently assigning vessels to berths in a busy port is a hard scheduling problem: decisions must be made in real time, under uncertainty about future arrivals, and with the goal of minimizing how long ships spend in the port. We present a learning-based approach in which an agent is trained, purely through trial and error, to perform these assignments one at a time as the vessels arrive. The agent represents the current port state as a graph, capturing relationships between waiting vessels, available berths, and ships still on their way, and learns which assignments are promising via graph-based attention. Our formulation incorporates vessel priorities, berth-dependent handling times, and a skip action that allows the agent to postpone assignments when beneficial. Across a range of port congestion levels, the trained agent outperforms classical heuristic rules, achieving on average a 20% reduction in priority-weighted turnaround cost relative to the best heuristic baseline.

Keywords: Berth Allocation Problem · Reinforcement Learning · Graph Neural Networks · Operational Research

1 Introduction

Berth Allocation represents one of the bottlenecks in maritime logistics, significantly increasing the time that vessels spend in virtual queues and, therefore, contributing substantially to emissions associated with port operations [10]. Indeed, emissions associated with port calls and anchorage waiting can reach levels comparable to the annual emissions of entire countries, as reported in the case of the Port of Rotterdam. This highlights the critical role of efficient berth allocation not only in improving port performance but also in advancing decarbonization efforts within maritime transport.

Efficient and intelligent port logistics are therefore essential to ensure the smooth operation of global supply chains while reducing both operational costs

J. de Armas and E. Lalla Ruiz (Eds.): LOGMS 2026, LNCS 16679, pp. 15–26, 2027.
https://doi.org/10.1007/978-3-032-30795-8_2

and environmental impact. Within this context, one of the core operational optimization problems is the Berth Allocation Problem (BAP), which consists of deciding to which berth each arriving vessel should be assigned and at what time, taking into account berth-dependent handling times and operational constraints. When vessels arrive dynamically over time rather than being in the port at the beginning of the planning horizon, the problem is referred to as the Dynamic Berth Allocation Problem (DBAP).

The BAP is an NP-hard problem [4], and its dynamic nature makes real-time decision-making particularly challenging. In practice, ports often rely on simple dispatching rules due to their speed and ease of implementation. However, these approaches typically fail to capture the global structure of the problem and may lead to suboptimal performance.

In recent years, learning-based optimization methods have emerged as a promising alternative to custom heuristics and metaheuristics. In particular, reinforcement learning (RL) provides a natural framework for modelling sequential decision-making under uncertainty, enabling agents to learn policies directly from interaction with the environment. Nevertheless, its application to maritime logistics problems remains relatively limited. Particularly, for dynamic scheduling problems, (deep) reinforcement learning approaches seem to offer advantages that are less explored structurally similar problems as the dynamic BAP.

Motivated by these challenges, this paper proposes a size-agnostic, graph-based reinforcement learning framework for the discrete BAP with vessel priorities and berth-dependent handling times. The main contributions of this work are as follows:

1. We introduce an MDP formulation of the discrete BAP that incorporates vessel priorities, berth-dependent handling times, and a skip action allowing the agent to defer assignments when beneficial.
2. We propose a Graph Neural Network (GNN)-based architecture capable of generalizing across instances with varying numbers of vessels and berths, integrating both local and global contextual information.
3. We conduct an empirical evaluation on 2700 randomly generated instances, demonstrating that the proposed method consistently outperforms classical dispatching heuristics.

2 Related Work

The BAP is classified along two axes: spatial layout (discrete, continuous, or hybrid) and temporal setting (static, when all vessels are known upfront, or dynamic, when they arrive over time). This work addresses the discrete dynamic variant (DDBAP). Early exact approaches for the DDBAP include a Lagrangian relaxation method [5] and subsequent Mixed-Integer Programming (MIP) extensions [3]; while optimal for small instances, these methods do not scale. Metaheuristics such as hybrid genetic algorithms [1] and bee colony optimization [9] improve scalability but still require per-instance computation and do not generalize across problem configurations.

In practice, ports rely on simple dispatching heuristics for their speed, but these ignore global scheduling structure and yield large optimality gaps under congestion. This has motivated the use of reinforcement learning to learn decision policies directly from experience. RL has shown strong results in combinatorial optimization (routing, scheduling), yet its application to maritime logistics remains limited. In [8], the agent selects among predefined heuristics at each step to resolve conflicts, using a fixed-size state representation tied to a specific number of berths. More recently, [6] propose a hierarchical multi-agent MDP for joint vessel selection, berth allocation, and crane assignment, while [7] train a size-agnostic model via evolutionary strategies for the continuous BAP.

Only [7] and [6] propose size-agnostic approaches, but neither fully addresses our setting: [7] lacks a skip action and explicit priority modelling, and [6] encodes only a simplified state without vessel priorities. In contrast, this work proposes a unified MDP with a graph-based size-agnostic state representation, explicit priority modelling, and a skip action, enabling robust generalization across varying port configurations.

3 Problem Formulation

We address the Dynamic Discrete Berth Allocation Problem (DDBAP) with vessel priorities and berth-dependent handling times. A port has a set of discrete berths $\mathcal{B} = \{1, \ldots, B\}$ and receives a set of vessels $\mathcal{V} = \{1, \ldots, V\}$ dynamically over a rolling planning horizon. Each vessel v is characterized by its arrival time $a_v \geq 0$, a berth-dependent handling time $h_{v,b} > 0$ for each berth $b \in \mathcal{B}$, and an integer priority weight $p_v \in \mathbb{Z}_{\geq 1}$. Four families of decision variables are introduced: the continuous start time $t_v \geq 0$; the binary berth-assignment $x_{v,b} \in \{0, 1\}$; the binary sequencing variable $y_{v,v'} \in \{0, 1\}$, equal to 1 iff v is served *immediately before* v' at the same berth; and the first/last-in-berth indicators $f_v, l_v \in \{0, 1\}$.

The resulting MIP model is adapted to consider the service time from [8]:

$$\min \quad \sum_{v \in \mathcal{V}} p_v \left(t_v - a_v + \sum_{b \in \mathcal{B}} h_{v,b} x_{v,b} \right) \tag{1}$$

$$\text{s.t.} \quad \sum_{b \in \mathcal{B}} x_{v,b} = 1 \qquad \forall v \in \mathcal{V} \tag{2}$$

$$f_v + \sum_{\substack{v' \in \mathcal{V} \\ v' \neq v}} y_{v',v} = 1 \qquad \forall v \in \mathcal{V} \tag{3}$$

$$l_v + \sum_{\substack{v' \in \mathcal{V} \\ v' \neq v}} y_{v,v'} = 1 \qquad \forall v \in \mathcal{V} \tag{4}$$

$$f_v + f_{v'} \leq 3 - x_{v,b} - x_{v',b} \qquad \forall b \in \mathcal{B},\ \forall v, v' \in \mathcal{V},\ v \neq v' \tag{5}$$

$$l_v + l_{v'} \leq 3 - x_{v,b} - x_{v',b} \qquad \forall b \in \mathcal{B},\ \forall v, v' \in \mathcal{V},\ v \neq v' \tag{6}$$

$$y_{v,v'} - 1 \leq x_{v,b} - x_{v',b} \leq 1 - y_{v,v'} \qquad \forall b \in \mathcal{B},\ \forall v, v' \in \mathcal{V},\ v \neq v' \tag{7}$$

$$t_v + \sum_{b \in \mathcal{B}} h_{v,b}\, x_{v,b} - M(1 - y_{v,v'}) \leq t_{v'} \qquad \forall v, v' \in \mathcal{V},\ v \neq v' \tag{8}$$

$$t_v \geq a_v \qquad \forall v \in \mathcal{V} \tag{9}$$

The objective function (1) minimizes total priority-weighted service time. Constraints (2) enforces a unique berth per vessel. Constraints (3)–(6) link sequencing variables to first/last-in-berth indicators, ensuring each berth has exactly one head and one tail. Constraints (7) couples ordering and assignment ($y_{v,v'} = 1$ only if v, v' share a berth), Constraints (8) enforces non-overlap via big-M, and Constraints (9) ensure service cannot start before arrival.

4 Markov Decision Process

In order to solve the DDBAP using reinforcement learning we formulate it as a Markov Decision Process (MDP) $(\mathcal{S}, \mathcal{A}, \mathcal{T}, \mathcal{R}, \gamma)$, where decisions are made sequentially as vessels arrive and berths become available.

4.1 State Space

At each decision step t, the state $s_t \in \mathcal{S}$ is represented by a single heterogeneous bipartite graph $G = (\mathcal{V}, \mathcal{B}, E)$ containing all vessels (both waiting and not-yet-arrived) and all berths as nodes, with edges whose features encode assignment costs and vessel status.

Vessel Nodes. Each vessel $v \in \mathcal{V}$ is described by a four-dimensional feature vector:

$$\mathbf{f}^{(v)} = \left[\, \tilde{w}_v,\ \tilde{a}_v,\ \tilde{p}_v,\ \tilde{q}_v \,\right], \tag{10}$$

where $\tilde{w}_v = \max(0,\, t_{\text{cur}} - a_v)/T$ is the normalized waiting time already accumulated (0 for vessels not yet arrived), $\tilde{a}_v = \max(0,\, a_v - t_{\text{cur}})/T$ is the normalized time until arrival (0 for arrived vessels), $\tilde{p}_v = p_v/p_{\max}$ is the normalized priority, and $\tilde{q}_v = \max_b(p_v/h_{v,b})/q_{\max}$ is the vessel's best achievable score across all berths, with T as the planning horizon, $p_{\max}$ as the maximum priority and $q_{\max}$ as the maximum weighted processing time and priority in the instance. Exactly one of $\tilde{w}_v$ and $\tilde{a}_v$ is non-zero at any time, encoding whether the vessel is already waiting or is still in transit

Berth Nodes. Each berth $b \in \mathcal{B}$ carries a three-dimensional feature vector:

$$\mathbf{f}^{(b)} = \left[\, \tilde{r}_b,\ \tilde{q}_b,\ o_b \,\right], \tag{11}$$

where $\tilde{r}_b = \max(0, f_b - t_{\text{cur}})/T$ is the normalized remaining time until the berth is free, $\tilde{q}_b = \max_v(p_v/h_{v,b})/q_{\max}$ is the best score achievable at this berth across all vessels, and $o_b \in \{0, 1\}$ is an occupancy indicator.

Edge Features. Every pair of (vessel, berth) is connected by an edge $(v, b) \in E$ with a six-dimensional feature vector:

$$\mathbf{e}_{vb} = \left[\, \tilde{s}_{vb},\, \tilde{c}_{vb},\, \tilde{h}_{vb},\, \mathbb{1}_{\text{valid}},\, \mathbb{1}_{\text{skip}},\, \mathbb{1}_{\text{future}} \,\right], \tag{12}$$

where $\tilde{s}_{vb} = (p_v/h_{v,b})/q_{\max}$ is the normalized ranking score for this (vessel, berth) pair, $\tilde{c}_{vb} = (\max(0, t_{\text{cur}} - a_v) \cdot p_v)/\mathcal{L}$ is the weighted waiting cost already accumulated by vessel v, normalized by a reference solution value $\mathcal{L}$, and the last three dimensions form a mutually exclusive one-hot status encoding: *valid* means the vessel has arrived and the edge is not forbidden (immediately actionable), *skip* means the vessel has arrived but this pair was skipped and is temporarily blocked, and *future* means the vessel has not yet arrived. Figure 1 illustrates the graph representation of a state in which three vessels have arrived, two more are coming and one of three berths is occupied. Due to a prior `Skip` action, vessel 2 cannot be assigned to berth 1.

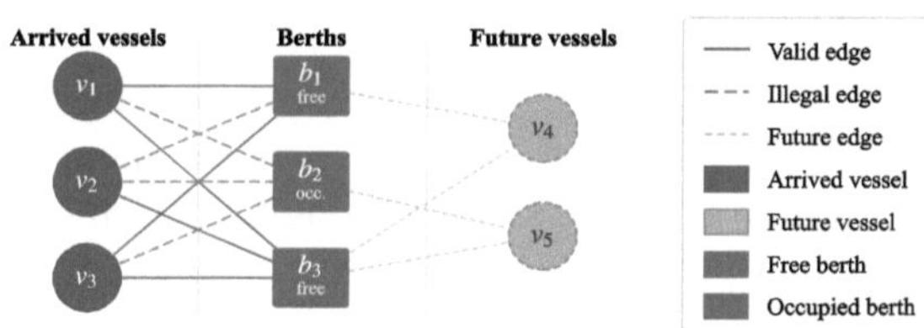

Fig. 1. Unified bipartite state graph example.

4.2 Action Space

At each state s_t, the agent selects an action from the set $\mathcal{A}(s_t) = \mathcal{A}^{\text{assign}}(s_t) \cup \{\texttt{Skip}\}$. Each action has a different impact on the environment.

Assignment Actions. A feasible assignment action is a pair (v, b) where v is an arrived vessel (i.e. $a_v \leq t_{\text{cur}}$) and $b \in \mathcal{B}$ is a free berth such that the corresponding edge (v, b) carries status $\mathbb{1}_{\text{valid}} = 1$ (not forbidden by a prior skip).

Skip Action. The agent may also choose to `Skip`, advancing the clock to the next relevant event, either a berth becoming free or a new vessel arriving, without making an assignment. This is necessary because it can be beneficial to wait for a future vessel before committing to an assignment.

Forbidden-Edge Masking. To make the `Skip` action learnable, whenever the `Skip` is taken, every edge (v, b) that is available at that step (vessel waiting, berth free) is marked *forbidden* for all subsequent states until either that vessel is assigned or berth b is re-occupied. When a vessel is assigned, all forbidden edges involving that vessel or berth are cleared. This encodes the constraint that re-considering a declined pair at a later time can only worsen the objective. If no future vessels remain and all berths are free, the forbidden set is cleared and `Skip` is masked. Additionally, if an available assignment dominates `Skip` (the vessel could be fully processed before the next event), `Skip` is also masked.

Transition. In an assignment of vessel v to berth b, the vessel node is removed from the graph and the time advances to $t_{\text{next}} = \max(\min_{v'}(a_{v'}), \min_{b'}(f_{b'}), t_{cur})$, where $\min_{v'}(a_{v'})$ is the earliest arrival among unassigned vessels not yet in port and $\min_{b'}(f_{b'})$ is the earliest time any occupied berth becomes free. In other words, the next decision point is as soon as *either* a new vessel is available *or* a berth opens up, whichever comes first, but never before the current time. On a `skip`, the vessel nodes remain unchanged and the clock advances only to the *next event*: whichever of (next vessel arrival, next berth becoming free) happens first strictly after t_{cur}, since by construction there is already at least one waiting vessel and one free berth at the time of the skip.

4.3 Reward

The reward signal is an incremental penalty based on changes in the objective function, providing a dense learning signal throughout each episode.

Assignment Reward. When the agent assigns vessel v to berth b at time t:

$$r_t^{\text{assign}} = -\frac{p_v h_{v,b} + \Delta W_t}{\mathcal{L}}, \tag{13}$$

where $p_v h_{v,b}$ is the priority-weighted handling cost, $\Delta W_t = \sum_{v' \neq v} p_{v'} \Delta w_{v',t}$ is the additional waiting-time cost incurred by queued vessels when the clock advances. Waiting time is tracked incrementally via a counter $\hat{w}_v$; only the new increment $\Delta w_{v,t} = (t_{\text{cur}} - a_v) - \hat{w}_v$ is taken into account per step to avoid double counting.

Skip Reward. When the agent takes `Skip`, advancing the clock by Δt:

$$r_t^{\text{skip}} = -\frac{\Delta W_t}{\mathcal{L}} \tag{14}$$

In both cases, $\mathcal{L}$ is a reference solution value that stabilizes training by scaling rewards across instances of different sizes.

5 Proposed Method

In this section, we present the proposed reinforcement learning approach for solving the berth allocation problem. The architecture is based on a Graph Neural Network, which encodes the problem as a bipartite graph and guides the decision-making process.

5.1 GNN Architecture

The agent consists of an encoder that processes the unified bipartite graph G (containing all vessels and all berths) and a decoder that assigns scores to candidate assignment actions via a two-branch edge scorer.

GNN Encoder. The graph is processed by a encoder consisting of $L = 3$ heterogeneous graph convolution layers built with Graph ATtention networks (GAT) [2] operating on the bipartite graph. At each layer ℓ, messages are passed in both directions (vessel → berth and berth → vessel):

$$\mathbf{h}_v^{(\ell)} = \mathrm{ELU}\Big(\mathrm{LN}\Big(\mathrm{GAT}_{(\ell)}^{v\to b}\big(\mathbf{h}_v^{(\ell-1)}, \mathbf{h}_b^{(\ell-1)}, \mathbf{e}_{vb}\big)\Big)\Big), \tag{15}$$

$$\mathbf{h}_b^{(\ell)} = \mathrm{ELU}\Big(\mathrm{LN}\Big(\mathrm{GAT}_{(\ell)}^{b\to v}\big(\mathbf{h}_b^{(\ell-1)}, \mathbf{h}_v^{(\ell-1)}, \mathbf{e}_{vb}\big)\Big)\Big), \tag{16}$$

where $\mathbf{e}_{vb} \in \mathbb{R}^5$ is the edge feature vector defined in Eq. (12), LN denotes Layer Normalization, and ELU is the Exponential Linear Unit activation. Residual connections are added from layer 2 onwards (once the feature dimension stabilises at d_h). All attention layers use $H = 4$ heads with mean aggregation, yielding output dimension d_h. The first layer projects raw features (vessel: $\mathbb{R}^4$, berth: $\mathbb{R}^3$) into $\mathbb{R}^{d_h}$; subsequent layers operate entirely in $\mathbb{R}^{d_h}$. The encoder produces:

- Per-node embeddings $\mathbf{H} \in \mathbb{R}^{(|\mathcal{V}|+|\mathcal{B}|)\times d_h}$ (vessels concatenated with berths).
- A global graph embedding $\mathbf{g} \in \mathbb{R}^{d_h}$ obtained via mean pooling over all nodes.

Edge Scoring (Actor). For each candidate vessel–berth pair (v, b) with edge status $\mathbb{1}_{\text{valid}} = 1$, a score is computed by summing two complementary branches:

$$\mathrm{score}(v,b) = \underbrace{\mathrm{MLP}_{\text{local}}\big(\mathbf{e}_{vb}^{(1:3)}\big)}_{\text{local ranking}} + \underbrace{\mathrm{MLP}_{\text{ctx}}\big([\,\mathbf{h}_v^{(L)} \,\|\, \mathbf{h}_b^{(L)}\,]\big)}_{\text{context}}, \tag{17}$$

where $\mathbf{e}_{vb}^{(1:3)} = [\tilde{s}_{vb}, \tilde{c}_{vb}, \tilde{h}_{vb}]$ are the first three (numeric) edge features. The *local branch* $\mathrm{MLP}_{\text{local}}$ has layers $[3 \to d_h \to 1]$ and captures the immediate assignment quality signal (WTSP score and accumulated waiting cost). The *context branch* $\mathrm{MLP}_{\text{ctx}}$ has layers $[2d_h \to d_h \to 1]$ and captures interactions such as berth congestion and future vessel arrivals encoded in the GNN embeddings. An additional `Skip` score $\mathrm{score}_{\text{skip}} \in \mathbb{R}$ is produced by a separate MLP with layers $[d_h \to d_h \to d_h/2 \to 1]$ taking the global graph embedding $\mathbf{g}$ as input.

Action-Masking and Distribution. Before computing the softmax distribution, all logits corresponding to invalid actions (occupied berths, skipped edges, future-vessel edges, or `Skip` when no future vessels remain and all berths are free) are set to $-\infty$. During training, an action is sampled from the policy; at evaluation, the argmax is taken (deterministic greedy policy). This design is *size-agnostic*: the GNN encoder operates on graphs of arbitrary size, so the same model can be applied to instances with different numbers of vessels and berths without re-training. For the trained model the hidden dimension d_h is set to 64.

Value Network (Critic). A separate value network estimates $V(s_t) = \mathrm{MLP}_{\mathrm{value}}(\mathbf{g})$ with layers $[d_h \to d_h \to d_h/2 \to 1]$ and ELU activations.

5.2 Training Procedure

The agent is trained with Proximal Policy Optimization. Training proceeds in batches: at the start of each batch, a fixed random seed is set and N_{inst} BAP instances are generated. Episodes are distributed across instances in round-robin fashion according to E_{inst}, interleaving learning updates across different problem realizations. For each episode the agent collects a full trajectory and computes discounted returns and GAE advantages ($\gamma = 0.99$, $\lambda = 0.95$), normalized to zero mean and unit variance. The actor and critic are then updated for $K = 4$ epochs using the clipped surrogate objective ($\epsilon = 0.2$), with a value loss coefficient $c_1 = 0.5$ and entropy bonus $c_2 = 0.01$. Gradients are clipped to a max norm of 0.5 and Adam is used with learning rate $\alpha = 10^{-4}$. The final model is selected as the checkpoint with the best performance on a held-out validation set.

6 Experimental Study

In this section, we first describe how the instances used for training, validation, and testing were generated. We then present the performance of the trained agent on both the validation and test sets, comparing it against an exact solver (when feasible within the imposed time limits) and four dispatching heuristics.

Instance Generation. All instance sets (training, validation, test) share the same generation procedure. Vessel arrivals follow the methodology of [8]: inter-arrival times are sampled from an exponential distribution with rate $\lambda = 1/I$, where $I = C \cdot \frac{\sum_{v,b} h_{v,b}}{BV^2}$ and $C > 0$ controls congestion (smaller C = higher congestion). Handling times are drawn from $\mathcal{U}[10, 200]$ and priorities from $\{1, \ldots, 10\}$. Training batches alternate between small (10 vessels, 3 berths) and medium (30 vessels, 5 berths) instances across $C \in \{0.5, 1.0, 2.0\}$, generating 12 instances per batch with $E_{\mathrm{inst}} = 5$ episodes each. The validation set contains six fixed instances (same sizes/congestions as training). Test instances cover all 27 combinations of $V \in \{80, 100, 120\}$, $B \in \{5, 10, 15\}$, and $C \in \{0.5, 1.0, 2.0\}$, with 100 independent replicates per combination (2 700 instances total).

Baselines. For a fair comparison, we evaluate the agent against four dispatching heuristics and additionally against the MIP solver Gurobi (1800 s timeout). **FCFS** assigns the earliest-arrived vessel to the available berth with the shortest processing time. **SPT** always selects the vessel-berth pair with the smallest handling time. **Priority** dispatches vessels in decreasing priority order, assigning each to the available berth with the shortest processing time. **WTSP** ranks all arrived-vessel/free-berth pairs by $p_v/h_{v,b}$ and selects the highest-scoring pair; this heuristic is used as the reference solution $\mathcal{L}$ for reward scaling. Regarding the MIP solver Gurobi, we allow 1800 s to evaluate how closely the method approaches optimal solutions. However, ports are extremely dynamic environments, requiring frequent re-optimization, which makes exact solvers like Gurobi impractical for real-time deployment. In contrast, both the heuristics and our agent can handle common sources of uncertainty in port operations, such as vessel delays, variable handling times, and other stochastic events, while requiring low computational time compared to MIP solvers, making them more suitable for operational use.

Table 1. Objective function and gap with respect to the best solution found by Gurobi of the heuristics and the agent on the validation set. † Gurobi time-limit reached.

Instance	Gurobi	FCFS	SPT	Priority	WTSP	Agent
1_10v3b_C05	306.50	+136%	+23%	+27%	+9%	**+5.2%**
2_10v3b_C1	512.50	+122%	+85%	+157%	+77%	**+3.5%**
3_10v3b_C2	449.40	+71%	+43%	+60%	+10%	**+0.0%**
4_30v5b_C05	329.47†	+244%	+59%	+189%	+69%	**+2.3%**
5_30v5b_C1	400.03†	+289%	+85%	+254%	+73%	**+3.6%**
6_30v5b_C2	414.07†	+164%	+32%	+135%	+33%	**+13%**

Results on the Validation Set. Table 1 reports the objective value and gap with respect to Gurobi for each validation instance. The agent outperforms all four heuristics on every instance; on instance 3 ($C = 2$) it recovers the proven optimal. On instances 4–6 (30 vessels) Gurobi hits its 1800 s time limit yet the agent remains competitive with or below that bound. WTSP is the strongest heuristic baseline, but the learned policy improves further by leveraging global context from the GNN embeddings.

Results on the Test Set. Table 2 reports the mean gap (%) with respect to the WTSP objective across 100 replicated instances for each of the 27 configurations. WTSP is the best-performing heuristic and is therefore used as the baseline for computing the gaps, instead of Gurobi, which does not produce feasible solutions for all instances within the timeout even though in some configurations the performance of Gurobi is better than the performance of the Agent. In addition, the table indicates, in parentheses, the percentage of instances for which Gurobi finds a feasible solution within the time limit. It is worth noting that Gurobi, with the given time, was only able to find the optimal solution for one instance. The proposed agent achieves the lowest or nearly the lowest gap in almost every configuration, consistently improving over standard heuristics. The relative improvement of the agent is more pronounced in less congested

Table 2. Mean gap (%) with respect to WTSP across 100 replicate instances per configuration. Best result per row in bold.

C	Vessels	Berths	FCFS	SPT	Priority	Agent	Gurobi	
0.5	80	5	264	13.2	162	**−9.4**	−8.2	(97%)
		10	319	6.9	214	−20.3	**−23.5**	(99%)
		15	280	1.5	193	−26.9	**−32.9**	(100%)
	100	5	283	13.5	176	**−7.8**	1.7	(85%)
		10	359	10.1	239	**−17.8**	−3.6	(82%)
		15	379	6.1	254	**−19.7**	−16.2	(95%)
	120	5	294	14.3	185	**−5.8**	27.2	(45%)
		10	401	11.4	265	**−13.5**	25.0	(52%)
		15	416	8.9	285	**−18.3**	3.1	(76%)
1.0	80	5	284	12.2	179	−9.2	**−11.4**	(100%)
		10	314	2.5	204	−24.6	**−32.5**	(100%)
		15	226	−4.0	163	−36.4	**−47.5**	(100%)
	100	5	303	13.9	191	**−7.7**	1.5	(94%)
		10	385	8.0	254	**−20.3**	−15.8	(87%)
		15	332	−1.1	226	−31.7	**−36.0**	(100%)
	120	5	312	15.3	195	**−6.5**	49.6	(43%)
		10	421	9.8	273	**−16.8**	22.4	(68%)
		15	417	2.3	282	**−27.3**	−2.9	(86%)
2.0	80	5	313	12.2	196	−10.3	**−14.0**	(99%)
		10	298	−3.3	192	−29.9	**−45.6**	(100%)
		15	99.3	−6.1	70.6	−46.1	**−56.7**	(100%)
	100	5	333	14.4	202	**−9.3**	2.4	(98%)
		10	393	0.8	261	−26.1	**−31.8**	(100%)
		15	232	−7.8	160	−41.6	**−52.6**	(99%)
	120	5	350	15.1	220	**−6.8**	81.8	(34%)
		10	468	4.1	307	**−21.3**	15.8	(70%)
		15	349	−6.3	231	−35.9	**−36.1**	(97%)
Overall mean			327	6.2	214	**−20.3**	−15.3	(85%)

settings, reaching up to 50% reduction in gap for instances with 80 vessels and 15 berths at low congestion ($C = 2.0$). In more congested scenarios, such as 120 vessels and 5 berths at $C = 0.5$, the agent still reduces the cost by roughly 6% relative to WTSP. Overall, across all instances, the agent yields a mean gap of approximately 20%, confirming its effectiveness in reducing the priority-weighted turnaround cost compared to standard heuristics.

7 Conclusion

We presented a size-agnostic graph-based reinforcement learning approach for the DDBAP. Representing the port state as a heterogeneous bipartite graph and encoding it with a multi-layer GAT, the agent captures both local assignment signals and global context without being limited by the number of vessels or berths. The MDP includes vessel priorities, berth-dependent handling times, and a skip action to defer assignments, enabling high-quality schedules. On the validation set, the agent achieves solutions close to those obtained by Gurobi when given 1800 s per instance. Experimental results on the test set, comprising 2,700 synthetic instances across 27 configurations, show that the agent consistently outperforms classical heuristics, with the largest gains observed under low congestion ($C = 2$), where greedy methods degrade the most. Across all instances, the agent achieves a mean gap of approximately 20% relative to the best heuristic. Nevertheless, the results are very promising only in synthetic data, therefore, extensive evaluation should be performed in the future, including real world data in order to evaluate the practical contribution of the proposed method. In addition, a large validation set with distributions different from the one used in training should also be considered in future works to make the model selection more robust. Finally, future work will also include extending to the continuous BAP, handling arrival-time uncertainty, and incorporating features such as shore power.

Acknowledgments. This work is part of the PortCall. Zero project within the NWO Perspective programme, project number P23.015, financed by the Netherlands Organisation for Scientific Research (NWO).

Disclosure of Interests. The authors have no competing interests to declare that are relevant to the content of this article.

References

1. Bacalhau, E.T., Casacio, L., de Azevedo, A.T.: New hybrid genetic algorithms to solve dynamic berth allocation problem. Expert Syst. Appl. **167**, 114198 (2021)
2. Brody, S., Alon, U., Yahav, E.: How attentive are graph attention networks?. arXiv preprint arXiv:2105.14491 (2021)
3. Buhrkal, K., Zuglian, S., Ropke, S., Larsen, J., Lusby, R.: Models for the discrete berth allocation problem: a computational comparison. Transp. Res. Part E: Logist. Transp. Rev. **47**(4), 461–473 (2011)
4. Hansen, P., Oguz, C.: A note on formulations of static and dynamic berth allocation problems. Les Cahiers du GERAD ISSN **711**, 2440 (2003)
5. Imai, A., Nishimura, E., Papadimitriou, S.: The dynamic berth allocation problem for a container port. Transp. Res. Part B: Methodol. **35**(4), 401–417 (2001)
6. Jo, S., Moon, I.: A hierarchical reinforcement learning approach for real-time berth allocation and quay crane scheduling. Int. J. Prod. Res. **63**(24), 10027–10052 (2025)
7. Li, S., Xu, P., Ding, Z., Kong, Z., Luo, W.: Evolutionary reinforcement learning with density-based behavioral diversity enhancement for berth allocation and crane assignment. Swarm Evol. Comput. **100**, 102241 (2026)

8. Lv, Y., Zou, M., Li, J., Liu, J.: Dynamic berth allocation under uncertainties based on deep reinforcement learning towards resilient ports. Ocean Coastal Manag. **252**, 107113 (2024)
9. Prencipe, L.P., Marinelli, M.: A novel mathematical formulation for solving the dynamic and discrete berth allocation problem by using the bee colony optimisation algorithm: A novel mathematical formulation for solving the dynamic and discrete berth allocation problem by using the bee colony optimisation algorithm. Appl. Intell. **51**(7), 4127–4142 (2021)
10. United Nations Conference on Trade and Development: Review of maritime transport 2024 (2024). https://unctad.org/publication/review-maritime-transport-2024

Neural Column Generation for Quay Crane Scheduling

Minsu Woo[1], Hyeonjeong Kim[1], Hoyoung Kim[1], Yanjie Zhou[2], and Sung Won Cho[1,3](✉)

[1] Department of Industrial Engineering, Dankook University, Cheonan 31116, South Korea
sungwon.cho@dankook.ac.kr
[2] School of Management, Zhengzhou University, Zhengzhou 450001, China
[3] Department of Management Engineering, Dankook University, Cheonan 31116, South Korea

Abstract. This paper proposes a neural column generation approach for the quay crane scheduling problem (QCSP) and integrates it into a complete branch-and-price (B&P) framework. The QCSP allocates quay cranes to vessels over discrete time periods under adjacency, workload, and capacity constraints. While commercial solvers can find feasible solutions to the compact MILP formulation quickly, the weak LP relaxation makes it difficult to prove optimality as the number of vessels grows. B&P provides tighter bounds through Dantzig-Wolfe decomposition, but the pricing subproblem, a vessel-level MIP, becomes the computational bottleneck. To accelerate the pricing step, a Transformer encoder-decoder is trained on exact pricing solutions to generate feasible columns autoregressively with feasibility masking that guarantees constraint satisfaction by construction. A hybrid neural-MIP pricing strategy is adopted to preserve exactness, with exact MIP pricing verifying LP optimality when the neural model fails to find a negative reduced cost column. Numerical experiments on real-world instances from Busan Port show that the proposed method proves optimality in 45 of 50 instances, compared with 34 for MIP-based B&P and 16 for direct MILP solving, while reducing per-iteration pricing cost by a factor of three to six.

Keywords: Quay crane scheduling · Column generation · Branch and price · Neural combinatorial optimization · Container terminal

1 Introduction

Maritime transport accounts for over 80% of global trade by volume, and containerized trade is projected to grow at an average annual rate of 2.3% through 2030 [1]. This growth places increasing pressure on container terminals to improve operational efficiency. Seaside operations at a terminal comprise three interrelated planning problems (berth allocation, quay crane assignment, and quay crane scheduling), among which quay crane scheduling most directly determines vessel handling time and overall terminal productivity [2].

J. de Armas and E. Lalla Ruiz (Eds.): LOGMS 2026, LNCS 16679, pp. 27–39, 2027.
https://doi.org/10.1007/978-3-032-30795-8_3

The quay crane scheduling problem (QCSP) allocates quay cranes (QCs) to vessels over discrete time periods to minimize QC operating costs. Because QCs run on a shared rail, those serving the same vessel must occupy adjacent positions, forming a contiguous block at every time slot. This adjacency requirement, combined with workload and crane capacity constraints, renders the problem NP-hard [3].

The standard approach formulates QCSP as a mixed-integer linear programming (MILP) and solves it with a commercial solver. Related quay crane planning models have used similar time-indexed crane-assignment variables and setup/overtime cost components [4]. Modern solvers find high-quality feasible solutions quickly through primal heuristics, yet the LP relaxation of the compact formulation yields weak dual bounds. As the number of vessels grows, closing the optimality gap within practical time limits becomes increasingly difficult. Branch-and-Price (B&P) provides tighter LP bounds through Dantzig-Wolfe decomposition [5]. However, the pricing subproblem—a vessel-level MIP—grows rapidly with the number of time slots and limits the scalability of B&P.

Prior exact algorithms for QCSP show that crane interference and vessel-level structure can be exploited through branch-and cut and branch-and-price frameworks [6–8]. Related B&P work has also addressed integrated berth allocation and quay crane assignment [9]. These studies motivate exact approaches that exploit QCSP structure, but their separation or pricing components can remain computational bottlenecks. We therefore use learned pricing to reduce the computational burden of the pricing step while preserving the certification mechanism of B&P.

In recent years, several studies have applied machine learning techniques to accelerate column generation (CG) and B&P. Morabit et al. [10] used a graph neural network to select promising columns rather than generate them directly. Shen et al. [11] proposed a pricing heuristic based on machine learning for graph coloring, where predictions guide sampling to generate high-quality columns and improve both CG and B&P performance. Hijazi et al. [12] trained a Transformer model to directly generate columns for parallel machine scheduling, preserving LP optimality through exact verification. However, the method of Hijazi et al. operates only at the LP relaxation level without extending to integer-optimal solutions through branch-and-bound, and experiments are conducted on synthetic instances.

Table positions the proposed method against selected QCSP exact algorithms and learning-based column generation studies. The main contributions are summarized as follows.

First, the proposed framework combines the QCSP setting, direct neural column generation, and integer-level B&P certification. A neural pricing model that directly generates columns is integrated into a full B&P algorithm that guarantees integer optimality. The neural model accelerates the pricing step, while exact MIP pricing is retained to verify LP optimality, so the overall framework remains exact. Compared with prior direct neural column generation studies that focus on LP relaxation, this work extends neural pricing to integer-level B&P through QCSP-specific feasibility masks, exact reduced-cost verification, and node-dependent branching constraints.

Second, the neural pricing model is applied to the QCSP, where the pricing subproblem is formulated as a MIP involving crane adjacency, workload, and capacity constraints. The model addresses this structure through a block-level autoregressive formulation with feasibility masking that guarantees valid columns by construction.

Third, numerical experiments are conducted on real-world operational data from Busan Port. The results demonstrate that the proposed method proves optimality in substantially more instances than both direct MILP solving and MIP-based B&P, while reducing per-iteration pricing cost by a factor of three to six.

2 Problem Description and Formulation

2.1 Problem Description

We consider N vessels $N = \{1, \ldots, N\}$ berthed at a quay served by Q QCs $\mathcal{J} = \{1, \ldots, Q\}$. Each vessel i has an estimated time of arrival ETA_i, estimated time of departure ETD_i, workload W_i in crane-time units, and bounds q_i^{min}, q_i^{max} on the number of QCs that may work simultaneously. The service time window is $\mathcal{T}_i = \{\text{ETA}_i, \ldots, \text{ETD}_i - 1\}$. Because cranes run on a shared rail, those assigned to the same vessel at any time slot must occupy adjacent positions, forming a contiguous block. Each crane can serve at most one vessel per time slot.

The objective minimizes total operating cost: a setup cost C^s incurred each time a QC begins a new work session on a vessel, and an overtime cost C^o for each crane-time unit beyond H consecutive regular slots. Table 1 summarizes the notation.

Table 1. Notation summary.

Symbol	Description
Parameters and sets	
N, i	Set of vessels $\{1, \ldots, N\}$ and vessel index
J, j	Set of QCs $\{1, \ldots, Q\}$ and crane index
$\mathcal{T}_i, t$	Service time slots $\{\text{ETA}_i, \ldots, \text{ETD}_i - 1\}$ and time index
B_i	Feasible crane blocks $\{(l, w) : q_i^{min} \le w \le q_i^{max}, 1 \le l \le Q - w + 1\}$
P_i, p	Set of columns (schedules) for vessel i and column index
c_p^i	Cost of column p for vessel i
a_{jt}^{ip}	1 if column p assigns crane j to vessel i at time t
$\text{ETA}_i, \text{ETD}_i$	Estimated time of arrival and departure of vessel i
W_i	Workload of vessel i in crane-time units
q_i^{max}, q_i^{min}	Max/min number of QCs assigned to vessel i
$\overline{q}$	Maximum crane count across all vessels, $\max_i q_i^{max}$
C^s, C^o	Setup cost and overtime cost per crane-time unit
H	Regular working-hour threshold before overtime applies

(continued)

Table 1. (*continued*)

Symbol	Description
$\overline{c}_i^*$	Optimal reduced cost of the pricing subproblem for vessel i
Decision variables	
$x_{ijt} \in \{0, 1\}$	1 if crane j serves vessel i at time t
$y_{it} \in \{0, 1\}$	1 if vessel i is active at time t
$s_{ijt} \in \{0, 1\}$	1 if crane j begins handling vessel i at time t
$e_{ijt} \in \{0, 1\}$	1 if crane j finishes handling vessel i at time t
$z_{ijt} \in [0, H]$	Consecutive work counter for overtime accounting
$\lambda_{ip} \geq 0$	Weight of column p for vessel i (RMP)
$y_{tlw} \in \{0, 1\}$	1 if block (l, w) selected at time t (pricing)
$u_{jt} \in \{0, 1\}$	1 if crane j is used at time t (pricing)
$\delta_t \in \{0, 1\}$	1 if vessel is idle at time t (pricing)
α_i	Dual variable for convexity constraint of vessel i
$\mu_{jt} \geq 0$	Dual variable for crane capacity constraint at (j, t)

2.2 MILP Formulation

Using the notation in Table 1, the QCSP is formulated as follows:

$$\text{(M1) Min} \quad \sum_{i \in N} \sum_{j \in J} \sum_{t \in \mathcal{T}_i} \left[C^s \cdot s_{ijt} + C^o \cdot \left(x_{ijt} - z_{ijt} \right) \right] \tag{1}$$

$$\text{s.t.} \quad \sum_{j \in J} \sum_{t \in \mathcal{T}_\rangle} x_{ijt} = W_i \quad \forall i \in N \tag{2}$$

$$\sum_{i: t \in \mathcal{T}_i} x_{ijt} \leq 1 \quad \forall j \in J, t \tag{3}$$

$$q_i^{\min} \cdot y_{it} \leq \sum_{j \in J} x_{ijt} \leq q_i^{max} \cdot y_{it} \quad \forall i, t \in \mathcal{T}_i \tag{4}$$

$$x_{ijt} \geq x_{ij't} + x_{ij''t} - 1 \quad \forall i, t \in \mathcal{T}_i, j' < j < j'' \tag{5}$$

$$x_{ijt} - x_{ij,t-1} = s_{ijt} - e_{ijt} \quad \forall i, j, t \in \mathcal{T}_i \backslash \{ETA_i\} \tag{6}$$

$$s_{ijt} \leq x_{ijt} \quad \forall i, j, t \in \mathcal{T}_i \tag{7}$$

$$s_{ijt} + e_{ijt} \leq 1 \quad \forall i, j, t \in \mathcal{T}_i \tag{8}$$

$$z_{ijt} \leq H \cdot s_{ijt} \quad \forall i, j, t \in \mathcal{T}_i \tag{9}$$

$$z_{ijt} \leq k + H \cdot x_{ij,t+k} \quad \forall i, j, t, k = 0, \ldots, h_{it} \tag{10}$$

$$x_{ijt}, y_{it}, s_{ijt}, e_{ijt} \in \{0, 1\}, \;\; 0 \leq z_{ijt} \leq H \tag{11}$$

Where $h_{it} =$ min (H, ETD$_i$ - t) -1.

The objective (1) minimizes total setup and overtime cost. Constraint (2) ensures each vessel's workload is completed. Constraint (3) limits each crane to at most one vessel per time slot. Constraint (4) enforces crane count bounds when vessel i is active. Constraint (5) enforces crane adjacency: for any three cranes $j' < j < j''$, if the outer two are assigned then the middle one must also be assigned, preventing gaps in the crane block. Constraints (6–8) track the start and end of each crane's work session through flow balance. Constraints (9–10) compute the consecutive work counter z_{ijt} for overtime accounting: the overtime term $C^o(x_{ijt} - z_{ijt})$ is positive only for work beyond H consecutive slots.

2.3 Dantzig-Wolfe Decomposition

All constraints except the crane capacity constraint (3) are vessel-separable; only (3) links vessels through shared QCs. We apply Dantzig-Wolfe decomposition [5], keeping the linking constraint in the master problem and generating feasible schedules (columns) for each vessel through a pricing subproblem. This decomposition at the vessel follows the same principle of column generation used in related quay crane planning [7]. Here, the pricing problem focuses on QCSP crane block scheduling for each vessel.

A column $p \in \mathcal{P}_i$ for vessel i specifies a contiguous crane block (l_t^p, w_t^p) at each $t \in \mathcal{T}_i$, satisfying all per-vessel constraints, with cost c_p^i computed from the objective of (M1). Let $a_{jt}^{ip} = 1$ if column p assigns crane j at time t. The restricted master problem (RMP) is:

$$\text{(M2)} \quad \text{Min} \sum_{i \in N} \sum_{p \in P_i} c_p^i \lambda_{ip} \tag{12}$$

$$\sum_{p \in P_i} \lambda_{ip} = 1 \quad \forall i \in N \ (\alpha_i) \tag{13}$$

$$\sum_{i \in N} \sum_{p \in P_i} a_{jt}^{ip} \lambda_{ip} \leq 1 \quad \forall j, t \ (\mu_{jt}) \tag{14}$$

$$\lambda_{ip} \geq 0 \quad \forall i, p \tag{15}$$

Given duals α_i *and* $\mu_{jt} \geq 0$, the pricing subproblem for vessel i finds a minimum reduced cost schedule. Using block-selection variables y_{tlw} and derived crane usage u_{jt}:

$$\text{SP}_i \quad \overline{c}_i^* = \text{Min} \sum_{j \in J} \sum_{t \in \mathcal{T}_i} \left[C^s s_{jt} + C^o \left(u_{jt} - z_{jt} \right) - \mu_{jt} u_{jt} \right] - \alpha_i \tag{16}$$

$$\text{s.t.} \quad \sum_{(l,w) \in B_i} y_{tlw} + \delta_t = 1 \quad \forall t \in \mathcal{T}_i \tag{17}$$

$$u_{jt} = \sum_{\substack{(l,w) \in B_i \\ l \leq j < l + w}} y_{tlw} \quad \forall j \in J, t \in \mathcal{T}_i \tag{18}$$

$$\sum_{j \in J} \sum_{t \in \mathcal{T}_i} u_{jt} = W_i \tag{19}$$

$$y_{tlw}, u_{jt}, \delta_t \in \{0, 1\}, s_{jt} \in \{0, 1\}, \ 0 \leq z_{jt} \leq H \tag{20}$$

where $s_{jt} = 1$ when crane j begins a new session ($u_{jt} = 1$ and $u_{j,\,t-1} = 0$), and overtime counters z_{jt} are bounded as in (M1) with u_{jt} replacing x_{ijt}. Each time slot selects exactly one block or idle (17, 18) derives per-crane usage from the block selection, inherently enforcing adjacency and crane count bounds through the definition of $\mathcal{B}_i$. Column generation alternates between solving (M2) and (SP$_i$) until $\overline{c_i^*} \geq 0$ for all i, yielding the LP relaxation bound.

3 Neural Branch-and-Price

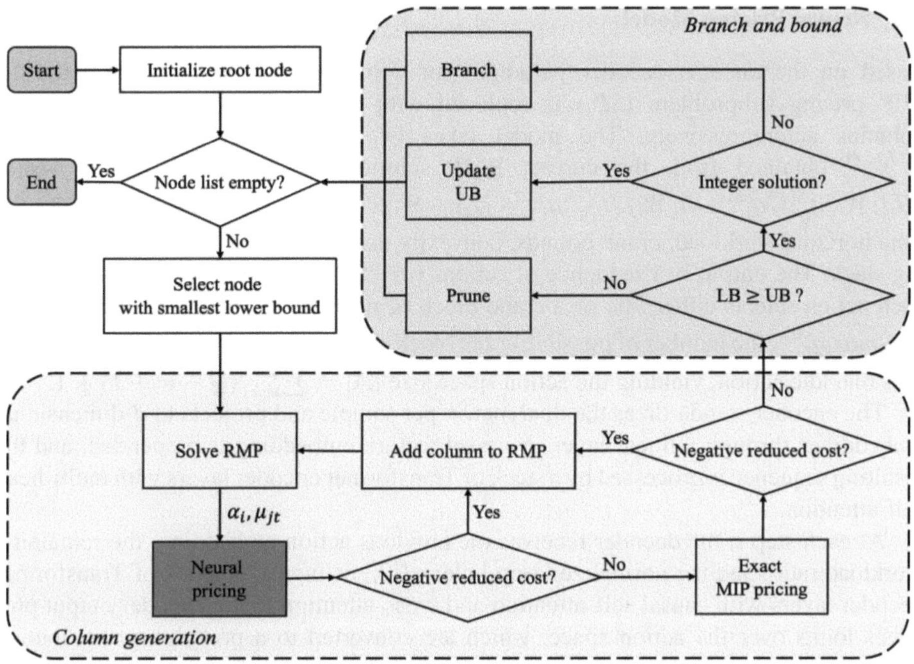

Fig. 1. Overview of the neural branch-and-price framework. The column generation loop alternates between RMP solving and pricing; the neural pricing model replaces the MIP subproblem, with exact MIP pricing serving as a verification step.

Figure 1 illustrates the overall procedure. The column pool is initialized with greedy heuristic columns, and column generation is carried out at each node of the branch-and-bound tree. At the root node, CG proceeds in two phases: Phase 1 drives the artificial variables to zero to establish LP feasibility, and Phase 2 optimizes the LP objective. Within the CG loop, the RMP is solved to obtain dual values (α_i, μ_{jt}), and the neural pricing model generates candidate columns. When no improving neural column is found, exact MIP pricing verifies optimality. After CG converges, the node is pruned if its lower bound exceeds the incumbent, or the RMP is solved as an integer problem to update the incumbent. Otherwise, branching is performed on the original variable x_{ijt} whose value, computed from the current λ solution, is most fractional, and node-specific branching constraints are imposed at each child node. The tree is explored in best-first order.

The initial column pool is constructed from greedy vessel schedules obtained by varying the number and placement of active time slots and the position of the crane block. Phase 1 uses artificial variables in the vessel convexity constraints and Phase 2 fixes them to zero; no dual stabilization, cutting planes, or strong branching are used. Since MIP B&P and Neural B&P share this same B&P scaffold, their comparison isolates the effect of the pricing module. Branching decisions on x_{ijt} are enforced as constraints on column sums in the RMP, as fixed u_{jt} values in MIP pricing, and by filtering sampled columns before evaluating reduced costs in neural pricing.

3.1 Neural Pricing Model

Based on the encoder-decoder paradigm for combinatorial optimization [10], the MIP pricing subproblem (SP_i) is replaced with a neural network that generates columns autoregressively. The model takes two inputs: the dual matrix $\mu \in \mathbb{R}^{|\mathcal{T}_i| \times Q}$ obtained from the current RMP solution, and a vessel feature vector $(|\mathcal{T}_i|, W_i, q_i^{min}, q_i^{max}, \alpha_i, W_i/|\mathcal{T}_i|, q_i^{max} \cdot |\mathcal{T}_i| - W_i, |\mathcal{T}_i| - \lceil W_i/q_i^{max} \rceil)$ that encodes the time horizon, workload, crane bounds, convexity dual, workload density, and scheduling slack. The output is a sequence of actions $(a_1, \ldots, a_{|\mathcal{T}_i|})$, one per time slot, where each action selects either idle or a crane block (l, w) from the feasible set $\mathcal{B}_i$. Letting $\overline{q} = max_i q_i^{max}$, the number of possible crane block configurations is $\sum_{w=1}^{\overline{q}} (Q - w + 1)$, plus one idle action, yielding the action space size $|\mathcal{A}| = \sum_{w=1}^{\overline{q}} (Q - w + 1) + 1$.

The encoder standardizes the dual matrix per sample and projects to d-dimensional embeddings through a linear layer. A vessel feature embedding is prepended, and the resulting sequence is processed by a stack of Transformer encoder layers with multi-head self-attention.

At each step t, the decoder receives the previous action embedding, the remaining workload ratio, and the normalized step index $t/|\mathcal{T}_i|$ as inputs. A stack of Transformer decoder layers with causal self-attention and cross-attention to the encoder output produces logits over the action space, which are converted to a probability distribution through a softmax operation.

To guarantee constraint satisfaction by construction, a feasibility mask $m_t \in \{0, 1\}^{|\mathcal{A}|}$ is applied at each decoding step. Let $R_t = W_i - \sum_{\mathcal{T}<t} w_{\mathcal{T}}$ denote the remaining workload. An action (l, w) is masked if: (i) $w > R_t$ (the block width exceeds the remaining workload); (ii) $w \notin [q_i^{min}, q_i^{max}]$ (the crane count violates the given bounds); or (iii) the remaining time slots are insufficient to complete $R_t - w$ at the maximum rate q_i^{max} (look-ahead infeasibility). The idle action is masked when $R_t > q_i^{max} \cdot (|\mathcal{T}_i| - t)$, meaning that any further idling would make it impossible to complete the workload. The masked logits are set to $-\infty$ before the softmax operation, ensuring that every sampled column is feasible. The mask enforces one block or idle per time slot, crane-count bounds, contiguity by block construction, and exact workload completion. Shared crane capacity remains a master constraint.

During inference, KV-caching is employed to achieve $O(T)$ autoregressive decoding. For each vessel, K candidate columns are sampled at a given temperature, and the column with the lowest reduced cost is selected.

3.2 Training Procedure

The training data is collected by running column generation with exact MIP pricing on synthetic QCSP instances, where the vessel parameters (arrival, departure, workload, crane bounds) are drawn from the empirical distribution of Busan Port data. Each pricing call produces an input-output pair: the current dual values (μ, α_i) and vessel parameters serve as the input, while the optimal block schedule is used as the target action sequence. The resulting dataset consists of 80,534 samples (68,457 training and 12,077 validation).

The model is trained using teacher forcing cross-entropy loss with the AdamW optimizer (learning rate 3×10^{-4}, weight decay 0.01, batch size 64), a cosine learning rate schedule (warmup 500 steps), gradient clipping at 1.0, and early stopping on validation loss (patience 20 epochs). On the validation set, the trained model achieves a per-action accuracy of 85.6%, a feasibility rate of 100%, and a mean (median) cost gap of 5.4% (0.0%) relative to the exact MIP pricing solution.

3.3 Hybrid Neural-MIP Pricing

Since neural pricing alone cannot guarantee CG convergence (the model may fail to identify a negative reduced cost column that exists), a hybrid strategy is adopted to preserve exactness. At each CG iteration, K columns are sampled from the neural model, and the column with the most negative reduced cost is added to the RMP. If no improving column is found among the K samples, a single round of exact MIP pricing is performed to verify the optimality of the current LP solution. When MIP pricing discovers improving columns, CG resumes with neural pricing. After n_f consecutive verification rounds without neural improvement, pricing switches to MIP for the remainder of the node. This design ensures exact LP bounds while delegating the bulk of pricing to the neural model. A node LP bound is accepted only after exact MIP pricing has verified that all vessel pricing subproblems have nonnegative reduced cost. Therefore, if the neural model misses an improving column, convergence may be delayed, but the resulting LP bound remains valid.

4 Numerical Experiments

4.1 Experimental Setup

The proposed method is evaluated on real-world operational data from Busan Port, South Korea, comprising 115 vessels with recorded arrival/departure times, cargo volumes, and QC specifications. Workloads are computed as $W_i = \lceil V_i/P \rceil$, where V_i is the cargo volume (in TEUs) and $P = 25$ TEUs per time slot is the QC productivity. Test instances of size $N \in \{10, 15, 20, 25, 30\}$ are generated at 10 evenly spaced starting indices, yielding 50 test instances. The terminal operates $Q = 11$ QCs with $\overline{q} = 7$, yielding $|\mathcal{A}| = 57$ actions. The cost parameters are $C^s = 253.7$, $C^0 = 31.7$, and $H = 8$.

The Transformer model has 3 encoder and 3 decoder layers with embedding dimension $d = 128$ and 4 attention heads (1.0 M parameters total). At inference, $K = 128$ candidate columns are sampled per vessel at temperature 0.8, and the fallback threshold is set to $n_f = 3$. All experiments are conducted on an Apple M4 Pro (24GB RAM) with Gurobi 13.0.1; neural inference runs on CPU.

Three methods are compared under a one-hour time limit: Baseline MILP, which solves (M1) directly; MIP B&P, B&P with exact MIP pricing; and Neural B&P, B&P with the proposed hybrid neural-MIP pricing.

4.2 Exact Method Comparison

The results are summarized in Table 2. Neural B&P proves optimality in 45 of 50 instances, compared with 34 for MIP B&P and 16 for Baseline MILP. For $N \leq 20$, Neural B&P achieves a perfect optimality rate (30/30), whereas MIP B&P leaves 4 instances unresolved and the MILP solver leaves 15. At $N = 25$, Neural B&P proves optimality in 9 out of 10 instances, compared with 5 for MIP B&P and 1 for Baseline MILP. At $N = 30$, Neural B&P fails to find a feasible integer solution in one instance within the time limit. Although the MILP solver finds feasible solutions in all cases through its primal heuristics, the weak LP relaxation of the compact formulation prevents it from closing the optimality gap. The B&P framework yields tighter LP bounds through Dantzig-Wolfe decomposition, and Neural B&P reduces runtime relative to MIP B&P in this controlled comparison, achieving a speedup of 7.4 times at $N = 10$ and 1.4 times at $N = 30$ compared to MIP B&P.

Table 2. Comparison of exact methods under a one-hour time limit

N	Baseline MILP			MIP B&P			Neural B&P		
	Feas	Opt	Time	Feas	Opt	Time	Feas	Opt	Time
10	10/10	8/10	872	10/10	10/10	214	10/10	10/10	29
15	10/10	4/10	2235	10/10	10/10	748	10/10	10/10	188
20	10/10	3/10	2818	10/10	6/10	1811	10/10	10/10	726
25	10/10	1/10	3540	7/10	5/10	2274	10/10	9/10	1136
30	10/10	0/10	3602	4/10	3/10	2919	9/10	6/10	2152
Total	50/50	16/50	–	41/50	34/50	–	49/50	45/50	–

Feas/Opt: instances with feasible solution found / proven optimal, out of 10. Time: average runtime (seconds). All methods use a one-hour time limit.

Figure 2 presents the cumulative number of optimally solved instances as a function of computation time. Neural B&P achieves better certification performance across most time budgets: within 5 min, it solves 28 instances, which is already close to MIP B&P's final count at the one-hour limit. The advantage is most pronounced in the 100–1800s range, where neural pricing avoids many of the expensive MIP pricing calls that limit MIP B&P.

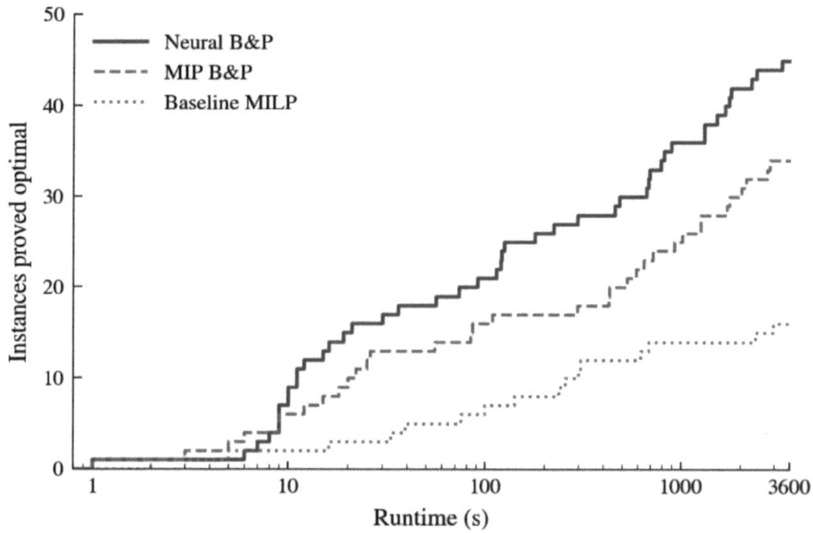

Fig. 2. Performance profile: cumulative instances proved optimal vs. runtime across all 50 main instances ($N = 10$–30).

4.3 Incumbent Quality Comparison

Table 3 complements the exact comparison in Table 2 by comparing incumbent quality against two reference heuristics on the same instance grid. The heuristic references are motivated by different QCSP heuristic paradigms. The first is an adapted Lagrangian relaxation (LR) heuristic for multi-ship QCSP [13]. In our adaptation, shared crane capacity constraints are moved into the objective through nonnegative multipliers. The resulting vessel subproblems are solved with the pricing MIP, and a restricted selection MIP over the accumulated schedules recovers a feasible solution. The second, Priority, is a constructive priority-rule heuristic for QCSP [14]. It orders vessels using arrival, workload, slack, and crane pressure scores, then constructs each vessel schedule by selecting feasible contiguous crane blocks on the shared crane capacity calendar, followed by local improvement through removing and reinserting vessels.

LR achieves small gaps on the instances for which it recovers a feasible solution, whereas Priority is more robust on larger instances but yields larger average gaps. Neural B&P provides the most reliable incumbents, finding feasible solutions in 49 of 50 instances with the smallest overall average gap of 0.06%. Because LR and Priority are reference heuristics for incumbent generation while Neural B&P is an exact B&P framework, Table 3 should be read as an incumbent-quality comparison that complements the optimality-certification results in Table 2.

Table 3. Incumbent quality comparison with reference heuristics.

N	LR [13]			Priority [14]			Neural B&P		
	Feas	Gap	Time	Feas	Gap	Time	Feas	Gap	Time
10	10/10	0.05%	71	10/10	0.23%	91	10/10	0.00%	29
15	9/10	0.17%	104	10/10	1.50%	149	10/10	0.00%	188
20	9/10	0.26%	146	10/10	1.70%	188	10/10	0.00%	726
25	7/10	0.18%	186	9/10	1.12%	198	10/10	0.01%	1136
30	5/10	0.30%	232	8/10	2.57%	346	9/10	0.30%	2152
Total	40/50	0.18%	–	47/50	1.38%	–	49/50	0.06%	–

Feas: feasible instances out of 10. Gap: average gap to the best-known incumbent over feasible cases. Time: average runtime (seconds). LR and Priority do not provide optimality certificates.

4.4 Pricing Efficiency Analysis

The per-iteration pricing costs are reported in Table 4. As N increases, the vessel-level MIP becomes more difficult to solve, and the MIP pricing cost rises from 3.66 s to 6.09 s per CG iteration. The neural pricing model reduces this cost to 0.60–2.17 s, corresponding to a 3 to 6 times speedup, while generating 94–99% of all columns. The hybrid strategy triggers a full MIP fallback only 0.2–2.4 times per instance on average, which indicates that the neural model reliably produces improving columns throughout the CG process.

Table 4. Pricing efficiency: per-iteration cost and neural model reliability.

N	MIP B&P	Neural B&P		$\mathrm{Col_N}$ (%)	Fallbacks
	Time/Iter	Time/Iter	Speedup		
15	3.66	0.60	6.1×	98.6	0.2
20	4.30	1.38	3.1×	93.7	0.9
25	4.93	1.67	3.0×	97.4	0.6
30	6.09	2.17	2.8×	96.0	2.4

Time/Iter: average pricing time per CG iteration (seconds). $\mathrm{Col_N}$: share of columns generated by the neural model (%). Fallbacks: average number of times pricing switches entirely to MIP per instance.

5 Conclusions

In this paper, a neural column generation approach was proposed for the QCSP and integrated into a complete B&P framework. A Transformer model with feasibility masking generates feasible columns autoregressively, and a hybrid neural-MIP strategy preserves the exactness of column generation. Numerical experiments on real-world instances from Busan Port show that the neural model generates 94–99% of all columns while reducing per-iteration pricing cost by 3–6 times, and the proposed method proves optimality at problem scales where both direct MILP solving and MIP-based B&P struggle within practical time limits.

Acknowledgments. This research was supported by Korea Institute of Marine Science & Technology Promotion (KIMST) funded by the Ministry of Oceans and Fisheries, Korea (RS-2024-00407024, International Joint R&D and Collaborative Demonstration of VDES).

Disclosure of Interests. The authors have no competing interests to declare that are relevant to the content of this article.

References

1. United Nations Conference on Trade and Development (UNCTAD): Review of Maritime Transport 2025: Staying the Course in Turbulent Waters. United Nations, Geneva (2025)
2. Bierwirth, C., Meisel, F.: A survey of berth allocation and quay crane scheduling problems in container terminals. Eur. J. Oper. Res. **202**(3), 615–627 (2010)
3. Kim, K.H., Park, Y.M.: A crane scheduling method for port container terminals. Eur. J. Oper. Res. **156**(3), 752–768 (2004)
4. Cho, S.W., Park, H.J., Lee, C.: An integrated method for berth allocation and quay crane assignment to allow for reassignment of vessels to other terminals. Marit. Econ.Logistics. **23**(1), 123–153 (2021)
5. Barnhart, C., Johnson, E.L., Nemhauser, G.L., Savelsbergh, M.W., Vance, P.H.: Branch-and-price: column generation for solving huge integer programs. Oper. Res. **46**(3), 316–329 (1998)
6. Moccia, L., Cordeau, J.-F., Gaudioso, M., Laporte, G.: A branch-and-cut algorithm for the quay crane scheduling problem in a container terminal. Nav. Res. Logist. **53**(1), 45–59 (2006)
7. Sun, D., Tang, L., Baldacci, R.: A benders decomposition-based framework for solving quay crane scheduling problems. Eur. J. Oper. Res. **273**(2), 504–515 (2019)
8. Sun, D., Tang, L., Baldacci, R., Chen, Z.: A decomposition method for the group-based quay crane scheduling problem. INFORMS J. Comput. **36**(2), 543–570 (2024)
9. Abou Kasm, O., Diabat, A.: The quay crane scheduling problem with non-crossing and safety clearance constraints: an exact solution approach. Comput. Oper. Res. **107**, 189–199 (2019)
10. Vacca, I., Salani, M., Bierlaire, M.: An exact algorithm for the integrated planning of berth allocation and quay crane assignment. Transp. Sci. **47**(2), 148–161 (2013)
11. Morabit, M., Desaulniers, G., Lodi, A.: Machine-learning-based column selection for column generation. Transp. Sci. **55**(4), 815–831 (2021)
12. Shen, Y., Sun, Y., Li, X., Eberhard, A., Ernst, A.: Enhancing column generation by a machine-learning-based pricing heuristic for graph coloring. Proceedings of the AAAI Conference on Artificial Intelligence, 36(9), 9926–9934 (2022)
13. Hijazi, A., Ozaltin, O., Uzsoy, R.: All you need is an improving column: Enhancing column generation for parallel machine scheduling via transformers. arXiv preprint https://arxiv.org/abs/2410.15601 (2024)
14. Al-Dhaheri, N., Diabat, A.: A Lagrangian relaxation-based heuristic for the multi-ship quay crane scheduling problem with ship stability constraints. Ann. Oper. Res. **248**(1–2), 1–34 (2017)
15. Bierwirth, C., Meisel, F.: A fast heuristic for quay crane scheduling with interference constraints. J. Sched. **12**(4), 345–360 (2009)

Power Flexible Scheduling of Quay Cranes and Automated Guided Vehicles in Container Terminals

S. Mahdi Homayouni(✉)

School of Business, Social and Decision Sciences, Constructor University, Campus Ring 1, 28759 Bremen, Germany
mhomayouni@constructor.university

Abstract. This paper investigates the integrated scheduling of quay cranes (QCs) and automated guided vehicles (AGVs) in container terminals under strict instantaneous peak power constraints. As modern terminals transition into energy "prosumers", the management of volatile power demands is critical to avoiding prohibitive peak-demand charges and ensuring grid stability. We propose a bi-objective optimization framework designed to minimize both the total completion time (makespan) and unproductive (deadhead) AGV travel, while adhering to a hard upper bound on instantaneous power consumption. Unlike traditional scheduling models, our approach explicitly accounts for the high-intensity power profiles of QCs during hoisting cycles. A bi-objective non-dominated sorting genetic algorithm (NSGA-II) is developed, featuring a specialized heuristic to dynamically time QC tasks without violating power limits. Computational experiments quantify the trade-off between operational productivity and energy constraints, demonstrating that significant peak-shaving can be achieved with marginal impacts on terminal throughput. These insights provide a practical decision-making tool for terminal operators seeking to balance logistical efficiency with energy sustainability.

Keywords: Container Terminal Operations · Quay Crane and AGV Coordination · Peak Power Management · Energy-Aware Scheduling · Multi-objective Optimization · NSGA-II

1 Introduction

Efficient container handling in modern container terminals is a sophisticated logistical challenge requiring the seamless synchronization of quay cranes (QCs), horizontal transport vehicles, and yard cranes. When a vessel berths, QCs discharge import containers onto transport vehicles, which then shuttle them to load/unload (LU) stations for yard storage. This process is reversed for export containers.

Automated guided vehicles (AGVs) have become a cornerstone of modern terminal operations, as seen in the Euromax (Rotterdam) and Pasir Panjang (Singapore) facilities. Because AGVs lack self-loading capabilities, their efficiency is

J. de Armas and E. Lalla Ruiz (Eds.): LOGMS 2026, LNCS 16679, pp. 40–50, 2027.
https://doi.org/10.1007/978-3-032-30795-8_4

strictly tethered to crane availability. This interdependence often leads to operational bottlenecks where AGVs idle awaiting a crane, or vice versa. Optimizing terminal throughput, therefore, requires an integrated scheduling approach. As noted in recent literature [3,6], this coordination involves three critical dimensions: (i) QC task timing, (ii) AGV-to-task assignment, and (iii) the specific dispatching and routing of those AGVs.

Parallel to these operational challenges, seaports are evolving into major energy hubs, both consuming and producing electricity from renewable sources [8]. However, the stochastic nature of port activities creates volatile instantaneous power demands. Unregulated peaks in demand can strain local grid infrastructure and lead to significant financial penalties. In many jurisdictions, electricity billing includes a substantial fixed capacity charge based on the highest recorded peak demand over a rolling 12-month period [5]. These peak demand charges can account for 25–30% of a terminal's total energy expenditure; thus, "peak shaving" is a vital economic lever.

QCs are the most energy-intensive assets in a terminal. A single QC may demand approximately 1500 kW during high-load hoisting operations, compared to significantly lower draws, roughly 200 kW, during horizontal trolley movements or empty spreads [10].

This paper investigates the integrated scheduling of QCs and AGVs under explicit peak power constraints. Our objective is twofold: to minimize the makespan (total completion time) while simultaneously reducing unproductive (deadhead) AGV travel. Unlike previous models that treat energy as a flexible cost, we model peak power as a hard constraint, reflecting the physical or contractual limits of the terminal's power supply.

The main contributions of this work are threefold: (i) we formulate a coordinated scheduling model for QCs and AGVs that strictly adheres to peak power thresholds, addressing a critical gap in sustainable port operations; (ii) we develop a bi-objective Non-dominated sorting genetic algorithm (NSGA-II) tailored with a specialized heuristic to manage task timing under power-limit interference; and (iii) we quantify the trade-offs between operational speed (makespan) and power constraints through extensive computational experiments.

The remainder of this paper is organized as follows: Sect. 2 details the problem definition. Section 3 describes the proposed NSGA-II approach. Section 4 presents the numerical results and sensitivity analysis. Finally, Sect. 5 concludes with directions for future research.

2 Problem Definition

Container ships arrive at ports and, based on ship and cargo characteristics, terminal operators determine berthing positions and QC assignments. The sequence of containers to be handled and the specific QC assigned to each are predetermined.

Unloading tasks involve moving a container from the ship to the yard. The process requires the QC to move empty to the ship's holding area, hoist down to

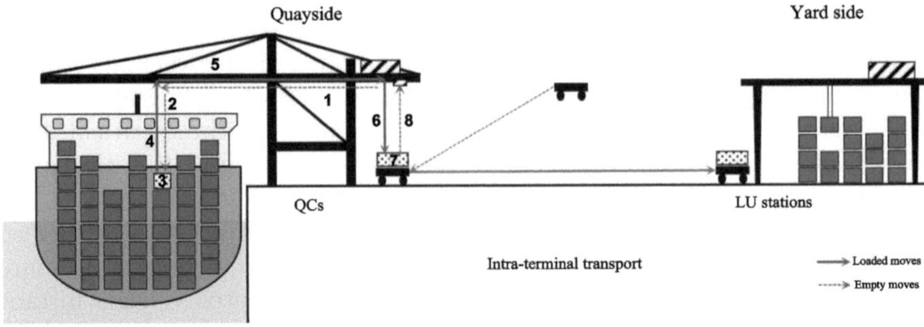

Fig. 1. Schematic of the operational sequence for an unloading task: (1) QC empty horizontal travel, (2) empty hoisting down to the container, (3) container pick-up, (4) loaded hoisting up, (5) loaded horizontal transfer to the quayside, (6) loaded hoisting down, (7) container release onto the AGV, and (8) empty hoisting up. Simultaneously, an empty AGV travels from its dwell point to the quayside.

the container, grab it, lift it to a safe height, move horizontally to the quayside, and hoist down. Concurrently, an empty AGV moves from its dwell point to the quayside. Once both the QC and AGV are available at the quayside, the QC drops the container onto the AGV, hoists up empty, and becomes ready for its next task. The AGV then transports the container to a predetermined LU station in the storage yard. The QC handling time for unloading is defined as the duration from the start of its empty move to the ship until the container is released onto the AGV. A schematic of this process is shown in Fig. 1.

Loading tasks involve moving containers from the storage yard to the ship. Containers are assumed available at LU stations, where they are picked up by AGVs and transported to the quayside. Once the AGV and the assigned QC are both available, the QC picks up the container, releasing the AGV. The QC then lifts the container, moves it onto the ship, hoists down to the holding space, and returns empty to the quayside. Thus, the QC handling time for loading is the interval from picking up the container from the AGV until the QC returns to the quayside, ready for its next assignment.

A transport task requires an AGV to carry a container from origin to destination. If the AGV's dwell point differs from the container's location, the task includes an empty leg (unproductive travel) from the dwell point to the pick-up location, followed by a loaded leg to the drop-off location. We assume AGVs remain at their last drop-off location (dwell point) until assigned a new task, and any AGV can be assigned to any container. QCs and AGVs perform tasks non-preemptively. Initial AGV locations, the terminal layout, and travel distances are predetermined.

Let $\mathcal{K}$ be the set of quay cranes. For any quay crane $k \in \mathcal{K}$, let n_k denote the number of tasks assigned to it. The ordered sequence of tasks assigned to QC_k is denoted by $\mathcal{J}_k$, where the tasks are indexed as: $\left(\sum_{i=1}^{k-1} n_i\right)+1, \ldots, \sum_{i=1}^{k} n_i \in \mathcal{J}_k$, with the standard convention that $\sum_{i=1}^{0} n_i = 0$. Furthermore, let $\mathcal{L}$ and $\mathcal{U}$ denote

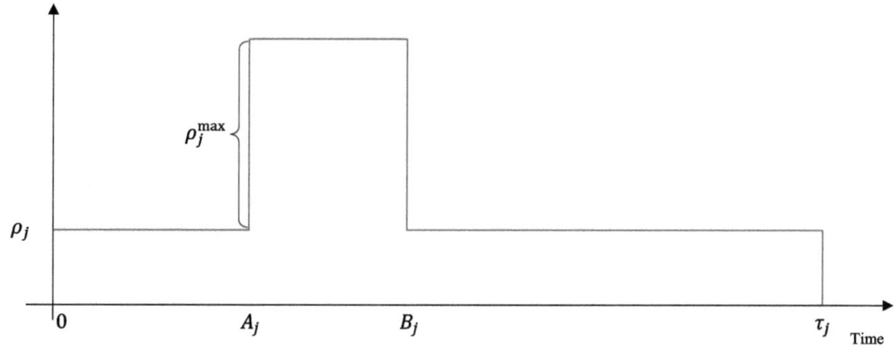

Fig. 2. The simplified instantaneous power consumption by a QC.

the sets of loading and unloading tasks, respectively. The set of all tasks in the horizon is defined as $\mathcal{J} = \mathcal{L} \cup \mathcal{U}$, which represents the union of all disjoint crane task sets, such that $\mathcal{J} = \bigcup_{k \in \mathcal{K}} \mathcal{J}_k$. Also, let $\mathcal{A}$ represent the set of identical AGVs traveling at varying constant speeds depending on whether they are loaded or empty.

QCs are the primary power consumers in this work. While handling task $j \in \mathcal{J}$ for duration τ_j, QC consumes a base power ρ_j. However, hoisting a container requires additional power ($\rho_j^{\max}$). The hoisting duration $[A_j, B_j]$ depends on the task type and the vertical distance (e.g., stack depth). Figure 2 illustrates this power profile. We assume idle power consumption for both QCs and AGVs is negligible.

We seek to minimize the makespan of all tasks ($\mathcal{C}$) and the total unproductive (deadhead) AGV travel distance ($\mathcal{D}$), as defined in Eqs. 1–3, where c_j is the completion time of task $j \in \mathcal{J}$, δ_{ij} is the empty distance between tasks i and j, δ_{aj} is the initial empty distance for AGV $a \in \mathcal{A}$, and x_{ij} and y_{aj} are binary variables if task $j \in \mathcal{J}$ is done by the same vehicle after task $i \in \mathcal{J}$ or if it is assigned to AGV $a \in \mathcal{A}$ as its first task.

$$\text{Minimize} \quad \{\mathcal{C}, \mathcal{D}\} \tag{1}$$

where

$$\mathcal{C} \geq c_j, \qquad \forall j \in \mathcal{J}, \tag{2}$$

$$\mathcal{D} = \sum_{i,j \in \mathcal{J}} (x_{ij}\delta_{ij}) + \sum_{a \in \mathcal{A}} \sum_{j \in \mathcal{J}} (y_{aj}\delta_{aj}), \tag{3}$$

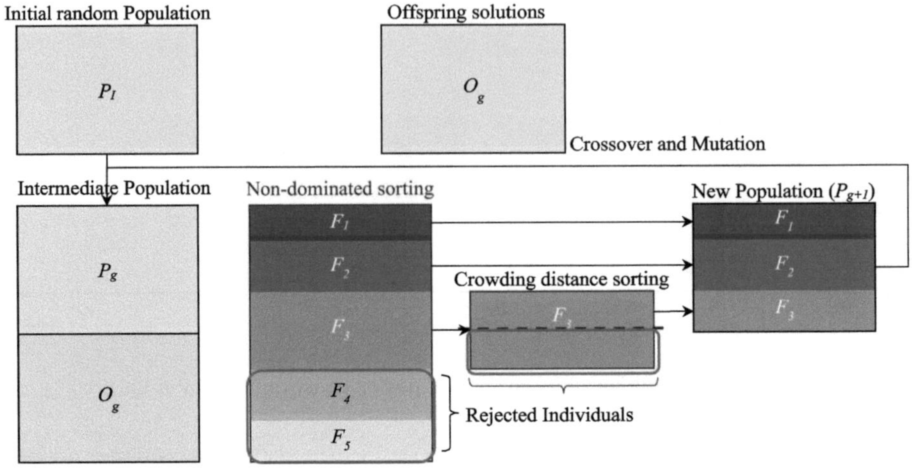

Fig. 3. Block diagram of the NSGA-II

3 The Proposed NSGA-II

The Non-dominated sorting genetic algorithm II (NSGA-II) is a widely used evolutionary algorithm for solving multi-objective optimization problems [2]. It is particularly effective in scheduling applications where conflicting objectives, such as minimizing makespan and energy consumption, must be balanced [4]. NSGA-II evolves a population of solutions across generations using non-dominated sorting, crowding distance, and elitism to maintain diversity and convergence toward the Pareto-optimal front (see Fig. 3).

Non-dominated sorting ranks individuals based on dominance relationships: an individual dominates another if it is better in at least one objective and not worse in any others. Ranks are assigned based on the number of dominating individuals; lower ranks indicate superior solutions. To maintain population diversity, the crowding distance operator selects individuals in less densely populated regions of the objective space.

3.1 Encoding and Decoding

A solution is represented by a two-part vector, each containing $|\mathcal{J}|$ elements, where $|\mathcal{J}|$ is the number of tasks in the horizon. The first part determines the order in which tasks are handled, while the second part assigns a specific AGV to each task.

Each element is a random key (RK), a real number in the interval $[0, 1]$. This scheme allows for efficient exploration of the solution space and quick identification of high-quality solutions. Figure 4. illustrates the encoding for an instance with 12 tasks and two AGVs.The decoding procedure for the first N elements utilizes the smallest position value (SPV) rule [1] to obtain a permutation by sorting

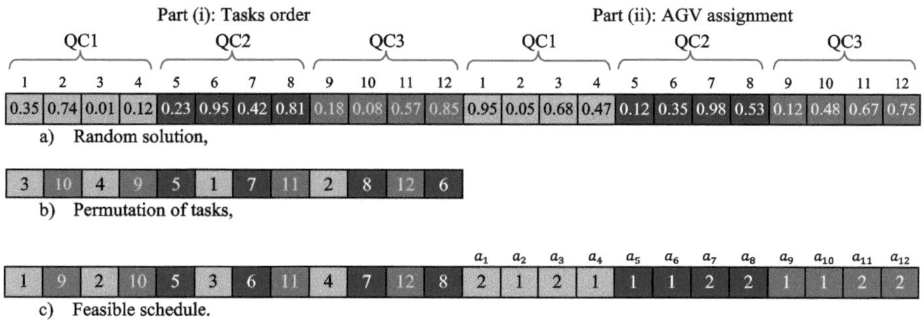

Fig. 4. Solution encoding and decoding for the illustrative problem instance with 12 containers, three QCs each of which is associated with four tasks, and two AGVs.

the RKs in ascending order. This sequence is then converted into a feasible operation sequence by sorting tasks for each QC to ensure precedence constraints. The second part of the chromosome assigns an AGV to each task j using the formula $\lceil \mathrm{RK}_j \times |\mathcal{A}| \rceil$. This procedure inherently satisfies precedence constraints, reducing the search space and eliminating the need for repair mechanisms.

3.2 Scheduling Strategy

Beyond sequencing and assignment, we must determine the start and completion times for all QC and AGV tasks. QC operations are contingent upon instantaneous power availability; if the grid limit is exceeded, the task must be postponed. Conversely, since AGVs in this model do not draw grid power during transport, their tasks initiate at the earliest possible start (EPS) time. We propose a priority scheduling scheme that: (i) follows the task order from the decoding stage, and (ii) initiates tasks at their EPS, provided power constraints are met.

This strategy is detailed in Algorithm 1. For unloading tasks (lines 5–16), a QC can ideally start as soon as it completes its previous task. If sufficient power is available for both the base load (ρ_j) and the hoisting peak ($\rho_j^{\max}$), the task is scheduled. The task concludes once the assigned AGV arrives at the quayside to receive the container. For loading tasks (lines 17–31), an AGV begins by moving to the yard LU area, picks up the container, and travels to the QC. The QC starts the handling process once it is free and the AGV has arrived, provided the power limit $\mathcal{P}_t^{\text{limit}}$ is respected. If power is insufficient at the EPS, the algorithm searches for the earliest subsequent time step where the constraint is satisfied.

3.3 Crossover and Mutation Operators

Offspring are generated via parameterized uniform crossover (PUC) [9]. PUC combines two parents and allows the swapping probability of each gene to be controlled, preserving high-quality genetic structures. Parents are selected through

Algorithm 1. The Scheduling Algorithm

Initialize the ordered set of tasks $\mathcal{O}$ and the assigned AGV, and total empty traveled distance $\mathcal{D} = 0$.
Initialize the current time and location of AGVs, $c_a = 0, l_a, a \in \mathcal{A}$ and current time of QCs, $c_k = 0, k \in \mathcal{K}$;
while $\mathcal{O} \neq \emptyset$ **do**
  Consider the first task in $\mathcal{O}$, j, and its assigned AGV, a_j;
  if $j \in \mathcal{U}$ **then**
    while task j is not scheduled **do**
      Set the current time as $\vartheta = c_{k_j}$;
      if $\rho_j \leq \mathcal{P}_t^{\text{limit}}, \forall t \in \{\vartheta, \ldots, \vartheta + \tau_j\}$ and $\rho_j^{\max} + \rho_j \leq \mathcal{P}_t^{\text{limit}}, \forall t \in \{\vartheta + A_j, \ldots \vartheta + B_j\}$ **then**
        Schedule the task, $s_j = \vartheta$; $c_j = c_{k_j} = \max\left\{s_j + \tau_j, c_{a_j} + \frac{\delta_{l_{a_j} k_j}}{v}\right\} + \Delta_j$;
        Update AGV a_j time and location, $c_{a_j} = c_j + \frac{d_j}{w}$, $l_{a_j} = u_j$;
        Update empty traveled distance, $\mathcal{D} += \delta_{l_{a_j} k_j}$;
        Update the remaining power, $\mathcal{P}_t^{\text{limit}} -= \rho_j, \forall t \in \{s_j, \ldots, s_j + \tau_j\}$, $\mathcal{P}_t^{\text{limit}} -= \rho_j^{\max}, \forall t \in \{s_j + A_j, \ldots, s_j + B_j\}$;
      else
        Update current time, $\vartheta += 1$
      end if
    end while
  else if $j \in \mathcal{L}$ **then**
    while task j is not scheduled **do**
      Update AGV a_j time and location, $c_{a_j} = c_{a_j} + \frac{\delta_{l_{a_j} u_j}}{v} + \frac{d_j}{w}$, $l_{a_j} = k_j$;
      Set the current time as $\vartheta = \max\{c_{k_j}, c_{a_j}\} + \Delta_j$;
      Update empty traveled distance, $\mathcal{D} += \delta_{l_{a_j} u_j}$;
      if $\rho_j \leq \mathcal{P}_t^{\text{limit}}, \forall t \in \{\vartheta, \ldots, \vartheta + \tau_j\}$ and $\rho_j^{\max} + \rho_j \leq \mathcal{P}_t^{\text{limit}}, \forall t \in \{\vartheta + A_j, \ldots \vartheta + B_j\}$ **then**
        Schedule the task, $s_j = \vartheta$, $c_j = c_{k_j} = s_j + \tau_j$, $c_{a_j} = s_j$;
        Update the remaining power, $\mathcal{P}_t^{\text{limit}} -= \rho_j, \forall t \in \{s_j, \ldots, s_j + \tau_j\}$, $\mathcal{P}_t^{\text{limit}} -= \rho_j^{\max}, \forall t \in \{s_j + A_j, \ldots, s_j + B_j\}$;
      else
        Update current time, $\vartheta += 1$
      end if
    end while
  end if
  Update the set of unscheduled operations, $\mathcal{O} = \mathcal{O} \setminus \{j\}$;
end while
Calculate $\mathcal{C} = \max\left(\max_{j \in \mathcal{U}}\{c_{a_j}\}, \max_{j \in \mathcal{L}}\{c_j\}\right)$
Return the schedule and the values of $\mathcal{C}$ and $\mathcal{D}$.

tournament selection: a subset of individuals is chosen at random, and the one with the best non-dominated rank (or highest crowding distance in case of a tie) is selected. This ensures selection pressure toward the Pareto front while maintaining diversity to avoid premature convergence.In the crossover proce-

0.35	0.74	0.01	0.12	0.23	0.95	0.42	0.81	0.18	0.08	0.57	0.85	0.95	0.05	0.68	0.47	0.12	0.35	0.98	0.53	0.12	0.48	0.67	0.75

a) Parent 1,

0.28	0.11	0.01	0.03	0.13	0.12	0.22	0.66	0.36	0.59	0.54	0.56	0.67	0.53	0.67	0.13	0.89	0.18	0.64	0.71	0.88	0.53	0.27	0.28

b) Parent 2,

0.30	0.39	0.70	0.71	0.97	0.35	0.97	0.53	0.10	0.51	0.39	0.52	0.95	0.95	0.70	0.40	0.96	0.40	0.10	0.03	0.29	0.23	0.56	0.30

c) Mapping vector,

0.35	0.74	0.01	0.03	0.13	0.95	0.22	0.66	0.18	0.59	0.57	0.56	0.67	0.53	0.67	0.47	0.89	0.35	0.98	0.53	0.12	0.48	0.27	0.75

d) Offspring 1,

0.28	0.11	0.01	0.12	0.23	0.12	0.42	0.81	0.36	0.08	0.54	0.85	0.95	0.05	0.68	0.13	0.12	0.18	0.64	0.71	0.88	0.53	0.67	0.28

e) Offspring 2.

Fig. 5. The parameterized uniform crossover operator generates two offspring from the two selected parents.

dure, each gene in the offspring has a 0.5 probability of being inherited from either parent. A mapping vector of random numbers determines the inheritance for each position, as shown in Fig. 5.

The mutation operator selects individuals from the population and applies one of two logic paths based on a random threshold. If the random value is less than 0.5, two elements in the sequencing part of the vector are swapped. Otherwise, a random cell in the assignment part is replaced by its complement $(1 - \mathrm{RK}_j)$. These mutations allow the algorithm to explore different task sequences or reassign tasks to different AGVs.

4 Results

We evaluate the performance of the proposed NSGA-II and the heuristic scheduling algorithm on a set of 10 medium and large-sized problem instances (DL01–DL10) as defined in [3]. These instances involve 40 to 160 containers handled by 8 to 16 QCs and transported by 4 to 8 AGVs. Consistent with [3], the average speeds for AGVs are set at 6 m/s when traveling empty and 3 m/s when carrying a 40-tonne load. Regarding power consumption, a typical QC is assumed to consume 1500 kW during container hoisting and 200 kW during horizontal movement or lowering of the spreader [5].

The solution algorithm was implemented in Python® 3.8 and executed on a 3.20 GHz Intel Core i7-8700 PC with 24 GB RAM. To calibrate the NSGA-II, control parameters were set based on literature recommendations [3,7]: the population size was set to 500, the mutation rate to 20%, and the crossover probability to 0.5.

To analyze the impact of peak power limitations on terminal efficiency, we first solved all instances while disregarding power limits (the unconstrained scenario). Subsequently, we imposed a hard instantaneous power limit of 4500 kW, mathematically restricting the system to a maximum of three simultaneous hoisting tasks, and re-solved all instances.

Table 1 reports the makespan ($\mathcal{C}$) and total unproductive traveling distance ($\mathcal{D}$) for the two extreme solutions on the Pareto front: the minimum makespan ($\mathcal{C}^*$) and the minimum unproductive distance ($\mathcal{D}^*$). These results are presented for both the no-limit (NL) and power-limit (PL) scenarios. To quantify the impact of the power constraint, we calculate the percentage gaps using Eqs. (4) and (5).

$$\delta_{\mathcal{C}^*} = 100 \times \sqrt{\left(\frac{\mathcal{C}^*_{\mathrm{PL}} - \mathcal{C}^*_{\mathrm{NL}}}{\mathcal{C}^*_{\mathrm{NL}}}\right)^2 + \left(\frac{\mathcal{D}_{\mathrm{PL}} - \mathcal{D}_{\mathrm{NL}}}{\mathcal{D}_{\mathrm{NL}}}\right)^2}, \tag{4}$$

$$\delta_{\mathcal{D}^*} = 100 \times \sqrt{\left(\frac{\mathcal{C}_{\mathrm{PL}} - \mathcal{C}_{\mathrm{NL}}}{\mathcal{C}_{\mathrm{NL}}}\right)^2 + \left(\frac{\mathcal{D}^*_{\mathrm{PL}} - \mathcal{D}^*_{\mathrm{NL}}}{\mathcal{D}^*_{\mathrm{NL}}}\right)^2}. \tag{5}$$

On average, the optimal makespan ($\mathcal{C}^*$) solutions degraded by 7.0% when the power limit was applied. Similarly, the $\mathcal{D}^*$ solutions showed an average degradation of 7.4%. These results highlight the trade-off between energy-conscious scheduling and operational throughput.

Table 1. Extreme solutions for problem instances without power constraints and with a power constraint of 4500 kW.

Ins.	Q-T-A	No Power Limit				Power Limit = 4500 kW				GAPs	
		$\mathcal{C}^*_{\mathrm{NL}}$	$\mathcal{D}_{\mathrm{NL}}$	$\mathcal{C}_{\mathrm{NL}}$	$\mathcal{D}^*_{\mathrm{NL}}$	$\mathcal{C}^*_{\mathrm{PL}}$	$\mathcal{D}_{\mathrm{PL}}$	$\mathcal{C}_{\mathrm{PL}}$	$\mathcal{D}^*_{\mathrm{PL}}$	$\delta_{\mathcal{C}^*}$	$\delta_{\mathcal{D}^*}$
DL01	8-40-4	1887	8100	2281	4750	1974	7200	2182	5150	12.0	9.5
DL02	8-80-4	3844	13400	4487	10600	3947	12300	4309	10250	8.6	5.2
DL03	10-50-5	1886	9600	2176	7650	1895	9050	1943	8550	5.7	15.9
DL04	10-100-5	3903	21650	4324	18250	4153	21200	4174	18455	6.7	3.6
DL05	12-60-6	2621	14550	3011	11000	2871	15000	2761	11110	10.0	8.4
DL06	12-120-6	5699	25150	6338	24500	5949	24520	6908	25080	5.1	9.3
DL07	14-70-7	3076	16850	3658	11200	3326	16400	3928	11580	8.6	8.1
DL08	14-140-7	8151	31410	9138	28350	8401	30960	9408	28730	3.4	3.2
DL09	16-80-8	3839	18750	4201	16380	4089	18300	4471	16760	6.9	6.8
DL10	16-160-8	8195	32730	8428	29840	8445	32280	8698	30220	3.3	3.4
Mean										**7.0**	**7.4**

Q-T-A: Number of QCs, tasks, and AGVs involved in each problem instance

The results demonstrate that while imposing a 4500 kW limit does introduce delays, the degradation in terminal productivity is relatively small (approx. 7%) compared to the potential reduction in peak power demand.

Interestingly, the impact of the power limit varies with instance size. In larger instances such as DL10, the gap ($\delta_{\mathcal{C}^*}$) is as low as 3.3%, suggesting that in complex systems with many cranes and vehicles, there is more "natural" flexibility to stagger high-power tasks without significantly extending the total makespan.

For terminal managers, this indicates that peak shaving via scheduling is a viable strategy for reducing electricity capacity charges. The NSGA-II effectively "smooths" the power demand by identifying windows where QCs can perform low-power horizontal movements while other cranes are performing high-power hoists. This allows the terminal to operate within strict grid limitations with only a marginal impact on vessel turnaround time.

5 Conclusion

This study investigated the integrated scheduling of quay crane operations and automated guided vehicle transport tasks under strict instantaneous peak power constraints. By addressing the dual objectives of minimizing makespan and reducing unproductive AGV travel, the research provides a framework for terminal operations that balances logistical throughput with the increasing economic and technical pressures of power demand management.

The development of a bi-objective NSGA-II, coupled with a specialized decoding heuristic, demonstrated that power-flexible scheduling can be achieved without resorting to computationally expensive repair mechanisms. Our results confirm that peak power limits act as a critical driver of terminal efficiency; while tighter constraints inherently increase makespan, the proposed algorithm identifies "sweet-spot" solutions where substantial peak shaving is achieved with only marginal impacts on productivity. From a sustainability perspective, this highlights the immense potential for terminal operators to support broader energy grid stability. By acting as a flexible load through intelligent task synchronization, terminals can avoid resource-heavy infrastructure expansion while directly reducing their carbon footprint during peak demand hours.

The practical implications of this work extend directly to sustainable port policy and port managers navigating the transition to electrified, "smart" terminals. Crucially, the ability to operate efficiently under strict power constraints is a prerequisite for integrating volatile renewable energy sources into terminal grids. The framework's capacity to quantify the trade-off between energy limits and vessel turnaround time serves as a vital decision-support tool for achieving long-term green maritime goals.

Future research will focus on developing exact solution methods, such as mixed-integer linear programming, to provide benchmark Pareto fronts for the proposed metaheuristic. Additionally, we intend to explore more dynamic scenarios, including time-of-use (ToU) electricity pricing and the inclusion of battery energy storage systems within the AGV fleet, further enhancing the power flexibility of modern container terminals.

Disclosure of Interests. The author has no competing interests to declare that are relevant to the content of this article.

References

1. Bean, J.C.: Genetic algorithms and random keys for sequencing and optimization. ORSA J. Comput. **6**(2), 154–160 (1994)
2. Deb, K., Pratap, A., Agarwal, S., Meyarivan, T.: A fast and elitist multiobjective genetic algorithm: NSGA-ii. IEEE Trans. Evol. Comput. **6**(2), 182–197 (2002)
3. Fontes, D.B., Homayouni, S.M.: A bi-objective multi-population biased random key genetic algorithm for joint scheduling quay cranes and speed adjustable vehicles in container terminals. Flex. Serv. Manuf. J. **35**(1), 241–268 (2023)
4. Fontes, D.B., Homayouni, S.M., Fernandes, J.C.: Energy-efficient job shop scheduling problem with transport resources considering speed adjustable resources. Int. J. Prod. Res. **62**(3), 867–890 (2024)
5. Geerlings, H., Heij, R., van Duin, R.: Opportunities for peak shaving the energy demand of ship-to-shore quay cranes at container terminals. J. Shipping Trade **3**, 1–20 (2018)
6. Homayouni, S.M., Fontes, D.B.M.M.: Metaheuristics for maritime operations. Wiley Online Library (2018)
7. Homayouni, S.M., Fontes, D.B., Gonçalves, J.F.: A multistart biased random key genetic algorithm for the flexible job shop scheduling problem with transportation. Int. Trans. Oper. Res. **30**(2), 688–716 (2023)
8. Pieńkowski, D.: Rethinking the concept of prosuming: a critical and integrative perspective. Energy Res. Social Sci. **74**, 101967 (2021)
9. Singh, G., Gupta, N.: A study of crossover operators in genetic algorithms. In: Frontiers in Nature-Inspired Industrial Optimization, pp. 17–32 (2022)
10. Tran, T., Nahavandi, S., Reid, R.: Power demand and energy usage of container crane-comparison between ac and dc drives. In: 43rd International Universities Power Engineering Conference, pp. 1–5. IEEE (2008)

Collaborative Optimization of Berth Allocation and Stockyard Selection in Coal Terminals: An Adaptive Hybrid Metaheuristic Approach Under Weather Uncertainty

Yiheng Zhou[2], Qianli Ma[1,2], Zhihao Zhu[1], and Baiyu Ma[3](✉)

[1] School of Maritime Economics and Management, Dalian Maritime University, 1 Linghai Road, Dalian 116026, Liaoning, China

[2] Collaborative Innovation Center for Transport Studies, Dalian Maritime University, 1 Linghai Road, Dalian 116026, Liaoning, China

[3] School of Transportation and Electrical Engineering, Dalian University of Science and Technology, Dalian 116026, Liaoning, China

Abstract. This study addresses the collaborative optimization of berth allocation and stockyard selection in coal export terminals, a critical challenge for global energy logistics given the significant disruptions caused by weather uncertainties. The research background stems from the limitations of traditional static scheduling models, which often fail to integrate offshore and onshore decisions effectively under dynamic environmental conditions. To bridge this gap, a comprehensive mixed-integer programming model incorporating a Weather Risk Index is developed to quantify the impact of adverse weather on equipment efficiency and vessel operations. Methodologically, an innovative Adaptive Hybrid Metaheuristic Algorithm is proposed, which synergistically combines the global search capability of a Genetic Algorithm with the local refinement strength of Variable Neighborhood Search through a dynamic feedback mechanism and a unified encoding scheme. Numerical experiments using real-world data demonstrate that this approach significantly outperforms conventional heuristics, reducing the average objective value by approximately 14.4% for large-scale fleets. The significance of this work lies in providing a robust decision-support tool that enhances operational resilience and efficiency, offering port managers a scientific framework for dynamic scheduling and the formulation of targeted meteorological response strategies, thereby strengthening the coal supply chain.

Keywords: Berth Allocation · Stockyard Selection · Weather Uncertainty · Adaptive Hybrid Metaheuristic · Coal Export Terminals

1 Introduction

Coal remains a cornerstone of global energy, and in China, the "north-to-south coal transportation" pattern makes the operational efficiency of export terminals critical to trade costs. Berth allocation and stack location selection are interdependent core links whose

J. de Armas and E. Lalla Ruiz (Eds.): LOGMS 2026, LNCS 16679, pp. 51–61, 2027.
https://doi.org/10.1007/978-3-032-30795-8_5

collaborative optimization is key to terminal productivity. While information technology has advanced port scheduling, practical operations face significant uncertainties, particularly adverse weather, which can render static models ineffective. This study constructs a comprehensive optimization model considering weather impacts to provide decision support for port managers.

The Berth Allocation Problem (BAP), a core focus of maritime logistics research, aims to optimize ship-berth assignments under constraints like ship size and tidal effects to reduce waiting time and improve throughput. Dong Yin et al. (2022) proposed a novel method for static discrete BAP in large-scale time-sensitive shipping, while Yu et al. (2023) developed a dynamic BAP model to address uncertainties in ship arrival times and loading capacities. Agra et al. (2022) further advanced this field with a distributionally robust two-stage model to minimize expected delays under uncertain processing times. Furthermore, tidal constraints, as a key physical limitation in port operations, have been extensively incorporated in related research. For instance, Xu et al. (2012) considered tides as a critical constraint when constructing a robust optimization model to handle uncertainties in vessel delays and handling times; studies by Lalla-Ruiz et al. have also systematically examined the impact of tides on berth allocation and scheduling. However, most existing BAP studies lack sufficient integration of weather-related uncertainties. Regarding yard resource allocation, container yards have been extensively explored—Wang et al. (2023) proposed flexible storage strategies accounting for demand uncertainty—whereas research on dry bulk yards remains scarce. Ai et al. (2023) applied deep reinforcement learning to optimize berth and yard scheduling for bulk terminals, and Cheimanoff et al. (2023) developed metaheuristic approaches for integrated production and storage yard allocation, yet weather constraints are rarely considered in dry bulk yard studies. For port scheduling uncertainties, Golias et al. (2011) constructed a bi-objective mixed-integer programming model for BAP to address uncertain handling times, while Guo et al. (2021) integrated weather awareness into BAP via machine learning to improve plan robustness. Yan et al. (2019) proposed a berth-flow network method for dynamic BAP with random arrivals, and Xu et al. (2012) developed a robust optimization model with ship time buffers to mitigate delays.

In summary, existing research has made significant progress in BAP, yard allocation, and uncertainty mitigation, forming a rich body of work particularly in handling tides, processing time, and arrival randomness. Nevertheless, the collaborative optimization of berth allocation and dry bulk yard selection under comprehensive weather constraints—systematically modeling weather as a dynamic factor affecting both offshore (berthing) and onshore (yard equipment) operations—remains a largely unexplored research gap. This study aims to bridge this gap by constructing a mixed-integer programming model incorporating a Weather Risk Index and a dynamic operational attenuation mechanism, and proposing a novel Adaptive Hybrid Metaheuristic Algorithm, thereby providing an innovative solution and decision support for the integrated scheduling of coal export terminals under comprehensive weather constraints.

2 Problem Description and Mathematical Model

This study focuses on a large coal export terminal in northern China characterized by a semi-discrete berth layout and fixed equipment. The cargo flow follows a sequence from land transportation to ship loading (Fig. 1).

2.1 Core Constraints

This study focuses on a large coal export terminal in northern China characterized by a semi-discrete berth layout and fixed equipment. The cargo flow follows a sequence from land transportation to ship loading (Fig. 1).

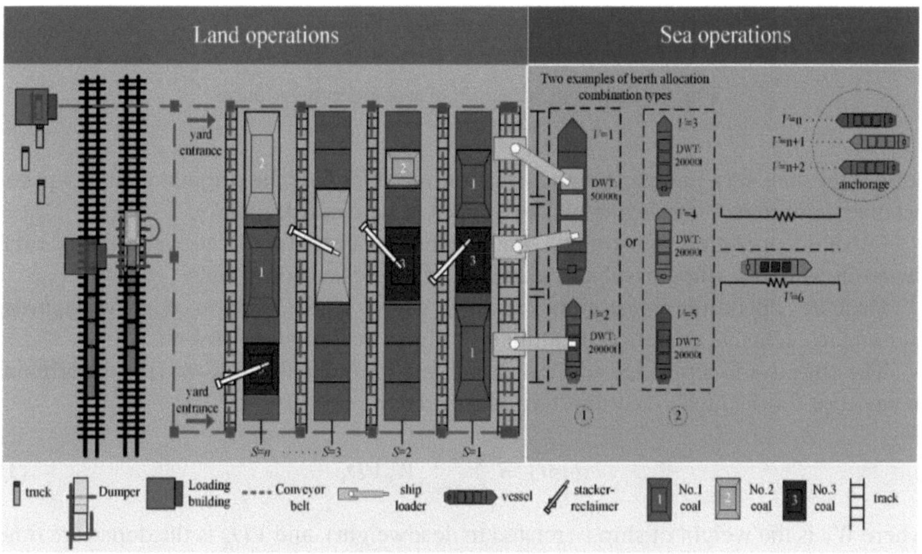

Fig. 1. Schematic diagram of terminal layout

We consider three interrelated constraint types:

1. Offshore: Ship-berth-tide interactions where loaded ships must depart at high tide (Fig. 2).
2. Onshore: Equipment exclusivity where one stacker-reclaimer serves one material pad at a time.
3. Weather: Adverse conditions that suspend berthing or reduce equipment efficiency.

The model assumes pre-known coal types and arrival times, sufficient yard space, and standardized equipment specifications.

2.2 Establishment of the Basic Model

A mixed-integer programming model is constructed with the objective of minimizing the weighted total departure time of all ships (heavier ships have higher weights). The model

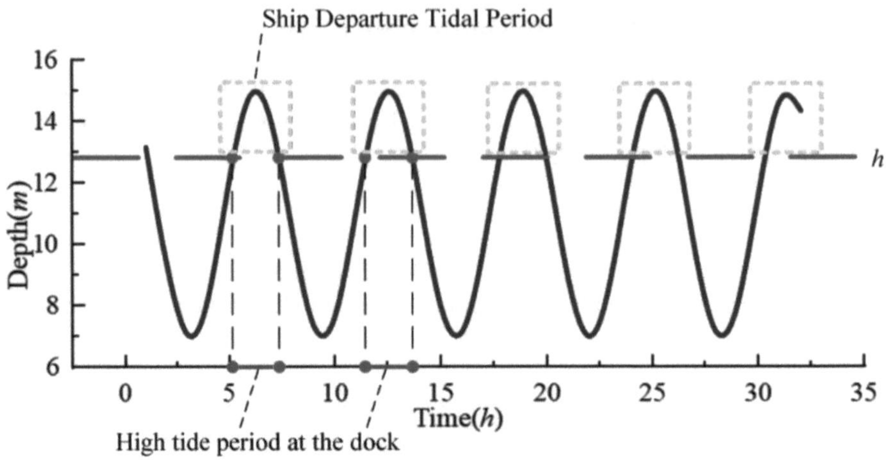

Fig. 2. Schematic diagram of water depth variation.

defines the core sets, parameters and decision variables (see the original manuscript for detailed definitions), and formulates two types of hard constraints:

Offshore operation constraints: Include berth occupation non-overlapping, tidal departure window, ship arrival and loading time sequence constraints;

Onshore operation constraints: Include cargo stack location non-overlapping, equipment exclusive operation, loading task time calculation constraints.

The objective function and core constraints are formulated as follows (see the original manuscript for detailed constraint formulas and numbering):

$$\min G = \sum\nolimits_{v=1}^{|V|} W_v VD_v \tag{1}$$

where W_v is the weight of ship v (related to deadweight), and VD_v is the departure time of ship v.

2.3 Constraints Considering Weather Conditions

To improve the model's practical applicability, weather condition parameters and dynamic decision variables are introduced to quantify the impact of weather on offshore and onshore operations, and the original model is adjusted and expanded:

Weather impact on offshore operations: Ship berthing/unberthing must meet wind speed, wave height and visibility thresholds; loading/unloading operations avoid high-WRI time periods.

Weather impact on onshore operations: Precipitation and strong wind reduce stacker-reclaimer efficiency or stop its operation, and prolong cargo transportation time.

Model expansion: Define WRI calculation formula (coupling wind speed, wave height, visibility and precipitation) and loading/unloading efficiency attenuation formula (coupling precipitation and wind speed), and add corresponding safety constraints and dynamic efficiency adjustment constraints to the model.

The core calculation formulas are as follows:

$$R_t = \alpha \frac{windsp_t}{\text{wind\_max}} + \beta \frac{waveht_t}{\text{wave\_max}} + \gamma max\left(1 - \frac{vis_t}{\text{vis\_min}}, 0\right) + \delta \frac{pre_t}{\text{pre\_max}} \quad \forall t \in T \tag{2}$$

where $windsp_t$, $waveht_t$, vis_t and pre_t are the normalized values of wind speed, wave height, visibility and precipitation at time t, and αk is the weight coefficient;

$$TL_{E_i}^t = TL_{E_i}\left(1 - \lambda \frac{pre_t}{\text{pre\_max}}\right)\left(1 - \mu \frac{windsp_t}{\text{wind\_max}}\right) \quad \forall i \in I, \forall t \in T \tag{3}$$

where $TL_{E_i}^t$ is the efficiency of loading task i at time t, TL_{E_i} is the normal efficiency, and λ, μ are the attenuation coefficients of precipitation and wind speed.

3 Solution Approach

The constructed model is a dynamic nonlinear mixed-integer programming problem with strong coupling of decision variables, random weather factors and complex hard constraints. This study adopts exact solver + heuristic algorithms for solving, and proposes a novel Adaptive Hybrid Metaheuristic Algorithm (AHMA) by fusing the advantages of Genetic Algorithm (GA) and Variable Neighborhood Search (VNS).

3.1 Solution by Gurobipy

The Gurobi optimizer (gurobipy library) is used for precise solution in the PyCharm environment, with constraint linearization and scenario tree sampling for random factors. Gurobi can obtain a strict optimal solution within 2 h through parallel computing and branch-and-cut algorithm, which serves as a benchmark for verifying the model's correctness and the effectiveness of heuristic algorithms.

3.2 Solution by Genetic Algorithm (GA)

A GA with hierarchical coding structure is designed for the problem, which decouples the solution into maritime (berth-time assignment) and land (stack location allocation) operations. The algorithm adopts a greedy-randomized initial population, a fitness function with weather constraint penalty terms, and tailored selection/crossover/mutation operations to handle spatiotemporal constraints. The WRI is integrated into the fitness evaluation to dynamically adjust operational duration, realizing global search for near-optimal solutions.

3.3 Solution by Variable Neighborhood Search (VNS) Algorithm

A VNS algorithm with three specialized neighborhood structures is proposed: Berth Exchange (N1), Stack Translation (N2) and Time Adjustment (N3). The algorithm initiates with a greedy feasible solution, and adopts a Tabu Search strategy to avoid cycling. It dynamically modifies the objective function with penalty terms for weather constraints, and its adaptive neighborhood selection mechanism ensures the model's feasibility under tidal and weather fluctuations, realizing local refined optimization of solutions.

3.4 Adaptive Hybrid Metaheuristic Algorithm (AHMA)

A novel AHMA is proposed by fusing the global exploration capability of GA and the local exploitation power of VNS, with core innovations in adaptive hybrid strategy, unified encoding scheme and dynamic weather response mechanism.

3.4.1 Algorithmic Principle and Hybrid Strategy

AHMA adopts a tight feedback loop hybrid mechanism: GA generates a diverse population for global exploration, and VNS intensively refines promising solutions (high fitness or high weather constraint violations) from the GA population. The algorithm dynamically adjusts the hybrid strategy and neighborhood selection based on the real-time WRI—e.g., prioritizing N3 (Time Adjustment) under high WRI to ensure scheduling feasibility.

3.4.2 Encoding Scheme

A unified three-layer coding schema is designed to integrate berth, yard and temporal decisions (Fig. 3):

1. Berth Gene: Vector encoding the berth interval assigned to each ship;
2. Yard Gene: Matrix encoding the stack location interval for each loading task;
3. Temporal Gene: List encoding berthing/unberthing time of ships and start/completion time of loading tasks.

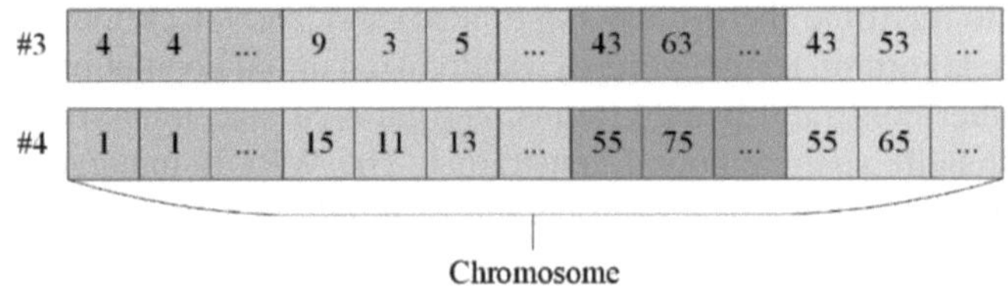

Fig. 3. Chromosome coding

3.4.3 Core Hybrid Workflow

AHMA's workflow includes GA-based global exploration, adaptive solution routing, VNS-based local intensification and parameter adaptation, with a pseudocode describing the iterative process (see the original manuscript for details). The algorithm maintains elitism in population update, and real-time updates WRI based on weather data to adjust the search strategy dynamically.

3.4.4 Distinctive Hybridization Features

AHMA achieves efficient synergy through three mechanisms: solution feedback loop, adaptive solution routing and dynamic neighborhood selection. These mechanisms enable the algorithm to balance global exploration and local exploitation, and adapt to dynamic weather uncertainties, significantly improving solution quality and robustness.

4 Numerical Experiments

Numerical experiments are conducted based on the actual operational data of a northern Chinese coal export terminal, to verify the performance of GA, VNS, AHMA and Gurobi, and analyze the model's robustness under weather constraints. The experiment runs on an Intel Core i7-9750H CPU (16GB RAM), with the model implemented by Gurobi 12.0.0 and heuristic algorithms programmed in Python 3.11.8.

4.1 Analysis of Algorithm Results

4.1.1 Analysis of Adaptive Hybrid Metaheuristic Algorithm (AHMA)

Sensitivity analysis of AHMA's key parameters shows that the algorithm has remarkable stability and low parameter sensitivity across all fleet scales (Table 1):

1. AOV fluctuates slightly under different parameter combinations;
2. Larger PS reduces ACG but increases AST;
3. AHMA's convergence curve shows rapid initial decline and gradual stabilization, verifying the effectiveness of the hybrid strategy (Fig. 4).

4.1.2 Comparison of Results from Different Algorithms

A comprehensive comparison of Gurobi, GA, VNS and AHMA is conducted across different fleet configurations featuring 10, 30 and 50 ships with varying large ship ratios (Fig. 5, Table 2), with key findings as follows: Gurobi can obtain the theoretical optimal solution for small-scale fleets yet incurs an extremely high computational cost, and it is unable to solve medium and large-scale fleet problems due to significant computational complexity; VNS converges the fastest but tends to fall into local optima, leading to the worst solution quality; GA strikes a balance between solution quality and computational speed but experiences convergence stagnation in the later iterations when handling large-scale fleets; AHMA outperforms both GA and VNS across all fleet scales, as it achieves a near-optimal solution for small-scale fleets and reduces the average objective value by approximately 14.4% against GA and approximately 17.0% against VNS for the large-scale fleet with 50 ships, with only a slight increase in computational time that is acceptable for practical applications.

Table 1. Sensitivity Comparison of Adaptive Hybrid Metaheuristic Algorithm Parameters

(PS;CP;MP)	Small scale fleets			Medium scale fleets			Large scale fleets		
	AOV	ACG	AST(s)	AOV	ACG	AST(s)	AOV	ACG	AST(s)
100;0.8;0.03	47.0	113.3	32.7	152.4	206.7	126.2	**288.8**	212.0	309.9
100;0.8;0.05	47.1	105.0	32.5	153.7	188.3	128.1	301.0	208.0	309.1
100;0.8;0.10	46.9	108.3	**32.2**	154.5	204.0	123.7	307.0	206.0	333.7
100;0.85;0.03	47.3	102.3	34.0	151.2	213.3	122.1	296.9	197.6	340.2
100;0.85;0.05	47.0	106.7	32.2	150.9	212.0	123.4	297.5	211.0	319.9
100;0.85;0.10	46.9	98.7	33.7	157.1	200.0	123.3	305.5	199.3	324.1
100;0.9;0.03	**46.8**	106.7	36.4	154.7	212.7	**117.3**	298.7	208.0	320.2
100;0.9;0.05	46.9	100.3	37.3	153.0	197.7	124.0	298.3	218.3	**295.9**
100;0.9;0.10	46.9	104.7	37.5	153.7	197.7	125.0	301.5	201.7	308.7
200;0.8;0.03	46.9	92.7	52.0	153.7	190.0	186.3	294.0	206.0	457.9
200;0.8;0.05	46.9	95.3	52.2	151.3	198.7	191.6	297.2	228.0	454.7
200;0.8;0.10	47.0	86.7	49.9	151.3	190.3	190.1	303.7	198.7	480.5
200;0.85;0.03	46.9	98.3	50.0	153.6	199.7	193.5	295.0	206.3	467.2
200;0.85;0.05	48.0	95.3	54.5	156.6	193.3	185.5	292.3	205.3	463.8
200;0.85;0.10	46.9	93.7	50.3	153.3	206.3	189.6	304.6	211.7	460.7
200;0.9;0.03	47.0	87.7	50.9	152.8	194.3	188.6	301.8	196.7	471.9
200;0.9;0.05	47.0	82.0	53.0	155.2	191.0	189.5	295.5	209.7	459.8
200;0.9;0.10	47.7	93.7	49.9	153.5	190.3	191.4	300.0	206.0	460.5
300;0.8;0.03	46.9	88.7	67.9	151.4	202.7	256.2	297.2	216.7	606.6
300;0.8;0.05	46.9	87.7	67.0	**150.8**	**185.0**	260.6	301.0	205.3	618.3
300;0.8;0.10	47.0	88.3	66.0	150.6	203.7	255.0	294.2	224.3	612.2
300;0.85;0.03	47.0	**81.0**	66.8	151.2	180.3	258.9	299.3	194.3	623.3
300;0.85;0.05	47.1	87.0	66.9	154.1	191.0	256.7	301.3	212.3	622.5
300;0.85;0.10	47.0	83.3	66.0	151.9	211.0	254.6	297.0	200.7	616.3
300;0.9;0.03	47.3	94.0	65.2	152.7	201.3	259.3	300.8	**194.0**	629.7
300;0.9;0.05	46.9	80.7	66.0	153.3	185.3	260.2	300.3	206.0	628.0
300;0.9;0.10	46.9	94.3	65.6	152.0	190.0	259.6	293.2	210.3	625.4

Notes: (PS: Population Size, CP: Crossover Probability, MP: Mutation Probability, AOV: Average Objective Value, ACG: Average Convergence Generations, AST: Average Solution Time)

4.2 Sensitivity Analysis of Environmental Thresholds

A sensitivity analysis is conducted on the key weather thresholds of wind speed, wave height and precipitation to evaluate the model's robustness (Fig. 6), and a significant scale-gradient effect is revealed: large-scale fleets exhibit an objective value volatility of

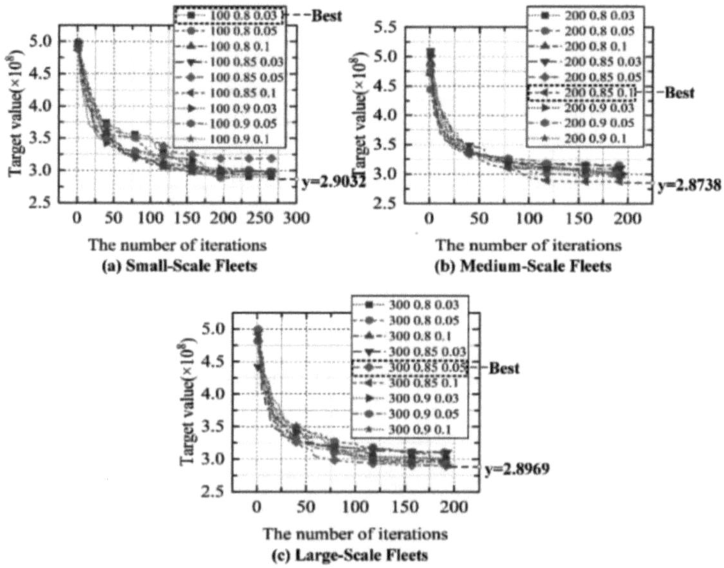

Fig. 4. Objective value vs. Iteration curves for large scale fleets under different AHMA parameters

Table 2 Result comparison among different algorithms

Case Details		Gurobi		GA		VNS		AHMA	
Ships	Large Ships	Obj ($\times 10^6$)	Time (s)	Obj ($\times 10^6$)	Time (s)	Obj ($\times 10^6$)	Time (s)	Obj ($\times 10^6$)	Time (s)
10	2	29.1	2,542.49	36.7	14.28	37.3	0.76	36.6	24.91
30	6	-	-	111.8	87.38	117.4	6.33	105.1	78.62
50	10			272.4	147.74	281.0	19.27	233.5	182.49
10	4	38.5	3,143.60	57.2	15.58	59.6	0.93	47.1	26.46
30	12	-	-	180.3	77.80	182.4	8.57	153.2	94.68
50	20	-	-	358.7	157.53	362.2	29.58	312.5	236.72

less than 3% and have strong resilience to weather fluctuations due to resource redundancy and advanced technology, medium-scale fleets show an objective value volatility of approximately 6.7% and are in a critical state that requires targeted moisture-proof and weather-resistant measures, and small-scale fleets feature a rigid objective value close to 50 million with a volatility of up to 33%, which stems from insufficient weather-resistant equipment and limited operational flexibility. These findings indicate that port managers need to formulate hierarchical meteorological response strategies tailored to different fleet sizes, where large-scale fleets prioritize efficiency enhancement while small and medium-scale fleets focus on safeguarding basic operational safety thresholds.

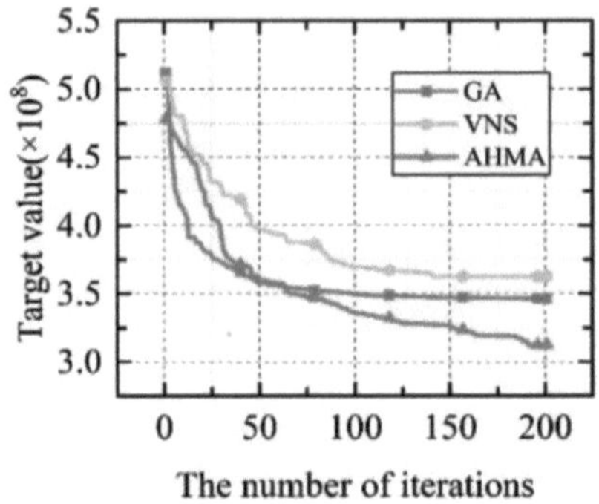

Fig. 5. Algorithm Iteration Comparison Chart

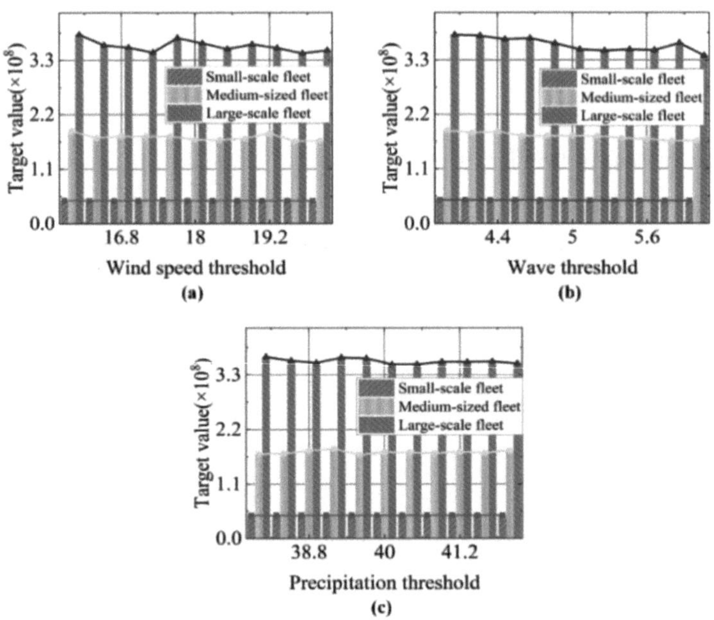

Fig. 6. Influence of different weather thresholds on different fleet sizes

5 Conclusion

This study develops a dynamic collaborative optimization framework for the integrated berth allocation and stack location selection of coal export terminals to overcome the drawbacks of traditional static scheduling under weather uncertainty. Its core innovations and findings include constructing a weather-constrained MIP model with a Weather Risk Index and dynamic operational attenuation mechanism to capture weather impacts on port operations, proposing a novel Adaptive Hybrid Metaheuristic Algorithm (AHMA) that fuses GA and VNS and outperforms traditional heuristic algorithms in solution quality and robustness, and verifying via actual port data that the model cuts the average vessel waiting time by 38.7% for a 30-vessel fleet while identifying a scale-gradient effect in fleet resilience to weather fluctuations, with the model also able to provide scientific decision support for port dynamic scheduling and guide targeted meteorological response strategy formulation to boost the efficiency and resilience of the global coal supply chain. For future research, the model and algorithm will be optimized and extended in four aspects: integrating multi-source weather forecasting data to enhance real-time scheduling capability, combining deep reinforcement learning to improve real-time performance and adaptability, incorporating carbon emission reduction objectives to align with green port development, and extending the model to the collaborative optimization of multi-port and multi-modal transportation for coal logistics.

References

Agra, A., Rodrigues, F.: Distributionally robust optimization for the berth allocation problem under uncertainty. Transp. Res. B Methodol. **164**, 1–24 (2022)

Ai, T., Huang, L., Song, R.J., Huang, H.F., Jiao, F., Ma, W.G.: An improved deep reinforcement learning approach: a case study for optimisation of berth and yard scheduling for bulk cargo terminal. Adv. Prod. Eng. Manage. **18**(3) (2023)

Cheimanoff, N., Féniès, P., Kitri, M.N., Tchernev, N.: Exact and metaheuristic approaches to solve the integrated production scheduling, berth allocation and storage yard allocation problem. Comput. Oper. Res. **153**, 106174 (2023)

Golias, M.M.: A bi-objective berth allocation formulation to account for vessel handling time uncertainty. Marit. Econ. logistics. **13**(4), 419–441 (2011)

Guo, L., Wang, J., Zheng, J.: Berth allocation problem with uncertain vessel handling times considering weather conditions. Comput. Ind. Eng. **158**, 107417 (2021)

Wang, W., Lin, S., Zhen, L.: Flexible storage yard management in container terminals under uncertainty. Comput. Ind. Eng. **186**, 109753 (2023)

Yin, D., Niu, Y., Yang, J., Yu, S.: Static and discrete berth allocation for large-scale marine-loading problem by using iterative variable grouping genetic algorithm. J. Mar. Sci. Eng. **10**(9), 1294 (2022)

Yu, M., Lv, Y., Wang, Y., Ji, X.: Enhanced ant colony algorithm for discrete dynamic berth allocation in a case container terminal. J. Mar. Sci. Eng. **11**(10), 1931 (2023)

Yan, S., Lu, C.C., Hsieh, J.H., Lin, H.C.: A dynamic and flexible berth allocation model with stochastic vessel arrival times. Netw. Spat. Econ. **19**(3), 903–927 (2019)

Xu, Y., Chen, Q., Quan, X.: Robust berth scheduling with uncertain vessel delay and handling time. Ann. Oper. Res. **192**(1), 123–140 (2012)

Interpretable DDQN Rule Selection for Truck–Crane Dispatching in a High-Fidelity Port Simulation

Yihan Liu(✉) and Rauno Heikkilä

Faculty of Technology, University of Oulu, Oulu, Finland
{Yihan.Liu,rauno.heikkila}@oulu.fi

Abstract. Dispatching decisions in automated container terminals propagate directly into crane utilization, truck queuing, and terminal-wide congestion, making truck–crane coordination a primary determinant of operational throughput. This paper presents a closed-loop DDQN dispatcher that learns a state-dependent rule-selection policy through sustained interaction with a Unity-based simulation integrating AGX vehicle dynamics. Because travel time variability and congestion effects emerge from physical maneuver constraints and vehicle interactions rather than from idealized travel-time assumptions, the evaluation reflects execution-level realism unavailable in discrete-event simulators. The trained dispatcher is benchmarked against rule-based and heuristic baselines across fleet sizes of 6, 8, and 10 trucks, spanning the transition from lightly loaded to congestion-dominated operating regimes. Across this scaling range, DDQN achieves approximately 27% throughput gains and 19% reductions in average waiting time relative to the strongest baselines, maintaining these advantages across all load conditions and demonstrating that the rule-selection strategy transfers robustly within the evaluated simulation environment.

Keywords: Automated container terminal · Truck Dispatching · Double Deep Q-Network

1 Introduction

Truck–crane coordination is a central operational decision in container terminals: when a crane completes service and requests the next truck, a dispatcher must dynamically assign an idle truck to minimize system-wide congestion. In practice, dispatching is most implemented through interpretable rules—shortest-distance selection, urgency-based priority, or queue-length variants—that are computationally cheap and operationally transparent. These rules are, however, regime-dependent: a distance-minimizing rule improves efficiency under light load yet induces queue imbalance as congestion builds, whereas urgency-driven assignment reduces starvation at the cost of travel efficiency when the system is underutilized.

Recent research has explored learning-based dispatching to improve adaptivity under stochastic delays and queue-state transitions. Real2Sim frameworks train dispatch agents

J. de Armas and E. Lalla Ruiz (Eds.): LOGMS 2026, LNCS 16679, pp. 62–73, 2027.
https://doi.org/10.1007/978-3-032-30795-8_6

in simulators designed to capture non-linear dynamics observed in real terminals [1]; DQN-family methods have been applied to terminal truck scheduling [2] and can outperform fixed heuristics when state features and reward signals are carefully aligned. A recent DDQN study further demonstrates that encoding heuristic strategies as discrete actions improves both learning stability and final performance over DQN and single-rule baselines [3]. Despite these advances, two evaluation gaps persist at conference scale. First, end-to-end learned dispatchers that output direct assignments sacrifice policy interpretability and require large action spaces that slow learning and hinder engineering adoption. Second, many evaluations rely on simplified travel-time assumptions, even though real-yard delays are strongly shaped by maneuver feasibility, reversing constraints, and interaction-induced stop-and-go dynamics.

This paper addresses both gaps through a pragmatic design. We train a DDQN dispatcher that selects among a compact set of interpretable dispatch rules, yielding a regime-switching policy whose decisions remain readable to engineers rather than emerging from an opaque allocator. Evaluation is conducted within a Unity-based simulation integrating AGX vehicle dynamics, so congestion and maneuver constraints emerge directly from execution rather than from parameterized travel-time models. Experiments are structured as a scaling study over 6, 8, and 10 trucks, characterizing how policy behavior and KPI profiles shift as the system transitions across load regimes.

Our contributions are threefold: (i) a DDQN rule-selection dispatcher for truck–crane coordination that produces an interpretable regime-switching policy; (ii) a closed-loop evaluation in a high-fidelity Unity+AGX simulation that couples dispatch decisions with physically constrained vehicle execution; and (iii) a scalability analysis linking congestion regime transitions to learned rule-switching behavior across fleet sizes.

2 Related Work

2.1 Terminal Dispatch Optimization and Learning-Based Scheduling

Terminal truck–crane scheduling has been addressed through rule-based control, metaheuristic search, and learning-based methods. Rule-based dispatching dominates in practice for its transparency and low computational cost, but fixed rules degrade under dynamic conditions. Metaheuristic approaches—including adaptive particle swarm optimization for integrated crane and truck scheduling [4] —achieve competitive results on static instances yet require re-optimization when operating conditions shift. Simulation-based optimization has further evaluated ensemble equipment scheduling under operational constraints [5].

The closest work to ours is the recent DDQN study that encodes heuristic strategies as discrete actions [3]. Our study differs by coupling interpretable rule selection with Unity+AGX closed-loop execution and by evaluating the learned policy across 6/8/10-truck workload regimes.

2.2 High-Fidelity and Scalable Evaluation

Typical terminal dispatch evaluations rely on discrete-event simulators with idealized travel-time assumptions. While sufficient for high-level throughput analysis, such models often underestimate execution-level constraints—maneuver feasibility, braking limits, and vehicle interaction dynamics—that dominate performance under congestion [1]. Real2Sim research shows that simulators capturing nonlinear dynamics enable more robust evaluation of learning-based strategies. However, a second evaluation gap persists: most studies assess dispatch policies under a single workload configuration, missing whether policies transfer across regimes. As fleet size grows, dominant delay mechanisms shift from travel inefficiency to sustained queueing, and policies optimized for one regime may fail under another [3].

We address both gaps via a dual design: high-fidelity dispatch–execution coupling and systematic fleet-scaling tests. We build a 1:1 Unity reconstruction of the Port of Oulu from satellite imagery and integrate AGX vehicle dynamics so execution effects arise from physics rather than travel-time parameterization. We then evaluate the learned policy under 6, 8, and 10 trucks to track how dispatch behavior and KPIs shift from light load to congestion.

3 Method

We propose a closed-loop dispatch framework that combines an interpretable rule set with DDQN-based rule selection in a high-fidelity Unity simulator. At each dispatch epoch, the simulator encodes the system into a fixed-length state vector, and the agent chooses an action a_t, that indexes one of six dispatch rules. The selected rule assigns an idle truck to the requesting crane, and the simulator executes the assignment until the next epoch. During the execution interval, the simulator computes KPI-based quantities and produces the reward. The resulting transition tuple is used to update DDQN with experience replay and a target network. Figure 1 summarizes the end-to-end pipeline; Sects. 3.1–3.3 detail the rule-based action space, state, reward, and learning.

3.1 Dispatch Epochs and Rule-Based Action Space

We perform dispatching at discrete epochs indexed by t. At each epoch, the simulator exposes a state vector $s_t \in \mathbb{R}^{25}$ and expects a dispatch decision. Rather than a direct truck-to-crane assignment, the agent selects an action a_t that indexes a dispatch rule R_{a_t} from a small, interpretable rule set R with $|R\,| = 6$. Let T_t denote the set of eligible idle trucks at epoch t, and let c_t denote the crane that requests service at epoch t. The selected rule maps (T_t, c_t) to a single concrete truck assignment i_t^*, written as

$$i_t^* \leftarrow R_{a_t}(T_t, c_t) \tag{1}$$

To define individual rules, let $p(i) \in \mathbb{R}^2$ denote the position of truck i, $p(c_t) \in \mathbb{R}^2$ for crane c_t, and $\text{Wait}(i, t)$ the idle-wait time of truck i at epoch t. The Random rule samples

Algorithm 1. DDQN dispatch algorithm flow

Input: rule set $\mathcal{R}$ with $|\mathcal{R}| = 6$; discount factor γ; replay capacity M; reward weights $w_{\text{time}}, w_{\text{idle}}, w_{\text{wait}}, w_{\text{done}}$

Output: trained policy $\pi(s) = \arg\max_a Q_\theta(s, a)$

Initialize $Q_\theta(s, a)$, $Q_{\theta^-}(s, a)$, replay buffer $\mathcal{D} \leftarrow \emptyset$, and exploration ϵ; start Unity–Python TCP (JSON);

for episode $= 1$ **to** E **do**

  Reset simulator; observe $s_0 \in \mathbb{R}^{25}$; set $t \leftarrow 0$, $r_{-1} \leftarrow 0$, $d_{-1} \leftarrow 0$; send $\{s_0, r_{-1}, d_{-1}\}$ and receive a_0;

  while $d_t = 0$ **do**

    Map $a_t \mapsto R_{a_t}$; form $\mathcal{T}_t$ and requesting crane c_t; set $i_t^* \leftarrow R_{a_t}(\mathcal{T}_t, c_t)$; execute and observe s_{t+1};

    Compute $N_{\text{idle}}(t)$, $N_{\text{wait}}(t)$, $N_{\text{done}}(t)$ and set $r_t \leftarrow w_{\text{time}} + w_{\text{idle}} N_{\text{idle}}(t) + w_{\text{wait}} N_{\text{wait}}(t) + w_{\text{done}} N_{\text{done}}(t)$; determine d_t;

    Send $\{s_{t+1}, r_t, d_t\}$; store $(s_t, a_t, r_t, s_{t+1}, d_t)$ into $\mathcal{D}$ (evict oldest if $|\mathcal{D}| > M$);

    if $|\mathcal{D}|$ *is sufficient* **then**

      Sample (s, a, r, s', d); set $a^* \leftarrow \arg\max_{a'} Q_\theta(s', a')$ and $y \leftarrow r + \gamma(1 - d) Q_{\theta^-}(s', a^*)$; update θ by minimizing $(Q_\theta(s, a) - y)^2$; periodically set $\theta^- \leftarrow \theta$; decay ϵ;

    if $d_t = 0$ **then**

      Select a_{t+1} by ϵ-greedy on $Q_\theta(s_{t+1}, \cdot)$ and return it to Unity;

    $t \leftarrow t + 1$;

return $\pi(s) = \arg\max_a Q_\theta(s, a)$;

Fig. 1. DDQN dispatch algorithm flow

i_t^* uniformly from T_t. The ShortestDistance rule selects the truck minimizing squared Euclidean distance and the ShortestQueue rule minimizes a travel-time proxy.

$$i_t^* = \arg\min_{i \in T_t} \|p(i) - p(c_t)\|^2, \; i_t^* = \arg\min_{i \in T_t} \left(\frac{\|p(i) - p(c_t)\|}{v_i} + q_i \right) \tag{2}$$

which v_i is the truck-specific speed estimate and q_i is the expected waiting time at the assigned crane. The MostUrgent rule chooses the truck with the longest idle-wait time:

$$i_t^* = argmax_{i \in T_t} \text{Wait}(i, t) \tag{3}$$

The Dedicated rule restricts candidates by a binding constraint and samples within the preferred subset when it is non-empty. Using integer IDs, the preferred subset is

$$T_t^{\text{pref}} = \{i \in T_t \mid (i mod 2) = (\text{ID}(c_t) \text{mod} 2)\} \tag{4}$$

and the rule samples uniformly from T_t^{pref} if $T_t^{\text{pref}} \neq \varnothing$, otherwise it falls back to Random. Finally, the ManualHeuristic rule computes a weighted score using normalized distance and normalized waiting time plus a random term. Let $d_i = \|p(i) - p(c_t)\|$, let $w_i = \text{Wait}(i, t)$, let $u_i \sim \mathcal{U}(0, 1)$, and define

$$\tilde{d}_i = \frac{d_i}{\max_{j \in T_t} d_j + \varepsilon}, \qquad \tilde{w}_i = \frac{w_i}{\max_{j \in T_t} w_j + \varepsilon} \tag{5}$$

where $\varepsilon > 0$ prevents division by zero. The heuristic score is

$$\text{Score}(i) = \alpha_d \tilde{d}_i + \alpha_w \tilde{w}_i + \alpha_r u_i, \quad i_t^* = argmax_{i \in T_t} \text{Score}(i) \tag{6}$$

where $\alpha_d < 0$ penalizes long distances, $\alpha_w > 0$ prioritizes long-waiting trucks, and $\alpha_r > 0$ adds mild stochasticity.

3.2 State Vector and KPI-Aligned Reward

Each state $s_t \in \mathbb{R}^{25}$ component is either a count feature or a normalized continuous statistic. Continuous variables x are normalized by:

$$\text{Norm}\left(x; x\text{clip}\left(\frac{x - x_{min}}{xmin_{max}, 0, 1()}\right)\text{max}_{min}\right. \tag{7}$$

where clip(·, 0, 1) truncates to [0, 1] and $\varepsilon > 0$ is a small constant. The 25 features consist of five resource-status variables, four distance statistics, four waiting-time statistics, four crane-utilization values, four task-progress variables, and four conflict/progress indicators. This compact representation captures the major congestion and inefficiency sources that dispatch decisions can influence.

The reward r_t is computed from KPI-driven counts over the execution interval of epoch t. Let $N_{\text{idle}}(t)$ denote the number of idle cranes (including both A and B cranes) during the epoch t interval, $N_{\text{wait}}(t)$ the waiting truck count, and $N_{\text{done}}(t)$ the number of job completions during the interval. The reward is:

$$r_t = w_{\text{time}} + w_{\text{idle}} N_{\text{idle}}(t) + w_{\text{wait}} N_{\text{wait}}(t) + w_{\text{done}} N_{\text{done}}(t) \tag{8}$$

where $w_{\text{time}} < 0$ is a constant time penalty encouraging faster completion, $w_{\text{idle}} < 0$ penalizes crane idleness, $w_{\text{wait}} < 0$ penalizes truck waiting, and $w_{\text{done}} > 0$ rewards completed jobs. Conflict events $N_{\text{conf}}(t)$ are tracked as a safety and congestion proxy included in the state; a conflict penalty term with weight $w_{\text{conf}} < 0$ can be appended to the reward if needed, but the current formulation above is used for stable learning.

3.3 DDQN Training with Unity-Python Closed-Loop Integration

The policy over rule indices is learned using DDQN. Let $Q_\theta(s, a)$ be the online action-value function parameterized by θ, and let $Q_{\theta^-}(s, a)$ be a periodically updated target network parameterized by θ^-. For each transition $(s_t, a_t, r_t, s_{t+1}, d_t)$, where $d_t \in \{0, 1\}$ indicates whether the episode terminates after reaching s_{t+1}, DDQN computes the bootstrap target by selecting the greedy next action using the online network and evaluating it using the target network:

$$a^*_{t+1} = argmax_{a'} Q_\theta\left(s_{t+1}, a'\right), \quad y_t = r_t + \gamma(1 - d_t) Q_{\theta^-}\left(s_{t+1}, a^*_{t+1}\right) \tag{9}$$

where $\gamma \in (0, 1)$ is the discount factor. The online parameters θ are updated by minimizing the mean-squared temporal-difference error:

$$\mathcal{L}(\theta) = \mathbb{E}\left[(Q_\theta(s_t, a_t) - y_t)^2\right]. \tag{10}$$

Figure 2 illustrates the MLP (Multilayer Perceptron) architecture used for both Q_θ and Q_{θ^-}, and how DDQN computes the target by selecting a^*_{t+1} with the online network and evaluating it with the target network.

Action selection follows an ϵ -greedy policy, where $\epsilon \in \{0, 1\}$ is the exploration probability:

$$a_t = \begin{cases} \text{Uniform}\{0, \ldots, |R| - 1\}, & \text{with probability } \varepsilon, \\ \arg\max_a Q_\theta(s_t, a), & \text{otherwise.} \end{cases} \tag{11}$$

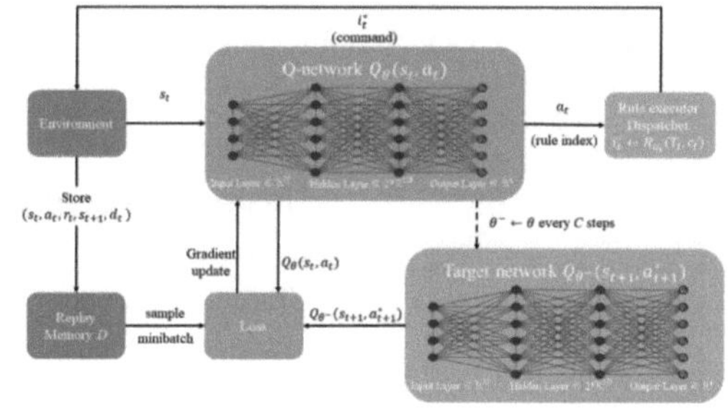

Fig. 2. MLP Architecture: Online and Target Q-Networks

The closed-loop interaction between Unity and Python is implemented via TCP socket with newline-delimited JSON. Unity sends the state–action–reward–next-state tuple $\{s_{t+1}, r_t, d_t\}$ after each epoch, and the Python trainer stores t in an experience replay buffer D, performs DDQN updates on sampled minibatches, periodically synchronizes the target network, and returns the next action a_{t+1} to Unity. Unity maps the action to the corresponding named rule $R_{a_{t+1}}$ and applies it at the next dispatch epoch.

4 Experiments

4.1 Network Training Convergence

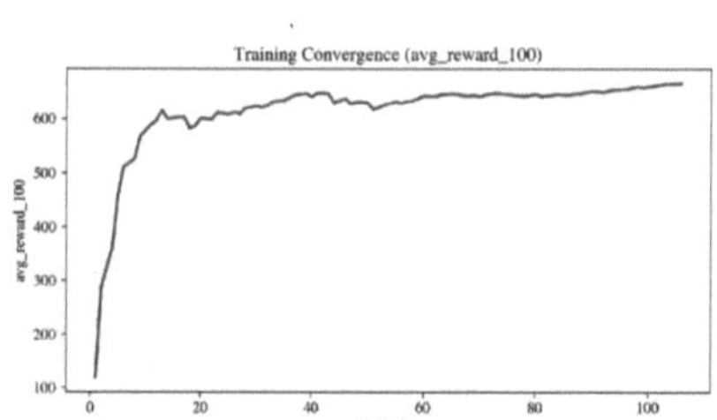

Fig. 3. Training Convergence of DDQN

Following the protocol defined in Sect. 3.3, we train DDQN by interacting with the Unity simulator for 105 episodes and record episode reward R, the exploration rate ϵ, and the training loss. Convergence is evaluated using a moving-average reward curve to reduce per-episode variance from stochastic dispatch outcomes and simulator timing. Figure 3 shows that ϵ decays from its initial value to the minimum by training end. Mean episode reward increases from approximately 616 in the first 10 episodes to approximately 758 in the last 10 episodes, with the moving-average reaching approximately 690 at training end. The moving-average curve flattens substantially after the mid-training stage, while ϵ has already reached its minimum, indicating that rule-selection behavior is no longer dominated by random exploration and has stabilized under the fixed training configuration. Table 1 lists the complete DDQN hyperparameters.

Table 1. DDQN training parameters

Parameter	Value	Parameter	Value
State dimension d	25	Replay buffer capacity $\|D\|$	10000
Action space size $\|R\|$	6	Target update period K	100 steps
Discount factor γ	0.99	Exploration decay λ_ϵ	0.995
Learning rate α	0.001	Hidden layer sizes (MLP) h_1, h_2	128,128
Mini-batch size B	64		
Reward weights (ω_{time}, ω_{idle}, ω_{wait}, ω_{done})	(−0.01, −0.1, −0.05, 10.0)	ManualHeuristic weights (α_d, α_ω, α_r)	(−0.5,0.3,0.2)

4.2 Simulation Environment and Protocol

All experiments are conducted in a Unity-based simulation of the Port of Oulu, reconstructed at 1:1 scale from satellite imagery and site layouts. The simulated terminal incorporates realistic lane geometry, yard topology, and heavy-truck motion constraints, so travel times, queuing, and interaction delays emerge from the environment rather than from simplified assumptions. Figure 4 shows the main two-stage layout comprises an A-side ship-side operation area and a B-side yard-side area, connected by internal transport routes. Trucks execute dispatch assignments via a global path planner based on the Theta* algorithm, which computes any-angle shortest paths on a grid map and tracks the planned route in Unity.

Fig. 4. Port of Oulu Terminal Layout

The main experimental configuration contains four cranes and six trucks. Cranes are divided into two service stages: CraneA ($T_A = 75s + \eta$) for pickup and loading, CraneB ($T_B = 70s + \eta$) for drop-off and unloading, with two cranes per stage. Crane service duration is modeled as a fixed base time plus independent zero-mean uniform noise ($\eta \sim \mathcal{U}(-5s, 5s)$) sampled once per service operation, preserving real-world stochasticity while maintaining controlled evaluation conditions. Each job requires a truck to visit an A-crane then a B-crane to complete one full task cycle. Each simulation run is terminated by a 20-min time budget or upon completing 12 tasks, so all methods are compared under an identical stopping rule.

To test scalability beyond the training configuration, extended experiments are conducted with 8 and 10 trucks, keeping the same crane set and yard layout. These tests compare DDQN against the two strongest heuristic baselines identified in the main experiments, isolating whether the learned switching logic remains robust as inter-truck contention increases. Every configuration is repeated across 15 independent runs with different random seeds; means and standard deviations are reported over runs.

4.3 Evaluation Metrics

Performance is quantified using four KPIs: throughput, average waiting time, average cycle time, and crane utilization. Let N_{done} be the number of completed tasks. Let t_{start} the time of first loading start, and t_{end} be the time when the last task completes unloading. the time of last unloading completion. Makespan and throughput are:

$$T_{\text{mk}} = t_{\text{end}} - t_{\text{start}},\ \text{TP} = \frac{60 N_{\text{done}}}{T_{\text{mk}}} \tag{12}$$

Truck waiting time is recorded separately at the two service stages. For visit j to stage A, let $t_{\text{arr},A}^{(j)}$ be the truck arrival time and $t_{\text{srv},A}^{(j)}$ be the time when loading starts. Stage B waiting time is defined analogously. We use the mean of the two-stage:

$$\bar{W} = \frac{1}{2}\left(\frac{1}{n_A}\sum\nolimits_{j=1}^{n_A}\left(t_{\text{srv},A}^{(j)} - t_{\text{arr},A}^{(j)}\right) + \frac{1}{n_B}\sum\nolimits_{j=1}^{n_B}\left(t_{\text{srv},B}^{(j)} - t_{\text{arr},B}^{(j)}\right)\right). \tag{13}$$

Each task k has an assignment time $t_{\text{asgn}}^{(k)}$ (when dispatch starts this job) and a completion time $t_{\text{done}}^{(k)}$ (when unloading finishes). The cycle time and its average are

$$\text{CT}^{(k)} = t_{\text{done}}^{(k)} - t_{\text{asgn}}^{(k)},\ \overline{\text{CT}} = \frac{1}{N_{\text{done}}}\sum\nolimits_{k=1}^{N_{\text{done}}} \text{CT}^{(k)} \tag{14}$$

Crane utilization is computed from the fraction of time each crane is busy during the full episode elapsed time T_{epi} (the run duration). For crane c, let its total busy time be B_c, which is accumulated over all loading/unloading service intervals. The utilization of crane c and the average utilization over all cranes C are

$$U_c = \frac{B_c}{T_{\text{epi}}},\ \bar{U} = \frac{1}{|C|}\sum\nolimits_{c \in C} U_c \tag{15}$$

A higher TP and $\bar{U}$ are desirable, while lower $\bar{W}$ and $\overline{\text{CT}}$ indicate reduced congestion and faster end-to-end completion. These KPIs align with the reward design in Sect. 3.2, which encourages more task completions while penalizing waiting and idling increments between dispatch epochs.

5 Results and Discussion

5.1 Main Results in the 6-Truck Setting

Figure 5 compares DDQN with all baseline rules under the main setting (4 cranes, 6 trucks, 20 min, target 12 tasks). DDQN achieves the highest scores on all four KPIs. Mean throughput reaches approximately 0.58 tasks/min. ManualHeuristic, the strongest fixed-rule baseline on throughput, reaches approximately 0.46 tasks/min—a gap of roughly 27%. Mean average waiting time falls to approximately 60.7 s under DDQN, compared with approximately 74.8 s for ShortestDistance—the best-performing baseline on this metric—a reduction of approximately 19%. Mean cycle time decreases to approximately 170.9 s from approximately 205.5 s under Random, a reduction of approximately 17%. Crane utilization reaches approximately 0.215, versus approximately 0.175 for ManualHeuristic, an increase of approximately 23%.

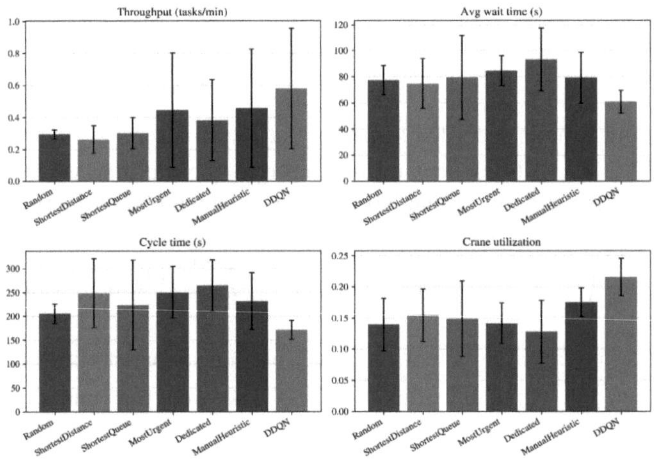

Fig. 5. KPI Comparison Across Dispatching Methods (6 Trucks)

Crane utilization is defined as $U_c = B_c/T_{\text{epi}}$ depends on run duration (early completion vs. full 20-min budget). Random's competitive cycle-time reflects only completed early tasks, while DDQN includes all 12 tasks; thus, the 17% improvement reflects genuine congestion suppression.

These results are consistent with, but do not verify, a rule-switching interpretation. A learned selector can choose different fixed rules as queue and distance states change, whereas each baseline applies one rule throughout the run. Direct attribution of the performance gap to regime switching would require rule-frequency analysis conditioned on queue states; we therefore treat this mechanism as a plausible explanation rather than a demonstrated cause.

5.2 Scalability Across Fleet Sizes

Figure 6 shows that increasing the fleet from 6 to 10 trucks, while keeping the crane count and yard layout unchanged, progressively shifts the dominant delay mechanism from travel inefficiency to sustained queuing and inter-truck conflicts. Waiting time captures this transition most clearly. DDQN holds mean average waiting time within 58–60 s across all three fleet sizes. The fixed heuristics show a monotonically increasing trend: at 10 trucks, the strongest heuristic baselines reach approximately 100 s or above. The divergence suggests that the learned policy sustains balanced service access and suppresses queue explosion as contention intensifies. To keep the scaling analysis compact, the 8- and 10-truck experiments focus on the two strongest heuristic baselines identified in the 6-truck setting. This design provides a conservative challenger comparison, but it does not constitute a full re-ranking of all heuristic rules across fleet sizes.

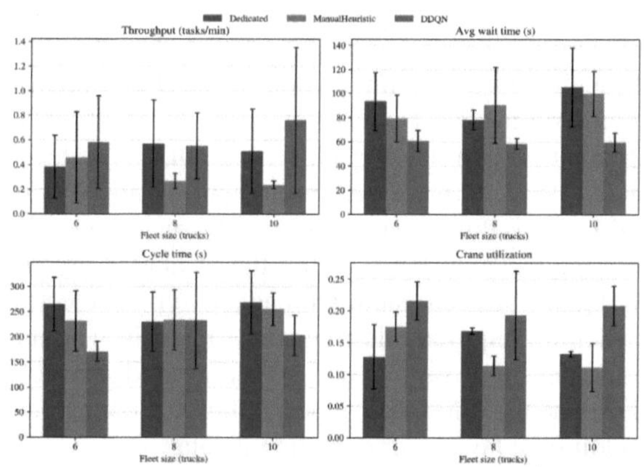

Fig. 6. KPI Scalability Across Fleet Sizes (6/8/10 Trucks)

Throughput comparisons reveal a more nuanced pattern. At 8 trucks—a transitional regime where the yard is busy but not yet saturated—DDQN and Dedicated produce comparable throughput. Dedicated's binding assignment structure reduces conflict probability and yields stable service patterns in this regime; stochastic service-time noise further limits the resolving power of throughput comparisons near equilibrium loading. DDQN nonetheless maintains lower waiting time and higher crane utilization at 8 trucks, indicating that congestion control differs even when throughput appears comparable.

At 10 trucks, the throughput gap widens substantially. DDQN reaches approximately 0.76 tasks/min; Dedicated reaches approximately 0.51 tasks/min and ManualHeuristic approximately 0.24 tasks/min. Crane utilization and waiting time follow the same direction. Dedicated's performance decline at 10 trucks is consistent with assignment overconstraint: when the preferred subset becomes unavailable under high contention, the binding rule withholds crane capacity that could otherwise be used. ManualHeuristic's fixed scoring weights cannot shift emphasis from distance to queue balance when queue imbalance becomes the primary delay source. DDQN's relative robustness under these conditions aligns with adaptive rule switching—though confirming this interpretation requires rule-selection frequency data.

The cross-fleet pattern indicates that DDQN's throughput, utilization, and waiting-time advantages are most pronounced above the congestion threshold, observed here between 8 and 10 trucks under the single-port, controlled-service-time experimental setup. Where the gap narrows—throughput at 8 trucks—the system remains in a transitional regime where a well-calibrated fixed rule can still match adaptive performance. These results are bounded to the evaluated yard configuration, fleet sizes, and task protocol; their generalization beyond this scope requires additional experimental validation.

6 Conclusion

This paper presented a DDQN-based dispatcher that selects among interpretable dispatch rules for truck–crane coordination in an automated container terminal. The dispatcher is trained through closed-loop interaction with a Unity+AGX simulation, where travel delays and congestion arise from vehicle-motion constraints rather than from fixed travel-time assumptions. In the 6-truck setting, DDQN reduced average waiting time by approximately 19% and increased throughput by approximately 27% relative to the strongest fixed-rule baselines; across the 6/8/10-truck range, the results remained consistent with cross-regime robustness within the evaluated layout and service-time setting. The observed gains are consistent with adaptive rule selection, but direct attribution to regime switching requires rule-frequency analysis. The main limitations are the predefined rule set, the single port layout, and controlled service-time assumptions; future work should expand the rule space, report policy-switching patterns, and validate the method across additional layouts or operational data.

Acknowledgments. We acknowledge the financial support of the Finnish Ministry of Education and Culture through the Intelligent Work Machines Doctoral Education Pilot Program (IWM VN/3137/2024-OKM-4), Merenkulun säätiö Foundation and Finnish Foundation for Technology Promotion.

Disclosure of Interests. The authors have no competing interests to declare that are relevant to the content of this article.

References

1. Jin, J., Cui, T., Bai, R., Qu, R.: Container port truck dispatching optimization using Real2Sim based deep reinforcement learning. Eur. J. Oper. Res. **315**, 161–175 (2024). https://doi.org/10.1016/j.ejor.2023.11.038
2. Zheng, X., Liang, C., Wang, Y., Shi, J., Lim, G.: Multi-AGV dynamic scheduling in an automated container terminal: a deep reinforcement learning approach. Mathematics. **10**, 4575 (2022). https://doi.org/10.3390/math10234575
3. Cheng, S., Liu, Q., Jin, H., Zhang, R., Ma, L., Kwong, C.F.: Collaborative optimization of truck scheduling in container terminals using graph theory and DDQN. Sci. Rep. **15**, 6950 (2025). https://doi.org/10.1038/s41598-025-91140-7

4. Hop, D.C., Van Hop, N., Anh, T.T.M.: Adaptive particle swarm optimization for integrated quay crane and yard truck scheduling problem. Comput. Ind. Eng. **153**, 107075 (2021). https://doi.org/10.1016/j.cie.2020.107075
5. Kastner, M., Nellen, N., Schwientek, A., Jahn, C.: Integrated simulation-based optimization of operational decisions at container terminals. Algorithms. **14**, 42 (2021). https://doi.org/10.3390/a14020042

Assignment of Orders in Horizontal Transport at Sea-Port Container Terminals

Simon Ilenburg, Florian Möhle(✉), Svenja Witte, Hermann Lödding, and Carlos Jahn

Hamburg University of Technology, Institute of Production Management and Technology, Hamburg 21073, Germany
{simon.ilenburg,florian.moehle,svenja.witte,loedding, carlos.jahn}@tuhh.de

Abstract. Quay cranes (QCs) represent the primary operational bottleneck at seaport container terminals due to their high capital intensity and role as critical nodes in global supply chains. Their productivity is strictly dependent on the efficient coordination of horizontal transport, specifically the assignment of transport orders to terminal trucks (TTs). While many terminals still rely on fixed TT-to-QC assignments, this approach often lacks the flexibility to handle disruptions and fluctuating workloads. This paper investigates the potential of a flexible, multi-criteria assignment procedure – considering work-in-process, travel distances, and QC waiting times – compared to traditional fixed assignments. The performance is evaluated using Logistic Operating Curves (LOCs), which map QC productivity against the number of deployed TTs. The results demonstrate that flexible assignment significantly outperforms fixed assignment in underload scenarios (low TT availability or high travel speeds), showing productivity gains of up to 17.85% during vehicle disruptions. However, this advantage diminishes as transport capacity increases. In high-utilization overload zones, the flexible method falls slightly below fixed assignment performance. This discrepancy is attributed to the timing of order assignment; making decisions when a previous task is completed, rather than at the last possible second, limits the system's ability to react to real-time fluctuations. The study concludes that flexible assignment increases robustness during transport shortages, but achieving theoretical productivity benchmarks requires shifting toward late-assignment strategies.

Keywords: Container Terminal · Productivity · Flexible Assignment · Logistic Operating Curves

1 Introduction

Global seaports are critical nodes in international supply chains, where small efficiency losses can ripple into significant delays and costs. Container terminals are under rising pressure to increase throughput while meeting stricter targets on reliability, safety, and emissions. A key operational lever is the tight coordination between quay cranes (QCs) and horizontal transport because QC productivity directly depends on timely vehicle

J. de Armas and E. Lalla Ruiz (Eds.): LOGMS 2026, LNCS 16679, pp. 74–84, 2027.
https://doi.org/10.1007/978-3-032-30795-8_7

availability and thus influences the handling time of the vessels. As a result, any idle time at the QC side directly translates into substantial productivity, handling time and cost losses. In this setting, order assignment, deciding which transport orders are served by which vehicles and when, becomes a challenge, especially under dynamic conditions. This work addresses possible improvements for the assignment of transport orders to terminal trucks (TTs). To reliably assess how assignment decisions affect QC productivity, the authors employ a discrete event simulation model that captures terminal operations under varying conditions using different assignment procedures. The resulting simulated productivity of QCs depending on the number of TTs used is plotted and compared in the form of simulated Logistic Operating Curves (LOCs), as already presented by previous publications [1, 2]. The aim of this paper is not to develop a new flexible assignment method, it rather is to test an already existing method. With the LOCs the already existing flexible assignment method will be compared with a fixed assignment of the TTs.

2 Theoretical Background and State of Research

Chap. 2 begins by outlining the theoretical foundations of container terminals, with particular emphasis on the key aspects and limitations relevant to this study. In the subsequent subsections, the fundamentals of LOCs from the field of production logistics are introduced and discussed. These concepts are then contextualized within the container terminal environment, with a specific focus on terminal productivity and the interaction between QCs and TTs.

2.1 Container Terminals

Container terminals are complex systems and are divided into different functional areas. These include the seaside handling area between vessel and terminal, the storage area in the yard and the landside handling area including rail loading. Various combinations of equipment can be used for the processes at container terminals. This paper focuses on the transport process between the QCs and the yard block. In particular it considers TTs to be used for the horizontal transport as they are still widely used in practice and play a key role in coordinating container flows between quay and yard [3]. QCs are the core resource of container terminals and above all, the work mode of the horizontal transport is crucial for the productivity of QCs. QCs are expensive and usually constitute the main operational bottleneck. Their productivity therefore has a major impact on overall terminal performance. In quayside operations, the basic process consists of loading containers from the terminal onto a vessel and unloading containers from a vessel to the terminal. In this process, the QCs perform the vertical handling at the quay by lifting containers between the vessel and the landside transfer point, while TTs provide the horizontal transport between the QCs and the yard block. As a result, the workflow of QCs and TTs depend on each other e.g. QCs can only keep on working productively if a TT is available to pick up or drop off the respective container. Otherwise waiting times and productivity losses of the QCs occur [3].

In terms of fixed assignment, a group of TTs is assigned to a specific QC and carries out transport orders exclusively for that QC. In comparison to that, the literature has already dealt extensively with new assignment methods. One method with great potential is the assignment procedure developed by Schwientek [3].

This procedure takes several aspects and criteria into account according to which an order can be assigned for horizontal transport. One aim of the procedure is to find the best suitable QC for a TT at the moment of the order assignment to improve the processes at the terminal. To do this, (1) the number of TTs currently assigned to the QCs is considered. For both the import and export processes, all TTs are counted as assigned to a specific QC that are on their way to the QC, are in the queue at the QC, or are currently being served by the QC. In the export process, all TTs that are on their way to the block storage area or are waiting at the block storage area to pick up a container for the respective QC are additionally assigned to a QC. (2) Another aspect that is considered is the distance to the QC. This results in shorter travel distances for the TT to the QC, saving time and thereby increasing the terminal's efficiency. To implement this, the QCs that are closest to the TT at the time of order assignment are given higher chances to get the TT assigned. (3) The waiting time of the QC is another factor after which the TTs are assigned. In this context, the waiting time does not mean that a QC has to wait for a TT. It refers to the time that has elapsed since the last TT was assigned to the respective QC instead. This is implemented to prevent a QC from remaining unvisited by another TT for too long. The number of assigned TTs, distance and waiting time are calculated for each QC that has active transport orders. This calculation is performed at the point in time when a TT has completed its previous transport order. The three criteria are given equal weight and no differentiated weighting of the three criteria is applied, as the available data and literature does not allow for an empirically substantiated prioritization of individual criteria, and equal weighting thus represented the most methodologically transparent approach.

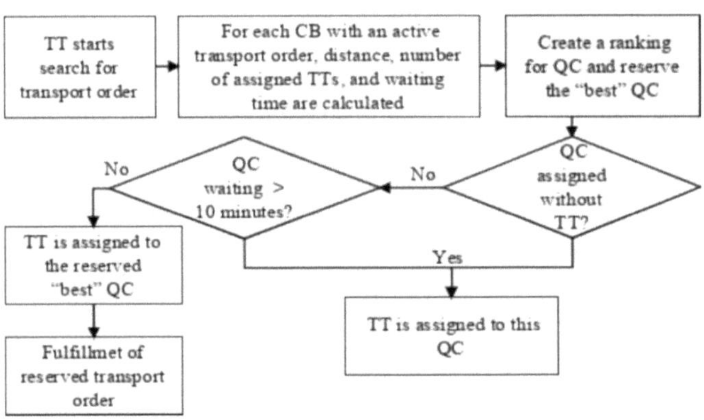

Fig. 1. Flexible assignment of TTs

A ranking is then created for each individual criterion. In the ranking for distance, the QC with the shortest distance to the TT is assigned the lowest value and the QC with the longest distance to the TT is assigned the highest value. In the number of assigned TTs ranking, the QC with the lowest number of assigned TTs is given the lowest value and the QC with the highest number of TTs is given the highest value. Similarly, for the waiting time, the lowest value is assigned to the QC with the longest waiting time and the highest value to the QC with the shortest waiting time. The individual values are then added up for each QC. The next transport order of the QC with the lowest total value is then assigned to the TT. If two or more QCs share the lowest value, one of these QCs is randomly assigned to the TT. However, in two cases, QCs are given priority regardless of their ranking. If a QC has not been assigned a TT for more than 10 min, this QC is prioritized and the TT is automatically assigned to that QC. This also happens if there is a QC that does not have a TT assigned to it at the time of assignment. These two priorities are assigned to prevent processes from grinding to a halt at the respective QCs. The two prioritized cases would have a significant impact on productivity due to prolonged unproductivity of the QCs, which would not occur in practice. Therefore, prioritization prevents these two cases from occurring in the simulation. If there is no QC with active transport orders at a given time, the TT drives to a parking space at the terminal. The described process of the flexible assignment method is also shown in Fig. 1.

This paper discusses the commonly used fixed assignment of TTs to a fixed assigned QC and compares it with the flexible assignment method as well as an ideal reference. To describe this relationship, the authors have already made use of production planning and control methods, such as LOCs.

2.2 Logistic Operating Curves

LOCs, commonly applied in production logistics, depict logistical objectives – such as the mean output rate, the mean capacity utilization, or the mean throughput time – as functions of a control variable like mean work in process [4]. LOCs represent a broad spectrum of achievable operating points obtained by varying the mean work in process. The typical relationship between mean work in process and mean output rate is characterized as follows: At low mean work in process, only a low output rate can be attained. As mean work in process increases, the output rate grows proportionally within the so-called underload zone. In the subsequent transition zone, the output rate increases more slowly, gradually approaching its maximum value depending on the system's capacity. Within the overload zone – where sufficient work is always available and no interruptions occur due to a lack of work in process – the output rate remains approximately constant at its maximum level [4].

These diagrams reveal inherent trade-offs among multiple conflicting objectives, particularly between output rate and throughput time. Therefore, companies must strategically position themselves, and LOCs serve as valuable tools in this decision-making process [4].

Moreover, LOCs can be effectively applied in the context of seaport container terminals. For instance, logistical objectives such as the productivity of QCs or vessel handling times can be plotted against the number of equipment used for horizontal transport, such as TTs. The derivation of such LOCs typically follows a deductive-experimental methodology [4].

Following this approach, the authors have derived an approximate operating curve describing the relationship between QC productivity and the mean work in process resulting of the number of vehicles deployed for horizontal transport [1].

When multiple workstations operate in parallel, queuing theory demonstrates that employing a shared common queue serving all parallel workstations reduces workstation waiting times and thereby leads to higher mean output rates for the same mean work in process [5]. In other words, utilizing a shared queue instead of individual queues per workstation decreases the mean buffer work in process necessary to attain a defined output rate [6]. This insight also holds significant potential for seaport container terminals. If, instead of fixed vehicle assignments for horizontal transport – which lead to queues at each QC – a flexible assignment method enabling a shared queue can be developed, it can be expected that fewer horizontal transport vehicles will suffice to achieve high QC productivity. The authors have already identified an operating curve corresponding to a system with a shared queue, thereby highlighting the potential of this approach [7].

2.3 Research Gap

While the potential, as previously demonstrated, is substantial and a number of assignment methods have already been developed to address this it remains unclear whether these will realize the potential. Current mathematical optimization approaches predominantly rely either on exact algorithms [8], which depend on particular problem instances, and cannot cope with deviations caused by stochastic factors, or on heuristics [9]. The latter, due to their complexity, are also often unsuitable for practical application. As a result, these methods fail to provide a solution that is both operationally feasible and generally applicable within seaport container terminals. Schwientek's procedure attempts to address these issues through a simple yet efficient rule [3]. However, it is uncertain whether this procedure actually realizes the described potential from shared queues. Furthermore, the influence of disruptions such as of QCs and TTs on the procedure is to be investigated in particular. The simulation model presented in this paper is therefore developed to enable the evaluation of Schwientek's order assignment procedure for TTs to QCs.

3 Methodology

In order to make use of the flexible assignment procedure for the existing use case, the Design Science Research Methodology according to Hevner [10] is used.

In the relevance cycle of the method, requirements and use cases for the assignment procedure are defined based on the simulation model. The model later represents the application environment for the selected assignment procedure. For the Rigor Cycle, an established assignment procedure is selected from the existing knowledge base. As already described above, the assignment method of Schwientek [3] is selected in this context. The assignment procedure is then implemented in the context of the design cycle in the existing simulation model so that it can be used for further research and new insights can be gained for the existing knowledge base. A discrete event simulation is used to evaluate the assignment procedure. Simulation experiments are performed with different scenarios in which various parameters are varied. This is done so that the two assignment methods can be evaluated and compared under different conditions. In the simulation runs, the speeds of the TTs and QCs, as well as the number of TTs, are varied.

In addition, simulation runs with disruptions are performed to reflect real conditions at a container terminal. In practice, disruptions at container terminals can occur for a variety of reasons. These may include severe weather, strikes, technical issues, or illness. In the simulation, the disruptions are modeled with a limited availability of the QCs and TTs. With active disruptions, both TTs and QCs are only available for 80% of the simulation time. The mean time to repair for a disruption is defined as five minutes. During the disruptions the QCs and TTs are not able to move, thus delaying the processes. On top of that, the number of TTs are being varied. Simulation runs are conducted with 8, 16, 24, 32 and 40 TTs, to compare the performance of both assignment methods with different levels of TT supply. The number of QCs is taken from our sample terminal and is set for 8 QCs in all simulations. Simultaneously, all the handling times and distances are constant throughout all simulation scenarios and will not be varied. For the distances and the general terminal layout, the MSC Terminal Valencia is the sample terminal. Due to its modular design and decoupled components, the simulation model scales well with growing input sizes and can be readily adapted or extended to incorporate additional components or processes.

For every possible parameter combination, 50 simulation runs are carried out. As a comparative value for the assignment methods, the box moves/h of the QCs are recorded depending on the number of TTs used in these runs. In regard to computational complexity, the 50 simulation runs for each combination take on average six hours. With the results and statistical values saved as excel files, the storage requirements for the simulation results are limited. LOCs are then used to compare the two assignment methods. The results of this comparison and evaluation will be discussed in the next chapter.

4 Results

The results section of this paper is divided into four parts. In the initial segment, the simulation outcomes, or more precisely, the QC productivity derived therefrom, are presented on an aggregate basis across the diverse simulation scenarios. This enables the illustration of a QC productivity LOC against the number of TTs for each assignment procedure. The second part of the study presents the results of a specific simulation experiment (Experiment 4). This scenario is the baseline, and it employs the standard speeds of QCs and TTs. It is also assumed that both systems are free from disruptions. The third part of this study presents the results of Experiment 1. The present experiment is characterized by reduced availability of operational systems, which consequently reflects disruptions in operational processes. The fourth part of the study presents the results of the sensitivity analysis of the simulation parameters. All further experiments and their results can be found in Ilenburg et al.[1]

The Results from averaged QC productivities over all scenarios demonstrates that the mean QC productivity under flexible assignment outperforms fixed assignment when the number of TTs is low. Utilizing a ratio of 1 TT per QC (8 TTs in total), the mean QC productivity for flexible assignment is 12.81 box moves per hour. This figure is 13.36% higher than the 11.3 box moves per hour achieved with fixed assignment. However, this

[1] Ilenburg, S., Möhle, F., Witte, S.: Performance Metrics and Approximations for Container Terminal Horizontal Transport (LOGMS Data), (2026). https://doi.org/10.15480/882.16938.

advantage is diminished as the number of vehicles increases. It has been demonstrated that, at a rate of two TTs per QC (16 TTs in total), the productivity of 20.61 box moves per hour is 4.48% above the fixed assignment level of 19.73 box moves per hour. reduces this benefit to a marginal 0.4%, with 24.5 box moves per hour compared to 24.4 box moves per hour. As TT capacity continues to increase, mean QC productivity remains at a comparable level but falls slightly below that of fixed assignment, showing minor negative deviations such as −0.36% with 26.19 and 26.28 box moves per hour at 4 TTs per QC and − 0.37% with 26.83 and 26.93 box moves per hour at higher capacities.

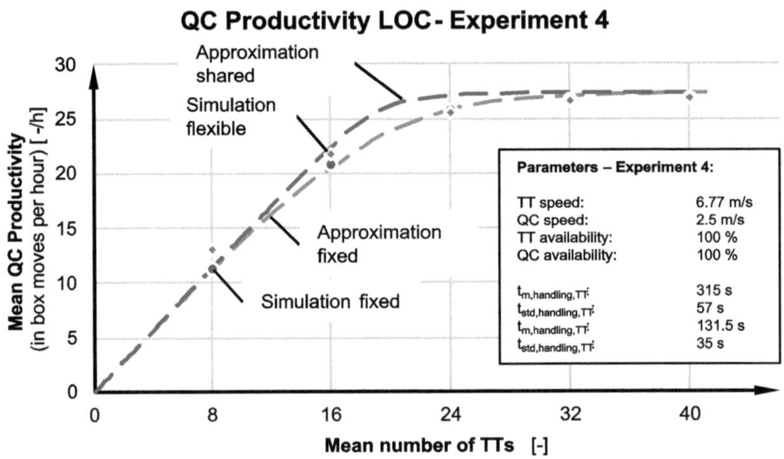

Fig. 2. Mean Productivity LOCs of the reference scenario (experiment 4) and approximated LOCs for flexible and fixed assignment

The reference scenario (Experiment 4), defined by the absence of technical disruptions and low operating speeds for both TTs and QCs, reveals a similar pattern and is shown in Fig. 2. In this instance, the flexible assignment method demonstrated a 15.24% improvement over the fixed assignment at 1 TT per QC and a 4.75% enhancement at 2 TTs per QC. Notably, the margin remained below 2% for higher vehicle counts. It is important to note that, given 1 TT per QC and the flexible assignment procedure, the simulation point lies above the approximation for shared queues. The theoretical curve under discussion is derived from the assumption that all transport orders can be handled by any QC, allowing TTs to be assigned at the last possible moment. This theoretical ideal facilitates a real-time response to fluctuations in demand. A similar picture emerges for experiment 1, which differs from Experiment 4 in that fewer TTs and QCs are available, as shown in Fig. 3. In this instance, too, greater productivity is observed with flexible assignment than with fixed assignment with 1 TTs per QC (6.59%) and 2 TTs per QC (2.74%).

In addition, as illustrated in Experiment 4, the QC productivity at 1 TT per QC exceeds the approximate curve for shared queues. However, the productivity gains

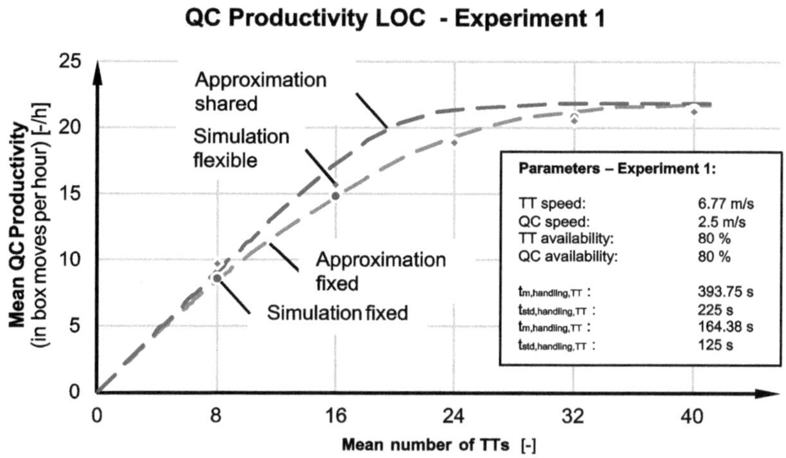

Fig. 3. Mean Productivity LOCs of Experiment 1 with reduced availability and approximated LOCs for flexible and fixed assignment

observed in this experiment are comparatively modest in comparison to those documented in Experiment 4. It is evident that, with a greater number of TTs per QC, the flexible and fixed assignment systems are approximately equivalent in this context.

Sensitivity analyses indicate that increasing TT speed reduces the initial advantage of fixed assignment to 11.64% at one TT per QC, compared to the baseline experiment. Since higher travel speeds reduce the total number of TTs required, the advantage decreases at two TTs per QC and turns into a negative deviation of 1.33%. Conversely, when only the QC speed is increased, the benefit of combined assignment is more pronounced, reaching 16.97% at one TT per QC, 9.71% at two TTs per QC and 2.92% at three TTs per QC. The strategy is most effective when TTs are subject to technical disruptions for 20% of the time, with the advantage rising to 17.85% at 1 TT per QC before declining sharply. However, when QC availability is restricted to 80% due to disruptions, the advantage of flexible assignment over fixed assignment is less significant, yielding 10.72% at one TT per QC and 1.88% at two TTs per QC.

Overall, these results demonstrate that flexible assignment is superior to fixed assignment when horizontal transport availability is the limiting factor. However, as transport capacity increases, this advantage dissipates until fixed assignment becomes slightly more efficient at high productivity and QC utilization levels. Furthermore, the findings suggest that the approximation equations for fixed assignment introduced previously align closely with the simulation data points. While the theoretical improvement potential, represented by the approximation curve for a shared queue, serves as a benchmark, this is not realized at higher TT counts. Rather, the productivity values for flexible assignment converge towards the fixed assignment approximation curve as the system becomes more saturated.

5 Discussion and Outlook

This section of the paper critically examines the results achieved. On a positive note, the assignment method selected for use with the DSRM in this paper has been successfully adapted and integrated. The LOC method, which compares productivity in terms of box moves per hour for the QCs, has proven to be an effective method for comparing different assignment strategies.

The simulation results provide valuable insights into the performance of the investigated assignment strategies. (1) The findings confirm that the flexible assignment method offers advantages over fixed assignment. This is consistent with Schwientek's existing findings [3]. However, the results of this study also show that the higher productivity of flexible assignments compared to fixed assignments depends heavily on the number of TTs available. The advantages of flexible assignment mainly arise when the transport demand of the QCs cannot be met by the available TTs. This underload state can be caused by factors such as longer TT travel times relative to QC cycle times, technical disruptions affecting the TTs or an insufficient number of vehicles deployed overall. In these instances, the flexible assignment utilizes a ranking system based on the number of assigned TTs, travel times and QC waiting times to leverage its strengths. By orienting itself towards the actual demand of the QCs, the method compensates for stochastic fluctuations more effectively than the fixed assignment method. However, when QC demand is fully met – referred to here as the 'overload' state – the advantage over the fixed assignment disappears. In fact, fixed assignment is superior in this range due to its simplicity. However, the flexible assignment method presented in this paper outperforms all of the authors' previously tested assignment methods—which considered only one of the three factors—in every respect. As a result, it consistently achieves a higher number of moves per h for the QCs than a purely distance-based or purely work in process-based assignment of TTs.

Contrary to initial expectations, flexible assignment also underperforms compared to fixed assignment in the transition zone between underload and overload. Since the assignment occurs at an early stage, the system is unable to exploit its full potential to react to demand fluctuations. Since TTs are assigned to a new transport order and a specific QC when the previous transport order is completed, the decision is based on the system's values at that moment in time. However, the actual demand of the QCs may have changed by the time the TTs arrive, due to fluctuating handling times or technical disruptions. This limitation is particularly evident when the results are compared to the approximation curve for a shared queue. The fact that the simulated mean QC productivity for flexible assignment remains significantly below this approximation, and even below the level for fixed assignment, in both the transition zone and the overload zone, demonstrates that the method fails to unlock productivity potential. As these specific ranges are of particular interest to terminal operators because they represent high utilization levels of expensive QCs, this strategy is not considered practical.

(2) Interestingly, however, it is precisely the outliers described in the Results section that demonstrate the potential of the assignment procedure. For example, with one TT per QC, the productivity of both Experiment 4 and Experiment 1 lies above the approximate LOC for shared queues. While this LOC shows the potential of short-term assignment to accommodate demand fluctuations, it assumes that the mean handling times of the TTs

will not change. Taking route lengths into account, the flexible method implemented here leads to trucks preferring shorter routes, resulting in shorter mean travel distances and thus shorter handling times for the TTs. This is also demonstrated by Schwientek's studies [3]. These shorter handling times ensure that productivity remains above the LOC, even when there are few TTs available, with shared queues assumed to be ideal.

(3) In addition to mean QC productivity, this procedure's central objective is robustness against technical disruptions. The results of Experiment 1, which involved reduced availability of TTs and QCs, are shown in Fig. 3. As the results show, the method has advantages over fixed assignment, particularly when TT availability is low. This benefit is also evident when TTs are temporarily unavailable due to disruptions. Consequently, flexible assignment is more advantageous when disruptions lead to a significant deficit in transport capacity. Conversely, QC disruptions, which lower the mean transport demand, prevent the method from utilizing its strengths. In this regard, the procedure reacts more robustly to TT disruptions, provided there is not an excess of TTs. It only demonstrates resilience to QC disruptions if there were already insufficient TTs prior to the failure.

In addition to evaluating the robustness of the assignment procedure, the simulation study further supports the authors' previous findings regarding the development of approximation equations for fixed assignment [7]. The approximation curves demonstrate a high level of alignment with the results of this study, which further validates their accuracy in cases beyond the initial evaluation.

While shared-queue benchmarks indicate substantial improvement potential, the evaluation revealed that this cannot be realized with the applied procedure. In terms of mean QC productivity and robustness against disruptions, the new method offers no clear advantage in the examined scenarios. One reason for this underperformance is the timing of the assignment. In order to respond as precisely as possible to QC demand, assignments should be made as late as possible. Furthermore, the procedure does not sufficiently consider disruptions and therefore has no advantage over fixed assignment in terms of robustness against disturbances.

In practice, terminal operators could benefit from a hybrid assignment logic that maintains the simplicity of fixed assignment during stable, high-utilization periods while automatically pivoting to flexible procedures during technical disruptions or resource shortages. Such adaptive control would significantly enhance operational robustness against stochastic fluctuations in daily terminal routines without unnecessarily increasing system complexity during stable phases.

The insights gained from this simulation study form the basis of our ongoing research and the development of more advanced assignment strategies. While the flexible assignment method does not meet performance expectations in high utilization ranges, these results help to improve our understanding of the assignment procedures and their advantages. Instead, they provide valuable diagnostic information by identifying the precise bottleneck in the current dispatching logic: the timing of the assignment. The study clearly demonstrates that late assignment is the decisive factor in unlocking the productivity potential observed in the theoretical shared queue model. However, it also shows that shorter distances lead to shorter journey times and thus shift the possible LOCs. Consequently, the authors are currently developing a new assignment procedure for TTs and QCs that specifically incorporates these requirements. By deferring the assignment decision until the last possible moment, the new method aims to respond to stochastic disruptions and handling fluctuations, thereby bridging the gap between current practical limitations and theoretical efficiency.

Acknowledgments. This study is funded by the Deutsche Forschungsgemeinschaft (DFG, German Research Foundation) - project no. 508626914.

Disclosure of Interests. The authors have no competing interests to declare that are relevant to the content of this article.

References

1. Möhle, F., Koch, S., Jahn, C., Lödding, H.: Modelling of logistics objectives at the sea side of container terminals. In: Mizuyama, H., Morinaga, E., Nonaka, T., Kaihara, T., von Cieminski, G., Romero, D. (eds.) Advances in Production Management Systems. Cyber-Physical-Human Production Systems: Human-AI Collaboration and beyond, pp. 249–263. Springer Nature, Switzerland, Cham (2025). https://doi.org/10.1007/978-3-032-03550-9_17
2. Witte, S., Möhle, F., Ilenburg, S., Lödding, H., Jahn, C.: Simulation-based analysis of conflicting objectives of quay cranes and terminal trucks at container terminals. Simulation Produktion und Logistik. **2025** (2025)
3. Schwientek, A.K.: Effiziente Auftragszuordnung im Horizontaltransport von Seehafen-Containerterminals. Fraunhofer Verlag, Stuttgart (2021)
4. Lödding, H.: Handbook of Manufacturing Control: Fundamentals, Description, Configuration. Springer, Heidelberg (2013). https://doi.org/10.1007/978-3-642-24458-2
5. Hopp, W.J., Spearman, M.L.: Factory Physics, Third edn. Waveland Press (2011)
6. Smith, D.R., Whitt, W.: Resource sharing for efficiency in traffic systems. Bell Syst. Tech. J. **60**, 39–55 (1981). https://doi.org/10.1002/j.1538-7305.1981.tb00221.x
7. Möhle, F., Jahn, C., Lödding, H.: Logistic operating curves for closed queueing systems: enhancing container terminal productivity through shared queues. In: Advances in Production Management Systems. Cyber-Physical-Human Production Systems: Human-AI Collaboration and beyond. Springer Nature Switzerland, Cham
8. Ji, S., Ji, J.L., Ji, M.J., Kong, L.R., Gao, Z.D.: Spatiotemporally coordinated scheduling of suspended monorail vehicles and AGVs under a double cycling strategy in automated container terminals. Transp. Res. Part E logistics Transp. Rev. (2026). https://doi.org/10.1016/j.tre.2025.104485
9. Hu, Y.J., Dong, L.C., Xu, L.: Multi-AGV dispatching and routing problem based on a three-stage decomposition method. Math. Biosci. Eng. MBE. (2020). https://doi.org/10.3934/mbe.2020279
10. Hevner, R.A., March, S.T., Park, J., Ram, S.: Design science in information systems research. Manag. Inf. Syst. Q. **28**, 75 (2004)

Green Shipping and Energy Transition

Emission Reallocation Under Maritime Carbon Pricing: Evidence from EU-Related Shipping

Xinyue Pu[1], Xi Lin[2], Jingyang Du[1], and Xiwen Bai[1](✉)

[1] Department of Industrial Engineering, Tsinghua University, Beijing 100084, People's Republic of China
xiwenbai@tsinghua.edu.cn

[2] Department of Civil and Environmental Engineering, University of Michigan, Ann Arbor, MI 48104, USA

Abstract. The extension of the European Union Emissions Trading System (EU ETS) to maritime transport represents an early large-scale regional attempt to apply economy-wide carbon pricing to global shipping. By regulating emissions at the level of sailing segments, however, the policy may induce unintended shipping network adjustments. Here we reveal how this design can incentivize evasive hub-and-spoke transshipment, leading to a reallocation of emissions rather than a proportional reduction at the global level. Using multi-source, large-scale shipping data, we document a systematic shift toward hub-and-spoke transshipment. With a stylized network model, we characterize the incentive mechanisms underlying this behavior and identify the conditions under which transshipment dominates direct shipping, generating carbon leakage. Applying our framework to 7791 demand pairs on major trades of Europe imports, we find that although only about 11.71% of routes adopt transshipment, they account for over 41.92% of cargo volume. Relative to an ETS counterfactual without evasive adjustments, this reconfiguration raises total corridor-level emissions by approximately 1.94%, reduces aggregate EU ETS exposure by up to 34.77%, and erodes 7.24% of the emissions abatement that the ETS would otherwise achieve. These results suggest that market responses to carbon pricing can substantially reshape the effectiveness of regional maritime climate regulation, with implications for the design of future carbon policies in global transport.

Keywords: EU Emissions Trading System · Hub-and-spoke transshipment · Shipping networks

1 Introduction

Maritime transportation carries more than four-fifths of world merchandise by volume [8], but is also a major source of greenhouse gas emissions. Under business-as-usual scenarios, shipping CO_2 emissions are projected to remain

J. de Armas and E. Lalla Ruiz (Eds.): LOGMS 2026, LNCS 16679, pp. 87–97, 2027.
https://doi.org/10.1007/978-3-032-30795-8_8

10%–30% above 2008 levels by 2050 [7], conflicting with the International Maritime Organization's (IMO) mid-century net-zero target [3].

In response, market-based climate regulation has expanded into maritime transport. A prominent example is the European Union Emissions Trading System (EU ETS), which in 2024 became one of the first major carbon markets to cover international shipping [2]. Under current rules, 100% of emissions from voyages between EU ports and 50% from voyages between EU and non-EU ports are covered. By pricing emissions, the EU ETS is intended to promote cleaner fuels, lower speeds, and more efficient operations.

Yet carriers may also respond by reconfiguring service networks to reduce regulatory exposure [10]. Such adjustments include hub-and-spoke services, more transshipment, shifting port calls to nearby non-EU hubs, and changes in sailing speed and schedules. While these strategies reduce compliance costs, they may also increase emissions outside the regulated region, creating a trade-off between regional abatement and global environmental outcomes [1,5]. This raises a central question: does carbon pricing reduce total emissions or mainly shift them across space? We refer to this mechanism as *emission reallocation*, whereby emissions decline inside the regulated region but rise elsewhere through endogenous adjustments in routing, speed, and network structure. Assessing this mechanism is central to evaluating the climate effectiveness of regional maritime carbon regulation.

Recent studies have examined the implications of emissions trading in shipping, including compliance costs, allowance-price effects, carbon-leakage risks, and policy-design trade-offs [1,5]. However, less is known about how observed vessel operations, transshipment activity, and route-level emission outcomes jointly evolve after implementation. High-frequency AIS data remain underused for identifying changes in routing, port calls, and service structure.

This study addresses two questions: (i) how do shipping firms adjust routing, speed, and network configuration under carbon pricing? and (ii) do these adjustments reduce total emissions or mainly reallocate them beyond the regulated region? To answer them, we combine a stylized theoretical model with large-scale AIS data to examine operational and network responses to the EU ETS. Our contribution is to combine post-implementation AIS evidence with a stylized mechanism to assess whether maritime carbon pricing reduces emissions or reallocates them across regions.

2 Empirical Evidence and Analytical Framework

This section presents evidence, mechanism, and results, with detailed data and methods deferred to Sect. 4.

2.1 Evasive Hub-and-Spoke Transshipment Triggered by the EU ETS

The EU ETS regulates maritime emissions at the voyage-segment level, assigning carbon liabilities to sailing legs rather than end-to-end cargo movements. These rules became binding for maritime transport on January 1, 2024. Segment-based regulation creates incentives to reduce ETS-covered sailing by limiting EU port calls or shifting traffic away from ETS-liable segments. To constrain *simple voyage segmentation through intermediate port calls*, the EU designates a list of *neighboring transshipment ports*, including Tanger Med and Port Said, for which intermediate calls do not interrupt ETS liability. This limits evasive behavior based on port-call sequencing by a single vessel, but not broader network reorganization. In particular, *evasive hub-and-spoke transshipment* involving vessel switching at non-EU hubs remains unaddressed: cargo is transferred to feeder vessels so that only a small share of the voyage remains ETS-covered. Because ETS obligations are assessed at the vessel–leg level rather than the cargo or service level, such adjustments remain compliant yet economically evasive.

Comparing 2023 with 2024, vessels show distinct port-calling patterns across EU ports, nearby non-EU transshipment ports, and other ports (Fig. 1a,b). At EU ports, large vessels make fewer calls but stay longer in 2024. At nearby non-EU ports, large-vessel call frequencies remain broadly stable while port-call durations increase substantially. In the absence of rising call frequencies, longer stays are consistent with intensified transshipment rather than technical stops or simple route truncation. At the same time, feeder vessels increase both call frequencies and call durations on routes connecting these ports to EU destinations. These patterns are unlikely to reflect trade-demand shifts, as aggregate EU import and export volumes remain broadly stable.

Routing behavior supports this interpretation. Under the EU ETS, large vessels calling at transshipment ports are less likely to subsequently enter the EU and, conditional on entry, call at fewer EU ports (Fig. 1c). Meanwhile, feeder services between transshipment ports and EU ports become more frequent, and a growing share of voyages terminates after transshipment. Taken together, these patterns are consistent with increased hub-and-spoke transshipment after the EU ETS extension, rather than simple route truncation alone. Since these descriptive patterns cannot by themselves establish the full network-level adjustment mechanism, we next develop a stylized model to characterize the underlying incentives.

2.2 Incentive Structure and Mechanisms of Evasive Transshipment

Evasive hub-and-spoke transshipment arises as a cost-minimizing response to the heterogeneous marginal carbon costs created by the EU ETS. Large mainline vessels are more energy-efficient than feeders but incur larger absolute carbon liabilities on ETS-covered segments, whereas feeders face lower per-voyage carbon costs. This asymmetry creates an incentive to minimize the ETS-covered share of a route. We model a shipping service as a route between an origin and a destination. Direct shipping is a single leg, whereas transshipment splits the route into an ETS-covered feeder leg and a non-covered mainline leg, following the stylized three-node structure in Fig. 2a. Let $x \in (0,1)$ denote the ETS-covered share of route distance, with the remaining $1-x$ served by the mainline vessel outside the

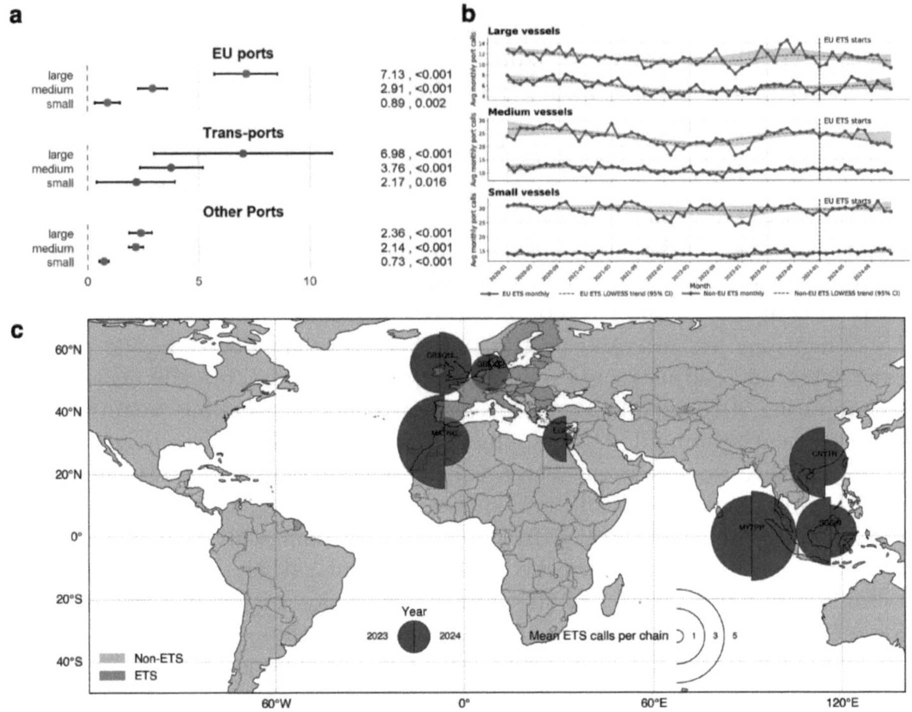

Fig. 1. Empirical evidence of increasing hub-and-spoke transshipment after the EU ETS extension to maritime transport. a Triple-difference estimates of changes in berthing duration across port types and vessel classes after EU ETS implementation. Vessel classes are defined by nominal capacity: small vessels (0–3,000 TEU), medium vessels (3,000–12,000 TEU), and large vessels (above 12,000 TEU). Estimates are reported for EU ports, nearby non-EU transshipment ports, and other ports worldwide, with 95% confidence intervals. **b** Port-call behavior at EU ETS ports and neighboring non-EU transshipment ports (2020–2024). Port-call counts by vessel size class are shown separately for the two port groups. **c** Average number of ETS port calls following the last non-ETS port of call (2023–2024). For each last non-ETS port, the pie chart shows the mean number of subsequent ETS-covered port calls per vessel chain, with colors indicating the year. Port codes correspond to CNYTN (Yantian), SGSIN (Singapore), MYTPP (Tanjung Pelepas), EGPSD (Port Said), MATNG (Tanger Med), GBSOU (Southampton), and GBFXT (Felixstowe).

ETS. The carrier chooses between direct shipping and transshipment by comparing total operating costs, including time-charter costs, fuel use, and carbon liabilities on ETS-covered segments. Transshipment becomes optimal when the carbon-cost savings from shifting the mainline leg outside ETS coverage exceed the feeder's lower energy efficiency and the additional handling cost. On long-haul trades such as Far East–Europe, this condition is readily satisfied when x is small.

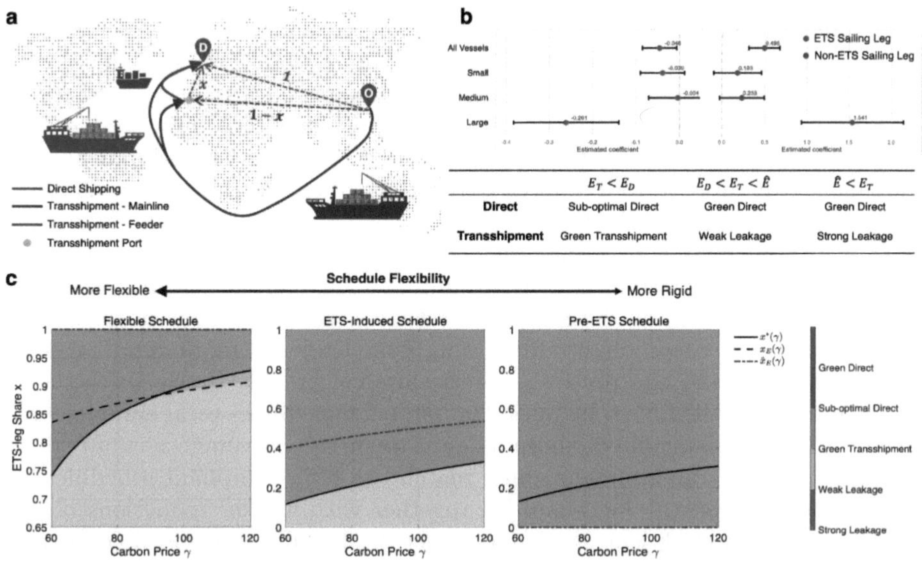

Fig. 2. Structure, behavioral adjustment, and potential carbon leakage under evasive transshipment. **a** Stylized framework of carrier routing under the EU ETS. Direct shipping exposes the full route to ETS coverage, whereas transshipment splits the journey into a non-ETS mainline segment and an ETS-covered feeder segment, with x denoting the ETS-covered share. **b** Estimated speed compensation and illustrative emission outcomes. Top: Estimates from Eq. (1) show that large vessels reduce speed on ETS-covered segments while increasing speed outside the ETS. Vessel classes are defined by nominal capacity: small vessels (0–3,000 TEU), medium vessels (3,000–12,000 TEU), and large vessels (above 12,000 TEU). Bottom: Routing choices and associated emissions under alternative strategies. Here, E_T denotes emissions under transshipment, E_D denotes emissions from direct shipping under the EU ETS, and $\hat{E}$ denotes emissions from direct shipping before the EU ETS. **c** Phase diagram of routing choices and emission outcomes under different levels of schedule flexibility and carbon prices. The optimal ETS exposure share x^* increases with carbon prices, while the emission regime depends on schedule constraints. Here, x_E and $\hat{x}_E$ denote the thresholds separating weak and strong leakage. Green transshipment arises only in a narrow range with high ETS exposure, whereas greater schedule rigidity makes transshipment increasingly associated with weak or strong leakage.

When carriers can freely adjust sailing speeds and schedules, evasive transshipment shifts ETS exposure to the short feeder leg. Because feeders are less emission-efficient, their cost-minimizing speed on the ETS-covered segment is lower than that of an ETS-compliant mainline vessel on the direct route. Yet despite sailing more slowly, the feeder can still generate higher ETS-liable unit-cargo emissions on this short segment. This gives rise to **weak carbon leakage**: global emissions remain below the pre-regulation baseline, but ETS-induced abatement is substantially reduced because the long-haul leg is shifted outside the regulated region.

In practice, carriers cannot freely adjust speeds and schedules. Service frequency, port-call windows, and fleet rotation impose binding operational constraints. Empirically, vessels slow down on ETS-covered legs and speed up on non-ETS legs to maintain service performance, a behavioral response we term *speed compensation* (Fig. 2b, top). Combined with evasive transshipment, this adjustment can raise non-ETS speeds, and thus emissions, above pre-ETS levels, producing **strong carbon leakage**.

To capture these constraints, we consider two scheduling environments defined by the transit-time constraint imposed on transshipment relative to direct shipping. Under an *ETS-induced schedule*, transshipment preserves the transit time of ETS-compliant direct shipping. Under a more rigid *pre-ETS schedule*, it preserves the pre-ETS direct-shipping transit time. As shown in Fig. 2c, under fully flexible schedules, transshipment reduces total emissions relative to ETS-compliant direct shipping only when ETS coverage x is unrealistically large. When transshipment must match the ETS-compliant schedule, the loss of abatement on the long-haul leg together with weaker reductions on the feeder leg leads to weak leakage. Under stricter schedules, the speed compensation required on the non-ETS segment leads to strong leakage.

2.3 Emission Reallocation Under Evasive Transshipment

Across major EU import corridors, evasive transshipment primarily affects long-haul, high-volume trades for which ETS coverage is low enough to make rerouting attractive. We construct a corridor sample for Atlantic and Far East–EU shipping lines, the two main components of EU inbound maritime trade. Based on the ports involved in these corridors, we identify 478 origin–destination demand pairs and examine route-level decisions under the baseline scenario. As shown in Fig. 3a, evasive transshipment arises on only a limited subset of routes and is concentrated on long-haul Far East–EU trades with low ETS exposure (below 2.33%). Accordingly, no Atlantic routes switch under baseline conditions. The ring plot in Fig. 3b shows that although only 11.71% of routes in this sample adopt transshipment, they account for 41.92% of associated TEU demand.

At the aggregate level, evasive transshipment substantially reduces carriers' ETS exposure and weakens the emissions-reduction effect of the EU ETS. We extend the analysis from the major corridors to all EU import trades, comprising 7,791 demand pairs. Relative to ETS-compliant direct shipping, routes that switch to transshipment generate on average 1.93% more emissions, implying an additional 76.98 ktCO_2 per year in aggregate (Fig. 3b). For these routes, emissions within EU waters rise by 12.99%, while emissions outside the EU increase by 1.67%, because the EU leg previously served by large mainline vessels is replaced by smaller, less fuel-efficient feeder ships. Overall, for switching routes, evasive transshipment weakens the emissions-reduction effect of the EU ETS by 7.24%. Under projected trade growth, this annual increase could rise to 137.71 ktCO_2 by 2050. At the level of all EU imports, evasive transshipment also lowers aggregate EU ETS exposure by 34.77% (about 3.86 MtCO_2 per year).

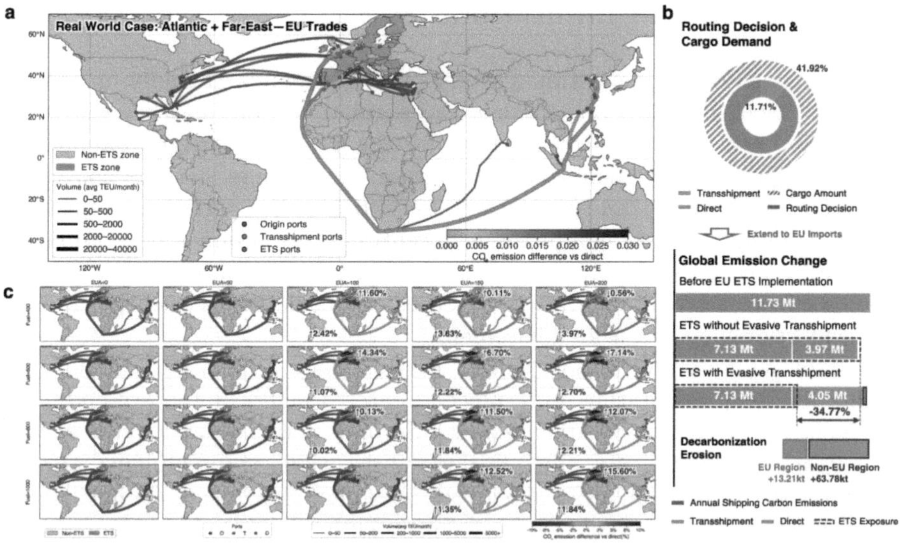

Fig. 3. Emission reallocation under evasive transshipment. a Per-unit cargo emission changes induced by evasive transshipment under observed market conditions on Atlantic and Far East–EU shipping routes. Grey routes correspond to demand pairs choosing direct shipping, while highlighted routes indicate transshipment choices. Baseline parameters are calibrated at a carbon price (EUA) of 95 USD per tonne, a fuel price of 600 USD per tonne, and a transshipment cost of 70 USD per TEU. **b** Cargo rerouting, emission increments, and policy erosion under evasive transshipment. The upper ring chart summarizes the shares of routes and cargo volumes adopting transshipment under baseline estimation. The lower panel reports key quantitative indices of evasive transshipment and the regional decomposition of induced emission changes in EU and non-EU regions. **c** Sensitivity analysis of emission reallocation under alternative combinations of carbon prices and fuel costs for EU imports. Each panel reports routing choices and associated emission changes across demand pairs. Regional percentage changes in emissions, measured relative to the ETS-compliant direct-shipping benchmark, are annotated within each panel.

The prevalence of evasive transshipment and the resulting regional emission reallocation are highly sensitive to carbon and fuel prices. Figure 3c shows that evasive transshipment becomes attractive on a much larger set of routes and cargo flows as carbon prices rise and fuel costs fall. In historically plausible scenarios, this mechanism can even generate regional abatement within the ETS while increasing emissions elsewhere. For example, when the EUA price reaches 200 USD and the fuel price falls to 400 USD per tonne, 60.47% of shipping routes switch to transshipment, accounting for 82.92% of total cargo volume. Under this configuration, emissions within EU waters decline by 0.56%, while emissions outside EU waters increase by 3.97%.

3 Discussion and Limitations

Our findings show that maritime carbon pricing depends not only on the carbon price itself, but also on whether the regulatory unit matches the operational unit optimized by carriers. Because the EU ETS assigns liabilities to sailing segments rather than end-to-end cargo movements, carriers can reduce ETS exposure through transshipment, vessel substitution, and speed adjustment while remaining formally compliant. Concentrated on commercially important long-haul trades, this adaptive response can generate disproportionate cargo and emission effects, so reductions in regulated emissions do not necessarily translate into proportional system-wide abatement.

Several policy implications follow. First, policy evaluation should move beyond leg-level accounting and place greater weight on end-to-end cargo movements and system-wide emissions. Second, monitoring should account for network responses, including feeder substitution, transshipment through nearby non-EU hubs, and adjustments on unregulated segments. Third, regional carbon-pricing schemes may require complementary accounting rules or cross-jurisdictional coordination to better align regulated emissions with the full transport chain optimized by carriers.

This study has several limitations. The network model is intentionally stylized to isolate the incentive mechanism created by segment-based carbon pricing, and abstracts from carrier competition, alliance-level service design, port capacity constraints, and detailed fleet deployment decisions. The empirical analysis focuses on EU-related corridors because the EU ETS is currently the relevant carbon-pricing scheme for international shipping; the estimated magnitudes may therefore differ under other regulatory designs or future global measures. Finally, the transshipment cost parameter is calibrated using confidential industry information, so the underlying operator-level records cannot be disclosed. We interpret the results as mechanism-level evidence rather than a full equilibrium prediction.

4 Data and Methods

Dataset. This study combines vessel movement, ship characteristics, and cargo shipment data to characterize global container shipping operations. We use global AIS data for container ships from 2016 to 2024 from MarineTraffic, providing vessel identifiers, timestamps, positions, and speeds. Vessel characteristics are obtained from Clarkson's and cover the full container-ship fleet. To measure cargo flows, we use Container Trade Statistics (CTS) data from January 2023 to October 2024, covering EU-related containerized trade by 18 major shipping lines. The dataset contains 2,062,037 shipment records, 97,097,152 containers, and 80,441 origin–destination port pairs. In 2024 alone, it covers 67,988 port pairs and implies an annualized trade volume of 26.2 million TEU, equivalent to about 87.79% of total EU container import and export flows [9]. Sailing distances are computed using the `searoute` Python package based on realistic maritime routes between representative port locations identified from observed port calls. Fuel consumption and emissions are estimated using IMO guidelines and related industry sources,[1] including standard speed–power relationships, specific fuel oil consumption, and fuel-based CO_2 emission factors [4].

Empirical Evidence. To examine how the EU ETS affects vessel operations, we analyze two margins: sailing speed and port calls. We test whether vessels slow down on ETS-covered legs while speeding up on non-EU legs, and whether they spend longer at EU and potential transshipment ports. For sailing speed, we estimate a generalized difference-in-differences (DiD) framework:

$$\begin{cases} S_{ijt} = \beta_0 + \beta_1(treat_i \times post_t) + \beta_2(redsea_i \times post_t) + \beta_3 X_{jt} + \lambda_t + \delta_i + \varepsilon_{ijt}, \\ S_{\text{nonEU},ijt} = \beta_0 + \beta_1(treat_j \times post_t) + \beta_2(redsea_i \times post_t) + \beta_3 X_{jt} + \lambda_t + \delta_i + \varepsilon_{ijt}, \end{cases}$$

where the first specification examines ETS-covered legs, with $treat_i$ indicating whether leg i is ETS-covered, while the second examines non-EU legs, where $treat_j$ is vessel-level ETS exposure, measured as the share of ETS-covered legs in vessel j's post-policy operations. $post_t$ indicates the introduction of the EU ETS, X_{jt} includes vessel characteristics, $redsea_i \times post_t$ absorbs Red Sea rerouting effects, λ_t are quarter fixed effects, and δ_i are origin–destination fixed effects. The coefficient β_1 captures ETS-induced slowdown in the first specification and compensatory acceleration in the second. For port operations, we estimate a generalized triple-difference design by port type and vessel size:

$$\begin{aligned} berth\_duration_{pjt} = {} & \alpha_1(port_p \times ship_j \times post_t) \\ & + \beta_1(port_p \times ship_j) + \beta_2(port_p \times post_t) + \beta_3(ship_j \times post_t) \\ & + \gamma_1 port_p + \gamma_2 ship_j + \gamma_3 post_t + \varepsilon_{pjt}, \end{aligned}$$

where $berth\_duration_{pjt}$ is the average berthing duration of vessel j at port p in period t. The triple interaction captures the differential post-policy change across port–vessel-size combinations.

Stylized Modeling for Evasive Transshipment. We model the carrier's choice between direct shipping and evasive transshipment through unit cargo operating costs, comprising time-charter cost $H(\cdot)$, fuel consumption $B_i(\cdot)$, and ETS-liable emissions $E_i(\cdot)$, where $i = 1, 2$ denote the mainline and feeder vessels. We use the standard forms

$$H(v) = \frac{\theta}{v}, B_i(v) = \frac{a_i v^{b_i - 1}}{Q_i}, E_i(v) = \tau B_i(v), \tag{1}$$

where θ is the unit-TEU time-charter rate, $a_i > 0$ and $b_i > 1$ parameterize unit-distance bunker consumption (see, e.g., [6]), Q_i is vessel capacity, and τ is the

[1] The transshipment cost is calibrated using confidential industry data obtained from shipping operators and treated as a fixed per-TEU handling cost in the baseline analysis. This treatment reflects the fact that such charges are relatively stable compared with carbon and fuel prices, which are the main sources of short- to medium-term variation in the routing incentive considered here.

emission factor of Marine Diesel Oil (MDO). To capture efficiency differences, we impose $a_1 v^{b_1-1} > a_2 v^{b_2-1}$ and $\frac{a_1 v^{b_1-1}}{Q_1} < \frac{a_2 v^{b_2-1}}{Q_2}$ for all $v > 0$. For direct shipping at speed v, the full route is ETS-covered:

$$C_{\mathrm{D}}(v) = H(v) + \beta B_1(v) + \gamma E_1(v), \tag{2}$$

where β and γ denote fuel and carbon prices. Under transshipment, only the feeder leg of length x is ETS-covered. With mainline speed v_1, feeder speed v_2, and transshipment cost S_T, unit cost is

$$C_T(v_1, v_2; x) = \underbrace{(1-x)\left(H\left(v_1\right) + \beta B_1(v_1)\right)}_{C_{L_1}} + \underbrace{x\left(H\left(v_2\right) + \beta B_2(v_2) + \gamma E_2(v_2)\right)}_{C_{L_2}} + S_T.$$

Let v^* and (v_1^*, v_2^*) denote the optimal speeds under direct shipping and transshipment. Evasive transshipment occurs when $C_{\mathrm{T}}(v_1^*, v_2^*; x) \leq C_{\mathrm{D}}(v^*)$, implying a critical ETS-coverage threshold

$$x^* = \frac{C_D(v^*) - C_{L_1}(v_1^*) - S_T}{C_{L_2}(v_2^*) - C_{L_1}(v_1^*)}, \tag{3}$$

where C_{L_1} and C_{L_2} denote the costs on the unregulated and regulated segments. Smaller ETS-covered shares therefore make a route more vulnerable to evasive transshipment. Let $\hat{v}^*$ denote the optimal direct-shipping speed without ETS. Under free schedules,

$$v^* = \left(\frac{\theta Q_1}{a_1(b_1-1)(\beta+\tau\gamma)}\right)^{1/b_1}, \qquad \hat{v}^* = \left(\frac{\theta Q_1}{\beta a_1(b_1-1)}\right)^{1/b_1}, \tag{4}$$

with $\hat{v}^* = v_1^* > v^* > v_2^*$. Under schedule constraints, transshipment speeds are instead pinned down by time-matching conditions: under ETS-induced schedules, $\frac{1}{v^*} = \frac{1-x}{v_1} + \frac{x}{v_2}, \quad x \in (0,1)$, and under pre-ETS schedules, $\frac{1}{\hat{v}^*} = \frac{1-x}{v_1} + \frac{x}{v_2}, \quad x \in (0,1)$.

Global Emission Under Evasive Transshipment. To quantify the network-level emission effects of evasive transshipment, we combine the stylized routing framework with a calibrated emission model and apply it to observed trade flows on major EU-related corridors. Shipping demand is derived from the CTS database, covering all origin–destination pairs with EU ports as destinations and ports on the Atlantic and Far East–EU corridors as origins, and aggregated to monthly average TEU volumes.

For each demand pair, we compare direct shipping with hub-and-spoke transshipment. Under direct shipping, a large mainline vessel serves the full route. Under transshipment, the route is split into a non-ETS mainline segment served by a large vessel and an ETS-covered feeder segment served by a smaller vessel. In both cases, vessels choose cost-minimizing sailing speeds based on per-TEU generalized costs, including time, fuel, and ETS-related carbon costs, subject to pre-ETS schedule consistency and, where applicable, a per-TEU transshipment cost. Carriers choose the lower-cost option for each route. Emissions are then calculated on a per-TEU basis and aggregated using observed monthly demand to quantify how ETS-induced rerouting reallocates emissions between EU and non-EU segments under baseline and alternative carbon price and fuel cost scenarios.

References

1. Christodoulou, A., Cullinane, K.: The prospects for, and implications of, emissions trading in shipping. Maritime Econ. Logist. **26**(1), 168–184 (2024)
2. European Commission: Directive (eu) 2023/959 amending directive 2003/87/ec establishing a system for greenhouse gas emission allowance trading within the european union. Legal directive, European Commission, Brussels, Belgium (2023), cELEX: 32023L0959. https://eur-lex.europa.eu/legal-content/EN/TXT/PDF/?uri=CELEX:32023L0959
3. IMO: 2023 imo strategy on reduction of ghg emissions from ships. Strategy report, International Maritime Organization (IMO) (2023). Accessed 07 July 2023. https://www.imo.org/en/OurWork/Environment/Pages/2023-IMO-Strategy-on-Reduction-of-GHG-Emissions-from-Ships.aspx
4. International Maritime Organization: Fourth IMO greenhouse gas study 2020 (2020). https://www.maritimecyprus.com/wp-content/uploads/2021/03/4th-IMO-GHG-Study-2020.pdf
5. Kotzampasakis, M.: Maritime emissions trading in the EU: systematic literature review and policy assessment. Transp. Policy **165**, 28–41 (2025)
6. Lin, X., Pu, X., Bai, X.: On the efficiency impacts of berthing priority provision. Transp. Sci. **58**(3), 578–596 (2024)
7. MEPC, R.: 2023 IMO strategy on reduction of GHG emissions from ships (2023)
8. UNCTAD: Review of maritime transport 2023: towards a green and just transition. LLC Stylus Publishing (2023)
9. UNCTAD: 2024 Review of Maritime Transport: Navigating Maritime Chokepoints. United Nations Publications (2024)
10. Verschuur, J., Koks, E.E., Hall, J.: Ports' criticality in international trade and global supply-chains. Nat. Commun. **13**(1), 4351 (2022)

Container Liner Fleet Planning under FuelEU Maritime: Banking and Borrowing

Joseph Seong-Hyun Cho and Jasmine Siu Lee Lam(✉)

Department of Technology, Management and Economics, Technical University of Denmark, Kongens Lyngby 2800, Denmark
jasmlam@dtu.dk

Abstract. This study examines container liner fleet planning under the FuelEU Maritime regulation, focusing on banking and borrowing mechanisms. A mixed-integer linear programming model is developed to determine optimal vessel purchase and retrofit decisions under greenhouse gas (GHG) intensity constraints and different shares of EU port calls. Results show that penalty levels drive green transition, as low penalties sustain diesel use and higher penalties accelerate retrofitting. Banking enables the accumulation of compliance surpluses and supports earlier transition to low-carbon vessels, while borrowing is mainly used prior to retrofit to anticipate these surpluses. However, bio-methanol does not meet post-2050 targets, indicating that additional decarbonization measures, such as greener fuels or more advanced vessel technologies, are required. The incentive for green transition is relatively weaker for shipping companies operating routes with a lower share of EU port calls.

Keywords: FuelEU Maritime · Fleet renewal · Alternative fuels · Banking and borrowing · Maritime decarbonization

1 Introduction

The FuelEU Maritime Regulation (EU) 2023/1805, which entered into force on 1 January 2025, sets limits on the well-to-wake (WtW) greenhouse gas (GHG) intensity of energy used onboard ships calling at EU ports [1]. The regulation introduces a compliance structure that combines progressively tightening targets with flexibility mechanisms, including banking and borrowing of compliance balance. These features create new strategic challenges for fleet planning. Shipping companies must decide when to retrofit or replace vessels while managing intertemporal compliance through banking and borrowing. In addition, compliance depends on voyage composition, as the regulation applies differently to intra-EU and extra-EU legs.

Although prior studies have examined fleet transition under environmental constraints [2–4], they do not fully reflect how FuelEU Maritime operates in practice [2]. analyzes fleet composition under a binding carbon cap, while [3] considers environmental impact minimization as an objective [4]. incorporates environmental regulation

J. de Armas and E. Lalla Ruiz (Eds.): LOGMS 2026, LNCS 16679, pp. 98–108, 2027.
https://doi.org/10.1007/978-3-032-30795-8_9

into fleet planning through carbon taxing and cap-and-trade mechanisms based on well-to-wake and tank-to-wake emissions. However, these studies do not explicitly model FuelEU Maritime compliance targets, annual compliance balances, the associated banking and borrowing mechanisms, or differentiated regulatory coverage across EU-related routes. This paper addresses this gap by directly incorporating these policy-specific features into fleet planning, thereby enabling an analysis of how banking, borrowing, and penalty levels influence investment decisions and the timing of decarbonization. Only a limited number of studies, such as [5], have considered similar mechanisms in supply chain contexts, but not in fleet planning.

This study analyzes how banking and borrowing affect fleet transition decisions and how route composition influences the timing and type of green technology adoption under FuelEU Maritime.

2 Problem Statement and Model Formulation

2.1 Problem Statement

We consider a container liner shipping company operating a set of routes with fixed annual demand. Each route is served by vessels operating in repeated cycles, and a subset of routes includes EU port calls, making them subject to the FuelEU Maritime regulation.

The company initially operates a fleet of diesel-powered vessels. It must decide when to retrofit existing vessels or invest in new vessels using alternative fuels. The candidate fuel options considered in this study are bio-LNG, bio-methanol, and ammonia, which are among the most prominent low-carbon fuel alternatives in maritime transport [2, 4]. Each vessel operates on a single fuel type.

Under FuelEU Maritime, compliance is assessed annually at the vessel level based on lifecycle (well-to-wake, WtW) GHG intensity. The actual GHG intensity of a vessel is defined as

$$g_{ship} = \frac{\sum_k (E_k \bullet GHG_k)}{\sum_k E_k} \tag{1}$$

where E_k denotes the annual energy consumption of fuel k (MJ) and GHG_k represents the corresponding WtW GHG intensity (gCO2e/MJ).

The regulatory target is determined by applying a reduction factor to a reference intensity. The reference value corresponds to the average WtW GHG intensity of the fleet in 2020, calculated based on the EU Monitoring, Reporting and Verification (EU MRV) system, and is set to 91.16gCO2e/MJ [1]. The resulting target intensities for selected milestone years are summarized in Table 1.

The compliance balance is defined as the difference between the target and actual GHG intensity multiplied by the total energy consumption. A positive balance represents a compliance surplus, while a negative balance indicates a deficit.

FuelEU Maritime provides flexibility mechanisms to manage compliance. Banking allows surplus to be carried forward to future years without expiration. Borrowing enables a deficit in the current year to be covered by anticipated surplus in the following year, subject to regulatory constraints. In particular, borrowing is limited to 2% of

Table 1. Target GHG intensity

Year	Reduction factor	Target intensity (gCO2e/MJ)
2025	2%	89.34
2030	6%	85.69
2035	14.5%	77.95
2040	31%	62.90
2045	62%	34.64
2050	80%	18.23

the annual target and cannot be used in two consecutive years. Any borrowed amount must be repaid in the subsequent year with a 10% premium. If the compliance balance remains negative after applying these mechanisms, a penalty is imposed, corresponding to approximately €700 per ton of CO2 equivalent [1] (Table 2).

Table 2. Notations for sets, parameters, and variables

Sets	
$K = \{1, \ldots, \lvert K\rvert\}$	Set of fuel/propulsion types
$R = \{1, \ldots, \lvert R\rvert\}$	Set of routes
V	Set of vessel slots
$T = \{0, \ldots, T^{\max}\}$	Set of planning periods (years)
$T^{'} = \{0, \ldots, T^{\max} - 1\}$	Set of transition periods (years)
$F \subseteq K \times K$	Set of feasible retrofit pairs
$\mathbb{Z}^{+}$	Set of nonnegative integers
Parameter	
a_v^{init}	Initial age of vessel slot v
$\underline{A}^{ret}, \overline{A}^{ret}$	Lower and upper age bounds for retrofit eligibility
A^{max}	Maximum vessel age
c_{kr}^{fuel}	Fuel cost per voyage of type k on route r
c_{kr}^{oper}	Non-fuel operating cost per voyage of type k
c^{pen}	Penalty rate per tonne of compliance deficit
c_{kt}^{pur}	Purchase cost of ship type k
c_{ijt}^{ret}	Retrofit cost from ship type i to j
c_k^{scr}	Scrap value of ship type k at age 25
Cap_k	Capacity (TEU) per voyage of ship type k
D_{rt}	Demand (TEU) on route r in year t

(continued)

Table 2. (*continued*)

Sets	
E_{kr}	Energy consumption per voyage of ship type k on route r
g_k	Well-to-wake GHG intensity (gCO2e/MJ)
I_t^{tar}	Target GHG intensity in year t
M	Sufficiently large constant
s_{kv}^{init}	Initial state; equals 1 if slot v initially contains a ship of type k
$\overline{V}_{kr}$	Maximum annual number of voyages of ship type k on route r
δ_t	Discount factor in year t
ρ	Borrowing premium
β	Borrowing cap ratio
$\alpha_r \in [0, 1]$	A route-specific weighting parameter
Variable	
y_{krt}	Binary indicating ship type k is deployed on route r in year t
x_{krtv}	Number of voyages performed by v using type k on route r in t
v_{ktv}^{state}	Binary indicating vessel slot v is occupied by a ship of type k in t
v_{tv}^{active}	Binary indicating vessel slot v is occupied by a ship in t
v_{tv}^{age}	Age of the ship assigned to slot v in year t
v_{ktv}^{new}	Binary indicating a new ship of type k is introduced into slot v at the end of year t and becomes active in year t + 1
v_{ktv}^{scr}	Binary indicating a ship in slot v is scrapped at the end of year t
v_{ijtv}^{retro}	Binary indicating a ship in slot v is retrofitted from type i to j
q_{tv}	Repayment obligation in year t due to borrowing in year t-1
def_{tv}	Compliance deficit of slot v in year t
sup_{tv}	Compliance surplus of slot v in year t
z_{tv}	Cumulative banked surplus in year t
use_{tv}	Amount of banked surplus used in year t
y_{tv}^{b}	Binary for borrowing decision in year t
b_{tv}	Borrowed compliance amount in year t
η_{tv}	Penalized deficit in year t
ϕ_{tv}	Binary preventing simultaneous deficit and surplus

2.2 Model Formulation

A mixed-integer linear programming (MILP) model is developed to capture the fleet planning problem under FuelEU Maritime regulation. The model determines optimal fleet composition, retrofit timing, and operational decisions over the planning horizon while accounting for regulatory compliance mechanisms.

The objective is to minimize the total discounted cost over the planning horizon, including fuel, operation, vessel purchase, retrofit, and FuelEU penalty costs, minus scrap revenues.

$$\min \sum_{t\in T} \delta_t \left[\sum_{k\in K} \sum_{r\in R} \sum_{v\in V} \left(c_{kr}^{\mathrm{fuel}} + c_{kr}^{\mathrm{oper}} \right) x_{krtv} \right.$$
$$\left. + \sum_{k\in K} \sum_{v\in V} c_k^{\mathrm{pur}} v_{k,t,v}^{new} + \sum_{(i,j)\in F} \sum_{v\in V} c_{ijt}^{\mathrm{ret}} v_{ijtv}^{retro} - \sum_{k\in K} \sum_{v\in V} c_k^{\mathrm{scr}} v_{ktv}^{scrap} + \sum_{v\in V} c^{pen} \eta_{tv} \right] \tag{2}$$

Fleet Deployment and Voyage Constraints.

$$\sum_{k\in K} y_{krt} = 1, \ \forall r, t \tag{3}$$

$$v_{ktv}^{state} \le y_{krt}, \ \forall k, r, t, v \tag{4}$$

$$x_{krtv} \le \overline{V}_{kr} \, v_{ktv}^{state}, \ \forall k, r, t, v \tag{5}$$

$$\sum_{k\in K} \sum_{v\in V} \mathrm{Cap}_k x_{krtv} \ge \mathrm{D}_{rt}, \ \forall r, t \tag{6}$$

Constraints (3)–(6) define the deployment and operational decisions of the fleet. Constraint (3) ensures that exactly one vessel type is selected for each route and year. Constraint (4) links the vessel state to the route-level deployment decision. Constraint (5) limits the number of voyages by the maximum annual voyages per vessel. Constraint (6) ensures that the total transport capacity satisfies the demand on each route.

Fleet Renewal Constraints.

$$\sum_{k\in K} v_{ktv}^{state} = v_{tv}^{active}, \ \forall t, v \tag{7}$$

$$v_{k0v}^{state} = s_{kv}^{init}, \ \forall k, v \tag{8}$$

$$v_{0v}^{age} = a_v^{init}, \ \forall v \tag{9}$$

$$v_{ktv}^{scrap} \le v_{ktv}^{state}, \ \forall k, t, v \tag{10}$$

$$\sum_{(i,j)\in F} v_{ijtv}^{retro} \le 1, \ \forall t, v \tag{11}$$

$$v_{ijtv}^{retro} \leq v_{itv}^{state}, \ \forall (i,j) \in F, t, v \tag{12}$$

$$\sum_{k \in K} v_{ktv}^{new} \leq 1, \ \forall t, v \tag{13}$$

$$\sum_{k \in K} v_{ktv}^{new} \leq \sum_{k \in K} v_{ktv}^{scrap} + \left(1 - v_{tv}^{active}\right), \ \forall t, v \tag{14}$$

$$v_{tv}^{age} \geq \underline{A}^{ret} - M\left(1 - v_{ijtv}^{retro}\right), \ \forall (i,j) \in F, t, v \tag{15}$$

$$v_{tv}^{age} \leq \overline{A}^{ret} - M\left(1 - v_{ijtv}^{retro}\right), \ \forall (i,j) \in F, t, v \tag{16}$$

$$v_{t+1,v}^{active} = v_{tv}^{active} - \sum_{k \in K} v_{ktv}^{scrap} + \sum_{k \in K} v_{ktv}^{new}, \ \forall t, v \tag{17}$$

$$v_{k,t+1,v}^{state} = v_{ktv}^{state} - \sum_{j:(k,j) \in F} v_{kjtv}^{retro} + \sum_{i:(i,k) \in F} v_{iktv}^{retro} - v_{ktv}^{scrap} + v_{ktv}^{new}, \ \forall k, t, v \tag{18}$$

$$v_{t+1,v}^{age} \leq v_{tv}^{age} + 1 + M\left(\sum_{k \in K} v_{ktv}^{scrap} + \sum_{k \in K} v_{ktv}^{new}\right), \ \forall t, v \tag{19}$$

$$v_{t+1,v}^{age} \geq v_{tv}^{age} + 1 - M\left(\sum_{k \in K} v_{ktv}^{scrap} + \sum_{k \in K} v_{ktv}^{new}\right), \ \forall t, v \tag{20}$$

$$v_{t+1,v}^{age} \leq M\left(1 - \sum_{k \in K} v_{ktv}^{new}\right), \ \forall t, v \tag{21}$$

$$v_{tv}^{age} \leq M v_{tv}^{active}, \ \forall t, v \tag{22}$$

$$v_{tv}^{age} - A^{max} \leq M \sum_{k \in K} v_{ktv}^{scrap}, \ \forall t, v \tag{23}$$

$$v_{t+1,v}^{age} \leq A^{max}, \ \forall t, v \tag{24}$$

Constraints (7)–(24) describe fleet transition over time. Constraint (7) links vessel state and slot occupancy. Constraints (8)–(9) define the initial fleet configuration and vessel ages. Constraint (10) allows scrapping only for vessels currently occupying the slot. Constraints (11)–(12) govern retrofit feasibility and ensure consistency with vessel type. Constraints (13)–(14) restrict newbuilding decisions to at most one vessel per slot and require either scrapping or an empty slot. Constraints (15)–(16) enforce retrofit feasibility within the admissible age window. Constraints (17)–(18) update slot activity and type transitions over time. Constraints (19)–(21) describe vessel age dynamics, including ageing and reset after newbuilding. Constraints (22)–(24) ensure consistency between vessel activity and age, and enforce the maximum vessel lifetime.

FuelEU Compliance Balance with Banking and Borrowing

$$def_{tv} - sup_{tv} = \sum_{k\in K}\sum_{r\in R}\alpha_r\left(g_k - I_t^{\text{tar}}\right)E_{kr}x_{krtv} + q_{tv},\ \ \forall t, v \tag{25}$$

$$def_{tv} \le M\,\phi_{tv},\ \ \forall t, v \tag{26}$$

$$sup_{tv} \le M\,(1 - \phi_{tv}),\ \ \forall t, v \tag{27}$$

$$def_{tv} \le Mv_{tv}^{active},\ \ \forall t, v \tag{28}$$

$$sup_{tv} \le Mv_{tv}^{active},\ \ \forall t, v \tag{29}$$

$$z_{tv} \le Mv_{tv}^{active},\ \ \forall t, v \tag{30}$$

$$use_{tv} \le Mv_{tv}^{active},\ \ \forall t, v \tag{31}$$

$$b_{tv} \le Mv_{tv}^{active},\ \ \forall t, v \tag{32}$$

$$\eta_{tv} \le Mv_{tv}^{active},\ \ \forall t, v \tag{33}$$

$$z_{0v} = 0,\ \ \forall v \tag{34}$$

$$z_{t+1,v} \le z_{tv} + sup_{tv} - use_{tv},\ \ \forall t, v \tag{35}$$

$$z_{t+1,v} \ge z_{tv} + sup_{tv} - use_{tv} - M\sum_{k\in K} v_{ktv}^{new},\ \ \forall t, v \tag{36}$$

$$z_{t+1,v} \le M\left(1 - \sum_{k\in K} v_{ktv}^{new}\right),\ \ \forall t, v \tag{37}$$

$$use_{tv} \le z_{tv},\ \ \forall t, v \tag{38}$$

$$use_{tv} \le def_{tv},\ \ \forall t, v \tag{39}$$

$$b_{tv} \le \beta I_t^{\text{tar}}\sum_{k\in K}\sum_{r\in R} E_{kr}x_{krtv},\ \ \forall t, v \tag{40}$$

$$b_{tv} \le def_{tv},\ \ \forall t, v \tag{41}$$

$$b_{tv} \le M\,y_{tv}^{b},\ \ \forall t, v \tag{42}$$

$$y^b_{tv} + y^b_{t-1,v} \leq 1, \ \ \forall t \setminus \{0\}, v \tag{43}$$

$$q_{0v} = 0, \ \ \forall v \tag{44}$$

$$q_{t+1,v} = \rho \, b_{tv}, \ \ \forall t, v \tag{45}$$

$$y^b_{T^{\max},v} = 0, \ \ \forall v \tag{46}$$

$$\eta_{tv} = def_{tv} - use_{tv} - b_{tv}, \ \ \forall t, v \tag{47}$$

Constraints (25)–(47) model compliance with FuelEU Maritime. Constraint (25) defines the compliance balance, where a route-dependent weight reflects the share of energy subject to EU regulation. A positive balance is treated as a surplus, which can be banked and carried forward for future compliance, while a negative balance is treated as a deficit. Constraints (26)–(27) ensure that deficit and surplus cannot be simultaneously positive. Constraints (28)–(33) enforce that compliance-related variables are zero when the vessel is inactive. The banking mechanism, represented by Constraints (34)–(39), allows surplus to be preserved and used in later periods, but only up to the available bank and without transferring it to a newly purchased vessel. The borrowing mechanism, represented by Constraints (40)–(46), allows a limited share of the current deficit to be deferred to the next period, subject to the regulatory cap, repayment requirement, and the restriction against consecutive borrowing. The remaining deficit after banking and borrowing is penalized through Constraint (47). A sufficiently large Big-M value ($M = 10^6$) is used throughout the formulation.

3 Case Study and Results

3.1 Input Parameters

For the case study, we consider a hypothetical shipping company operating a 4,000-TEU diesel-powered container vessel providing a liner service. The route demand is satisfied through repeated voyages along a fixed port rotation. The sailing distance is assumed to be 1,193 nautical miles based on a representative route reported in [6].

All ports in the base case are assumed to be located within Europe, implying that 100% of the voyage is subject to FuelEU Maritime. To examine the impact of regulatory coverage, an additional scenario is considered in which 75% of the route is subject to EU regulation.

All vessel types are assumed to operate at a constant speed of 15 knots, which yields a maximum of 4.6 voyages per year based on the route length. The annual demand is fixed at 89,960 TEU [6]. Fuel consumption, vessel purchase, and retrofit costs are based on the formulations in [4], while operating costs are approximately 10% of fuel costs. FuelEU penalty costs are incorporated following [1], and additional scenarios are used to examine the impact of higher penalty levels. The WtW GHG intensities of alternative fuels are obtained from [2].

Vessels are assumed to be scrapped once they reach the maximum service age of 25 years. The scrap value is assumed as 10% of the vessel purchase cost, reflecting residual steel value. Retrofit timing is a key decision due to trade-offs over the vessel lifetime: early retrofit is inefficient as the existing propulsion system retains value and regulatory targets are still relatively lenient, while late retrofit restricts cost recovery due to the short remaining service life. Accordingly, retrofitting is assumed to occur within the mid-life window of 10–17 years under a 25-year vessel lifetime [7].

3.2 Results

The impact of banking and borrowing is strongly driven by the penalty level. As shown in Table 3, under a low penalty level of €700, the shipping company retains the diesel-fueled vessel until age 24, pays the compliance penalty, and subsequently acquires a bio-methanol vessel in 2045, with this timing aligned with the tightening of regulatory requirements that render continued diesel operation less favorable; in contrast, when the penalty level exceeds €1200, retrofitting becomes the preferred strategy, and a further increase to €1600 accelerates the timing of retrofit.

Table 3. Fleet transition outcomes under different penalty levels (initial age of fleet = 5)

Penalty level (€ per deficit)		700	1200	1600
Retrofit	Ship type	No retrofit	Bio-methanol	Bio-methanol
	Year	-	2035	2030
Acquire	Ship type	Bio-methanol	Bio-methanol	Bio-methanol
	Year	2045	2046	2046

Prior to 2050, bio-methanol vessels generate substantial compliance surpluses. As shown in Table 3, under a penalty level of €1200, retrofitting to bio-methanol occurs in 2035, resulting in a cumulative banked surplus of 53,728 before the vessel is scrapped in 2045. Under a higher penalty level of €1600, the retrofit is advanced to 2030, yielding a larger cumulative surplus of 83,954.

In the present case study, which considers a single-vessel setting, these surpluses remain unused and are effectively discarded. However, in practice, such surpluses could be utilized through pooling mechanisms, thereby representing a valuable resource. This implies that the potential to share surplus compliance across vessels may serve as an additional incentive for earlier retrofitting. In particular, earlier adoption leads to a larger GHG intensity gap relative to the target, enabling greater accumulation of banked surplus.

After 2050, bio-methanol vessels no longer comply with the net-zero GHG target and begin to generate annual compliance deficits. This is because the target GHG intensity from 2050 is 18.23gCO_2e/MJ, whereas the GHG intensity of bio-methanol remains at 32.2gCO_2e/MJ. This indicates that further decarbonization measures will be necessary beyond 2050. Potential strategies include transitioning to lower-intensity fuels such as e-methanol, with an approximate intensity of 0.97gCO_2e/MJ, or investing in cleaner vessels upon fleet renewal.

The incentive to adopt low-carbon vessels decreases when a liner shipping company operates routes with a lower share of EU port calls. Under FuelEU Maritime, energy consumption is weighted by route type: 100% for intra-EU legs, 50% for EU–non-EU legs, and 0% for non-EU legs in the compliance calculation. As shown in Table 4, when 75% of the route is covered by FuelEU regulation, green transition is significantly delayed. Under a penalty level of €700, diesel vessels are retained and even replaced by new diesel vessels, while no retrofit occurs under €1200. Only at €1600 does retrofitting occur, and at a later timing than in the fully regulated case.

Table 4. Fleet transition outcomes under 75% FuelEU coverage (initial age of fleet = 5)

Penalty level (€ per deficit)		700	1200	1600
Retrofit	Ship type	No retrofit	No retrofit	Bio-methanol
	Year	-	-	2035
Acquire	Ship type	Diesel	Bio-methanol	Bio-methanol
	Year	2046	2045	2046

4 Conclusion

This study analyzes container liner fleet planning under FuelEU Maritime using a MILP model with banking and borrowing mechanisms. The results show that penalty levels drive transition decisions, as low penalties sustain diesel use while higher penalties accelerate retrofitting. Banking supports earlier transition by enabling the accumulation of compliance surpluses, while borrowing is mainly used prior to retrofit in anticipation of these surpluses.

Bio-methanol generates substantial surpluses before 2050 but does not meet post-2050 targets, indicating that additional decarbonization measures, such as cleaner fuels or more advanced vessel technologies, are required. The incentive for green transition is weaker for shipping companies operating routes with a lower share of EU port calls.

Future work may consider multi-vessel settings, and multi-route operations with varying shares of EU port calls. In addition, alternative fuel pathways beyond bio-methanol could be explored. For example, although ammonia is currently less competitive due to its relatively high lifecycle emissions when produced from natural gas, it may become an attractive option with the transition to low-carbon production pathways, without requiring further retrofits. Broader sensitivity analyses, baseline strategy comparisons, and uncertainty in demand, fuel prices, and technology costs are also left for future research.

References

1. European Union: Regulation (EU) 2023/1805 of the European Parliament and of the council of 13 September 2023 on the use of renewable and low-carbon fuels in maritime transport, and amending directive 2009/16/EC. Off. J. Eur. Union. **50**, 48–100 (2023)

2. Loennechen, O., Fagerholt, K., Lagemann, B., Stålhane, M.: Maritime fleet composition under future greenhouse gas emission restrictions and uncertain fuel prices. Marit. Transport Res. **6**, 100103 (2024)
3. Lagemann, B., Lagouvardou, S., Lindstad, E., Fagerholt, K., Psaraftis, H.N., Erikstad, S.O.: Optimal ship lifetime fuel and power system selection under uncertainty. Transp. Res. Part D: Transp. Environ. **119**, 103748 (2023)
4. Wang, Y., Iris, Ç.: Transition to near-zero emission shipping fleet powered by alternative fuels under uncertainty. Transp. Res. Part D: Transp. Environ. **142**, 104689 (2025)
5. Wang, M., Ye, B., Lin, S., Wang, C., Zhang, P.: Sustainable supply chain planning with the flexible provisions of inter-period emission credits borrowing and banking under a multi-period carbon trading scheme. J. Clean. Prod. **445**, 141406 (2024)
6. Wang, S., Meng, Q.: Liner ship fleet deployment with container transshipment operations. Transp. Res. Part E Logist. Transp. Rev. **48**(2), 470–484 (2012)
7. Garbatov, Y., Georgiev, P., Yalamov, D.: Risk-based retrofitting analysis employing the carbon intensity indicator. Ocean Eng. **289**, 116283 (2023)

The Governance of Green Terminals: Hold-Up Risks and Optimal Mechanism Design for Onshore Power Supply in Mediterranean Gateway Ports

J. M. Aliaga(✉)

ESCI-UPF, Pompeu Fabra University, Barcelona, Spain
josemiguel.aliaga@esci.upf.edu

Abstract. The decarbonisation of maritime transport is routinely framed as an engineering and regulatory compliance exercise. This paper argues that such framing masks a deeper problem: the deployment of Onshore Power Supply (OPS) infrastructure in European ports constitutes, at its core, a microeconomic coordination failure of the hold-up variety. Despite the FuelEU Maritime mandate requiring physical connection from 2030, neither the Alternative Fuels Infrastructure Regulation nor FuelEU Maritime specifies the commercial terms of the electricity transfer, leaving tariff determination to bilateral negotiation between Port Authorities bearing large, irreversible capital expenditures and highly concentrated shipping alliances retaining ex-post strategic flexibility to evade connection.

We develop a model of bilateral investment under incomplete contracting to formalise this friction. Our framework departs from prior work in three respects. First, we position the model within the bilateral hold-up tradition of Klein, Crawford and Alchian [18] and Tirole [29], rather than the asset-ownership branch of the property rights literature [11,13], thereby avoiding a conflation that has characterised earlier applications of incomplete contracting to port infrastructure. Second, we treat evasion as a probabilistic strategy: a shipping line that claims technical non-compliance faces detection by port state control with probability θ and incurs the FuelEU non-compliance penalty F, enriching the outside option beyond the standard fuel-and-carbon cost formulation. Third, we derive the optimal two-part tariff analytically from model primitives. The mechanism—a fixed surcharge K^* embedded in statutory vessel access dues and a connection rebate R^* set equal to the cooperative surplus net of a participation margin—is shown to satisfy incentive compatibility and individual rationality for both parties, with closed-form comparative statics with respect to CAPEX, call volume, enforcement probability and market prices.

Parameterising the model with early-2026 Mediterranean ECA and EU ETS data for a representative gateway terminal, we demonstrate that linear pricing fails robustly across a wide matrix of EUA and MGO price scenarios, and that the derived Bonus-Malus mechanism restores the social optimum. We further characterise the boundary conditions

J. de Armas and E. Lalla Ruiz (Eds.): LOGMS 2026, LNCS 16679, pp. 109–119, 2027.
https://doi.org/10.1007/978-3-032-30795-8_10

under which the mechanism breaks down for transshipment hubs and offer policy guidance for port classification-specific regulation.

Keywords: Onshore Power Supply · hold-up problem · incomplete contracts · two-part tariff · FuelEU Maritime · EU ETS · Mediterranean ECA · port governance · Bonus-Malus

1 Introduction

The maritime shipping industry accounts for approximately 3 percent of global anthropogenic greenhouse gas emissions [3,15]. The European Union's response culminates, on the infrastructure side, in the mandatory deployment of Onshore Power Supply (OPS) at core Trans-European Transport Network (TEN-T) ports under the Alternative Fuels Infrastructure Regulation (AFIR, Regulation (EU) 2023/1804) [8] and, on the demand side, in the obligation for container and passenger vessels to connect to shore-side electricity while at berth under FuelEU Maritime (Regulation (EU) 2023/1805) [9]. Both obligations take legal effect from 1 January 2030.

The policy logic is seductive in its simplicity: mandate the supply of infrastructure, mandate its use, and the investment problem is solved. This paper argues that such reasoning conflates a regulatory compliance problem with an underlying microeconomic coordination failure that regulation alone cannot resolve. Specifically, we demonstrate that the 2030 mandate creates what we call an *illusion of compliance*—a regulatory architecture that mandates physical connection while leaving the economic governance of the electricity transfer entirely to bilateral negotiation between Port Authorities and highly concentrated global shipping alliances.

The hold-up problem in infrastructure investment is well established. Klein, Crawford and Alchian [18] showed that relation-specific sunk investments create ex-post appropriable quasi-rents; Williamson [30] generalised this within the transaction cost framework. Our setting maps onto the bilateral hold-up formulation of Tirole [29] and the infrastructure analysis of Basso, Jara-Díaz and Tovar [1]. We depart from the existing OPS literature [17,28,31] in three respects: (i) we treat the mandate as incomplete rather than decisive; (ii) we model evasion as probabilistic, incorporating the expected FuelEU non-compliance penalty into the outside option; and (iii) we derive the optimal two-part tariff analytically from model primitives, yielding closed-form comparative statics. We are careful to distinguish our framework from the Grossman-Hart-Moore property rights approach [11,13]: the relevant instrument here is tariff design, not asset ownership. Our paper is methodologically closer to the mechanism design tradition of Laffont and Tirole [19] applied to infrastructure pricing. While the analytical apparatus is drawn from the economics of incomplete contracting, the implications are directly operational—governing terminal concession design, vessel access due parameterisation, and the interaction between port state control enforcement and infrastructure financing.

The remainder of the paper is structured as follows. Section 2 describes the regulatory architecture. Section 3 develops the theoretical model. Section 4 presents the empirical calibration, sensitivity analysis and mechanism derivation. Section 5 draws out policy implications. Section 6 concludes.

2 Regulatory Architecture: Mediterranean 2026

Three overlapping instruments define the parties' outside options. *Med SOx ECA* (in force May 2025): vessels must use fuel with sulphur content $\leq 0.10\%$ m/m, forcing a switch to costly MGO for at-berth hoteling [16,20,26]. *EU ETS* (100% compliance from 2026): EUAs must be surrendered for all at-berth emissions in EU ports regardless of voyage origin, adding a dynamic carbon penalty [14]. *FuelEU Maritime / AFIR* (2030): ports must provide OPS capacity; vessels must connect and achieve zero at-berth emissions, subject to per-call non-compliance penalties [8,9]. The critical lacuna is that neither regulation specifies the commercial terms of the electricity transfer, leaving tariff determination to bilateral negotiation [12,17]. This regulatory vacuum is the origin of the hold-up problem we study.

3 A Bilateral Hold-Up Model of OPS Investment

We formalise the interaction between a Port Authority (P) and a representative Shipping Line (S) as a bilateral hold-up problem under incomplete contracting. We emphasise that our framework belongs to the transaction-cost branch of the incomplete contracting literature—the bilateral hold-up tradition initiated by Klein, Crawford and Alchian [18] and formalised by Tirole [29]—rather than to the property rights branch associated with Grossman and Hart [11] and Hart and Moore [13].

3.1 Environment, Timing and Information

Consider a two-period model, $t \in \{0, 1\}$, with the following sequence of events.

At $t = 0$ (the Investment Phase), the Port Authority undertakes a non-contractible, relation-specific investment $i_P \geq 0$ in high-voltage subterranean grid infrastructure and frequency converters. The total capital expenditure is $C(i_P)$, where $C'(i_P) > 0$ and $C''(i_P) > 0$, reflecting increasing marginal cost of infrastructure capacity. The investment is irreversible and has negligible salvage value outside the terminal.

At $t = 1$ (the Operational Phase), the Shipping Line arrives at the port for a scheduled call. The vessel's total electrical energy demand during hoteling is $E = P_{\text{ship}} \times T_{\text{call}}$, where P_{ship} is the required auxiliary power and T_{call} is the port-call duration. The Port Authority sets commercial terms; the Shipping Line decides whether to connect or to exercise its outside option.

Both parties are risk-neutral and information is symmetric with respect to the observable components of the outside option. Three simplifying assumptions are adopted: risk neutrality (abstracting from insurance motives), a representative agent on each side (suppressing fleet heterogeneity—relaxed in future work via screening models), and a static two-period structure (abstracting from repeated interaction and renegotiation).

3.2 The Cooperative Surplus

If the Shipping Line connects to shore power, the first-best cost of energy provision is $E \times MC$, where MC denotes the marginal cost of grid electricity inclusive of wholesale prices and high-voltage access tariffs. The cooperative surplus from connection is positive if and only if:

$$\Delta(\theta) \; = \; O_S(\theta) - E \times MC \; > \; 0, \tag{1}$$

where $O_S(\theta)$ is the expected cost of the shipping line's outside option, derived in Sect. 3.3. The core economic problem is distributional: how to allocate $\Delta(\theta)$ such that the Port Authority recovers $C(i_P^*)$ without inducing the Shipping Line to evade.

3.3 The Outside Option with Probabilistic Enforcement

A Shipping Line that attempts to evade connection is detected by port state control with probability $\theta \in [0,1]$ and faces a penalty F (EUR per non-compliant call), and evades successfully with probability $(1-\theta)$, incurring only the fuel and carbon costs of hoteling on MGO. The expected cost of the evasion strategy is:

$$O_S(\theta) \; = \; E\big(\rho_{\text{MGO}}\, C_{\text{MGO}} + \rho_{\text{CO}_2}\, P_{\text{ETS}}\big) + \theta\, F, \tag{2}$$

where ρ_{MGO} is the specific fuel oil consumption factor (tons/MWh), C_{MGO} is the MGO spot price, ρ_{CO_2} is the CO_2 emission conversion factor (tCO_2/tMGO), P_{ETS} is the prevailing EUA price, and F is the regulatory penalty. Equation (2) nests the binary evasion model as the limiting case $\theta = 0$. The term θF directly augments the cooperative surplus in equation (1): stronger enforcement is a complement to mechanism design in OPS governance.

3.4 The Failure of Linear Pricing

Suppose the Port Authority recovers its investment through a linear utility tariff P_{OPS} per MWh. The Shipping Line's Incentive Compatibility Constraint (ICC) for voluntary connection is:

$$E \times P_{\text{OPS}} \; \leq \; O_S(\theta). \tag{3}$$

Substituting equation (2), the maximum linear price compatible with voluntary compliance is:

$$P_{\text{OPS}}^{\max} \leq \rho_{\text{MGO}}\, C_{\text{MGO}} + \rho_{\text{CO}_2}\, P_{\text{ETS}} + \frac{\theta F}{E}. \tag{4}$$

The hold-up failure arises when the markup required to recover $C(i_P)$ pushes P_{OPS} above this threshold. Linear pricing conflates two economically distinct objectives: (i) recovering a fixed sunk infrastructure cost, and (ii) efficiently allocating variable electricity consumption at marginal cost. These objectives are inherently in tension under linear pricing, and the tension is resolved at the expense of the ICC.

3.5 The Optimal Mechanism: Derivation of the Two-Part Tariff

We seek a mechanism $\{K, R, P_e\}$ satisfying three conditions simultaneously: (i) the Shipping Line's ICC (connection preferred to evasion); (ii) the Port Authority's participation constraint (CAPEX recovery); and (iii) the Shipping Line's individual rationality. The mechanism takes the form of a universal surcharge K on all arriving vessels via the statutory T1 due, a rebate R exclusively for connecting vessels, and a marginal electricity price P_e.

The ICC requires $(T_1 + K - R) + E\,P_e \leq (T_1 + K) + O_S(\theta)$, which is satisfied for any $R \geq 0$ when $P_e = MC < O_S(\theta)/E$. CAPEX recovery requires:

$$N\,K \geq C(i_P^*) \quad \Longrightarrow \quad K^* = \frac{C(i_P^*)}{N}. \tag{5}$$

Setting $P_e^* = MC$ and leaving participation margin $\varepsilon > 0$ with the Shipping Line:

$$R^* = \Delta(\theta) - \varepsilon. \tag{6}$$

The mechanism $\{K^*, R^*, MC\}$ is incentive-compatible and individually rational for both parties. We do not claim uniqueness; the two-part structure is strongly motivated by the problem logic (pricing above MC distorts the connection decision; pricing below MC is not self-sustaining), but a formal proof lies beyond the scope of this paper. Key properties: $\Delta(\theta)$ is strictly increasing in θ (enforcement and mechanism design are complements); the mechanism is self-financing iff $\Delta(\theta) \geq K^*$ (public co-financing required otherwise); K^* decreases in N and R^* increases in θ.

4 Empirical Calibration, Sensitivity Analysis and Mechanism Parameterisation

We parameterise the model using early-2026 data for the Mediterranean. The representative vessel is an Ultra Large Container Vessel (ULCV) of 15 000 TEU.[1] Following IMO (2020) [15] emissions inventories and the technical parameters in Zis et al. [31], auxiliary power demand is set at $P_{\text{ship}} = 6$ MW and average port-call duration at $T_{\text{call}} = 24$ hours, yielding $E = 144$ MWh per call.

[1] The calibration uses representative parameters drawn from the literature rather than port-specific data. Barcelona (Spain) represents the natural candidate for a full empirical application, given its status as the leading Mediterranean gateway terminal and the availability of Puertos del Estado tariff data; we leave this extension to future work.

4.1 Calibrating the Outside Option

Applying equation (2): MGO at EUR 635/ton ([27]) with $\rho_{\mathrm{MGO}} = 0.21$ t/MWh gives a fuel cost of EUR 19 202; combustion of 30.24 t MGO yields 96.95 tCO_2, attracting an EU ETS charge of EUR 7 077 at EUR 73/tCO_2 ([7]); the expected FuelEU penalty is $\theta F = 0.30 \times$ EUR 12 000 = EUR 3 600, where $\theta = 0.30$ is a conservative baseline informed by port state control deficiency rates in the Paris MOU (2024) [25] and treated as a sensitivity parameter (see Table 2). Aggregating via equation (2):

$$O_S(0.30) = 19\,202 + 7\,077 + 3\,600 = \text{EUR } 29\,879 \text{ per call.} \tag{7}$$

With MC = EUR 75/MWh (OMIE/CNMC, 2026 [5,24]), the first-best connection cost is EUR 10 800 per call. From equation (1):

$$\Delta(0.30) = 29\,879 - 10\,800 = \text{EUR } 19\,079 \text{ per call.} \tag{8}$$

4.2 Calibration Parameters

Table 1 summarises all calibration parameters.

Table 1. Calibration parameters, early-2026 Mediterranean baseline.

Parameter	Symbol	Value	Source
ULCV energy demand	E	144 MWh	[15]
MGO spot price	C_{MGO}	EUR 635/ton	[27]
SFOC factor	ρ_{MGO}	0.21 t/MWh	[15]
CO_2 emission factor	ρ_{CO_2}	3.206 tCO_2/tMGO	[15]
EUA carbon price	P_{ETS}	EUR 73/tCO_2	[7]
Grid marginal cost	MC	EUR 75/MWh	[5,24]
FuelEU non-compliance penalty	F	EUR 12 000/call	[9]
Enforcement probability	θ	0.30	[25]
Outside option (baseline)	$O_S(0.30)$	EUR 29 879	Eq. (7)
Cooperative surplus	$\Delta(0.30)$	EUR 19 079	Eq. (8)

4.3 Sensitivity Analysis: Robustness of the Cooperative Surplus

EUA prices ranged between EUR 40 and EUR 105 over 2022–2026 [7,14]; MGO prices are similarly volatile [20]. Table 2 reports Δ across a matrix of price scenarios and enforcement intensities, using EUR 200/MWh as an illustrative linear tariff benchmark consistent with port utility markups documented in [12]; note that $P_{\mathrm{OPS}}^{\max} = O_S(\theta)/E \approx$ EUR 207/MWh, so any markup sufficient to recover CAPEX exceeds this ceiling.

Table 2. Cooperative surplus Δ under alternative EUA/MGO price scenarios and enforcement intensities. Linear pricing at EUR 200/MWh implies a connection cost of EUR 28 800, which exceeds O_S under all scenarios.

EUA (EUR/t)	MGO (EUR/t)	Δ	Δ	Δ	Linear viable?
		θ=0	θ=0.30	θ=0.50	
40	550	EUR 8 350	EUR 11 950	EUR 14 350	No
40	635	EUR 10 141	EUR 13 741	EUR 16 141	No
73	635	EUR 15 479	EUR 19 079	EUR 21 479	No
100	700	EUR 20 980	EUR 24 580	EUR 26 980	No
73	800	EUR 20 669	EUR 24 269	EUR 26 669	No

Three findings emerge. First, linear pricing at P_{OPS} = EUR 200/MWh violates the ICC under every scenario: the mechanism failure is structural, not calibration-specific. Second, the cooperative surplus is robustly positive throughout, confirming that the two-part tariff is self-financing even under adverse market conditions. Third, enforcement intensity matters quantitatively: moving from $\theta = 0$ to $\theta = 0.50$ adds EUR 3 600–6 000 to Δ per call.

Table 3 reports K^* across CAPEX (EUR 5M–35M, annualised at 5% over 20 years) and call volume N (100–400); † denotes configurations where $K^* > \Delta(0.30)$ = EUR 19 079 and public co-financing is required.

Table 3. Required per-call surcharge K^* (EUR) across CAPEX and call-volume scenarios. † denotes configurations where $K^* > \Delta(0.30)$ and public co-financing is required. Annualisation: 20 years, 5% cost of capital.

CAPEX	Annual qualifying calls (N)			
	$N = 100$	$N = 200$	$N = 300$	$N = 400$
EUR 5M	EUR 4 006	EUR 2 003	EUR 1 335	EUR 1 002
EUR 10M	EUR 8 012	EUR 4 006	EUR 2 671	EUR 2 003
EUR 15M	EUR 12 018	EUR 6 009	EUR 4 006	EUR 3 005
EUR 20M	EUR 16 024†	EUR 8 012	EUR 5 341	EUR 4 006
EUR 35M	EUR 28 042†	EUR 14 021†	EUR 9 347	EUR 7 011

The mechanism is self-financing for $N \geq 200$ at CAPEX $\leq$ EUR 20M, and for $N \geq 300$ at CAPEX $\leq$ EUR 35M, covering the realistic range for Mediterranean gateway terminals where ULCV call volumes typically exceed 300 per year.

4.4 Mechanism Parameterisation

For $C(i_P^*)$ = EUR 15M (annualised at 5% over 20 years, $\approx$ EUR 1,200,000/year) and $N = 200$ calls, Eq. (5) gives K^* = EUR 6,000/call and Eq. (6) gives $R^* =$

EUR 18,979. The payoff comparison is:

$$\text{Cost (evasion)} = T_1 + 6\,000 + 29\,879 = T_1 + \text{EUR } 35\,879, \tag{9}$$

$$\text{Cost (connection)} = T_1 + 6\,000 - 18\,979 + 10\,800 = T_1 - \text{EUR } 2\,179. \tag{10}$$

Connection dominates evasion by EUR 38 058; the port recovers EUR 1,200,000 annually; electricity is priced at cost. Note that $R^* > K^*$ is not paradoxical: K^* is levied on *all* N vessels and recovers CAPEX independently; R^* is paid only to connecting vessels from the cooperative surplus, not the surcharge revenue (no cross-subsidy).

5 Policy Implications

5.1 Mandating Non-linear Tariffs and Redesigning Concessions

The primary implication is normative: port utility charges must evolve from linear markups to two-part tariff structures. The Spanish *Puertos del Estado* T1 system provides a natural vehicle; K^* and R^* can be embedded as conditional line items within existing T1 fee schedules. ESPO should develop harmonised guidelines across TEN-T ports ahead of the 2030 mandate. Concurrently, terminal operators—frequently vertically integrated with shipping alliances [10,22]—are better positioned than Port Authorities to internalise the OPS cooperative surplus and should co-finance CAPEX in exchange for concession tenure extensions [4,21].

5.2 Boundary Conditions and Enforcement

The mechanism requires captive hinterland demand [23]: at gateway terminals (Barcelona, Genoa, Piraeus) carriers cannot reroute without prohibitive costs, so the hold-up is one-sided. At pure transshipment hubs (Algeciras, Malta, Gioia Tauro) the outside option includes rerouting to Tanger-Med, escaping both the OPS surcharge and the EU ETS liability; this requires network-level instruments (a maritime CBAM or differentiated public subsidies) beyond the scope of port tariff design. Finally, enforcement and mechanism design are complements: each increment of $\theta = +0.20$ adds EUR 2 400/call to the cooperative surplus; Port State Control authorities should be resourced to verify OPS connection logs under the Paris MOU framework [25].

6 Concluding Remarks

The 2030 FuelEU Maritime and AFIR mandates dictate physical OPS connection but leave the commercial terms of the electricity transfer to bilateral negotiation, creating a hold-up that regulation alone cannot resolve. This paper makes three contributions: (i) it characterises the OPS investment problem as a bilateral hold-up in the Tirolean tradition; (ii) it extends prior formulations by treating evasion as probabilistic, identifying enforcement intensity as a policy complement to tariff design; and (iii) it derives the optimal two-part tariff analytically from model primitives (5)–(6), yielding closed-form comparative statics. Future work should relax symmetric information via screening models for a heterogeneous fleet [19], incorporate peak-load pricing and battery storage, and analyse spatial competition between ports on T1 fees and OPS tariffs [2,6].

Acknowledgments. The author thanks participants at the ESCI-UPF Maritime Economics seminar for helpful comments. No external funding was received for this research. The practical implication is direct: OPS mandates must be complemented by non-linear tariff structures and credible enforcement to avoid the hold-up trap—regulation alone is necessary but not sufficient.

Disclosure of Interests. The author has no competing interests to declare that are relevant to the content of this article.

References

1. Basso, L.J., Jara-Díaz, S.R., Tovar, B.: Investment and pricing in relation-specific transport infrastructure. Econ. Transp. **18**, 1–14 (2019). https://doi.org/10.1016/j.ecotra.2019.02.001
2. Basso, L.J., Zhang, A.: Pricing versus slot policies when airport profits matter. Transp. Res. Part B: Methodol. **44**(3), 381–391 (2010). https://doi.org/10.1016/j.trb.2009.10.002
3. Bouman, E.A., Lindstad, E., Rialland, A.I., Strømman, A.H.: State-of-the-art technologies, measures, and potential for reducing GHG emissions from shipping. Transp. Res. Part D: Transp. Environ. **52**, 408–421 (2017). https://doi.org/10.1016/j.trd.2017.03.022
4. Brooks, M.R., Cullinane, K. (eds.): Devolution, Port Governance and Port Performance, Research in Transportation Economics, vol. 17. Elsevier, London (2007)
5. CNMC: Metodología de cálculo de los peajes de transporte y distribución de electricidad. Technical report, Comisión Nacional de Mercados y la Competencia, Madrid (2025)
6. De Langen, P.W., Pallis, A.A.: Entry barriers in seaports. Marit. Policy Manag. **34**(5), 427–440 (2007). https://doi.org/10.1080/03088830701585069
7. EEX: European emission allowances (EUA) market data. Technical report, European Energy Exchange, Leipzig (2026)
8. European Union: Regulation (EU) 2023/1804 of the European parliament and of the council on the deployment of alternative fuels infrastructure (AFIR). Official Journal of the European Union **L 234**, 1–65 (2023)
9. European Union: Regulation (EU) 2023/1805 of the European parliament and of the council on the use of renewable and low-carbon fuels in maritime transport (FuelEU maritime). Official Journal of the European Union **L 234**, 48–100 (2023)
10. Franc, P., Van der Horst, M.: Understanding hinterland service integration by shipping lines and terminal operators. J. Transp. Geogr. **18**(4), 557–566 (2010). https://doi.org/10.1016/j.jtrangeo.2010.03.004

11. Grossman, S.J., Hart, O.D.: The costs and benefits of ownership: a theory of vertical and lateral integration. J. Polit. Econ. **94**(4), 691–719 (1986). https://doi.org/10.1086/261404
12. Haralambides, H.E.: Gigantism in container shipping, ports and global logistics: a time-lapse into the future. Maritime Econ. Logist. **21**(1), 1–60 (2019). https://doi.org/10.1057/s41278-018-00116-0
13. Hart, O., Moore, J.: Property rights and the nature of the firm. J. Polit. Econ. **98**(6), 1119–1158 (1990). https://doi.org/10.1086/261729
14. Hermeling, C., Klement, J.H., Steinbacher, K.: First experiences with the EU shipping monitoring, reporting and verification system. Transp. Res. Part D: Transp. Environ. **39**, 179–190 (2015). https://doi.org/10.1016/j.trd.2015.06.001
15. IMO: Fourth IMO GHG study 2020. Technical report, International Maritime Organization, London (2020)
16. IMO: Designation of the mediterranean sea as an emission control area for sulphur oxides (Med SOx ECA), London (2022). Mepc 78/17, International Maritime Organization
17. Innes, A., Monios, J.: Stranded assets and the interplay between the port and shipping sectors in the energy transition. Mar. Policy **94**, 166–177 (2018). https://doi.org/10.1016/j.marpol.2018.05.018
18. Klein, B., Crawford, R.A., Alchian, A.A.: Vertical integration, appropriable rents, and the competitive contracting process. J. Law Econ. **21**(2), 297–326 (1978). https://doi.org/10.1086/466922
19. Laffont, J.J., Tirole, J.: A Theory of Incentives in Procurement and Regulation. MIT Press, Cambridge (1993)
20. Lindstad, H.E., Asbjørnslett, B.E., Strømman, A.H.: Reductions in greenhouse gas emissions and cost by shipping at lower speeds. Energy Policy **39**(6), 3456–3464 (2015). https://doi.org/10.1016/j.enpol.2011.03.044
21. Notteboom, T., De Langen, P., Jacobs, W.: Institutional plasticity and path dependence in seaports. Geoforum **43**(2), 284–295 (2013). https://doi.org/10.1016/j.geoforum.2011.09.002
22. Notteboom, T., Rodrigue, J.P.: Port regionalization: towards a new phase in port development. Marit. Policy Manag. **32**(3), 297–313 (2005). https://doi.org/10.1080/03088830500139885
23. Notteboom, T.E.: Spatial dynamics in the container terminal market of the Low Countries. Tijdschr. Econ. Soc. Geogr. **101**(5), 530–547 (2010). https://doi.org/10.1111/j.1467-9663.2009.00556.x
24. OMIE: Spanish electricity market — wholesale prices 2026. Tech. rep., Operador del Mercado Ibérico de Energía, Madrid (2026)
25. Paris, MOU: Annual report on port state control 2023. Technical report, Paris Memorandum of Understanding on Port State Control (2024)
26. Psaraftis, H.N., Kontovas, C.A.: Speed models for energy-efficient maritime transportation: a taxonomy and survey. Transp. Res. Part C: Emerg. Technol. **26**, 331–351 (2013). https://doi.org/10.1016/j.trc.2012.09.012
27. Ship & Bunker: Global bunker fuel prices — ARA hub spot price MGO 0.1%. Market data report, March 2026 (2026)
28. Sys, C., Vanelslander, T., Adriaenssen, A., Van Rillaer, I.: International emission regulation in sea transport: economic feasibility and impact. Transp. Res. Part D: Transp. Environ. **45**, 139–150 (2016). https://doi.org/10.1016/j.trd.2015.06.009
29. Tirole, J.: Procurement and renegotiation. J. Polit. Econ. **94**(2), 235–259 (1986). https://doi.org/10.1086/261368

30. Williamson, O.E.: The Economic Institutions of Capitalism: Firms, Markets, Relational Contracting. Free Press, New York (1985)
31. Zis, T., North, R.J., Angeloudis, P., Ochieng, W.Y., Bell, M.G.H.: Evaluation of cold ironing and speed reduction policies to reduce ship emissions near and at ports. Maritime Econ. Logist. **21**(4), 491–507 (2019). https://doi.org/10.1057/s41278-017-0077-0

Digitalisation of Onshore Power Supply: A Data-Driven Management Tool for the Port of Barcelona

Guillem Bonilla Martin[1], Sara Hatami[1(✉)], Jesus Viscarri[1], and Ana Arevalo[2]

[1] Department of Management, Universitat Politècnica de Catalunya, BarcelonaTech, Barcelona, Spain
guillem.bonilla.martin@estudiantat.upc.edu, {sara.hatami, jesus.viscarri}@upc.edu

[2] ShorePower Department, Autoritat Portuaria de Barcelona (APB), Barcelona, Spain
ana.arevalo@portdebarcelona.cat

Abstract. The maritime industry faces stringent decarbonisation mandates to eliminate greenhouse gas and pollutant emissions generated during vessel hotelling. Onshore Power Supply (OPS) is the most technologically mature solution, allowing docked ships to connect to the terrestrial grid. However, despite its environmental efficacy, the widespread adoption of OPS is hindered by significant economic barriers. In particular, port authorities lack dedicated digital tools to manage the volatile wholesale electricity market (OMIE, the operator of the Iberian wholesale electricity market) and the complexity of high-voltage regulatory tariffs, such as the Spanish 6.1TD access tariff.

This paper addresses this operational gap by developing an Information Management System (IMS) for the OPS pilot project at the Barcelona Europe South Terminal (BEST) in the Port of Barcelona. The system is built on a Python-based microservices architecture and automates the processing of smart meter data, integrates real-time OMIE spot prices, and applies multi-period tariff structures to generate accurate and predictive billing.

Furthermore, the system includes an automated auditing module based on Portable Document Format (PDF) data extraction to validate utility invoices and reduce revenue leakage. Experimental results from an operational simulation demonstrate that accurate cost calculation enables reliable OPS billing and that OPS can be economically competitive with Marine Gas Oil (MGO) under real operating conditions. These findings indicate that the large-scale deployment of OPS depends not only on physical electrification, but also on advanced digital systems capable of managing economic complexity and supporting decision-making.

Keywords: Onshore Power Supply (OPS) · Smart Ports · Energy Management Systems · Maritime Decarbonization · Live Electricity Pricing

J. de Armas and E. Lalla Ruiz (Eds.): LOGMS 2026, LNCS 16679, pp. 120–131, 2027.
https://doi.org/10.1007/978-3-032-30795-8_11

1 Introduction

Maritime transport constitutes the backbone of global trade, yet it remains a significant source of greenhouse gas (GHG) emissions and local air pollutants, particularly during the "hotelling" phase at port [1]. During this period, vessels rely on auxiliary diesel engines to maintain onboard operations, emitting high levels of NOx, SOx, and particulate matter directly into coastal urban environments [9]. Onshore Power Supply (OPS), also known as cold ironing, is widely recognized as the most technologically mature solution to mitigate these emissions, enabling docked vessels to replace onboard fossil fuel generation with electricity supplied from the terrestrial grid.

The deployment of OPS is no longer driven solely by environmental concerns, but increasingly by regulatory pressure. European policies such as the Alternative Fuels Infrastructure Regulation (AFIR) and the FuelEU Maritime initiative are transforming OPS into a strategic—and progressively mandatory—component of port decarbonisation [3,4]. From a technical perspective, OPS systems rely on complex high-voltage infrastructure defined by the IEC/ISO/IEEE 80005-1 standard, which governs the transformation of grid electricity (typically 25 kV, 50 Hz) into ship-compatible power (6.6 kV, 60 Hz) through static frequency converters [5].

Despite this technological maturity and regulatory momentum, the large-scale deployment of OPS remains significantly constrained by economic barriers [2,3]. The implementation of OPS infrastructure requires substantial capital expenditure (CAPEX), while operational expenditure (OPEX) is highly sensitive to fluctuations in wholesale electricity markets [3]. This combination of high upfront investment and volatile operational costs introduces significant financial uncertainty for port authorities, particularly as they transition from traditional infrastructure managers to active energy service providers.

To manage the increasing electrical loads introduced by OPS and broader electrification, maritime ports are evolving into "Smart Ports" through digitalisation and the deployment of Energy Management Systems (EMS) [6]. Most studies on smart ports focus on the technical management of energy, including load forecasting, peak shaving, and the integration of renewable sources [6]. However, these approaches primarily address engineering challenges and do not sufficiently consider the financial and economic management required for the effective operation of OPS systems.

A review of the existing literature indicates a limited availability of specialized digital frameworks for the economic management, billing, and auditing of OPS services. While OPS is essential for port decarbonisation, its economic sustainability depends on the accurate management of variable energy costs, a challenge that is not adequately addressed by conventional port management systems.

This gap becomes critical in real operational environments, where port authorities must simultaneously handle volatile wholesale electricity markets, complex regulatory tariff structures (such as the Spanish 6.1TD), and high-frequency telemetry data from smart meters. In the absence of automated and integrated digital tools, these processes are typically managed through manual or semi-automated workflows, increasing the risk of errors, inefficiencies, and financial losses.

Addressing this gap is essential to ensure that OPS evolves from a subsidized environmental solution into a financially sustainable and competitive service. Accordingly, this paper proposes and implements a customized Information Management System (IMS) designed to integrate real-time market data, automate tariff modelling, and enable accurate billing and auditing processes within port environments. The system is validated through its application to the OPS pilot at the BEST terminal in the Port of Barcelona, demonstrating its capability to support data-driven operational and economic decision-making.

The main contributions of this work are as follows. First, the paper presents the development of an Information Management System (IMS) tailored to the economic and operational management of OPS in port environments. Second, it integrates heterogeneous data sources—including smart meter telemetry, real-time electricity market prices, and regulatory tariff structures—to enable accurate cost modelling and billing. Finally, the system is applied and validated in a real OPS pilot at the BEST terminal in the Port of Barcelona, demonstrating its applicability and effectiveness in supporting decision-making under real market conditions.

The remainder of this paper is structured as follows. Section 2 defines the operational problem and outlines the key challenges associated with OPS deployment. Section 3 presents the proposed methodology and system architecture. Section 4 describes the experimental results and evaluates the performance of the system in a real-world scenario. Finally, Sect. 5 concludes the paper and discusses the main findings and future work.

2 Problem Definition

While the broader academic literature highlights a theoretical gap in the financial management of smart ports, this paper addresses a concrete, operational challenge currently faced by port authorities during the implementation of OPS pilot projects. Specifically, this study focuses on the electrification of the BEST container terminal at the Port of Barcelona.

The physical deployment of the high-voltage shore connection infrastructure, transforming terrestrial 25 kV grid power to the 6.6 kV maritime standard and converting the European 50 Hz frequency to 60 Hz via static converters, has been successfully engineered in compliance with the IEC/ISO/IEEE 80005-1 standard. However, the transition from physical infrastructure deployment to sustainable day-to-day operation remains critically constrained by the absence of dedicated digital frameworks for economic and administrative management.

The electrical supply architecture of the OPS system considered in this study is presented in Fig. 1. This figure provides a high-level overview of the energy flow from the terrestrial grid to the vessel, contextualizing the operational environment in which the proposed system is deployed.

This operational gap is not merely technological but systemic, arising from the need to coordinate multiple heterogeneous data sources, regulatory constraints, and volatile market signals within a unified decision-making framework.

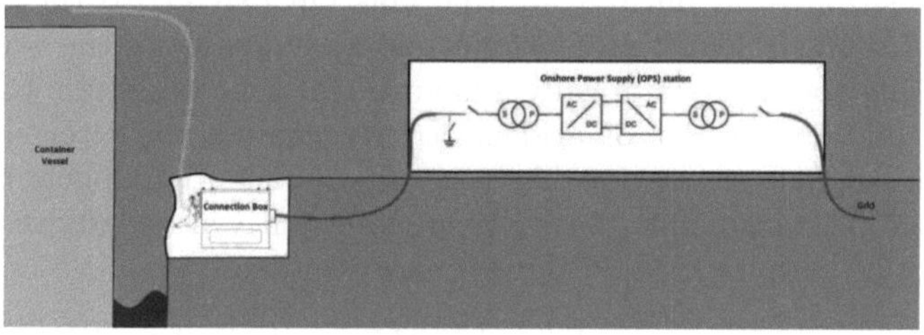

Fig. 1. Electrical supply diagram for ships

Currently, port authorities acting as localized utility providers for docked vessels face four critical operational problems:

1. **Exposure to Wholesale Market Volatility:** The cost-competitiveness of OPS heavily relies on the spot prices of the wholesale Spanish electricity market (OMIE). Without automated Application Programming Interface (API) integration to synchronize real-time quarter-hourly prices with vessel connection telemetry, predicting and calculating the true cost of energy is practically impossible, leading to high financial risk and blind billings for the port.
   This challenge is fundamentally driven by the need to integrate volatile time-series market data with high-frequency consumption measurements, requiring continuous temporal synchronization and dynamic cost recalculation.
2. **Complex High-Voltage Tariff Structures:** Industrial energy consumption is governed by rigid regulatory frameworks, such as the Spanish 6.1TD access tariff, which divides energy and capacity costs into six highly dynamic temporal periods (P1 to P6). Under this tariff, each period is defined as a set of hourly time slots that vary according to the day of the week and the month of the year. Traditional administrative methods cannot properly and efficiently process massive telemetry datasets to accurately assign costs to these changing periods.
   This difficulty arises from the discrete and non-linear nature of tariff structures, which require algorithmic mapping between timestamped consumption data and dynamically shifting regulatory periods, a task that cannot be reliably performed using manual or spreadsheet-based approaches.
3. **Inefficient Auditing and Revenue Leakage:** The auditing of complex utility invoices from energy retailers is currently a manual, error-prone process. The absence of automated tools capable of reading digital documents (extracting the Universal Supply Point Code (CUPS) and billed amounts via PDF scraping) to compare their data against actual smart-meter telemetry, results in delayed reconciliations and potential financial discrepancies.

This lack of automation reduces financial traceability and increases the risk of undetected billing errors, ultimately leading to systematic revenue leakage for port authorities.

4. **Lack of Transparent Competitiveness Metrics:** To incentivize shipowners to transition from burning Marine Gas Oil (MGO) to the use of shore power, ports must clearly prove the economic viability of the service. There is no existing tool to dynamically generate real-time economic balances that compare the volatile cost of grid electricity against the alternative cost of onboard fossil fuel generation. As a result, decision-making is impaired by the absence of transparent, data-driven competitiveness indicators, limiting OPS adoption despite its environmental advantages.

Therefore, the specific problem defined in this study is the critical necessity to engineer a customized IMS that bridges the gap between physical OPS infrastructure and its economic operability. More formally, the problem can be defined as the design of a data-driven system capable of synchronizing heterogeneous high-frequency data streams—including smart meter telemetry, quarter-hourly wholesale electricity prices, and multi-period regulatory tariff structures—in order to generate accurate, auditable, and real-time economic outputs under uncertainty.

This problem is inherently temporal and computational, as it requires the alignment and processing of multiple asynchronous time-series datasets within a unified cost calculation framework.

The objective is to develop a software solution capable of automating mass data ingestion, dynamic tariff modeling, invoice auditing, and the generation of visual operational economic balances, thereby ensuring the financial sustainability and competitiveness of port decarbonisation efforts.

Furthermore, this operational context effectively transforms port authorities into hybrid energy service providers exposed to real-time market risks and regulatory constraints. Existing port management systems and traditional EMS are not designed to handle this level of economic complexity, reinforcing the need for specialized digital solutions.

3 Methodology and System Architecture

To address the operational and financial gaps identified in the management of OPS, this study proposes the development of a specialized IMS. The methodology follows a system-oriented and data-driven design approach, structured into four sequential phases: (i) requirements definition based on operational constraints identified in the problem analysis, (ii) modular system design, (iii) implementation of data processing pipelines and integration mechanisms, and (iv) validation through real-world operational data.

This approach ensures that the proposed system is not only technically functional, but also aligned with real operational requirements, particularly in handling heterogeneous data sources, regulatory tariff structures, and real-time market volatility.

3.1 System Architecture

The IMS is built upon a modular, microservices-based architecture centralized through a web interface. Python3 was selected as the primary programming language due to its robust data science capabilities and its extensive ecosystem of libraries tailored for energy sector analytics.

In practice, the system adopts a modular monolithic architecture with clearly decoupled functional components, prioritizing simplicity, maintainability, and rapid deployment over fully distributed microservices complexity.

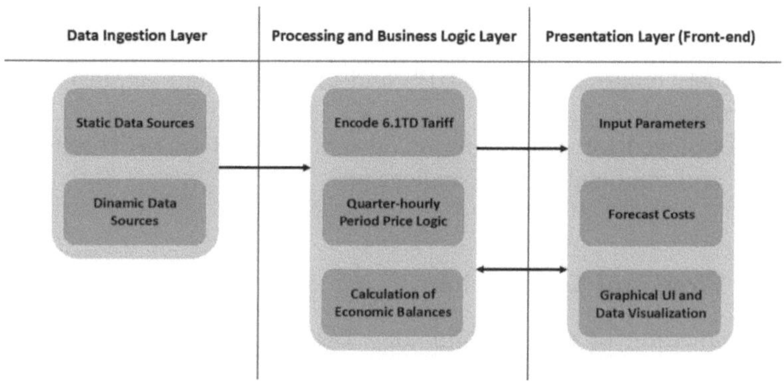

Fig. 2. System Architecture of the IMS

The system is logically divided into three layers:

1. **Data Ingestion Layer:** Responsible for ingesting static telemetry files (CSV/Excel) from port smart meters and establishing real-time connections with external APIs for dynamic data retrieval.
2. **Processing and Business Logic Layer:** A suite of algorithms and scripts that encode the complex 6.1TD access tariff rules, quarter-hourly period price logic, and the calculations of economic balances.
3. **Presentation Layer (Front-end):** An interactive graphical User Interface (UI) designed to allow port operators to input parameters, forecast costs, and visualize data without requiring complex web development maintenance.

The system architecture of the IMS comprises three layers, including the elements within each layer and the relationships between them, as shown in Fig. 2. This layered architecture enforces a clear separation of concerns, ensuring that data acquisition, transformation, and visualization processes remain independent, scalable, and easily extendable.

3.2 Technology Stack

The technical implementation relies on several open-source Python libraries to execute its core functionalities:

- **Streamlit:** Functions as the primary engine for the web application, transforming data scripts into an interactive, browser-accessible dashboard. Its selection is motivated by rapid prototyping capabilities and low maintenance overhead compared to traditional front-end frameworks.
- **Pandas:** Essential for manipulating large datasets (DataFrames). It is utilized to clean erroneous smart meter readings, resample time-series data, and align consumption metrics with regulatory tariff calendars.
- **OMIEData:** An automated extraction library designed to retrieve quarter-hourly marginal spot prices directly from the Iberian Energy Market (OMIE) servers.
- **PyPDF2:** Integrated into the auditing modules to perform automated text extraction (PDF scraping) on utility invoices, allowing the system to autonomously cross-reference CUPS and billed amounts against the system's own calculations.
- **Plotly:** Deployed for generating advanced, interactive multi-axis graphs for temporal and financial data visualisation.

3.3 Data Flow and Integration

The core innovation of the methodology lies in its automated data pipeline, which replaces historically fragmented and manual administrative tasks. Rather than isolated processing steps, the system implements a continuous and traceable data pipeline in which each stage performs a well-defined transformation of the input data.

The workflow is composed of the following stages:

- **Telemetry Processing:** The system automatically ingests smart meter data exports, detecting active energy columns and standardizing timestamp formats while proactively identifying and discarding corrupted data lines. A temporal normalization step aligns all measurements to a unified quarter-hour resolution, ensuring compatibility with market price signals.
- **Infrastructure API Integration (NouxCloud):** Through HTTP GET requests to the physical OPS infrastructure provider's API, the system retrieves the total energy supplied per vessel. A rule-based filtering mechanism (threshold >1000 kW) is applied to distinguish actual vessel connections from transient test loads, improving data reliability. This step ensures consistency between physical infrastructure data and metered consumption datasets.
- **Wholesale Market Integration:**
  This stage integrates real-time electricity prices from the OMIE market and aligns them with the port's energy consumption data at a quarter-hourly resolution. Each timestamped consumption value is matched with its corresponding market price through temporal synchronization. Subsequently, a rule-based mapping assigns each data point to its corresponding regulatory tariff period (P1–P6) based on calendar conditions (month, day, and hour).

This mapping process enables the aggregation of energy volumes and associated costs per tariff period, allowing accurate cost attribution under the 6.1TD tariff structure. The resulting dynamic cost is then applied to the port's real energy consumption data, enabling a highly precise OPEX forecasting model that adapts to real-time market volatility.

4 Experiments and Results

This section evaluates the performance of the proposed IMS through a realistic and operationally grounded case study based on data from the BEST terminal at the Port of Barcelona. The assessment focuses on the system's ability to support dynamic billing, generate operational economic balances, automate invoice auditing, and assist routine decision-making through integrated processing and visualization tools.

4.1 Evaluation Scope

The proposed IMS was assessed through four main evaluation dimensions: (i) dynamic billing capability under the Spanish 6.1TD tariff structure, (ii) economic viability analysis for both the port authority and the shipping line, (iii) automated validation of utility invoices against internally computed values, and (iv) operational support through automated data processing and graphical visualization. These evaluation dimensions are designed to reflect real operational requirements rather than purely theoretical performance metrics, ensuring the practical relevance of the results.

4.2 Dynamic Billing and Tariff 6.1TD Implementation

The system accurately models the Spanish 6.1TD high-voltage access tariff by dynamically assigning energy consumption to the corresponding regulatory periods (P1 to P6) according to month, day, and hour.

Unlike conventional static billing approaches, the IMS integrates real-time OMIE market prices via API, enabling dynamic cost allocation at a quarter-hour resolution. This allows the system to replace simplified or averaged pricing models with time-resolved cost calculations that reflect actual market conditions.

The IMS processes large-scale telemetry datasets and automatically computes period-specific weighted average prices, ensuring consistent alignment between measured consumption and tariff structure.

This capability represents a significant improvement over traditional manual or spreadsheet-based approaches, which are unable to handle high-frequency data and dynamic tariff structures with sufficient accuracy and consistency.

This is one of the most important features accomplished with the IMS, not only due to the 99% accuracy with which it is able to calculate the value of the electricity bill, but also because it allows the port to access these expense data much earlier than before. Typically, the electricity supplier sends the invoice 3 to 4 months after the billing period. In contrast, the system provides an early estimation of the bill, enabling economic balances and overall service management to be carried out without delay.

4.3 Operational Economic Balances (Case Study)

To validate the IMS under realistic conditions, an operational simulation was conducted using data from 1st to 30th of June 2025. During this period, the system registered a total energy consumption of 511,649.0 kWh.

The system generated two complementary economic balances, representing the perspectives of the port authority and the shipping line, respectively. These results are summarized in the UI, which illustrates the billing outputs and the corresponding economic balances generated by the IMS.

From the port authority perspective, total costs, including electricity expenditure, OPEX, and CAPEX, reached €89,183.17, while total revenues amounted to €102,474.60. This yielded a net positive balance of €13,291.43, indicating that OPS operation can be economically sustainable for the port under the evaluated conditions.

From the shipping line perspective, the estimated equivalent onboard Marine Gas Oil (MGO) generation cost was €68,566.35, assuming an average fuel price of €670 per ton, whereas the direct OPS invoice amounted to €102,474.60. Under baseline conditions, OPS therefore presents an initial cost disadvantage of €33,908.25 relative to onboard fuel-based generation. However, when incorporating the €100,000 (avg. value dependant on the hours of connection) environmental subsidy given to the shipping lines for the emissions saving, the economic balance is reversed, resulting in a net saving of €66,091.75 for the shipping line.

This result highlights that OPS competitiveness is not intrinsic, but highly dependent on external economic conditions, particularly regulatory incentives and energy market prices. As the OPS ecosystem matures, with increased infrastructure deployment and a higher number of connected vessels, economic management is expected to improve. Greater utilization rates and demand aggregation will enable more efficient cost allocation and pricing strategies, ultimately enhancing the overall competitiveness of OPS.

Although only one month is presented for illustrative purposes, the IMS was tested with data from multiple months during its development at the Port de Barcelona, yielding results consistent with previously validated manual calculations and supporting its robustness across time. The system is designed to be flexible and scalable, enabling future longitudinal and statistical analyses as more data become available. Nevertheless, it remains a validated prototype, and further real-time integration with infrastructure platforms is required.

4.4 Economic Drivers of OPS Competitiveness

The results indicate that OPS competitiveness is mainly influenced by three external factors: wholesale electricity price volatility (OMIE), marine fuel price levels, and the availability of environmental subsidies. In the evaluated scenario, OPS is not cost-competitive under baseline conditions. However, the introduction of a €100,000 subsidy is sufficient to reverse the economic balance in favor of shore power. This demonstrates that OPS viability is strongly conditional and cannot be assumed without considering market and regulatory context. Although a formal sensitivity analysis is outside the scope of this study, these results underline the necessity of dynamic financial modelling tools, such as the proposed IMS, to support decision-making under uncertainty.

The automated auditing module demonstrated the capability to process unstructured utility invoices. Using PDF parsing techniques (PyPDF2), the IMS extracts key billing parameters, including CUPS identifiers and total invoice amounts, and cross-references them with internally computed values derived from telemetry data and OMIE-based calculations. This functionality significantly reduces the risk of undetected billing discrepancies and revenue leakage.

4.5 Operational Processing and Visualization Capability

The IMS integrates automated data ingestion, cleaning, tariff mapping, and cost computation within a unified workflow. This replaces manual spreadsheet-based processes, improving consistency, reproducibility, and reducing human error.

Visualization tools are provided to support operational monitoring; however, they are considered a secondary feature and not a core contribution of the system.

4.6 Environmental Implications

The implementation of OPS guarantees a 100% reduction in local emissions of NOx, SOx, and particulate matter during vessel hotelling, as no MGO is used anymore to power the ship and the electricity used by the OPS is all from renewable energy sources. While this environmental benefit is inherent to OPS technology rather than the IMS itself, the proposed system acts as an enabling layer by making OPS economically and operationally viable. Given that approximately 72% of vessel NOx emissions occur during port stays [9], the deployment of OPS supported by IMS contributes significantly to urban air quality improvement in port areas such as Barcelona.

5 Conclusion

Onshore Power Supply (OPS) stands as an indispensable and technologically mature solution for maritime decarbonisation. However, its large-scale deployment is primarily constrained by economic and operational complexity rather than engineering limitations. Within the real operational context of the BEST terminal at the Port of Barcelona, this work demonstrates that zero-emission port operations require not only physical electrification, but also advanced digital systems capable of managing financial and regulatory uncertainty.

To address this gap, the proposed Information Management System (IMS) provides an integrated, data-driven framework that automates the processing of smart meter telemetry, incorporates real-time OMIE electricity prices, and models complex multi-period tariff structures such as the Spanish 6.1TD. By synchronizing heterogeneous high-frequency data, the system enables accurate, auditable, and time-resolved cost calculations under real market conditions, supporting both billing and operational decision-making.

The results confirm that OPS can be economically viable under specific conditions, particularly when supported by regulatory incentives. However, the findings also show that its competitiveness is highly sensitive to external factors such as electricity price volatility, fuel costs, and subsidy schemes, indicating that its economic feasibility is conditional rather than intrinsic. More broadly, this work highlights digitalisation as a key enabler for scalable OPS deployment, bridging the gap between infrastructure implementation and financially sustainable operation.

Nevertheless, several limitations must be acknowledged. The economic analysis is based on specific assumptions regarding fuel prices, electricity tariffs, and subsidy schemes, which may vary across regions and over time. The evaluation is limited to a single month (June 2025), restricting generalisability. However, the IMS is designed to be flexible and scalable, supporting future longitudinal and statistical analyses as more data become available. The current system represents a validated prototype, and further real-time integration with infrastructure platforms is still required.

Future research should focus on extending validation across multiple scenarios, incorporating stochastic modelling of electricity markets, and improving interoperability through standardized real-time data architectures. These developments will be essential to ensure scalability, robustness, and real-world applicability of digital financial management systems for OPS.

References

1. Innes, A., Monios, J.: Identifying the unique challenges of installing cold ironing at small and medium ports. Transp. Res. Part D Transp. Environ. **62**(1), 298–313 (2018)
2. Vaittinen, T.: Costs and Benefits of Shore Power: A Review of Economic Modelling. University of Helsinki, Helsinki (2025)
3. Bakar, N.N.A., Bazmohammadi, N., Vasquez, J.C., Guerrero, J.M.: Electrification of onshore power systems in maritime transportation towards decarbonization of ports. Renew. Sustain. Energy Rev. **178**(8), 1–16 (2023)
4. IEC/IEEE: Utility connections in port: High voltage shore connection (HVSC) systems-General requirements. International Electrotechnical Commission, Geneva
5. Bonilla, G.: Anàlisi del OPS a Barcelona i desenvolupament d'un SGI. Universitat Politècnica de Catalunya, Barcelona (2026)
6. Neugebauer, A., Heilig, L., Voss, S.: Digital Twin for resilience and sustainability assessment of port facility. In: International Conference on Maritime Logistics, pp. 1–13. Springer, Heidelberg (2024)

7. Ballini, E., Bozzo, R.: Feasibility study of a cold ironing system and district heating in port area. J. Marit. Res. **2**(2), 22–30 (2015)
8. Susilawati, A., et al.: Sustainable maritime of onshore power supply systems for ships in Thai ports. Energy Res. **1**(1), 1–10 (2024)
9. Port de Barcelona: Emissions from port activity. https://www.portdebarcelona.cat/en/sustainability/environmental-sustainability/environmental-actions/air/emissions-port-activity. Accessed 9 Apr 2026

Service Configuration Design for Green Bunkering Capture at Transshipment Hubs: Sequencing Queue Management, SIMOPS, and Availability

Ji-Won Lee(✉) and Joo-Won Lee

Korea Maritime Institute, 26, Haeyang-ro 301 beon-gil, Yeongdo-gu, Busan, South Korea
jiwon@kmi.re.kr

Abstract. The growth of alternative-fuel-capable vessels is creating new demand for green bunkering at major transshipment hubs, but port-side service systems have not developed at the same pace. In transshipment-linked settings, vessels already call for cargo handling, so the key issue is whether bunkering can be executed within the existing port call. Green bunkering capture is therefore a hub-internal service-design problem.

This paper examines how a hub should configure its service system under operational and investment constraints. It focuses on three controllable levers: queue management, simultaneous operations (SIMOPS), and bunkering vessel availability. To analyze this problem, the paper develops a two-layer model. Layer 1 maps service configurations into operational performance indicators, and Layer 2 embeds those indicators in a vessel choice model with three alternatives: bunkering at the focal hub, bunkering at a competing hub, or deferring.

The results show that service configuration is a first-order determinant of capture. SIMOPS is the dominant first-step intervention because it relaxes the feasibility constraint within the port-call window. Availability enhancement also improves capture, but once cost-effectiveness is considered it becomes a weaker first move, revealing an availability sequencing trap. Fuel price discounting is also found to be structurally less effective than service redesign. The findings suggest a clear early-stage sequence for transshipment hubs: establish SIMOPS capability first, improve queue coordination second, and expand dedicated asset availability third.

Keywords: green bunkering · service configuration · SIMOPS · transshipment hub · investment sequencing

1 Introduction

The growth of alternative-fuel-capable vessels is generating new demand for green bunkering at major transshipment hubs, but port-side service systems have not developed at the same pace. In transshipment-linked settings, vessels already call for cargo handling, so the key question is not whether the hub is on the network, but whether

J. de Armas and E. Lalla Ruiz (Eds.): LOGMS 2026, LNCS 16679, pp. 132–142, 2027.
https://doi.org/10.1007/978-3-032-30795-8_12

bunkering can be executed within the existing port call. Green bunkering capture is therefore not only a market issue but also a service-design problem [2, 5].

This paper examines how a hub should configure its internal service system to convert latent demand into realized capture under operational and investment constraints. It focuses on three controllable levers: queue management, which reduces waiting through coordination and scheduling; simultaneous operations (SIMOPS), which determine whether bunkering can be conducted within the cargo-handling window; and bunkering vessel availability, which captures supply readiness. These levers address different bottlenecks and differ in cost structure, so their priority is not self-evident [3, 8].

Existing studies analyze bunkering choice, fuel procurement, and infrastructure location, but usually treat port-side service quality as exogenous. As a result, they explain vessel response better than hub-side service design. This gap is particularly important in early-stage green bunkering, where feasibility and readiness may matter more than price [1, 4, 6, 9].

To address this gap, the paper develops a two-layer model. Layer 1 maps service configurations into operational performance indicators. Layer 2 embeds those indicators in a vessel choice model with three alternatives: bunkering at the focal hub, bunkering at a competing hub, or deferring. The paper makes three contributions. First, it shows that service configuration is a first-order determinant of capture. Second, it identifies SIMOPS as the dominant first-step intervention and reveals an availability sequencing trap once cost is considered. Third, it introduces a threshold-based ranking logic for intervention order under incomplete cost information.

2 Related Literature and Problem Positioning

Relevant studies fall into three streams: bunkering optimization, port and bunkering choice, and green bunkering operations. The first examines where and how much vessels should bunker. The second shows that price, congestion, reliability, and location affect port attractiveness. The third identifies technical and procedural constraints for fuels such as LNG and methanol, especially for SIMOPS and asset readiness [1, 3, 6, 9].

Their common limitation is that port-side service quality is usually treated as given. Waiting, feasibility, and reliability may enter as explanatory variables, but they are rarely modeled as outcomes of hub-side design. The literature therefore explains user response more clearly than provider-side service formation. In transshipment-linked green bunkering, this matters because capture depends heavily on whether service can be executed within the existing call window [4, 6, 10].

This paper addresses that gap by treating service configuration as an endogenous decision variable. It links queue management, SIMOPS, and asset availability to vessel choice through a two-layer framework. The contribution is thus both applied and methodological: it studies a relevant maritime logistics problem while shifting attention from exogenous service attributes to provider-side service-system design.

3 Model

3.1 Problem and Framework

The model evaluates how alternative service configurations affect a hub's ability to capture green bunkering demand. It connects two levels. At the hub level, service design shapes the operating conditions of bunkering. At the vessel level, heterogeneous users respond by bunkering at the focal hub, bunkering elsewhere, or deferring. The two-layer structure makes service configuration an endogenous design variable rather than a background condition.

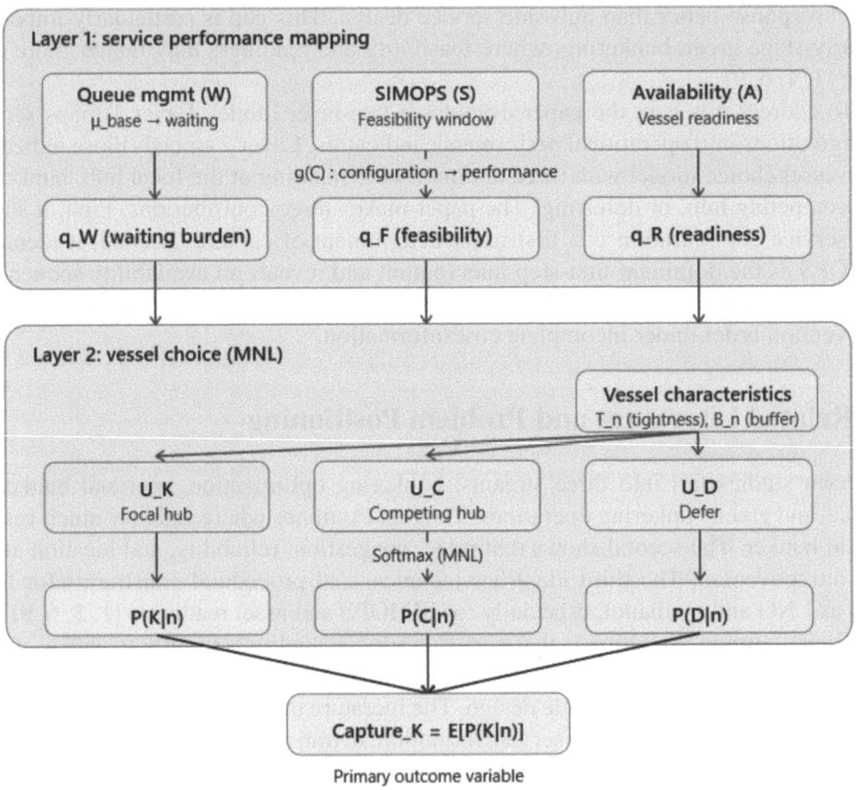

Fig. 1. Two-layer framework for green bunkering capture at a transshipment hub. **Source:** Author's elaboration

The overall logic of the model is illustrated in Figure 1. Layer 1 maps service interventions into operational performance indicators, and Layer 2 converts those indicators into vessel-level choice probabilities and expected capture.

3.2 Model Structure

Service Configuration Space. The model focuses on three levers: queue management intensity, SIMOPS capability, and bunkering vessel availability. Queue management reduces waiting through coordination and scheduling. SIMOPS determines whether bunkering can occur in parallel with cargo handling. Availability captures the readiness of bunkering assets. The analysis compares a small set of structured configurations from a minimum-service baseline to an integrated configuration [3, 8] (Table 1, 4, 5).

Table 1. Service configurations analyzed in the model

Config	Label	μ_base	S	A	Interpretation
C0	Baseline	1.00	0	0.40	No SIMOPS, limited assets
C1	Queue-managed	1.15	0	0.40	Better coordination
C2	SIMOPS-enabled	1.00	1	0.40	Parallel cargo/bunkering
C3	Availability-enhanced	1.00	0	0.80	More dedicated assets
C4	Integrated	1.15	1	0.80	All three improved

Layer 1: Operational Performance. Layer 1 converts service configurations into three indicators: waiting burden, service feasibility, and supply readiness. Effective service rate is

$$\mu_{\{eff\}} = \mu_{\{base\}} \cdot (1 + \eta_S \cdot S) \cdot (0.5 + 0.5 \cdot A) \tag{1}$$

With arrival rate λ, utilization is = min(/eff, 0.98). Expected waiting time is

$$W = w_0 + w_1\left(\frac{\rho^{\kappa}}{1 - \rho + \varepsilon}\right) \tag{2}$$

Waiting burden enters the choice model as = – ln(1+). Together, these terms capture how congestion and coordination affect the service environment faced by vessels [4, 10].

Feasibility captures whether bunkering can be completed within the port-call window:

$$q^{\{(n)\}}_{\{F\}} = \sigma\left(\theta_0 + \theta_S S - \theta_T T_n + \theta_{\{ST\}S} T_n\right) \tag{3}$$

where is vessel schedule tightness. Supply readiness is

$$q_R = A \cdot \exp(-\phi \cdot \rho) \tag{4}$$

These terms allow SIMOPS and readiness to affect capture through different operational channels, especially under tight call windows [3, 7].

Layer 2: Vessel Choice. Each vessel chooses among bunkering at the focal hub (), bunkering at a competing hub (), or deferring (). Utility for hub ∈{,} is

$$U_{\{j\}}^{\{(n)\}} = \alpha_j + \beta_P P_j + \beta_W q_{\{W,j\}} + \beta_F q_{\{F,j\}}^{\{(n)\}}$$

$$+\beta_R q_{\{R,j\}} + \gamma_T T_n + \gamma_B B_n \tag{5}$$

where is fuel price and is fuel buffer. Deferral utility is

$$U_D^n = \alpha_D + \delta_B B_n + \delta_T T_n \tag{6}$$

Choice probabilities follow the multinomial logit model. Capture is the average probability that vessels choose . Deferral is modeled explicitly because postponement is a meaningful response in early-stage green bunkering markets [1, 9].

Sequencing and Threshold Logic. The model computes marginal contributions relative to the baseline and compares alternative intervention orders. To account for incomplete cost information, it uses threshold-based cost-effectiveness. Let =/. SIMOPS dominates availability if

$$\frac{C_S}{C_A} < \frac{MC_S}{MC_A} \tag{7}$$

This avoids relying on weak point estimates for all intervention costs and instead identifies the cost conditions under which the ranking would reverse.

4 Results

4.1 Configuration Performance

Table 2 shows that structural position alone does not generate meaningful capture. Under the baseline configuration, the focal hub captures little demand and most vessels defer. Low uptake therefore reflects service inadequacy more than weak market potential.

Table 2. Performance of alternative service configurations

Config	Capture (K)	Competitor share	Defer share	Waiting (h)
C0	0.060	0.155	0.785	21.6
C1	0.135	0.143	0.723	11.6
C2	0.276	0.119	0.605	7.9
C3	0.242	0.125	0.633	8.1
C4	0.584	0.068	0.348	3.5

When the service system is strengthened, capture rises sharply and deferral falls. Most of this improvement comes from activating previously deferred demand rather than diverting large volumes from the competitor. This indicates that early-stage green bunkering competition is partly about making the service executable, not just redistributing an already active market.

4.2 Sequencing and Ranking Results

Table 3 reports marginal gains from the baseline. SIMOPS produces the largest first-step effect, availability ranks second, and queue management ranks third. The main implication is that the most binding early-stage bottleneck is feasibility within the port-call window rather than congestion alone (Figs. 2, 3, 4, 5).

Table 3. Marginal gains and first-step sequencing implications.

Item	Result
Queue: C0 → C1	+7.5 pp
SIMOPS: C0 → C2	+21.6 pp
Availability: C0 → C3	+18.2 pp
Integrated: C0 → C4	+52.4 pp
Best first step	SIMOPS
Interpretation	Feasibility is the binding bottleneck

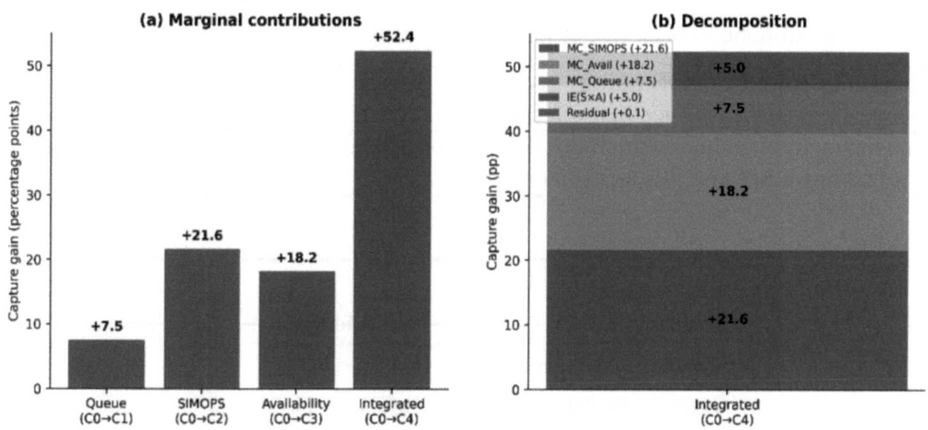

Fig. 2. Marginal capture gains of alternative service interventions and decomposition of the integrated gain.

Sequencing results confirm this. A SIMOPS-first path reaches a much higher interim capture level than either a queue-first or availability-first path. Thus, investment order affects transitional capture even when all paths eventually converge to the same integrated configuration, reinforcing the importance of feasibility within the port-call window [3].

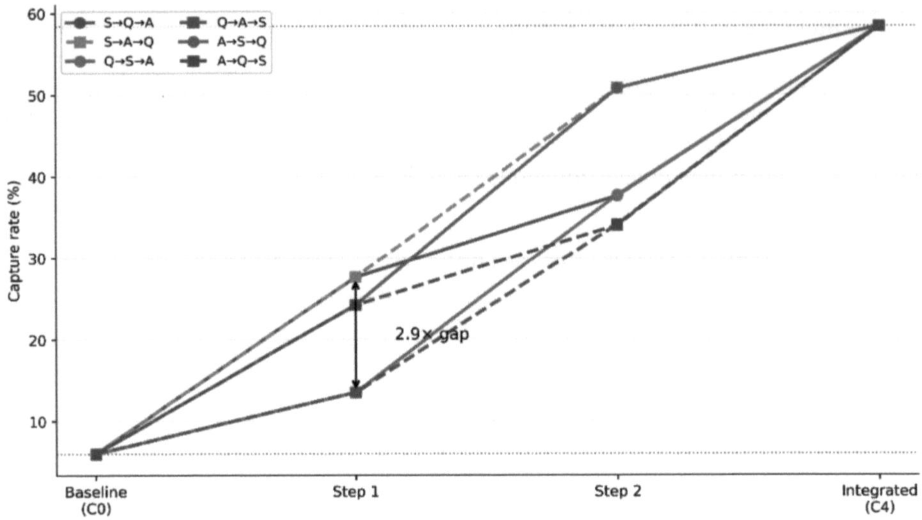

Fig. 3. Capture trajectories under alternative investment sequences toward the integrated configuration.

The practical implication of this sequencing result is that hubs should not interpret visible asset expansion as the natural first step of green bunkering development when the more binding bottleneck lies in service feasibility.

Threshold-Based Cost Ranking. Availability performs well in raw capture terms, but becomes less attractive once cost-effectiveness is considered. This creates the availability sequencing trap: an intervention that looks strong in performance terms becomes weak as a first move because it is asset-intensive [8].

Table 4. Threshold conditions for cost-effectiveness ranking

Comparison	Threshold Ratio
SIMOPS > Availability	$C_S/C_A < 118.8\%$
Queue > Availability	$C_W/C_A < 40.9\%$
SIMOPS > Queue	$C_S/C_W < 2.90\times$

This result matters because it replaces fragile point-estimate comparisons with reversal conditions. The practical question becomes whether one intervention could plausibly exceed the threshold needed to overturn the ranking.

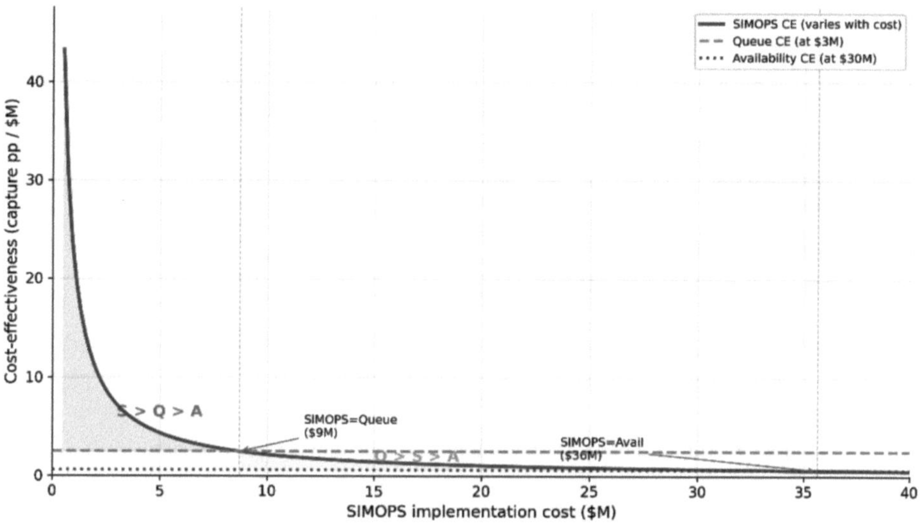

Fig. 4. Threshold map for the cost-effectiveness ranking of alternative interventions.

Service Redesign Versus Price Discounting. Price discounting has much weaker effects than service redesign. Even a substantial discount under baseline service conditions produces only a small fraction of the gain generated by SIMOPS or the integrated configuration.

Table 5. Capture gains from price discounting and service redesign

Strategy	ΔCapture (pp)
10% price discount	+0.5
20% price discount	+1.0
30% price discount	+1.5
SIMOPS only	+21.6
Integrated service	+52.4

The reason is structural: price cuts do not remove feasibility or readiness bottlenecks. In early-stage transshipment-linked green bunkering, operational capability formation is therefore more effective than price competition.

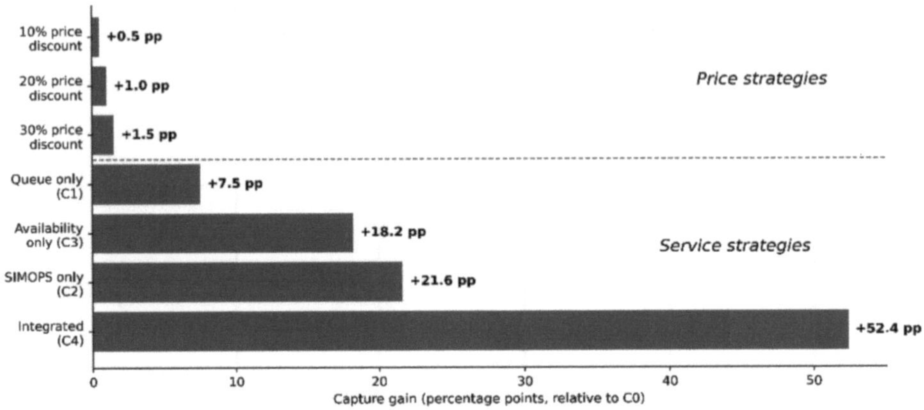

Fig. 5. Capture gains from price discounting and service redesign.

5 Robustness and Discussion

Robustness tests show that the main ranking logic is stable. Across parameter perturbations, stronger competition, and vessel subgroups, SIMOPS remains the strongest first-step intervention and the investment-adjusted ranking continues to place availability behind queue management. Absolute gains vary, but the ordering of priorities is preserved.

Some results are more conditional. In particular, the exact magnitude and sign of the SIMOPS–availability interaction can vary with behavioral assumptions. This means the model provides stronger confidence in the ranking of interventions than in the precise size of complementarities.

Managerial Implications. The main managerial implication is that hub operators should normally build procedural capability before visible asset scale. In practice, the model results support the following early-stage sequence: SIMOPS first, queue coordination second, and dedicated asset expansion third. This recommendation is tied directly to the model evidence that feasibility-enhancing capability delivers the strongest first-step gain, whereas asset expansion becomes less attractive once cost-effectiveness is considered. Price competition is also a weak early-stage strategy because discounts cannot resolve feasibility and readiness constraints [3, 8].

Methodological Implications. Methodologically, the paper contributes by endogenizing service configuration in a maritime choice setting and by applying threshold analysis under incomplete cost information. The model is calibrated, static, and stylized, so future work should extend it with richer data and dynamic capability formation. Even so, the main contribution is a stable ranking logic for sequencing interventions in an emerging service system.

Limitations. The model is calibrated rather than econometrically estimated, static rather than dynamic, and simplified in its behavioral structure. These limitations do not overturn the main result, but they do indicate the need for future work using richer operational data and dynamic inter-hub competition.

6 Conclusion

This paper analyzes green bunkering capture at transshipment hubs as a service-system design problem rather than as a passive outcome of market growth, port position, or fuel-price competition. By linking hub-side service configuration to vessel choice through a two-layer model, it shows that service capability is a first-order determinant of capture in early-stage green bunkering systems. Under the model setting, SIMOPS emerges as the dominant first-step intervention, availability enhancement becomes less attractive once cost-effectiveness is considered, and service redesign is substantially more effective than price discounting in the setting studied here.

The practical implication is clear: hubs should normally sequence capability formation procedurally before scaling it physically. More specifically, the model evidence suggests that feasibility-enhancing capability should be established before large-scale asset expansion. More broadly, the paper shows that application-driven operational research can support emerging maritime logistics services by treating service attributes as endogenous outputs of provider-side design. Future work should extend the framework with richer behavioral data and dynamic representations of capability formation, but the central insight remains that, in transshipment-linked green bunkering, the order in which operational bottlenecks are relaxed matters as much as the final service level itself.

Disclosure of Interests. The authors have no competing interests to declare that are relevant to the content of this article.

References

1. Aronietis, R., Sys, C., van Hassel, E., Vanelslander, T.: Investigating the bunkering choice determinants: the case of the port of Antwerp. J. Shipping Trade. **2**, 8 (2017)
2. DNV: LNG-fuelled container ships sustain alternative fuel share of global orderbook amid industry slowdown. DNV News (2026). https://www.dnv.com/news/2026/LNG-fuelled-container-ships-sustain-alternative-fuel-share-of-global-orderbook-amid-industry-slowdown/. Accessed 30 Apr 2026.
3. Fan, H., Enshaei, H., Jayasinghe, S.G., Wan, L., Fei, J.: Safety philosophy and risk analysis methodology for LNG bunkering simultaneous operations (SIMOPs): a literature review. Saf. Sci. **142**, 105398 (2021)
4. Fuentes, G., Wallace, S.W.: The effects of waiting times on the bunkering decision for tramp ships. Marit. Transp. Res. **6**, 100106 (2024)
5. International Maritime Organization: 2023 IMO strategy on reduction of GHG emissions from ships. Resolution MEPC.377(80), London (2023).
6. Chen, K., Yi, X., Xin, X., Shan, H.: Spatial evolution of liner bunkering hubs in Asia–Europe: green fuel adoption under demand and fuel price uncertainty. Transp. Policy. **178**, 103956 (2026). https://doi.org/10.1016/j.tranpol.2025.103956
7. Surinov, I., Shemonayev, V., Torskiy, V.: Simultaneous operations during LNG bunkering at LNG-powered vessels. TransNav: Int. J. Mar. Navig. Saf. Sea Transp. **19**(4), 1361–1370 (2025). https://doi.org/10.12716/1001.19.04.36

8. Sustainable Ships: The State of Methanol as Marine Fuel 2023. Sustainable Ships (2023). https://www.sustainable-ships.org/stories/2023/methanol-marine-fuel. Accessed 21 March 2026.
9. Wang, Y., Yeo, G.T., Ng, A.K.Y.: Choosing optimal bunkering ports for liner shipping companies: a hybrid fuzzy-Delphi-TOPSIS approach. Transp. Policy. **35**, 358–365 (2014)
10. Watanabe, E., Shibasaki, R.: Extraction of bunkering services from AIS data and their international comparisons. Sustainability. **15**(24), 16711 (2023)

Data-Driven Fuel Consumption Analysis for Maintenance Operations in Offshore Wind Farms

Komeyl Baghizadeh Polami[1], Julia Pahl[1(✉)], and Paulo Cesar Ribas[2]

[1] Department of Technology and Innovation, University of Southern Denmark, Odense, Denmark
{kob,julp}@iti.sdu.dk
[2] Faculty of Logistics, Molde University College, Molde, Norway
paulo.c.ribas@himolde.no

Abstract. This study presents a data-driven analysis of fuel consumption in offshore wind farm (OWF) maintenance operations using high-frequency engine logs, navigation records, met-ocean data, and operator-reported activity logs from a service offshore vessel (SOV). The results show that transit-related activities account for nearly three-quarters of total mission fuel consumption. Based on this finding, predictive modeling is focused on transit operations, where the greatest potential for fuel and emission reduction exists. Among the evaluated models, Random Forest (RF) achieved the best performance, with an R^2 of 0.857, MAE of 3.412 L/h, and RMSE of 8.917 L/h on unseen test data. Feature importance analysis shows that vessel speed is the dominant predictor, followed by wave-related variables. These findings indicate that weather-aware routing and speed selection can support lower fuel use, CO_2 emissions, and maintenance costs in OWF logistics.

Keywords: Offshore wind farms · Fuel consumption · Transit operations · Machine learning · Weather conditions

1 Introduction

The transition to renewable energy sources is essential for addressing climate change and meeting modern society's energy demands. Offshore wind farms (OWFs) have emerged as major contributors to this transition because they can exploit strong wind resources far from populated areas [1]. Efficient fuel consumption analysis for maintenance operations is critical for improving both the operational efficiency and sustainability of offshore wind energy systems. By optimizing maintenance activities and vessel fuel use, stakeholders can reduce costs while maintaining high service performance [2,3]. Although substantial advances have been made in OWF technology and infrastructure, fuel consumption during maintenance operations remains relatively underexplored. Existing literature has largely focused on wind farm design, environmental assessment, and monitoring

J. de Armas and E. Lalla Ruiz (Eds.): LOGMS 2026, LNCS 16679, pp. 143–155, 2027.
https://doi.org/10.1007/978-3-032-30795-8_13

systems. For example, prior studies have used multi-criteria decision-making to optimize turbine selection [4] and life-cycle cost analysis to evaluate offshore wind systems. Efficient logistics and operations in offshore wind farms are particularly important because vessels and maintenance activities constitute major contributors to both operational cost and energy use [5]. OWF logistics are highly time and fuel-sensitive due to the dispersed, remote, and weather-dependent nature of offshore sites, where even small delays or routing inefficiencies can substantially increase time at sea, fuel consumption, operating cost, and associated emissions [6]. In this context, the planning and execution of installation, operations and maintenance (O&M) and support vessel movements play a decisive role in project duration, turbine availability, and ultimately energy output. Empirical and methodological research in offshore wind and marine logistics has consistently identified weather windows, vessel routing, and maintenance scheduling as key determinants of both completion time and fuel expenditure. Accordingly, improvements in these elements can lead directly to meaningful reductions in downtime, fuel use, and overall cost of energy, while also supporting lower-emission offshore operations [7].

Despite the growing importance of OWF maintenance, the fuel consumption behavior of service vessels during daily operations is still insufficiently considered at a detailed activity level. Fuel consumption of vessels is nonlinear, with ship speed often exhibiting cubic or even higher-order relationships with fuel use [8]. In addition to speed, fuel consumption is influenced by a combination of operational and environmental factors whose effects are strongly interdependent [9]. As a result, accurate modeling of fuel consumption requires approaches capable of representing nonlinear relationships and interaction effects among operational, environmental, and vessel-motion variables. Consistent with this limitation, several maritime studies have reported that linear and polynomial regression models provide only moderate predictive capability of fuel consumption and are generally outperformed by more flexible approaches, particularly tree-based and neural network models, when modeling vessel fuel consumption under realistic operating conditions [10].

The present study addresses this need by constructing an integrated analytical framework based on high-frequency engine measurements, navigation data, met-ocean information, and operator-reported activity logs. Rather than inferring vessel states solely from movement patterns, the analysis uses operational reports as ground truth for labeling mission activities, thereby enabling a more reliable connection between fuel consumption and documented maintenance tasks. This study first characterizes fuel use across the full mission profile and then develops predictive models for transit operations, which are shown in the case study to constitute the dominant fuel-consuming regime. This framing allows the analysis to move beyond general speed–fuel relationships toward a more operationally interpretable assessment of energy use in offshore maintenance missions.

2 Methodology

The methodological framework consists of five steps. First, engine, navigation, met-ocean, and operator-report data are synchronized into a common time base. Second, operator reports are used to assign activity labels to each synchronized record. Third, fuel consumption and CO_2 emissions are calculated from measured engine fuel rates. Fourth, environmental and operational features are engineered from vessel course, speed, wave height, and wave direction. Fifth, supervised learning models are trained to predict transit fuel rate and to identify the operational and environmental variables most relevant for fuel use during transit operations. Figure 1 illustrates a daily OWF maintenance mission: A SOV departs from the home port, transits to the offshore wind farm, visits selected turbines for technician and equipment transfer, and returns to port after task completion. The proposed approach combines activity-level fuel accounting with supervised fuel-rate prediction. The descriptive analysis identifies which operational phases dominate total fuel use, while the predictive analysis focuses on transit operations because these phases account for the largest share of fuel consumption.

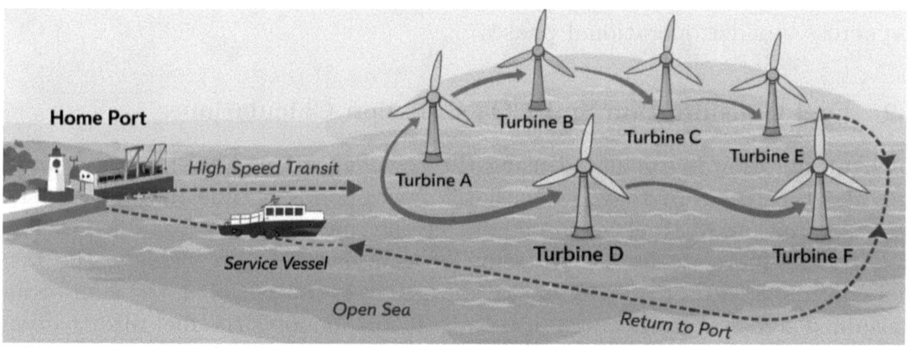

Fig. 1. Conceptual illustration of a daily OWF maintenance

2.1 Data Integration and Operation-Mode Labeling

The analysis integrates four data sources: high-frequency engine sensor data from the vessel's four main engines (10 Hz), onboard navigation records (three second intervals), met-ocean data from the Copernicus Marine Service (three hour resolution), and daily operational reports from the SOV provider. The engine dataset includes fuel rate, engine revolutions, boost pressure, and a logging timestamp field, *received_at*, which records when each engine message was received by the onboard data acquisition system. The navigation data provide vessel position, Speed Over Ground (SOG), and course, with timestamps based on GPS time. The met-ocean data provide significant wave height (VHM0), mean wave direction (VMDR), and wind-wave VHM0 from the nearest grid point, while the operator reports provide the reference activity windows for operation labeling. All timestamps are first normalized to UTC, and a constant offset is applied to the engine and navigation data to align them with the operator reports. The engine and navigation datasets are then merged using an as-of temporal join with a 1-s tolerance, and unmatched records are excluded. The merged dataset is subsequently enriched with met-ocean variables through a second as-of join with a 1-h tolerance, consistent with the three-h weather-data resolution. This produces a synchronized dataset containing engine, navigation, and environmental variables. Because rule-based labeling based solely on navigation or engine signals can misclassify offshore activities, the manual operational reports are treated as ground truth. Their activity start and end times are converted to UTC, cross-checked against the navigation data, and used to assign an operational label to each record, resulting in the categorical variable operation_mode. The physical variables used in the analysis, such as fuel rate, SOG, course, VHM0, and VMDR, originate from the engine, navigation, and met-ocean datasets. In contrast, the variables *operation_mode* and *merged category* are constructed in this study. The detailed operation labels are assigned by matching the operator-reported activity windows to the synchronized engine-navigation records. The merged categories are then created only for aggregation, visualization, and interpretation of fuel use across broader operational phases.

2.2 Fuel Consumption and CO_2 Emission Calculation

Fuel consumption is calculated using the vessel's engine (ENG) dataset, which provides the fuel rate together with the corresponding time information. For each observation, the fuel consumed during the time interval is obtained by multiplying the fuel rate by the duration of that interval. Accordingly, the total fuel consumption over a given operation or day is computed as the sum of fuel consumed across all consecutive intervals. If FR_i denotes the fuel rate at observation i in liters per hour, and Δt_i denotes the corresponding time interval in hours, then the fuel consumption for that interval is calculated as:

$$FC_i = FR_i \times \Delta t_i$$

The total fuel consumption is then obtained as:

$$FC = \sum_i FR_i \times \Delta t_i$$

Based on the available company information, the vessel fuel type is assumed to be Marine Gas Oil (MGO). CO_2 emissions are then estimated by multiplying the calculated fuel consumption by the emission factor of MGO, equal to 2.73 kg CO_2 per liter. Thus, if FC denotes fuel consumption in liters, the related CO_2 emission is calculated as:

$$CO_2 = 2.73 \times FC$$

2.3 Feature Engineering and Operation-Mode Preparation

To analyze the effect of sea conditions on fuel consumption, the relative wave direction is calculated from the angle between the vessel course and the incoming wave direction. Let ψ_v denote the vessel course angle and ψ_w denote the wave direction angle, both measured in degrees. The relative wave direction angle, denoted by θ_{rel}, is computed as

$$\theta_{\text{rel}} = \min\left(|\psi_v - \psi_w|,\, 360^\circ - |\psi_v - \psi_w|\right)$$

where $\theta_{\text{rel}} \in [0^\circ, 180^\circ]$ represents the smallest angular difference between the vessel heading and the incoming wave direction. Based on this relative angle, wave conditions are classified into five categories: head seas for $0^\circ \leq \theta_{\text{rel}} < 30^\circ$, bow quartering seas for $30^\circ \leq \theta_{\text{rel}} < 60^\circ$, beam seas for $60^\circ \leq \theta_{\text{rel}} < 120^\circ$, stern quartering seas for $120^\circ \leq \theta_{\text{rel}} < 150^\circ$, and following seas for $150^\circ \leq \theta_{\text{rel}} \leq 180^\circ$. Head seas increase resistance and fuel demand through pitching, bow quartering seas combine pitching and rolling, often requiring steering corrections. Beam seas cause strong rolling, reducing passenger comfort and stability. Stern quartering seas introduce roll and yaw, risking broaching, while following seas may reduce resistance but create control challenges. This classification captures the magnitude and directionality of environmental forcing, providing a basis for analyzing vessel performance under different sea states. The merged categories are used only for descriptive aggregation and visualization. They do not imply that all detailed activities within the same merged group have identical fuel efficiency. Fuel consumption, duration, and distance are first calculated for each detailed operation label and are then aggregated by summation. Distance-normalized fuel efficiency for a merged category is calculated as total fuel divided by total distance, rather than as an arithmetic average of the detailed-label efficiencies. In the predictive modeling stage, the analysis focuses on transit records, but the transit subcategories are retained through the operation-mode feature so that differences between port–site transit and transit between turbines are not removed.

A summary of the detailed operational modes used in the activity labeling and descriptive analysis is presented in Table 1.

3 Case Study and Results

Two data subsets are used for different purposes in the case study. The January 6, 2024 mission is used as an illustrative full-mission example because it contains all major operational phases, including port operations, port–site transit, transit between turbines, push operations, and standby. This mission is used for descriptive fuel and emission accounting. In contrast, the August–September 2024 records are used for supervised transit fuel-rate prediction because they provide a larger set of labeled transit observations for model training, testing, and validation. The total fuel consumption of 2238.6 L and the mission duration of 11.38 h refer only to the January 6 mission. The use of these two periods is not intended as a seasonal comparison.

Table 1. Definition of operational modes.

Detailed Label	Merged Category	Description
transit_with_PAX_to_site	Port–Site Transit	Port-to-site transit with technicians onboard
transit_with_PAX_to_TP	Transit Between Turbines	Transit Between Turbines with technicians
transit_without_PAX_to_TP	Transit Between Turbines	Transit Between Turbines without technicians
push_on_PAX_up	Push Operations	Push-on to embark technicians
push_on_PAX_down	Push Operations	Push-on to disembark technicians
push_on_cargo_up	Push Operations	Push-on for cargo or equipment transfer up
push_on_cargo_down	Push Operations	Push-on to receive cargo or equipment down
standby_in_field	Standby	DP hold or loitering within the wind farm
transit_with_PAX_to_port	Port–Site Transit	Site-to-port transit with technicians onboard
disembarkation_in_port	Port Operations	Quay maneuvers for disembarkation
offload_cargo_in_port	Port Operations	Quay operations for cargo or equipment offloading
shifting_in_port	Port Operations	Shift of berth or position within port
preparation_in_port	Port Operations	Pre-departure preparation, warm-up, and checks

3.1 Operational Profile and Fuel Efficiency Analysis

One day, more precisely January 6, 2024, is used as the illustrative full operational day for the descriptive analysis. On this day, seven of the 49 turbines were serviced during a mission lasting 11.38 h (683 min). Over the course of the mission, the vessel's four engines consumed a total of 2238.6 l of fuel. Some turbines were visited multiple times within the same day, indicating repeated technician drop-off and pick-up operations. Altogether, 14 maintenance operations were reconstructed over approximately six hours, yielding a high-resolution description of vessel movements and technician activity during the mission. Based on this reconstructed mission, the analysis pipeline is applied to characterize the vessel's operational profile and identify the activities with the highest fuel relevance. Table 2 presents the breakdown of time, speed, fuel rate, and fuel efficiency across 13 detailed operational modes.

Table 2. Aggregated performance metrics by operational mode for the analyzed mission, ordered according to the typical mission sequence from port to offshore operations and back to port.

Operational Mode	Duration (min)	Avg. Speed (knots)	Fuel Rate (l/h)	Data Records	Fuel Efficiency (l/NM)
disembarkation_in_port	2.0	0.05	15.81	184	318.87
offload_cargo_in_port	1.0	0.03	21.54	104	854.48
shifting_in_port	8.0	0.76	6.60	984	8.73
transit_with_PAX_to_site	90.0	8.14	105.17	16012	12.92
transit_with_PAX_to_TP	117.0	5.46	61.85	27092	11.32
transit_without_PAX_to_TP	27.0	5.64	62.94	5832	11.16
transit_with_PAX_to_other_vessel	28.0	3.91	40.25	6592	10.29
standby_in_field	219.0	1.20	4.27	51560	3.57
push_on_PAX_up	37.0	0.09	48.07	10796	506.96
push_on_PAX_down	18.0	0.14	41.55	4244	289.37
push_on_cargo_up	25.0	0.08	34.14	5876	432.56
push_on_cargo_down	19.0	0.10	36.63	4992	350.62
transit_with_PAX_to_port	92.0	7.64	99.22	19888	12.99

The results show that the longest portion of the mission is spent in standby in field (219 min), followed by different types of transit, which together accounted for more than five hours of the day. The highest average fuel rates occurred during high-speed transit, with `transit_with_PAX_to_site` reaching 105.2 l/h.

A more informative measure is fuel efficiency in liters per nautical mile (L/NM). Although high-speed transit is fuel-intensive, it remains relatively efficient for covering long distances, with values around 10.3–13.0 L/NM. In contrast, direct turbine-interface activities and certain port operations are extremely inefficient in distance-normalized terms. Push operations exhibit efficiencies between roughly 289 and 507 L/NM. The least efficient activity in the dataset is offload_cargo_in_port, at 854.48 L/NM. This occurs because the vessel burns substantial fuel to generate thrust and maintain controlled positioning while covering almost no distance. Therefore, the merged categories are not used to assume equal fuel efficiency within a group. They are used only to summarize total fuel use, duration, and distance at a higher operational level, while the detailed labels in Table 2 preserve the differences between individual activities.

To simplify interpretation, detailed operational labels are merged into broader categories:

- **Transit Between Turbines**: `transit_with_PAX_to_TP`, `transit_without_PAX_to_TP`
- **Push Operations**: `push_on_PAX_up`, `push_on_PAX_down`, `push_on_cargo_up`, `push_on_cargo_down`
- **Port–Site Transit**: `transit_with_PAX_to_port`, `transit_with_PAX_to_site`
- **Standby** : `standby_in_field`
- **Port Operations**: `shifting_in_port`, `disembarkation_in_port`, `offload_cargo_in_port`
- **Other Operations**: `transit_with_PAX_to_other_vessel`

This reduced operational space improves interpretability while remaining consistent with the original operator reports. Figure 2 and Fig. 3 show the total fuel consumption and mission duration by merged operation category. Transit phases dominate the total fuel budget, whereas standby occupies the largest share of mission time but consumes relatively little fuel.

The relative contribution of each merged category to total daily fuel use is shown in Fig. 4. Port–Site Transit accounts for 48.1% of total fuel consumption, while Transit Between Turbines adds a further 25.9%. Together, these two transit categories represent 73.9% of total daily fuel use. Push operations are highly inefficient in distance-normalized terms, but their contribution to total fuel consumption is smaller because of their shorter duration.

Based on this finding, the predictive modeling stage of the study focuses specifically on transit operations. This scope is chosen because transit phases represent the most fuel-intensive part of the mission and therefore offer the greatest practical potential for fuel savings, emission reduction, and operational improvement. The remaining operational modes are retained for descriptive analysis of the mission profile but are not included in the model-development stage.

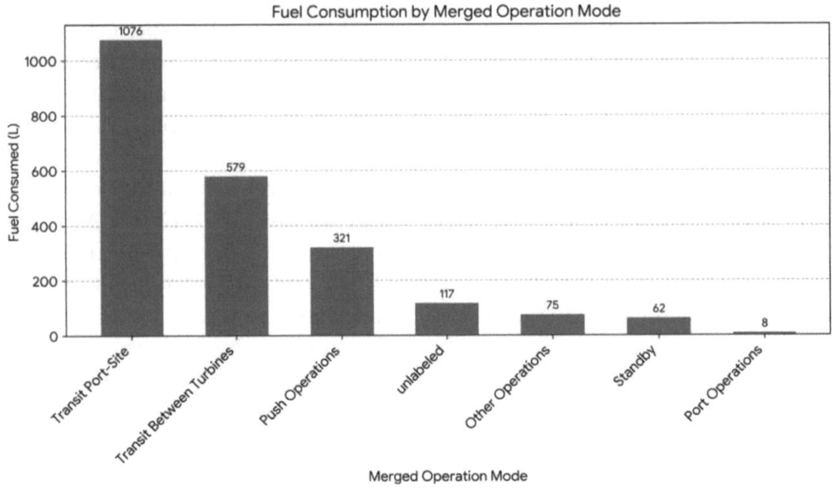

Fig. 2. Fuel consumption by merged operation category.

3.2 Transit Fuel-Rate Prediction Modeling

The objective of the supervised learning models is to predict the vessel's total fuel rate during transit operations, expressed in L/h, for each synchronized observation. The models do not directly predict total mission fuel consumption. Instead, predicted fuel rates can later be integrated over time to estimate fuel consumption for a transit leg or a complete mission:

$$\widehat{FC} = \sum_i \widehat{FR}_i \Delta t_i,$$

where $\widehat{FR}_i$ is the predicted fuel rate at observation i, and Δt_i is the corresponding time interval in hours.

The relationship between vessel speed and fuel rate during transit operations is examined using transit-related records collected from August to September 2024. Because the speed–fuel-rate relationship during transit is influenced by hydrodynamic resistance, weather conditions, and operational context, the analysis considers nonlinear and machine-learning-based approaches. A cubic polynomial model is used as a nonlinear benchmark and achieves an R^2 of 0.760 and an RMSE of 12.290 L/h, but it still struggles to capture the variability of transit fuel rate under changing environmental and operational conditions.

Support Vector Regression (SVR) with a radial basis function (RBF) kernel is also evaluated, but it performs poorly relative to the best alternatives, with higher prediction errors and weaker generalization. The analysis then moves to ensemble learning. The RF model is trained on 112,080 transit-related observations, which are split into 80% for training and 20% for testing. In addition, a separate validation set comprising 24,229 observations is used to further assess model performance. Although the analysis focuses only on transit operations, the

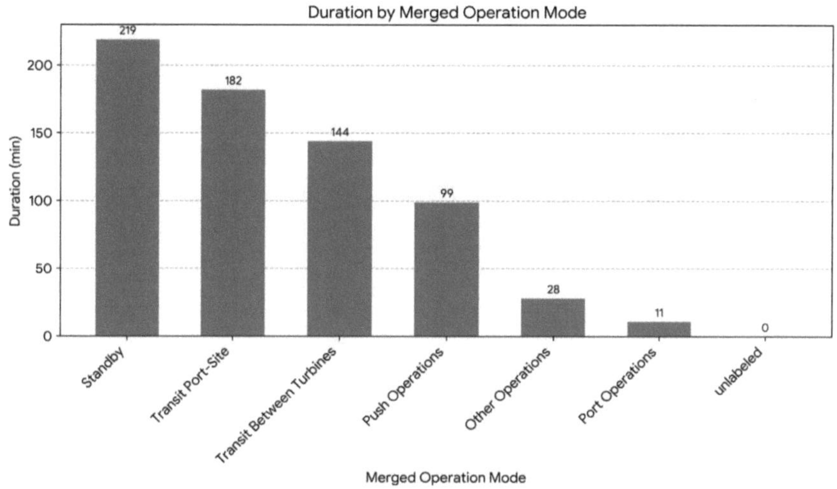

Fig. 3. Mission duration by merged operation category.

dataset still contains several transit subcategories, including port–site transit and Transit Between Turbines with and without technicians. Therefore, the operation mode code is retained to capture variation within transit activities. In addition to speed-based variables, the model includes speedoverground, speed_squared, speed_cubed, speed_category, and speed_x_mode; navigation-related variables including course, course_sin, and course_cos; and environmental variables including VHM0, VMDR, VHM0_WW, relative wave angle, directional wave force, and wave_angle_type. Among the evaluated models, RF achieves the best performance, with $R^2 = 0.857$, MAE = 3.412 l, and RMSE = 8.917 l. Although vessel speed is the dominant predictor, speed alone does not fully explain transit fuel-rate variation under changing operation modes and sea states. Therefore, the model includes speed-related variables, navigation variables, environmental variables, and operation-mode information. The model input variables are SOG, SOG^2, SOG^3, speed category, operation-mode code, the interaction between speed and operation mode, vessel course, sine and cosine transformations of course, VHM0, VMDR, VHM0_WW, relative wave angle, directional

Table 3. Performance of supervised fuel-rate prediction models for transit operations.

Model	MAE (L/h)	RMSE (L/h)	R^2
Cubic polynomial	11.297	12.290	0.760
SVR	18.423	25.123	0.678
Random Forest	**3.412**	**8.917**	**0.857**

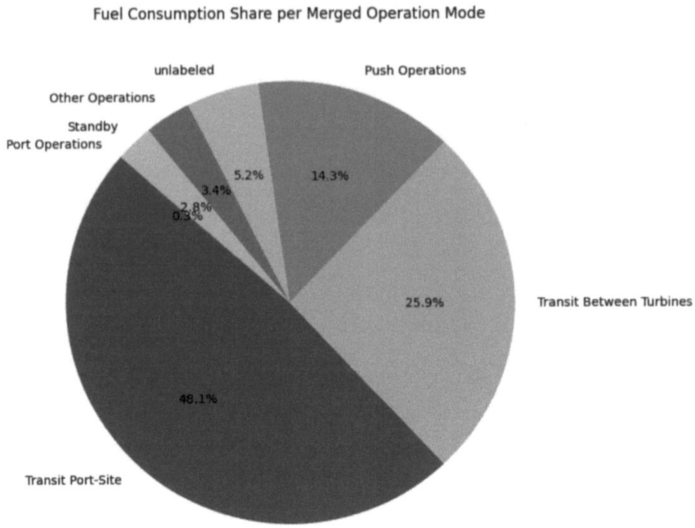

Fig. 4. Fuel consumption share by merged operation category.

wave force, and wave-angle type. The expected model output is the observed total fuel rate of the four main engines in L/h (Table 3).

3.3 Fuel and Emission Implications of Operational Categories

Based on the analyzed mission, the vessel consumed a total of 2238.6 l of fuel over 11.38 h, corresponding to an average consumption rate of approximately 196.7 l/h. Using the MGO emission factor of 2.73 kg CO_2/l, the total mission emissions are estimated at 6111.4 kg CO_2, equivalent to approximately 537.0 kg CO_2/h. The merged operational categories show that fuel use is highly concentrated in transit activities. Port–Site Transit consumed 1076 l, corresponding to 2937.5 kg CO_2, while Transit Between Turbines consumed 579 l, corresponding to 1580.7 kg CO_2. Together, these two transit categories account for 1655 l of fuel and 4518.2 kg CO_2, representing approximately 73.9% of total mission fuel use and emissions. By contrast, all non-transit categories combined account for only 583.6 l and 1593.2 kg CO_2, or about 26.1% of the total. Push operations consumed 321 l, equivalent to 876.3 kg CO_2, despite their relatively short duration. Standby accounted for only 62 l and 169.3 kg CO_2, while Port Operations contributed just 8 l and 21.8 kg CO_2. These results reinforce that the dominant opportunity for fuel and emission reduction lies in transit phases rather than in port or standby activities. These values represent a descriptive baseline for the scale of the fuel-saving opportunity. They should not be interpreted as direct outputs of the prediction model. For example, because transit activities consumed 1655 L of fuel in the analyzed mission, a hypothetical 5% reduction in measured transit fuel would correspond to 82.8 L of fuel and 225.9 kg CO_2, while a 10%

reduction would correspond to 165.5 L of fuel and 451.8 kg CO_2. These sensitivity values are included only to indicate the magnitude of potential savings. The predictive model is subsequently used to identify which operational and environmental variables should be considered when evaluating practical speed-selection and routing scenarios.

3.4 Feature Importance in Transit Fuel Prediction

The RF model interpreted in this section is the same fitted model evaluated in Sect. 3.2. Section 3.2 reports its predictive performance, whereas this section examines the relative contribution of the input variables to the model's transit fuel-rate predictions. No additional RF model is trained for the feature-importance analysis. The fitted model is analyzed using feature-importance values computed on the test set. The results, summarized in Table 4, show that vessel speed is by far the dominant predictor, followed by wave-related features.

Table 4. Random Forest feature importance on unseen transit test days.

Feature	Importance (%)
Speed (SOG)	77.6
Relative_wave_angle	10.1
Directional_wave_force	7.9
VMDR	1.6
VHM0_WW	1.4
VHM0	1.4

The feature-importance results should not be interpreted as a direct operational prescription, but as an indication of which variables are most relevant when evaluating alternative operating decisions. In practice, vessel speed is the main controllable variable, whereas wave height and wave direction are external conditions that cannot be changed directly. The trained model can therefore be used in a scenario-based manner: for a planned transit leg, the route, operation mode, and forecasted sea state are fixed, while alternative speed choices are evaluated and compared in terms of predicted fuel rate. Under adverse head-sea or bow-quartering conditions, the model supports lower speed settings or schedule adjustments when operational time windows allow. For inter-turbine movements, the same principle can support route sequencing by reducing unnecessary high-speed legs, especially when repeated legs are exposed to unfavorable relative wave angles. Thus, the practical value of the model is not that it confirms that lower speed reduces fuel use, but that it allows this speed–fuel trade-off to be evaluated conditionally under different wave and operational scenarios. Speed (SOG) alone explains 77.6% of the model's predictive importance, confirming that speed management is the primary operational element for reducing fuel consumption. Relative wave angle and directional wave force jointly contribute approximately 18%, showing that environmental conditions also shape vessel energy demand in a meaningful way. By contrast, the remaining wave descriptors have relatively minor marginal importance in the fitted model. These results suggest that fuel optimization efforts should focus first on speed selection and second on adapting operations to wave conditions. Possible actions include speed reduction under adverse conditions, improved mission timing, and route clustering to reduce unnecessary high-speed transit segments.

4 Conclusion

This study analyzed fuel consumption in OWF maintenance by integrating high-frequency engine logs, vessel trajectories, met-ocean data, and operator-reported activity labels. The results show that transit phases dominate total mission fuel use. Therefore, the predictive modeling stage focuses on transit operations, where the RF model provides the best fuel-rate prediction performance among the evaluated models. Speed-related variables explain most variance, while sea state and wave angle modulate fuel demand during transit. Operationally, the results suggest moderating speed in unfavorable sea states, clustering turbine visits to reduce long transits, and aligning departures with favorable wave directions to reduce fuel use, costs, and emissions. The findings are consistent with the offshore wind O&M literature, which identifies routing, weather windows, and vessel scheduling as important drivers of operational cost and emissions. However, the present study adds an activity-level empirical perspective by showing how fuel use is distributed across documented maintenance-operation phases using synchronized engine, navigation, met-ocean, and operator-report data. The results also support previous maritime fuel-consumption studies showing that the speed–fuel relationship is nonlinear and affected by environmental conditions. The contribution of the present work is therefore not the introduction of a new machine-learning algorithm, but the integration of operationally labeled vessel data with predictive modeling to identify where fuel-reduction efforts are most relevant in daily offshore wind maintenance missions.

The study has limitations: it is restricted to one vessel, operational context, and observation period, so generalization to other vessels, seasons, or wind farms should be cautious. The prediction target is short-horizon fuel rate, which must be integrated carefully when deriving daily totals or distance-normalized metrics. Low-speed or near-stationary activities can inflate liters-per-nautical-mile measures due to negligible distance accumulation.

Future work should extend validation across more vessels, farms, and seasons, apply leakage-safe temporal validation, quantify predictive uncertainty, benchmark additional models like gradient boosting, and complement feature importance analysis.

Acknowledgements. This research is funded by the Maritime Research Platform (MRP), A/S Dampskibsselskabet Orient's Fond. Furthermore, we thank the industrial partners for their availability, openness, and support.

References

1. Hadjoudj, Y., Pandit, R.: A review on data-centric decision tools for offshore wind operation and maintenance activities: challenges and opportunities. Energy Sci. Eng. (2022)
2. Tusar, M.I.H., Sarker, B.R.: Spare parts control strategies for offshore wind farms: a critical review and comparative study. Wind Eng. **46**(5), 1629–1656 (2022)
3. He, W., et al.: Accelerating efficient installation and optimization of battery energy storage system operations onboard vessels. Energies (2022)
4. Liu, L., Fu, Y., Ma, S., Huang, L., Wei, S., Pang, L.: Optimal scheduling strategy of operation and maintenance tasks for offhsore wind farm. IET Renew. Power Gener. (2019)
5. Baghizadeh, K., Pahl, J., Lützen, M., Rytter, N.G.M.: Using AIS data to analyze and optimize vessel operations for offshore wind farm maintenance. In: Spyrou, K.J., Themelis, N. (eds.) Innovations in Sustainable Maritime Technology—IMAM 2025, pp. 405–422. Springer Nature, Switzerland, Cham (2025)
6. Baumgärtner, D., Kaczenski, J.: Innovative benchmarking of offshore wind O&M strategies via AIS data analysis. J. Phys. Conf. Ser. (2024)
7. Kouloumpis, V., Azapagic, A.: A model for estimating life cycle environmental impacts of offshore wind electricity considering specific characteristics of wind farms. Sustain. Prod. Consumption (2022)
8. Zhao, C., Roberts, A., Cui, Y., Johanning, L.: Strategic deployment of service vessels for improved offshore wind farm maintenance and availability. Mar. Energy Res. (2024)
9. Taboada, J.V., Díaz-Casás, V., Yu, X.: Reliability and maintenance management analysis on offshore wind turbines. Energies (2021)
10. Lazakis, I., Khan, S.: An optimization framework for daily route planning and scheduling of maintenance vessel activities in offshore wind farms. Ocean Eng. **225**, 108752 (2021)

Energy Demand in Inland Waterway Transport Under Hydrodynamic Variability on the Rhine

Maryam Pourbeirami Hir[1(✉)], Floor P. Bakker[1], Alex Kirichek[1], Fedor Baart[1,2], and Mark van Koningsveld[1,3]

[1] Section of Rivers and Ports, Department of Hydraulic Engineering, Faculty of Civil Engineering and Geosciences, Delft University of Technology, Stevinweg 1, 2628 CN Delft, The Netherlands
m.pourbeiramihir@tudelft.nl
[2] Rijkswaterstaat, P.O. Box 2232, 3500 GE Utrecht, The Netherlands
[3] Van Oord Dredging and Marine Contractors B.V., Schaardijk 211, P.O. Box 8574, 3063 NH Rotterdam, The Netherlands

Abstract. Decarbonisation of inland waterway transport requires reliable estimates of propulsion energy use to support the design of zero-emission bunkering infrastructure. Existing approaches rely on averaged or static representations of energy demand, which fail to capture how vessel operations and waterway conditions interact along a corridor. As a result, peak energy requirements and their spatial concentration are systematically underestimated, leading to suboptimal infrastructure planning.

To address this, the study reconstructs vessel movements along the Rotterdam-Basel corridor using empirical trip data and observed hydrodynamic conditions for 2024. A discrete-event simulation is used to represent vessel operations, and battery-electric and hydrogen propulsion systems are evaluated under identical traffic and environmental conditions.

The results show that energy demand is a state-dependent outcome that varies along the corridor rather than a fixed vessel characteristic. Hydrodynamic properties, in particular current velocity, create a spatially heterogeneous demand pattern in which distinct waterway segments consistently concentrate energy use. Under adverse current velocities, these segments exhibit non-linear increases in propulsion requirements and define the upper bounds of corridor energy demand.

These findings show that average-based approaches fail to capture corridor-level properties and underestimate the infrastructure required to ensure operational feasibility. Corridor performance is governed by recurrent high-demand segments rather than mean energy use, suggesting that bunkering infrastructure planning should account for these recurrent high-demand locations rather than rely only on uniform spacing along the corridor.

J. de Armas and E. Lalla Ruiz (Eds.): LOGMS 2026, LNCS 16679, pp. 156–166, 2027.
https://doi.org/10.1007/978-3-032-30795-8_14

Keywords: Discrete-Event Simulation · Corridor Analysis · Transport Network Modelling · Energy Transition · IWT

1 Introduction

Recent maritime decarbonisation studies link fuel-use estimation with optimisation for strategic transition planning [1]. While these approaches integrate energy modelling with long-term fleet decisions, they primarily address seagoing vessels. Inland waterway transport (IWT) requires a complementary corridor-scale formulation as propulsion demand depends on current velocity, water depth, sailing direction, and vessel-waterway interaction. On the Rhine, discharge-driven changes in water levels, navigability, loading capacity, and vessel deployment redistribute transport effort along the corridor [2,3]. For zero-emission inland shipping, this redistribution is critical since charging and bunkering infrastructure need to be aligned with spatial and temporal concentrations of energy demand.

Most existing studies assess propulsion performance at the vessel level, where energy use is derived from technical characteristics under simplified or averaged conditions. These approaches typically neglect spatial variability in hydrodynamics and operational asymmetries between upstream and downstream sailing. As a result, they do not capture how river conditions and traffic dynamics shape energy demand at the corridor scale. In our earlier work, we developed a conceptual framework linking upstream energy supply with downstream demand for inland bunkering networks [4] and a simulation–optimisation framework for multi-fuel bunkering station siting along the Rotterdam–Mannheim corridor [5]. The latter, however, was based on a single-day snapshot under moderate discharge and did not account for current-induced variability in propulsion demand, which is the focus of the present paper. On the Rhine, this is particularly relevant, as discharge variations from tidal influence in the lower river to low-water constraints upstream affect sailing conditions and vessel deployment. Fuel consumption should therefore be understood as the result of the interaction between vessel characteristics, such as size and draught, together with propulsion configuration, and the waterway conditions along the corridor. Approaches based on averaged conditions consequently underestimate both peak demand and its spatial concentration.

This paper addresses this gap by answering the following research question: *How do hydrodynamic properties and vessel characteristics affect vessel energy use and sailing range at the corridor scale?* To this end, vessel movements along the Rotterdam-Basel corridor are simulated using a discrete-event model based on OpenTNSim for battery-electric and hydrogen propulsion. The analysis is conducted under spatial variations in water depth and current velocity. This approach enables the quantification of energy use along vessel trajectories and the assessment of how hydrodynamic conditions influence propulsion requirements across the corridor. The results provide insights into how variability in river conditions translates into spatial and temporal patterns of energy demand, providing a basis for infrastructure planning that reflects the dynamic nature of IWT systems.

2 System and Method

The modelling framework combines the waterway network, hydrodynamic conditions, and fleet data. These inputs are integrated within a discrete-event simulation to estimate energy use along the Rhine corridor (Fig. 1). Vessels are simulated along predefined routes, where local sailing conditions determine the resistance they experience. This resistance defines the propulsion power required to maintain motion, which is converted into energy use based on propulsion system characteristics.

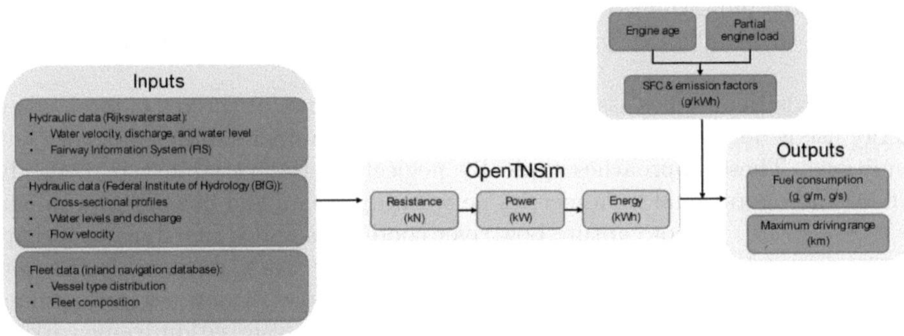

Fig. 1. Modelling framework linking the waterway network, hydrodynamic properties, and fleet data to energy use estimation. Vessel trajectories are simulated to compute resistance, propulsion power, and resulting energy consumption, enabling the assessment of sailing range along the corridor.

Vessel resistance follows Holtrop and Mennen [6], decomposing total resistance into frictional, wave, appendage, and residual components:

$$R_T = R_f(1 + k_1) + R_w + R_{app} + R_{res}. \tag{1}$$

The block coefficient is fixed at $C_B = 0.85$ (the upper applicability limit of the method) and the bulbous bow cross-section is set to zero, following standard practice for inland vessels. Frictional resistance is $R_f = \frac{1}{2}\rho_w V_s'^2 C_f S$, with C_f corrected for shallow-water effects [7] and wetted surface S [6]. The hull form factor $(1 + k_1)$ follows Watson [8]. Wave resistance accounts for shallow-water acceleration via the Karpov method [9], where the depth Froude number $Fr_h = V_s/\sqrt{gh_0}$ and depth-to-draught ratio h_0/D_s jointly determine the speed-correction coefficient α^{**} and the corrected ship speed V_s/α^{**}.

Current velocity U_c denotes the undisturbed current along the sailing direction. Positive values indicate favourable current and negative values indicate adverse current. Ship speed over ground is denoted by V_g, and ship speed through water is $V_s' = V_g - U_c$. This ship speed through water replaces V_s in the resistance terms. Brake power follows from inverting the propulsion-line efficiency chain [10]:

$$P_b = \frac{V_s' \, R_T}{\eta_o \, \eta_r \, \eta_h \, \eta_g \, \eta_t}, \tag{2}$$

with $\eta_g = 0.96$, $\eta_t = 0.98$, $\eta_r \approx 1.0$, and $\eta_o \in [0.55, 0.70]$. Hull efficiency is $\eta_h = (1-t)/(1-w)$, with wake fraction w [9] and thrust deduction $t = 0.6w(1 + 0.67w)$ for single-screw vessels. Hotel power is $P_{hotel} = 0.05\, P_{installed}$ [10], giving $P_{total} = P_b + P_{hotel}$.

Edge-level energy intensity is:

$$e_{i,e,p} = \frac{1}{\eta_{PS,p}\, V_{g,i,e}} \left[\frac{V_{s,i,e}' \, R_{T,i,e}}{\eta_o \eta_r \eta_h \eta_g \eta_t} + P_{hotel,i} \right], \tag{3}$$

where i, e, and p denote vessel, edge, and propulsion system, respectively. $V_{g,i,e}$ is speed over ground, $V_{s,i,e}' = V_{g,i,e} - U_c$ is ship speed through water, and $\eta_{PS,p}$ is propulsion-system conversion efficiency. Results are reported in kWh/km. For battery-electric propulsion, $\eta_{PS,batt} \approx 0.85$, accounting for battery, inverter, and motor losses, with a usable pack energy density of 160 Wh/kg. The model also reports the required electrical energy and the corresponding number of 2000 kWh battery-container equivalents. For hydrogen propulsion, $\eta_{PS,H_2} \approx 0.50$, accounting for PEM fuel-cell and motor losses, with a lower heating value of 33.3 kWh/kg and tank gravimetric storage of 5.7 wt% at 350 bar. Hydrogen demand is converted from the simulated energy requirement using the PEM fuel-cell representation in OpenTNSim and reported in kg.

The Rhine corridor is represented as a directed graph derived from Fairway Information Services (FIS) and European River Information Services (ERIS) network data, with 358 nodes at waterway locations and 716 edges defining navigable segments. The MATROOS database (Rijkswaterstaat) provides time-series water levels, current velocity, and discharge at fixed stations along the river. Steady-state profiles from the German Federal Institute of Hydrology (BfG), derived from a 1D SOBEK hydrodynamic model at approximately 100 m intervals, complement this with discharge-specific hydraulic conditions. Both datasets provide depth-averaged current velocities. A comparison with point measurements in the fairway indicates that depth-averaged values underestimate fairway current velocities by approximately 20%.

Three discharge scenarios (low, medium, high) are defined based on Lobith gauge conditions. Current-velocity magnitude and current direction are treated separately: in fluvial sections, flow is directed seaward; in tidal sections, direction depends on tidal phase (ebb or flood). Hydrodynamic properties are assigned at the node level and transferred to edges through spatial aggregation. Water depth along each edge is derived from Covadem bathymetric data, capturing spatial variation in under-keel clearance along the corridor. This allows resistance to respond to local depth conditions in addition to current velocity. In the tidal reaches, most observations correspond to the low-discharge scenario.

Medium-discharge values were interpolated from neighbouring stations within 5 km, introducing additional uncertainty in absolute magnitudes that does not affect the spatial identification of high-demand reaches.

Vessel data are derived from Inland Vessel Statistics (IVS, Rijkswaterstaat), covering origin–destination (OD) pairs, vessel characteristics, and trip timestamps for 2024. After cleaning and deduplication, approximately 265,000 trips are retained. OD pairs are mapped to network nodes, and routes are assigned using the shortest path with vessel-class compatibility according to the Conférence Européenne des Ministres des Transports (CEMT) classification. A limited number of vessel classes account for most corridor activity: M8 (97,606 trips), M6 (41,069), M9 (17,309), M3 (14,569), and M2 (13,335). Together, these classes represent approximately 70% of the cleaned trip sample; the remaining trips correspond to less common classes and are retained in the simulation. Speed over ground is derived from the Automatic Identification System (AIS) dataset combined with reconstructed route distances and, together with the local current velocity, yields the ship speed through water used in the resistance calculations.

The study focuses on hydrodynamic variability rather than on the independent effect of payload. Loaded and unloaded movements are retained in the traffic sample, but the same loading representation is applied across all hydrodynamic scenarios. This design keeps the fleet and traffic composition constant, so differences between scenarios reflect the effect of current velocity and waterway conditions rather than changes in payload.

3 Results and Discussion

Figure 2 shows energy use per kilometre as a non-linear, asymmetric function of current velocity for vessels sailing along the Rotterdam-Basel corridor. Under adverse current, energy use increases steeply, while under favourable current it falls more gradually.

The response can be approximated as a quadratic in current velocity:

$$E/\Delta x = a_0 + a_1 U_c + a_2 U_c^2, \tag{4}$$

where a_0 represents the baseline energy use at zero current, a_1 captures the directional asymmetry between favourable and adverse current, and a_2 reflects the non-linear $V_s'^2$ dependence of frictional and wave resistance, which propagates through Eqs. (1)–(2). The negative sign of a_1 and the positive sign of a_2 are preserved across vessel classes, so vessel geometry, draught, and operating speed scale the magnitude of the response without altering its dependence on U_c. The residual spread around the fitted curve reflects vessel heterogeneity in geometry, representative draught, and operating speed, which set the baseline level of energy use for each vessel.

The mechanism behind this asymmetry becomes clearer when current velocity is examined jointly with water depth (Fig. 3). Under favourable current, energy use decreases at a similar rate across all depths, and the three depth curves nearly coincide. Under adverse current, the response depends strongly

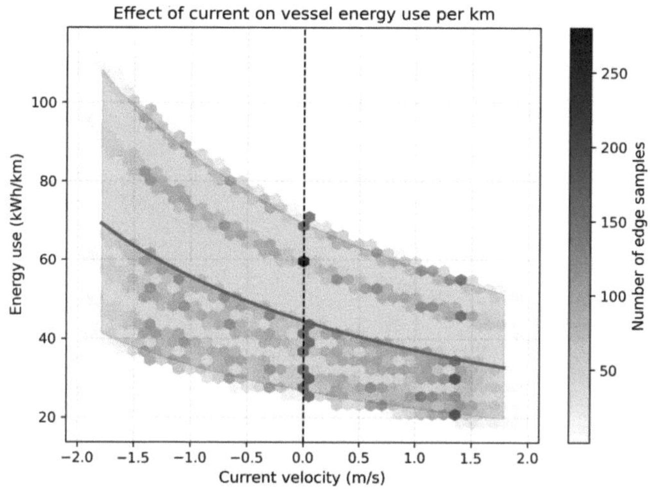

Fig. 2. Energy use per kilometre as a function of current velocity. The vertical dashed line marks neutral current. The fitted relationship is non-linear and asymmetric, with energy demand increasing sharply under adverse current and declining more gradually under favourable current. Hexagonal shading indicates the number of vessel-edge observations in each bin; the shaded band reflects variability across vessel classes.

on depth: at $h = 20$ m and $h = 8$ m the curves rise smoothly with current magnitude, whereas at $h = 4.5$ m the curve diverges sharply above approximately 1 m/s, reflecting the compounding effect of shallow-water resistance and increased ship speed through water. The asymmetry in Fig. 2 therefore originates not only from current direction but from the interaction between adverse current and limited under-keel clearance, which jointly amplify resistance non-linearly.

Corridor energy demand must be modelled as a state-dependent response, with current velocity and water depth jointly setting the baseline and vessel characteristics shaping the size of the effect. Operating speed and loading condition (represented through CEMT class, draught, and installed power) determine the baseline energy level for each vessel, while current velocity is the dominant source of corridor-scale *variability* in per-kilometre energy use.

Figure 4 translates this state-dependent response to the corridor scale. The two panels separate upstream sailing (Rotterdam to Basel) from downstream sailing (Basel to Rotterdam), and each panel shows the three discharge scenarios under both ebb and flood tidal phases. The directional contrast between the two panels is the most prominent feature: upstream sailing produces substantially higher and more variable energy demand than downstream sailing, confirming at the corridor scale the asymmetric response observed in Fig. 2.

The spatial pattern is consistent across discharge scenarios. Several reaches recur as local maxima, including the section around Kaub in the Middle Rhine and the lower-corridor reach approaching Rotterdam. In the upper Rhine between Iffezheim and Mainz, low-discharge conditions produce locally elevated

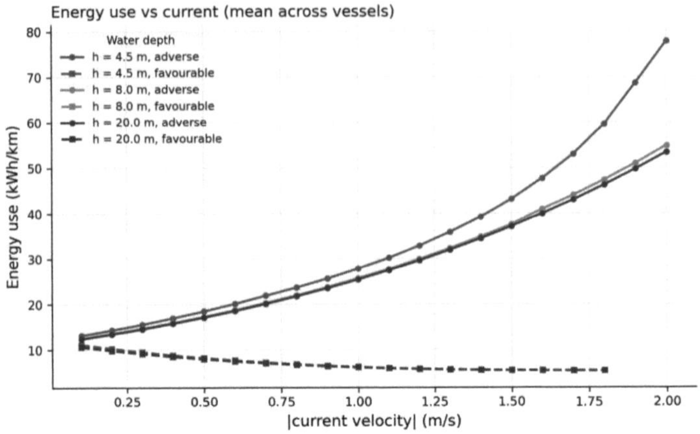

Fig. 3. Energy use per kilometre as a function of absolute current velocity, separated by water depth ($h = 4.5$, 8.0, and 20.0 m) and current direction (solid: adverse, dashed: favourable). Under favourable current, energy use is largely insensitive to depth. Under adverse current, the shallow-water case ($h = 4.5$ m) diverges sharply from deeper conditions, showing the compounding effect of shallow water and adverse current.

energy demand even though discharge is low, consistent with the depth effect identified in Fig. 3. Discharge therefore does not shift the location of the critical reaches, but it reshapes their intensity, with high-discharge ebb conditions producing the sharpest upstream peaks. The downstream panel remains comparatively flat over most of the route, but the tidal reach near Rotterdam exhibits sharp local spikes under flood conditions, where tidal current reverses against the sailing direction.

Figure 5 isolates the low-discharge scenario to compare favourable and adverse currents along the same corridor. The two trajectories are not separated by a constant offset; the gap changes along the river kilometres, and local extremes do not align between the two directions. Peaks under adverse current are not mirrored by equivalent reductions under favourable current. Each trajectory responds differently to the same spatial setting, reflecting a non-linear interaction between current direction, hydrodynamic properties of the waterway, and vessel operations. The effect of current is therefore not a simple reversal but a location-specific process.

These reaches act as operational bottlenecks that determine the maximum energy demand along the route. A corridor may look manageable on the basis of average energy use while still containing a few hydraulically demanding reaches that dominate propulsion requirements. Approaches based only on uniform spacing of charging or bunkering infrastructure may miss precisely these reaches; infrastructure planning should therefore consider the recurrence, location, and severity of high-demand reaches rather than rely on average conditions alone.

Figure 6 translates this corridor structure into the system-level constraint that ultimately governs operations: maximum sailing range. Range is a state-

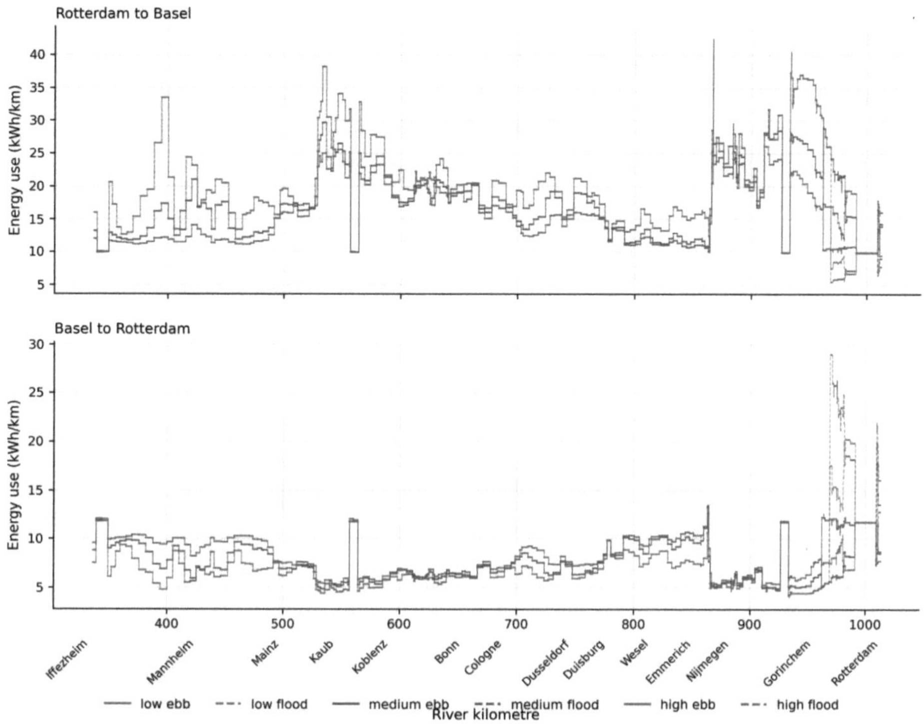

Fig. 4. Spatial distribution of energy use per kilometre along the Rhine corridor under low, medium, and high discharge conditions for both ebb and flood tidal phases. The upper panel shows upstream sailing from Rotterdam to Basel; the lower panel shows downstream sailing from Basel to Rotterdam. Hydrodynamic forcing generates persistent high-demand segments whose location is consistent across scenarios, while their intensity varies with discharge.

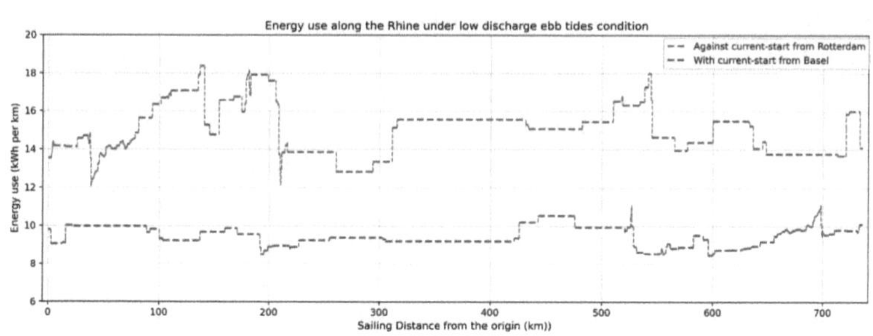

Fig. 5. Energy use per kilometre along the corridor under low discharge and ebb conditions, comparing favourable and adverse flow. Segment-specific divergence reveals persistent high-demand reaches where adverse flow amplifies propulsion requirements non-uniformly along the corridor.

dependent outcome shaped by propulsion technology and current velocity, not an intrinsic vessel characteristic. Across all vessel classes, sailing range is higher under favourable current than under adverse current, but the effect is not symmetric: the loss in range under adverse current is larger than the gain under favourable current. Adverse current therefore becomes the binding condition, defining the minimum achievable range and the effective operating envelope.

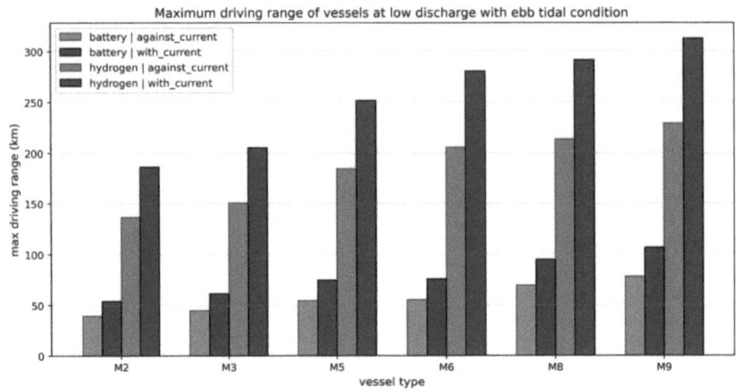

Fig. 6. Maximum sailing range for battery-electric and hydrogen vessels across vessel classes under low discharge and ebb tides. Differences between favourable and adverse current velocity illustrate the asymmetric impact of hydrodynamic properties on propulsion feasibility and sailing range.

The contrast between battery-electric and hydrogen propulsion is both quantitative and structural. Battery-electric vessels have shorter ranges and are more sensitive to adverse currents, so local peaks in energy demand translate directly into operational constraints. Hydrogen systems provide a wider feasibility envelope, and their greater onboard energy capacity buffers the effect of local demand peaks. That advantage does not remove the underlying asymmetry; however, smaller vessels and battery-electric systems remain especially sensitive to the location of charging or bunkering infrastructure. Increasing vessel size extends sailing range but does not change the structure of the constraint; high-demand reaches still define the effective operational limit.

These results point to different infrastructure logic for the two propulsion systems. Battery-electric operation would likely require a denser and more spatially responsive network, because feasibility is repeatedly constrained by local energy peaks. Hydrogen operation may allow a sparser network, but one that depends more heavily on the correct placement of fewer high-capacity nodes. The difference lies not only in the number of facilities required, but also in how hydrodynamic variability translates into network vulnerability.

4 Conclusion

Using 2024 empirical traffic and hydrodynamic data, this study develops a corridor-scale framework that explains how hydrodynamic variability, water depth, vessel characteristics, and propulsion-specific energy demand interact in IWT. The results show that energy demand is strongly state-dependent. Variations in current velocity affect energy intensity in asymmetric and non-linear ways, with the asymmetry driven jointly by current direction and water depth: shallow conditions and adverse current compound to amplify resistance non-linearly, while favourable current produces a smaller and depth-insensitive reduction. At the corridor scale, this state-dependent response concentrates demand along recurrent reaches whose location is consistent across discharge scenarios and whose intensity increases under adverse conditions. Infrastructure requirements are therefore shaped less by average demand than by the recurrence, location, and severity of these local bottlenecks.

Propulsion feasibility is likewise shaped by system state. Battery-electric systems are more constrained by limited sailing range and greater exposure to local demand peaks, pointing to a denser and more spatially responsive infrastructure network. Hydrogen systems offer a wider operational envelope but do not eliminate the underlying spatial variability; they shift infrastructure needs towards fewer but higher-capacity facilities. These differences point to distinct planning logics that cannot be captured through aggregate demand estimates or steady-state assumptions alone.

Several limitations point to natural extensions of this work. Payload is not modelled as an independent dynamic variable and the simplified loading representation supports comparison across hydrodynamic scenarios, but future work should incorporate trip-level payload and loading-dependent speed choices to separate payload effects from hydrodynamic effects more explicitly. Moreover, infrastructure placement is not optimised in this study. Facility siting under the identified high-demand reaches, including capacity sizing and queuing constraints, is a natural extension.

Acknowledgments. This research was conducted within the PATH2ZERO project, financed by the NWA L2-Thema 2020 Zero Emission Shipping (ZES) program of the Netherlands Organisation for Scientific Research (NWO), Grant NWA.1439.20.00.

Disclosure of Interests. The authors have no competing interests to declare that are relevant to the content of this article.

References

1. Zhou, L., Jin, J.G., Gao, Y., Iris, Ç., Bektaş, T., Chen, J.H.: Techno-economic optimization for containership green transition under net-zero emission target: a predict-then-optimize framework. Transp. Res. Part E Logistics Transp. Rev. **209**, 104731 (2026). https://doi.org/10.1016/j.tre.2026.104731
2. Vinke, F., Turpijn, B., van Gelder, P., van Koningsveld, M.: Inland shipping response to discharge extremes: a 10 years case study of the Rhine. Clim. Risk Manag. **43**, 100578 (2024)
3. Bakker, F.P., van der Werff, S., Baart, F., Kirichek, A., de Jong, S., van Koningsveld, M.: Port accessibility depends on cascading interactions between fleets, policies, infrastructure, and hydrodynamics. J. Mar. Sci. Eng. **12**(6), 1006 (2024)

4. Pourbeirami Hir, M., Kirichek, A., Pourmohammad-Zia, N., Jiang, M., van Koningsveld, M.: Zero-emission fueling infrastructure for IWT: optimizing the connection between upstream energy supply and downstream energy demand. In: Proceedings of the 4th International Conference on Modelling and Optimisation of Ship Energy Systems (MOSES 2023). TU Delft OPEN Publishing (2023)
5. Pourbeirami Hir, M., Kirichek, A., Pourmohammad-Zia, N., van Koningsveld, M.: Simulation-optimisation framework for multi-fuel bunkering in zero-emission inland waterway transport. In: Proceedings of the 16th International Conference on Computational Logistics (ICCL 2025). Springer (in press)
6. Holtrop, J., Mennen, G.G.J.: An approximate power prediction method. Int. Shipbuild. Prog. **29**(335), 166–170 (1982)
7. Zeng, Q., Thill, C., Hekkenberg, R., Rotteveel, E.: A method to determine the frictional resistance of inland ships in shallow water. Ocean Eng. **159**, 353–365 (2018)
8. Watson, D.G.M.: Practical Ship Design. Elsevier (1998)
9. Van Terwisga, T.: Weerstand en voortstuwing van bakken: een literatuurstudie, MARIN Report (1989)
10. van Koningsveld, M., Verheij, H.J., Taneja, P., de Vriend, H.J.: Ports and Waterways: Navigating the Changing World. TU Delft Open (2023)

Maritime Networks, Routing, and Hinterland Logistics

Container Management in the Norwegian Aluminium Industry: A Multi-commodity Network Flow Approach

Lukas Georg Österlin Dalhaug[1], Tobias Schwabe Jortveit[1], Didrik Næss[1], and Peter Schütz[1,2](✉)

[1] Department of Industrial Economics and Technology Management, Norwegian University of Science and Technology, Trondheim, Norway
peter.schutz@nhh.no

[2] Department of Business and Management Science, NHH Norwegian School of Economics, Bergen, Norway

Abstract. In this case study, we analyze the container logistics of a Norwegian aluminium producer. In particular we are interested in the necessary size of the fleet of containers and how different factors such as the initial number of containers, available vessel capacity and handling efficiency impact the overall costs of the system. The problem is formulated as a deterministic multi-commodity, multi-period network flow model and applied to the maritime logistics network of a Norwegian aluminum producer. The network consists of five production plants and eight European ports that are connected through shipping routes with regular schedules. The containers are used to transport different raw materials and byproducts and share vessel capacity with finished products. Our results indicate that number of available containers and efficient handling operations have a larger impact on the aluminium producer's overall costs than available vessel capacity.

Keywords: Container logistics · Multi-commodity network flow · Maritime transportation

1 Introduction

The global aluminium market is highly competitive with producers focussing on cost efficiency along the entire value chain. Aluminium producers are therefore increasingly paying more attention to the efficiency of their logistics operations to maintain cost discipline. In 2021, Hydro standardized its material transport by introducing RoRo ("Roll-on/Roll-off") vessels between the Norwegian production plants and European ports. The vessels operate with weekly schedules and mainly transport finished goods on cassettes from the production plants to the European ports and return to the production plants with raw materials in containers, sent from the European ports, but also in between the production plants. Overall, the transportation network must balance the flow of more than

J. de Armas and E. Lalla Ruiz (Eds.): LOGMS 2026, LNCS 16679, pp. 169–180, 2027.
https://doi.org/10.1007/978-3-032-30795-8_15

1.1 million tonnes of primary aluminium against the flow of containers with raw materials and byproducts, while observing vessel routes and schedules as well as vessel capacity and access to containers.

Container logistics, in particular empty container repositioning (ECR), is well explored in operations research. Recent comprehensive reviews document extensive work on network flow models, stochastic formulations, and robust optimization approaches primarily from shipping line and port operator perspectives [1,2]. Notable contributions include multi-commodity time-space network formulations [3,4] and a heterogeneous fleet positioning model [5]. More recently, uncertain demand has been included in the analysis, see e.g. [6]. However, one aspect is often overlooked: existing literature predominantly addresses ECR from the viewpoint of shipping companies or port operators whose core business involves container leasing and transportation. The perspective of an industrial producer, managing a fleet of containers in support of her own operations remains largely unexplored. With the case study presented in this paper, we aim to highlight some aspects that are of interest to an industrial producer.

The motivation for our research emerges from Hydro's operational challenges, increasing cost and environmental pressures. The company's Norwegian plants operate within a tightly interconnected logistics network where the flow of containers with raw materials and byproducts competes for limited vessel space with outbound finished products. Current manual planning processes cause several inefficiencies: a high proportion of empty container movements due to rigid flow structures and planning approaches focussing primarily on feasibility rather than cost optimization. In this study we aim to answer the following main questions

(1) Is Hydro's current fleet of containers sufficient to handle the necessary flow of raw materials and byproducts? In particular, is there an undersupply of specific container types?
(2) How sensitive are total costs and network decisions to key parameters such as number of available containers, vessel capacity and handling efficiency?

To answer these questions, we formulate a deterministic, multi-commodity network flow model. The model optimizes container movements across Hydro's five Norwegian plants and eight European ports over a 13-week planning horizon, accounting for heterogeneous container types with specific commodity mappings, explicit filling and emptying times, vessel scheduling and capacity constraints, trucking alternatives, storage limitations, and the option to purchase additional containers if necessary. We apply the model to a case study based on Hydro's real-world operations to provide answers to the research questions outlined above. In particular, we find that certain container types in Hydro's fleet are systematically undersupplied, while others appear to be in oversupply. Handling efficiency emerges as a critical cost driver. The results indicate that costs increase considerably if turnaround time surpasses 7 days. Vessel capacity on the other hand only shows limited impact on total costs, with even a 75% reduction in southbound capacity causing only a 4.8% increase in costs.

The remainder of this paper is structured as follows: In Sect. 2, we provide a more formal description of our problem. The mathematical model is presented in Sect. 3, before we introduce our case study in Sect. 4. The results are presented and discussed in Sect. 5. We conclude in Sect. 6.

2 Problem Description

We model the maritime transportation network and container flows as a multi-commodity network flow problem, including transshipments and capacity constraints over a finite planning horizon. The objective of the problem is to minimize the costs of satisfying demand. The problem focuses on the operational aspects of Hydro's operations, so factors such as vessel routes, vessel capacities, or plant production volumes cannot be modified.

The container transportation network consists of ports and routes. The set of ports comprises production plants as well as the shipping ports. Each port has a demand for containers of certain states (filled with a commodity or empty) and generates a supply of the opposite type after the required containers have been filled or emptied. Raw materials can be transported from any port to any port, whereas byproducts need to be transported from production ports to shipping ports. This drives the flow of containers through the network. Demand must be satisfied at all times. Ports can store only a limited number of containers and incur a holding cost per container. This storage capacity cannot be exceeded. Containers can be loaded and unloaded at all ports.

Containers are transported between ports by vessels. The vessels operate on fixed routes that follow weekly or biweekly schedules. Each route consists of a sequence of individual shipment legs between two ports. Each route has a fixed schedule where each leg departs at the same time in every round trip. The available vessel capacity for containers may vary on the same leg across different departures. Available vessel capacity cannot be exceeded. Each leg along a route is associated with a transportation cost per container.

Truck transportation is available as a supplementary transportation mode if shipping of containers is not possible. Trucks are assumed to be available at all times and in unlimited quantity. However, trucking is restricted to routes between production ports in Norway. Thus, none of the shipping ports are accessible by truck. Each truck can carry two standard container units, and all possible truck legs have an associated cost proportional to the distance traveled. This cost is always higher per container than transport by vessel.

There is an initial fleet of containers, but it is possible to buy additional containers. It is only possible to acquire new containers at the start of the planning period, but the purchased containers may become part of the container fleet throughout the planning period. These containers are assumed to be available in unlimited supply but are associated with a purchasing cost. All containers can be placed anywhere at the start of the planning period.

We consider a heterogeneous fleet of containers that are suitable for one or more commodities. Some containers can be used for transporting multiple commodities, whereas others can only transport one commodity. Note that a container can only carry one commodity at a time, i.e., commodities cannot be mixed in containers. Containers may however transport different commodities across different shipment legs, as long as they have been emptied and refilled in between. Whenever a container is filled with a commodity, Hydro incurs a filling cost. This cost represents the procurement or disposal cost of the commodity the container is filled with. We assume that the cost of emptying a container is zero. The emptying or filling of a container requires a handling time before the container becomes available again. The duration of this handling time can depend on the container type, the commodity it has carried, and the port where it is handled.

The planning horizon is divided into discrete time periods, with each day consisting of two periods of equal, 12 h durations. A vessel always arrives, unloads and/or loads, and departs within a single time period.

The overall objective of the problem is to minimize the costs related to the movement and storage of containers in the network. Costs originate from shipments of containers by vessel and truck, handling and storage of containers at both production plants and shipping ports, and purchasing of additional containers.

3 Model Formulation

We formulate the problem using a time-space network. The nodes of the network are thus combinations of ports and time periods. We distinguish between four types of arcs; shipping-, trucking-, storage-, and handling-arcs. Shipping- and trucking-arcs enables transport from one location to another across time and space. Storage- and handling-arcs enables movement only across time. Handling arcs have the special property of converting containers from one container type to another.

3.1 Notation

We first introduce the notation used in our model

Sets

$\mathcal{A}$	Set of arcs, $\mathcal{A} = \mathcal{A}^S \cup \mathcal{A}^T \cup \mathcal{A}^L \cup \mathcal{A}^H$
$\mathcal{A}^S$	Set of shipping arcs, $\{(p,t),(q,t+T^V_{pq})\}, p,q \in \mathcal{P}, t, t+T^V_{pq} \in \mathcal{T}$
$\mathcal{A}^T$	Set of trucking arcs, $\{(p,t),(q,t+T^T_{pq})\}, p,q, \in \mathcal{P}^P, t, t+T^T_{pq} \in \mathcal{T}$
$\mathcal{A}^L$	Set of storage arcs, $\{(p,t),(p,t+1)\}, p \in \mathcal{P}, t, t+1 \in \mathcal{T}$
$\mathcal{A}^H$	Set of handling arcs, $\{(p,t),(p,t+H^{cd}_p)\}, p \in \mathcal{P}, t, t+H^{cd}_p \in \mathcal{T}$
$\mathcal{C}$	Set of container types, $\mathcal{C} = \mathcal{C}^E \cup \mathcal{C}^F$
$\mathcal{C}^E$	Subset of empty container types, $\mathcal{C}^E \subset \mathcal{C}$
$\mathcal{C}^F$	Subset of full container types, $\mathcal{C}^F \subset \mathcal{C}$
$\mathcal{N}$	Set of nodes, $\{i = (p,t)\}, p \in \mathcal{P}, t \in \mathcal{T}$

$\mathcal{N}^1$	Subset of initial nodes, $\{i = (p, 1)\}, p \in \mathcal{P}$
$\mathcal{P}$	Set of ports
$\mathcal{P}^P$	Subset of production plants, $\mathcal{P}^P \subset \mathcal{P}$
$\mathcal{T}$	Set of time steps

Parameters

B^j	Maximum percentage of containers that can be filled at port j.
C^F	Cost of filling a container
C^L_{ci}	Cost of storing a container of type c at node i
C^P	Cost of purchasing a container
C^T_{ij}	Cost of trucking a container from node i to j
C^V_{ij}	Cost of shipping a container from node i to j
D^{cd}_{ij}	Demand for containers of type c in node i to be converted to type d in node j
F^c	Footprint of container type c
H^{cd}_p	Time to convert container of type c to type d at node p
I^L_i	Maximum storage capacity at node i
I^S_{ij}	Maximum shipping capacity from node i to j
M^c	Number of owned containers of type c
M^c_i	Maximum number of containers of type c in node $i \in \mathcal{N}^1$
T^T_{pq}	Travel time between port p and q for trucks
T^V_{pq}	Travel time between port p and q for vessels

Decision Variables

b^{cd}_{ij}	Containers of type c to convert (fill/empty) to type d from node i to j
d^c_i	Containers of type c to place in initial node $i \in \mathcal{N}^1$
e^c_i	Containers of type c to purchase and place in initial node $i \in \mathcal{N}^1$
x^c_{ij}	Containers of type c to ship from node i to j
y^c_{ij}	Containers of type c to truck from node i to j
z^c_{ij}	Containers of type c to store from node i to j

3.2 Mathematical Model

We now formulate our multi-commodity network flow problem. The model is given as

$$\min \sum_{c \in \mathcal{C}} \sum_{(i,j) \in \mathcal{A}^S} C^V_{ij} \cdot x^c_{ij} + \sum_{c \in \mathcal{C}} \sum_{(i,j) \in \mathcal{A}^T} C^T_{ij} \cdot y^c_{ij} + \sum_{c \in \mathcal{C}} \sum_{(i,j) \in \mathcal{A}^L} C^L_{ci} \cdot z^c_{ij}$$
$$+ \sum_{c \in \mathcal{C}} \sum_{i \in \mathcal{N}^1} C^P \cdot e^c_i + \sum_{(i,j) \in \mathcal{A}^H} \sum_{c \in \mathcal{C}} \sum_{d \in \mathcal{C}^F | c \neq d} C^F \cdot b^{cd}_{ij} \quad (1)$$

subject to

$$\sum_{c\in\mathcal{C}} F^c \cdot x_{ij}^c \le I_{ij}^S, \qquad (i,j)\in\mathcal{A}^S \tag{2}$$

$$\sum_{c\in\mathcal{C}} F^c \cdot z_{ij}^c \le I_i^L, \qquad (i,j)\in\mathcal{A}^L \tag{3}$$

$$\sum_{i\in\mathcal{N}^1} d_i^c = M^c, \qquad c\in\mathcal{C} \tag{4}$$

$$d_i^c \le M_i^c, \qquad c\in\mathcal{C}, i\in\mathcal{N}^1 \tag{5}$$

$$\sum_{(i,j)\in\mathcal{A}^S} x_{ij}^c + \sum_{(i,j)\in\mathcal{A}^T} y_{ij}^c + \sum_{(i,j)\in\mathcal{A}^L} z_{ij}^c + \sum_{(i,j)\in\mathcal{A}^H}\sum_{d\in\mathcal{C}^F|c\neq d} b_{ij}^{dc} = d_i^c + e_i^c - \sum_{(i,j)\in\mathcal{A}^H}\sum_{d\in\mathcal{C}|c\neq d} D_{ij}^{cd}, \qquad c\in\mathcal{C}, i\in\mathcal{N}^1, \tag{6}$$

$$\begin{aligned}\sum_{(i,j)\in\mathcal{A}^S} x_{ij}^c + \sum_{(i,j)\in\mathcal{A}^T} y_{ij}^c + \sum_{(i,j)\in\mathcal{A}^L} z_{ij}^c \\ + \sum_{(i,j)\in\mathcal{A}^H}\sum_{d\in\mathcal{C}|c\neq d} b_{ij}^{dc} + \sum_{(i,j)\in\mathcal{A}^H}\sum_{d\in\mathcal{C}|c\neq d} D_{ij}^{dc} = \\ \sum_{(j,k)\in\mathcal{A}^S} x_{jk}^c + \sum_{(j,k)\in\mathcal{A}^T} y_{jk}^c + \sum_{(j,k)\in\mathcal{A}^L} z_{jk}^c + \sum_{(j,k)\in\mathcal{A}^H}\sum_{d\in\mathcal{C}|c\neq d} b_{jk}^{cd} \\ + \sum_{(j,k)\in\mathcal{A}^H}\sum_{d\in\mathcal{C}|c\neq d} D_{jk}^{cd}, \qquad c\in\mathcal{C}, j\in\mathcal{N}\backslash\mathcal{N}^1,\end{aligned} \tag{7}$$

$$\sum_{(i,j)\in\mathcal{A}^H}\sum_{d\in\mathcal{C}|c\neq d} b_{ij}^{cd} \le B^j \sum_{i\in\mathcal{N}}\sum_{(i,j)\in\mathcal{A}^H}\sum_{d\in\mathcal{C}|c\neq d} b_{ij}^{cd}, \quad c\in\mathcal{C}, j\in\mathcal{N} \tag{8}$$

$$\begin{aligned} b_{ij}^{cd} &\in \mathbb{N}^+, && c,d\in\mathcal{C}|c\neq d, (i,j)\in\mathcal{A}^H \\ d_i^c &\in \mathbb{N}^+, && c\in\mathcal{C}, i\in\mathcal{N}^1 \\ e_i^c &\in \mathbb{N}^+, && c\in\mathcal{C}, i\in\mathcal{N}^1 \\ x_{ij}^c &\in \mathbb{N}^+, && c\in\mathcal{C}, (i,j)\in\mathcal{A}^S \\ y_{ij}^c &\in \mathbb{N}^+, && c\in\mathcal{C}, (i,j)\in\mathcal{A}^T \\ z_{ij}^c &\in \mathbb{N}^+, && c\in\mathcal{C}, (i,j)\in\mathcal{A}^L \end{aligned} \tag{9}$$

The objective function (1), sums the costs of shipping, trucking, storing, purchasing and filling containers.

Constraint (2) and (3) ensure the model does not ship more containers on the vessels or stores more containers in port than there is available space, respectively.

Constraints (4)–(6) initialize the system. Constraint (4) limits the initially placed containers to the available containers, while constraint (5) makes sure that each port is allocated no more containers in the first period than a predetermined number. Constraint (6) ensures the total flow of containers leaving any starting node is equal to the number of containers allocated to the starting node.

Constraint (7), is the central flow control constraint. It applies to all nodes that are not initial nodes, as these are handled by constraints (6). Equation (7) ensures that the number of containers coming to a node matches the number of containers leaving the node.

If the model was allowed to freely source raw material from shipping ports it would always choose the ports closest to the production plants to minimize transportation costs. The same can be said about what plants to transport byproducts from. In the real world, this can lead to reliance on a single supplier and increase the vulnerability of the logistics system. To create a more distributed pattern for these shipments, constraint (8) ensures shipments of full containers from ports are limited to a given percentage of all shipments. Note that by choosing B^j appropriately, this formulation still allows sourcing from a single port. The formulation also implies that production plants can decide when raw materials become available/are sourced from the terminal nodes.

As the model handles the flow of containers, all decision variables are positive integers, as one cannot ship fractional containers. Constraints (9) are the integer requirements for the decision variables.

4 Case Study

The case study is based on Hydro's operations. We model their logistics network using plants, ports and shipping routes as encountered in the real world. Other data, i.e. costs, initial container fleet, and demand have been estimated based on publicly available information for the production system. See [7] for more detailed information.

4.1 Logistics Network

Hydro's main European logistics network consists of five production plants in Norway and eight shipping ports in Europe. Finished goods are transported by ship on southbound routes from the plants to the shipping ports from where they are forwarded to the customers. Raw materials and byproducts are transported in containers on northbound routes from the shipping ports to the plants as well as on all routes between plants. The ports are served by eight vessels which operate the different routes on weekly schedules. As containers share vessel capacity with finished goods on southbound routes, but not northbound routes, we assume that there are no capacity restrictions for northbound transportation. The logistics network is illustrated in Fig. 1. Note that the colored arrows represent the routes sailed by the different vessels.

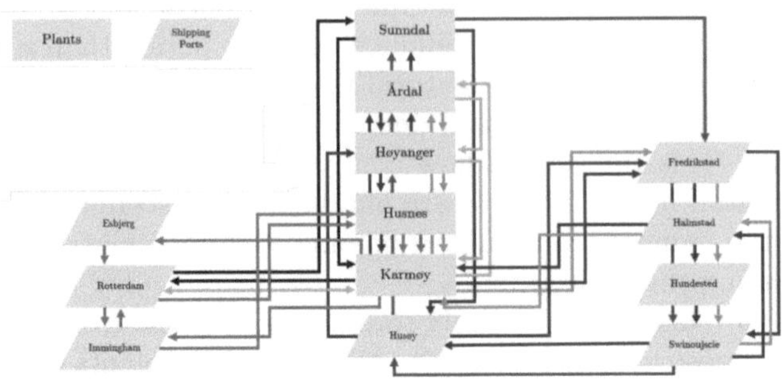

Fig. 1. Illustration of Hydro's logistics network [7].

4.2 Containers and Commodities

We consider a heterogeneous fleet of containers used to transport a total of five commodities. The commodities included here include anode butts, a byproduct from aluminium production that is mainly shipped between plants for recycling purposes, post-consumer scrap (PCS) that is shipped from shipping ports to the Høyanger plant for recycling, cathodes that are shipped from shipping ports to production plants, spent pot lining (SPL), a waste product that is shipped from plant to shipping ports, and crushed bath material that is also shipped as waste product from the plants to the shipping ports.

The fleet of containers consists of six different container types that can be used for transporting the different commodities. Only the 20ft standard container can be used to transport more than one commodity, whereas all other container types are dedicated to a single commodity. Note that a container can only carry one commodity at a time, i.e., mixing of commodities in a container is not permitted. Table 1 provides an overview over the different container types, their initial number and which commodities can be transported with them.

In the model, the subset of empty container types consists of the physical container types, whereas the subset of full container types consists of the combinations of physical container type with the commodities the container can be filled with.

4.3 Planning Horizon

We consider a planning horizon of 13 weeks. We assume perfect information during the planning horizon.

Table 1. Overview over the different container types, which commodities they transport, and how many are initially available [7].

Container Type	Commodity mapping	Number
20ft standard	Crushed bath material, PCS	182
20ft 1/2 Bulk	Anode butts	383
20ft 3/4 Bulk	Anode butts	44
20ft standard open side	Cathodes	36
20ft BK2-1/2 bulk	SPL	111
20ft BK2-3/4 bulk	SPL	14

5 Computational Results

In this section, we present the results from our analysis. We first introduce the instances we have solved, before discussing the results. The model has been implemented using Python 3.11 and gurobipy. Gurobi 12 has been used as commercial solver. All instances are solved with an optimality gap of less than 0.1%. A maximum runtime limit of 1 h was used, but most instances solve in less than 10 min.

5.1 Problem Instances

In addition to the benchmark instance based on the data provided in Sect. 4, we are solving instances where we vary one of the following three different parameters:

1. Number of initially available containers: we decrease the number of available containers by 10% and 20%. We also solve an instance with 10% more containers.
2. Available vessel capacity: we decrease the available vessel capacity on southbound routes by 25%, 50% and 75%.
3. Handling efficiency: we increase handling time (H_p^{cd}) by 250% and by 600%. We also solve an instance with a 50% decrease in handling time.

The purpose of these instances is to study the impact these parameters have on the required number of containers and the overall cost of operating the logistics system.

5.2 Results

Number of Initially Available Containers. Varying the number of initially available containers mainly impacts the number of containers that need to be purchased at the beginning of the planning horizon, especially for container types that are in undersupply. In general, the purchasing costs increase for the instance fewer containers and decrease for the instances with additional containers. The cost of storing containers increases in the number of available containers. On the other hand, shipping and trucking costs decrease when more containers are initially available. As a result, total costs increase by approx. 4% with 10% fewer containers, but decrease by 3% and 5% with an additional 10% and 20% more containers, respectively. Figure 2 provides a breakdown of the overall costs into the different cost components.

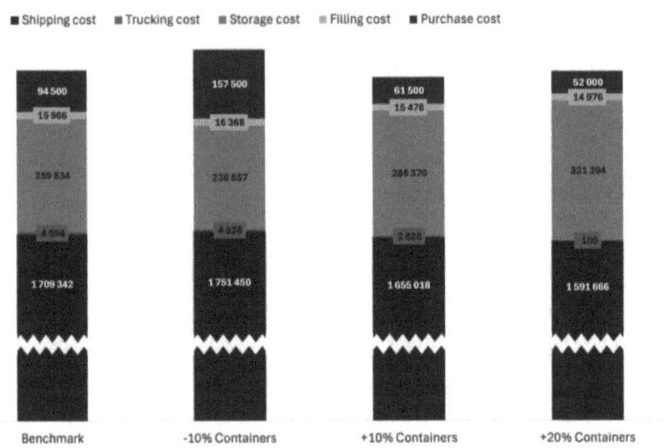

Fig. 2. Breakdown of costs for varying number of initially available containers.

Reduced Vessel Capacity. On southbound routes, containers share available vessel capacity with finished goods. As finished goods are prioritized over byproducts, the available capacity may change from departure to departure. From the results for the instances with reduced vessel capacity, we see that the impact on costs is rather small. An overall 75% reduction in available capacity only increases costs by approx. 4.8%. The increase in costs is mainly due an increase in shipping and trucking costs, implying less direct transportation of containers. An overview of the different cost components is shown in Fig. 3.

Handling Time Efficiency. Handling efficiency impacts turnaround time for containers. We model this by means of handling time H_p^{cd}. From the results we see that smaller changes in handling time do not have a large impact on costs. Even an increase in handling time by 250% (from 2 days to 7 days) only has a limited impact, mainly on the purchasing costs as the existing fleet of containers is no longer sufficient to handle the material flow. We see however that an increase of 600% has a massive impact on the cost as even more containers need to be purchased. This is likely due to the weekly schedules of the vessels serving the production ports. Smaller changes in handling time are absorbed in the schedules, whereas larger changes in handling time may lead to containers not being ready for the next departure and consequently trigger the purchasing of additional containers. Figure 4 illustrates the different cost components.

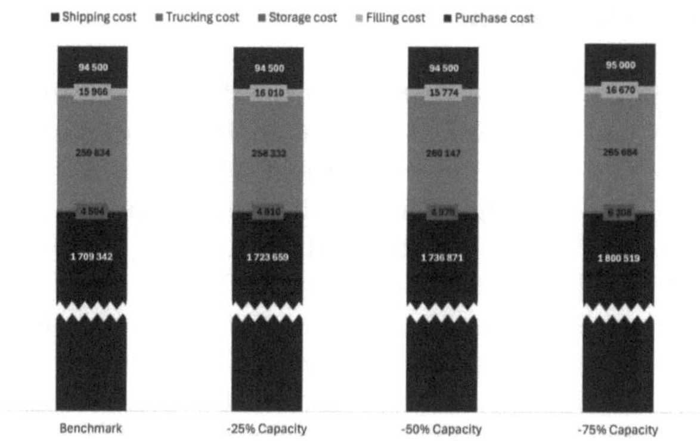

Fig. 3. Breakdown of costs for reduced vessel capacity on southbound routes.

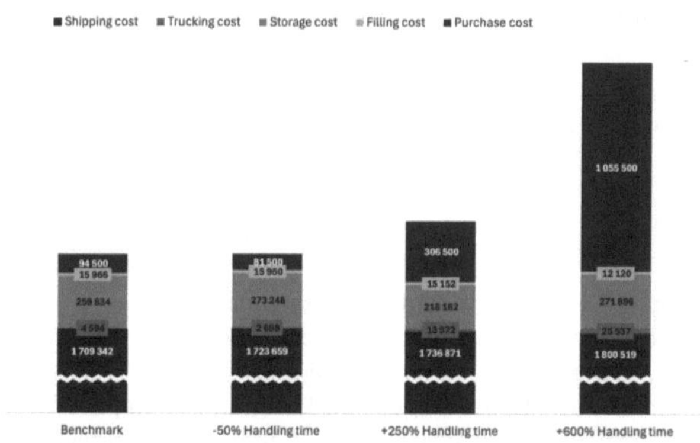

Fig. 4. Breakdown of costs for changes in container handling time.

Discussion. In all instances, Hydro incurs a procurement cost for additional containers. In particular, 20ft standard containers with open side for cathodes and 20ft standard containers for crushed bath material and PCS need to be procured. The number of other containers seems to be sufficient for current operations in most instances. We also see that transporting containers by truck is rarely used, indicating sufficient capacity on the vessels to reposition containers in time in most of the instances (with the exception of the most restrictive handling time instances). However, these results are obtained assuming perfect foresight for the planning horizon of 13 weeks. This assumption is likely not satisfied in the real world, possibly requiring a larger number of containers to maintain operations.

6 Concluding Remarks

The results in this paper indicate that size of the fleet of containers and efficient handling operations have the largest impact on Hydro's logistics costs. Available vessel capacity appears to be less critical. However, a major assumption for these results is perfect foresight. And while aluminium production usually is a stable process, making it possible to predict the need for raw materials and the production of byproducts, the availability of PCS in shipping ports is often unknown. A natural extension to the presented study is therefore to study the impact of this uncertainty. An updated analysis might indicate a fleet size different from the deterministic analysis presented in this paper. In general, a richer model capturing Hydro's real-world operations in more detail might also provide more useful insights for better container management decisions. Another potential extension of this work is to consider a tactical version of the problem and focus more on the design of routes and schedules for the vessels as well as their impact on Hydro's optimal fleet of containers.

Disclosure of Interests. The authors have no competing interests to declare that are relevant to the content of this article.

References

1. Song, D.-P., Dong, J.-X.: Empty container repositioning. In: Lee, C.-Y., Meng, Q. (eds.) Handbook of Ocean Container Transport Logistics. ISORMS, vol. 220, pp. 163–208. Springer, Cham (2015). https://doi.org/10.1007/978-3-319-11891-8_6
2. Abdelshafie, A., Salah, M., Kramberger, T., Dragan, D.: Repositioning and optimal re-allocation of empty containers: a review of methods, models, and applications. Sustainability **14**(11), 6655 (2022)
3. Di Francesco, M., Crainic, T.G., Zuddas, P.: The effect of multi-scenario policies on empty container repositioning. Transp. Res. Part E: Logist. Transp. Rev. **45**(5), 758–770 (2009)
4. Brouer, B. D., Pisinger, D., Spoorendonk, S.: Liner shipping cargo allocation with repositioning of empty containers. INFOR: Inf. Syst. Oper. Res. **49**(2), 109–124 (2011)
5. Moon, I., Do Ngoc, A.-D., Hur, Y.-S.: Positioning empty containers among multiple ports with leasing and purchasing considerations. OR Spectrum **32**(3), 765–786 (2010)
6. Xiang, X., Xu, X., Liu, C., Jia, S.: Liner fleet deployment and empty container repositioning under demand uncertainty: a robust optimization approach. Transp. Res. Part B: Methodol. **190**, 103088 (2024)
7. Dahlhaug, L.G.Ö., Jortveit, T.S., Næss, D.: Hydro aluminium AS' material logistics as a multi-commodity flow problem with empty container repositioning. Project report. Norwegian University of Science and Technology, Department of Industrial Economics and Technology Management. Trondheim, Norway (2025)

Shared-Load Container Drayage with Battery Swapping

Marco Ochoa-Barnuevo[1](✉), Fabian Akkerman[2], Eduardo Lalla-Ruiz[2], and Frederik Schulte[1]

[1] Delft University of Technology, Delft, The Netherlands
m.l.ochoabarnuevo@tudelft.nl
[2] University of Twente, Enschede, The Netherlands

Abstract. Container drayage refers to short-haul truck movements of containers between ports and nearby customers and is often characterized by poor asset utilization and high costs. Motivated by evolving digital less-than-container-load (LCL) practices of major forwarders, we investigate a shared-load container drayage setting in which a single sealed container serves multiple customers on the same route in both delivery and pickup operations. We formulate the problem as a mixed-integer linear program with clustered service, delivery-pickup sequencing, multi-trip routing, customer time windows, and electric-vehicle constraints through battery-capacity and swapping limitations. Computational results show that shared-load drayage can generate substantial cost savings relative to traditional one-load operations, mainly through reductions in fleet usage, and that these benefits are strongest under higher sharing levels and remain robust under EV-related restrictions.

Keywords: container drayage · shared-load routing · clustered vehicle routing · electric vehicles

1 Introduction

Container drayage denotes the short-distance transport of containers between ports and nearby customers, including factories, warehouses, and logistics centers, thus providing the first and last mile of containerized freight movement. Despite these short distances, drayage can account for up to 40% of overall container transport costs and is often characterized by empty or partially utilized trips [2]. This has motivated extensive research on improving drayage efficiency, traditionally by modeling the container drayage problem (CDP) as a routing and scheduling problem for dedicated container movements under time-window and terminal constraints, as in early intermodal pickup-and-delivery formulations such as [4].

New online booking platforms from major forwarders like Maersk and DHL have made less-than-container-load (LCL) as easy to book as a standard parcel. Inspired by these developments, we investigate a new CDP setting, referred to

J. de Armas and E. Lalla Ruiz (Eds.): LOGMS 2026, LNCS 16679, pp. 181–193, 2027.
https://doi.org/10.1007/978-3-032-30795-8_16

here as shared-load container drayage, for which a single container may serve multiple customers in the same delivery or pickup trip. In contrast to traditional drayage, where each container is typically dedicated to one customer, we allow container capacity to be shared across multiple consignees or shippers. We assume that these shared loads are formed upstream and do not address consolidation decisions: delivery containers are given as pre-assembled loads before dispatch and pickup requests correspond to predefined consolidated containers to be collected. Containers remain sealed and are only opened at customer locations during service. The routing problem, therefore, starts from a set of customer clusters, each associated with a delivery or pickup container, and seeks efficient tours that satisfy customer-specific time windows. This setting is consistent with emerging LCL services, such as those offered by Maersk [5], in which multiple shippers share container capacity and shipments are consolidated upstream before sealed containers are routed in drayage. It is also consistent with Physical Internet principles of modularity, load consolidation, shared capacity utilization, and reduced empty movements [6].

Related work has mainly focused on improving drayage efficiency through better asset utilization rather than through sharing customer loads within the same container. In drayage, [9] introduced flexible tasks in a multi-resource drayage setting (e.g., tractors, trailers, etc.) and showed system productivity can improve when operations are not tied to rigid one-task execution, and [10] demonstrated the value of empty-container sharing across carriers. Other studies enrich the loading and routing structure, for example through multi-load and heterogeneous-fleet settings [7], or through multi-trip planning combined with efficient empty-container reuse [3]. Collaboration has also been shown to reduce costs and emissions, although it mainly concerns shared operators or resources rather than multiple customers sharing the same container [8]. At the same time, electrification is becoming increasingly important in port-hinterland transport [1], and recent work has begun to extend electric vehicles (EV) routing and battery-swapping concepts to drayage contexts [11]. However, while the literature addresses dedicated drayage movements, empty-container reuse, collaboration, multi-load routing, and EV constraints, it does not study a drayage problem in which a single container is shared across multiple customers.

To address this gap, we formulate a shared-load container drayage problem as a mixed-integer linear program in Sect. 2 and evaluate its cost and operational implications under different customer distributions, time windows, and EV settings in Sect. 3. Section 4 concludes with the main findings and insights.

2 Problem Formulation

This section formalizes the shared-load container drayage setting introduced above and translates it into a routing problem. The focus is on how pre-defined container groupings and operational constraints can shape feasible truck tours efficiently.

Figure 1 illustrates the operational difference of the traditional one-load drayage with the proposed shared-load setting using a representative example.

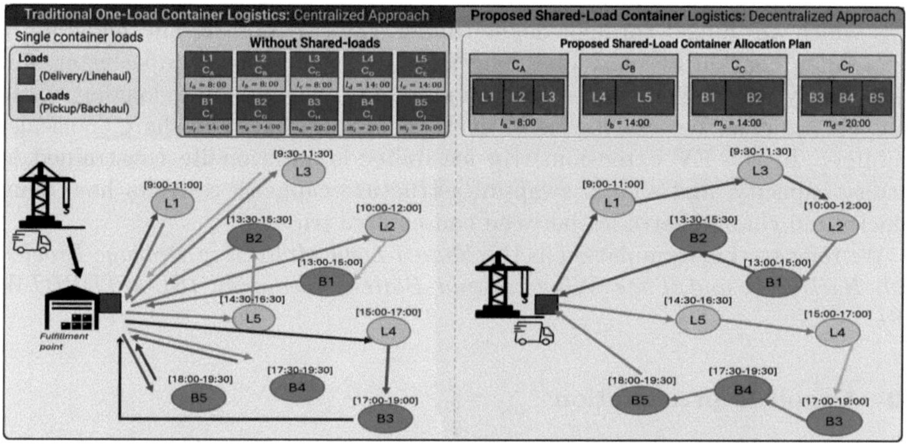

Fig. 1. Illustration of one-load vs. shared-load container drayage operations.

Under one-load operations (left), each container serves a single customer and requires a separate trip. For instance, a truck departs the terminal to serve customer L_1 with its time window [9:00, 11:00], returns, and then performs a separate trip for L_3 [9:30, 11:30]. Similarly, pickup requests such as such as B_1 [13:00, 15:00] and B_2 [13:30, 15:30] are also handled in separate routes. As a result, multiple trips are required, each with partially utilized container capacity. In contrast, under shared-load operations (right), containers are pre-assembled to serve multiple customers. For example, container C_A consolidates deliveries for L_1, L_2, and L_3. A single route can then visit $L_1 \rightarrow L_3 \rightarrow L_2$ within their respective time windows, progressively unloading the container. After completing deliveries, the same container can be reused to collect grouped pickup loads, such as B_1 and B_2, within their time windows. This reduces the number of required trips and increases container utilization while preserving feasibility with respect to time windows and operational constraints.

From a routing perspective, our problem is related to the VRP with backhauls through its delivery-before-pickup structure, and to the clustered VRP because customers assigned to the same container must be served consecutively within a trip.

2.1 Problem Definition (SL-MTDPBTW-BS)

We model the routing decision as a variant of the Vehicle Routing Problem with Time Windows, tailored to shared-load container drayage. We optimize the downstream routing given pre-defined shared-load containers. The objective is to assign and route a limited fleet of homogeneous trucks to execute both deliveries (*linehauls*) and pickups (*backhauls*). The model decides which vehicle serves which delivery and pickup clusters, in which trip they are served, and the customer visit sequence within each selected cluster. A vehicle can have multiple trips which are linked through depot timing; each trip starts and ends at the depot, may contain at most one delivery cluster and one pickup cluster, and must satisfy the delivery-before-pickup structure. Customers belonging to the same cluster must be served consecutively, reflecting that they share one sealed container. In the EV extension, trip feasibility is additionally constrained by battery capacity, and shared swap-infrastructure capacity restricts how many vehicles can change batteries between consecutive trips.

We refer to this formulation as the *Shared-Load Multi-Trip Drayage Problem with Backhauls and Time Windows and Battery Swapping (SL-MTDPBTW-BS)*.

2.2 Graph Representation

We consider a directed graph $G = (N, A)$ with node set $N = \{1\} \cup L \cup B \cup \{n\}$, where 1 and n denote the start and end depot, respectively, L and B denote the set of linehaul and backhaul customers. Each node $i \in N$ is associated with a service time s_i and a time window $[a_i, b_i]$. The arc set is $A = \{(i, j) : i, j \in N,\ i \neq j\}$; traversing arc (i, j) requires travel time t_{ij} and incurs travel cost c_{ij} (or equivalently a time-proportional cost defined below).

Customers are partitioned into clusters $C = C_L \cup C_B$. Each cluster $c \in C$ consists of a subset $N_c \subseteq L \cup B$ of customers that must be served *consecutively* within a single trip. For linehaul clusters $c \in C_L$, we impose a readiness time l_c. For backhaul clusters $c \in C_B$, we impose a strict return deadline m_c such that the vehicle must return to and service at the depot by m_c. A homogeneous fleet $k \in K$ performs depot-to-depot trips indexed by $t \in T$, and within any trip, linehaul service must precede backhaul service. Decision variables are grouped into routing, timing, assignment, and flow variables. Binary variables x_{ij}^{kt} indicate whether vehicle k traverses arc (i, j) in trip t, while z_c^{kt} assigns cluster c to vehicle–trip pair (k, t). Variables y_k and u_{kt} indicate vehicle and trip usage, respectively. Continuous variables $w_i^{kt} \geq 0$ and $late_i^{kt} \geq 0$ represent customer service start times and tardiness beyond b_i. To eliminate intra-cluster subtours, we use single-commodity flow within each cluster: $f_{ij}^{kt} \geq 0$ denotes flow on intra-cluster arc (i, j), and $r_i^{c,kt} \in \{0, 1\}$ selects the root customer of cluster c for vehicle–trip pair (k, t).

We use the following cost parameters: a fixed vehicle cost of $(c_t = 500)$, a travel cost of $(c_m = 1)$ per unit of travel time, and a lateness penalty of $(c_{\text{late}} = 5)$ per unit of delay, which applies only in the soft time window setting. To model bounded soft time windows, we allow a maximum tolerated violation $\Delta \geq 0$ (set to $\Delta = 200$ in our experiments); hard time windows are obtained by setting $\Delta = 0$.

To strengthen time-propagation constraints, we use arc-dependent constants M_{ij} based on earliest and latest feasible service times. Additional constants are defined using an upper bound on the planning horizon: M_i for customer time-window activation, M_d for depot time constraints, M^{link} for linking consecutive trips, and M_c^B to enforce backhaul return deadlines.

Preprocessing and Bounds. To reduce the problem size, we apply some preprocessing rules. The first cut removes arcs violating time-window feasibility, the second removes backhaul-to-linehaul transitions, which are forbidden due to the delivery–pickup structure. Thirdly, inter-cluster arcs between clusters of the same type are removed to preserve clustered service. Finally, arcs entering the start depot and leaving the end depot are excluded.

We derive bounds to tighten the formulation. The number of trips is bounded by sequentially constructing as many trips as possible with a single vehicle, each time selecting the earliest feasible delivery and pickup clusters while respecting time windows and the delivery–pickup policy. Moreover, the number of vehicles is bounded by pairing compatible delivery and pickup clusters into single trips, with the remaining clusters assigned to individual trips.

Objective. The objective combines vehicle usage, travel cost, and lateness penalties:

$$\min \sum_{k\in K} c_t y_k + \sum_{(i,j)\in A} \sum_{k\in K} \sum_{t\in T} c_m\, t_{ij}\, x_{ij}^{kt} + \sum_{i\in L\cup B} \sum_{k\in K} \sum_{t\in T} c_{late}\, late_i^{kt}. \tag{1}$$

Constraints

$$\sum_{j:(j,i)\in A} \sum_{k\in K} \sum_{t\in T} x_{ji}^{kt} = 1 \qquad \forall i \in L\cup B \tag{2}$$

$$\sum_{i:(i,j)\in A} x_{ij}^{kt} = \sum_{i:(j,i)\in A} x_{ji}^{kt} \qquad \forall j \in L\cup B,\ \forall k\in K,\ \forall t \in T \tag{3}$$

$$\sum_{j:(1,j)\in A} x_{1j}^{kt} = u_{kt} \qquad \forall k\in K,\ \forall t\in T \tag{4}$$

$$\sum_{i:(i,n)\in A} x_{in}^{kt} = u_{kt} \qquad \forall k\in K,\ \forall t\in T \tag{5}$$

$$\sum_{i\in N\setminus N_c} \sum_{j\in N_c:\ (i,j)\in A} x_{ij}^{kt} = z_c^{kt} \qquad \forall c\in C,\ \forall k\in K,\ \forall t\in T \tag{6}$$

$$\sum_{i\in N_c} \sum_{j\in N\setminus N_c:\ (i,j)\in A} x_{ij}^{kt} = z_c^{kt} \qquad \forall c\in C,\ \forall k\in K,\ \forall t\in T \tag{7}$$

$$\sum_{c\in C_L} z_c^{kt} \le 1 \qquad \forall k\in K,\ \forall t\in T \tag{8}$$

$$\sum_{c\in C_B} z_c^{kt} \le 1 \qquad \forall k\in K,\ \forall t\in T \tag{9}$$

$$\sum_{c\in C} z_c^{kt} \le 2u_{kt} \qquad \forall k\in K,\ \forall t\in T \tag{10}$$

$$z_c^{kt} \le u_{kt} \qquad \forall k \in K,\ \forall t \in T, \forall c \in C \tag{11}$$

$$\sum_{i \in N_c} r_i^{c,kt} = z_c^{kt} \qquad \forall c \in C,\ \forall k \in K,\ \forall t \in T \tag{12}$$

$$\sum_{j \in N_c \setminus \{i\}} (f_{ij}^{kt} - f_{ji}^{kt}) = |N_c|\, r_i^{c,kt} - z_c^{kt} \qquad \forall c \in C,\ \forall i \in N_c,\ \forall k \in K,\ \forall t \in T \tag{13}$$

$$f_{ij}^{kt} \le (|N_c| - 1) x_{ij}^{kt} \qquad \forall c \in C,\ \forall i,j \in N_c,\ i \ne j,\ \forall k \in K,\ \forall t \in T \tag{14}$$

$$\sum_{i \in N_c:\ (i,n) \in A} x_{in}^{kt} = z_c^{kt} \qquad \forall c \in C_B,\ \forall k \in K,\ \forall t \in T \tag{15}$$

$$w_j^{kt} \ge w_i^{kt} + s_i + t_{ij} - M_{ij}\big(1 - x_{ij}^{kt}\big) \qquad \forall (i,j) \in A,\ \forall k \in K,\ \forall t \in T \tag{16}$$

$$w_1^{k1} = 0 \qquad \forall k \in K \tag{17}$$

$$w_i^{kt} \ge a_i - a_i\, (1 - \sum_{j \in N \setminus \{n\}} x_{ji}^{kt}) \qquad \forall i \in N,\ \forall k \in K,\ \forall t \in T \tag{18}$$

$$w_i^{kt} \le b_i + \Delta + M_i(1 - \sum_{j \in N \setminus \{n\}} x_{ji}^{kt}) \qquad \forall i \in (L \cup B),\ \forall k \in K,\ \forall t \in T \tag{19}$$

$$late_i^{kt} \ge w_i^{kt} - b_i \qquad \forall i \in (L \cup B),\ \forall k \in K,\ \forall t \in T \tag{20}$$

$$w_n^{kt} + s_n \le b_n + M_d(1 - \sum_{j \in N \setminus \{n\}} x_{ji}^{kt}) \qquad \forall k \in K,\ \forall t \in T \tag{21}$$

$$w_1^{k,t+1} \ge w_n^{kt} + s_n + t_{n1} - M^{link}\Big(2 - \sum_{j:(1,j) \in A} x_{1j}^{k,t+1} - \sum_{i:(i,n) \in A} x_{in}^{kt}\Big) \qquad \forall k \in K,\ \forall t \in T \setminus \{|T|\} \tag{22}$$

$$w_n^{kt} + s_n \le m_c + M_c^B(1 - z_c^{kt}) \qquad \forall c \in C_B,\ \forall k \in K,\ \forall t \in \mathrm{T} \tag{23}$$

$$\sum_{(i,j) \in A:\ i \in L \cup B} x_{ij}^{kt} \ge u_{kt} \qquad \forall k \in K,\ \forall t \in \mathrm{T} \tag{24}$$

$$\sum_{(i,j) \in A:\ i \in L \cup B} x_{ij}^{kt} \le |N|\, u_{kt} \qquad \forall k \in K,\ \forall t \in \mathrm{T} \tag{25}$$

$$u_{kt} \le y_k \qquad \forall k \in K, \forall t \in \mathrm{T} \tag{26}$$

$$u_{kt} \le u_{k,t-1} \qquad \forall k \in K,\ \forall t > 1 \tag{27}$$

$$y_k \leq y_{k-1}, \qquad \sum_{t \in T} u_{kt} \leq \sum_{t \in T} u_{k-1,t} \qquad \forall k > 1 \tag{28}$$

Constraints (2)–(5) ensure that each customer is visited exactly once, trips start and end at the depot, and flow conservation holds within each trip. Constraints (6)–(7) ensure that, if a cluster is assigned to a vehicle-trip pair, the route enters that cluster exactly once from outside and leaves it exactly once to the outside. Together with the intra-cluster flow constraints (12)–(14), this makes the cluster behave as a consecutive service block. Constraints (8)–(9) restrict each trip to at most one linehaul cluster and at most one backhaul cluster, while constraints (10)–(11) link cluster assignment to trip activation. Constraints (12)–(14) eliminate subtours within clusters and enforce consecutive service of all customers belonging to a selected cluster. Constraint (15) ensures that after completing a backhaul cluster the vehicle returns directly to the end depot. Constraints (16)–(20) implement time propagation and time window feasibility (with parameter Δ allowing soft or hard windows). Constraint (21) bounds the depot return time of each trip, while constraint (22) links consecutive trips of the same vehicle by requiring trip $t+1$ to start only after trip t has returned to and completed service at the depot. Constraints (23) enforce cluster-specific return deadlines. Release times for delivery clusters are not enforced explicitly, as customer time windows are assumed to be consistent with cluster availability. Finally, constraints (24)–(28) activate trips and vehicles and apply symmetry-breaking to improve computational tractability.

2.3 Extension: Battery Swapping

To capture energy feasibility in electric drayage operations, we extend the model with a simplified battery swapping mechanism at the trip level.

Energy consumption on each arc is assumed to be linearly proportional to distance, i.e., $e_{ij} = \alpha d_{ij}$ for all $(i, j) \in A$, where α is a constant consumption rate defined as $\alpha = 0.5$. Let E_{kt} denote the state-of-charge (SOC) of vehicle k at the start of trip t, and let g_{kt} be the total energy consumption of that trip. Binary variables v_{kt} indicate whether a battery swap occurs between trips t and $t+1$. For this extension we define the following constraints:

$$g_{kt} = \sum_{(i,j) \in A} e_{ij} x_{ij}^{kt} \qquad \forall k \in K,\ \forall t \in T \tag{29}$$

$$g_{kt} \leq E_{kt} \qquad \forall k \in K,\ \forall t \in T \tag{30}$$

$$E_{k,t+1} \leq E^{cap} \qquad \forall k \in K,\ \forall t \in T \setminus \{|T|\} \tag{31}$$

$$E_{k,t+1} \leq E_{kt} - g_{kt} + E^{cap} \cdot v_{kt} \qquad \forall k \in K,\ \forall t \in T \setminus \{|T|\} \tag{32}$$

$$E_{k,t+1} \geq E^{cap} \cdot v_{kt} \qquad \forall k \in K,\ \forall t \in T \setminus \{|T|\} \tag{33}$$

$$E_{k,t+1} \geq E_{kt} - g_{kt} - E^{cap} \cdot v_{kt} \qquad \forall k \in K,\ \forall t \in T \setminus \{|T|\} \tag{34}$$

$$v_{kt} \leq u_{kt}, \quad v_{kt} \leq u_{k,t+1} \qquad \forall k \in K,\ \forall t \in T \setminus \{|T|\} \tag{35}$$

$$\sum_{k \in K} v_{kt} \leq V^{swap} \qquad \forall t \in T \setminus \{|T|\} \tag{36}$$

Constraints (29)–(31) define trip-level energy consumption and enforce feasibility with respect to available charge. Constraints (32)–(34) model the inter-trip SOC dynamics, capturing both battery depletion and full recharge under swapping. Constraints (35) ensure that swaps occur only between active trips, while constraint (36) limits the number of simultaneous swaps through a stage-based infrastructure capacity V^{swap}.

3 Computational Study

We evaluate the model through three experiments designed to isolate (i) the value of sharing, (ii) the role of temporal flexibility, and (iii) the impact of electrification constraints. Across all experiments, we compare $S1 = (1, 1)$, $S2 = (2, 2)$, and $S4 = (4, 4)$, where S denotes the maximum number of customers per container.

Experiment 1 varies instance size ($N \in \{25, 50, 100\}$), customer spatial structure (compact, mixed, dispersed layouts), and solving with hard/soft time windows to quantify the economic value of sharing. Experiment 2 fixes the layout (compact) and varies time-window width (base vs. widened) to isolate the effect of temporal flexibility. Experiment 3 fixes hard time windows and varies EV capacity ($\{0.6, 0.8, 1.0\}$) and swap availability (limited/unrestricted) to assess whether electrification constraints alter the value of sharing. Battery capacity levels are based on the distribution of energy needs across feasible routes, covering tight to generous ranges. Swap infrastructure is set to one station per 25 customers. All experiments run on a Linux cluster with Python 3.11 and Gurobi 10.0, using 8 threads on AMD Genoa 9654 cores (2.4 GHz) with 16 GB of memory per run. Computational performance is reported separately in Table 3 and

Instances are adapted from Solomon c101 by constructing clustered linehaul/backhaul customers. For each customer size and sharing level, many random seeds are tested: clusters are formed from nearby customers under time-window and depot-return feasibility, scored with geometric criteria, and filtered with feasibility checks. The best feasible profiles are kept as base instances, and widened time-window variants are obtained by doubling their time-window sizes.

3.1 Experiment 1: Is Load Sharing Economically Beneficial?

Figure 2 suggests that sharing is consistently beneficial, with $S4$ dominating all configurations. Relative to $S1$, cost reductions range from 27.9% to 62.3% (hard TW) and 31.7% to 62.3% (soft TW). In contrast, $S2$ is slightly worse than $S1$ for $N = 25$, as the small instance size could limit good pairings and may force inefficient two-customer combinations. However, $S2$ becomes clearly beneficial for $N = 50$ and $N = 100$, with reductions of about 30% and 47% under hard time windows and similar values under soft time windows. The cost breakdown shows that savings are mainly driven by fleet reduction, with additional but smaller travel savings, while lateness remains negligible under soft time windows.

This dependency on N indicates that partial sharing requires sufficient pairing opportunities to be effective, whereas full sharing ($S4$) can consistently exploit the available structure to reduce the number of trips and improve efficiency. Although $S1$ (and $S2$ for larger instances) has nonzero gaps and should be interpreted cautiously, the cost patterns are consistent across settings: $S4$ is always optimal and best, while $S2$ shifts from worse than $S1$ at $N = 25$ to better at $N \geq 50$, suggesting that the observed trends are largely driven by structural differences rather than solution quality.

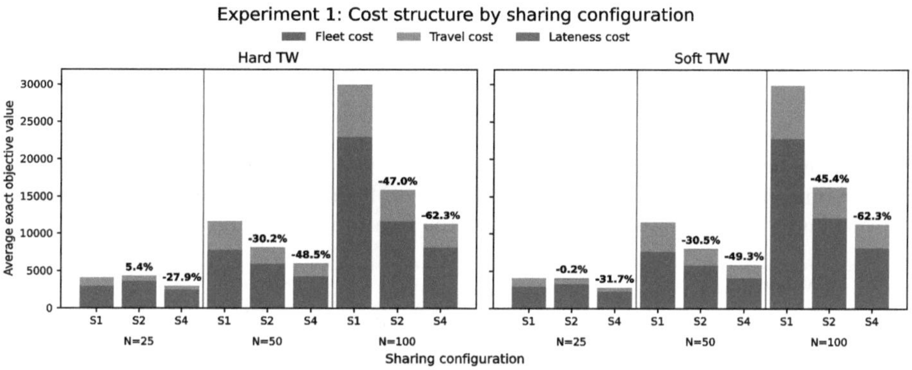

Fig. 2. Average cost breakdown in Experiment 1 for hard and soft time windows. Results are averaged over the three layouts. Percentage labels indicate the change in total cost relative to the no-sharing baseline $S1$.

3.2 Experiment 2: Does Wider Customer Flexibility Change the Value of Sharing?

These results for Experiment 2 consider only the compact layout. Table 1 shows that widening customer time windows reduces costs for $S1$ and $S2$, but has no effect on $S4$. For $N = 25$, costs decrease by 12% for $S1$ (both hard and soft) and by 11% and 20% for $S2$ under hard and soft time windows, respectively, while $S4$ remains unchanged. For $N = 50$, reductions are 8% and 5% for $S1$, and 10% and 6% for $S2$, again with no change for $S4$. Differences between hard and soft settings are small overall, with the largest effect for $S2$ at $N = 25$ under soft time windows. These results suggest that widening time windows can reduce costs for $S1$ and $S2$, likely by providing greater flexibility in routing and sequencing. However, since $S1$ and $S2$ cases still exhibit nonzero optimality gaps, the reported differences should be interpreted as indicative rather than exact. In contrast, widening time windows has no observable effect for $S4$ in the tested cases, indicating that the relative advantage of higher sharing levels is remains unchanged under increased flexibility.

Table 1. Experiment 2: impact of widening customer time windows on total cost. TWΔ% reports the percentage reduction from the base (B) to the widened (W) time-window (TW) setting. S–H (%) reports the percentage change from the hard to the soft regime for the corresponding setting.

Mode	N	$S1$			$S2$			$S4$		
		B-TW	W-TW	TWΔ%	B-TW	W-TW	TWΔ%	B-TW	W-TW	TWΔ%
Hard	25	3989.7	3504.2	12%	4223.3	3751.0	11%	2925.1	2925.1	0%
Soft	25	3989.7	3504.2	12%	4223.3	3377.5	20%	2925.1	2925.1	0%
S–H (%)		0%	0%		0%	10%		0%	0%	
Hard	50	11166.0	10272.5	8%	8592.4	7705.1	10%	6319.6	6319.6	0%
Soft	50	10813.4	10272.5	5%	8223.0	7705.1	6%	6319.6	6319.6	0%
S–H (%)		3%	0%		4%	0%		0%	0%	

Table 2. Experiment 3: impact of EV capacity (EvC) and swap-infrastructure limitation (SLim: limited, NoLim: unrestricted) on total cost. SΔ% reports the percentage increase under limited swap infrastructure relative to the no-limit case.

N	EvC	$S1$			$S2$			$S4$		
		NoLim	SLim	SΔ%	NoLim	SLim	SΔ%	NoLim	SLim	SΔ%
25	0.6	4155.8	5260.3	27%	4354.9	4354.9	0%	3286.0	3286.0	0%
25	0.8	4089.0	4534.6	11%	4310.4	4310.4	0%	2942.0	2942.0	0%
25	1.0	4081.6	4098.2	0%	4303.6	4303.6	0%	2942.0	2942.0	0%
50	0.6	11756.5	12803.1	9%	8153.1	8158.8	0%	6011.8	6168.0	3%
50	0.8	11082.5	12431.0	12%	8116.7	8118.9	0%	5996.3	5996.3	0%
50	1.0	11628.7	12049.8	4%	8116.7	8118.9	0%	5987.9	5987.9	0%

3.3 Experiment 3: Do Electrification Constraints Change the Value of Sharing?

Table 2 shows that limited swap infrastructure mainly affects $S1$. For $N = 25$, the cost increase relative to the no-limit case is 27% at EV capacity 0.6, 11% at 0.8, and negligible at 1.0; for $N = 50$, the corresponding increases are 9%, 12%, and 4%. In contrast, $S2$ is largely unaffected in the reported results, and $S4$ shows only minor changes, with a small increase of about 3% at $N = 50$ and capacity 0.6. Across all EV settings, $S4$ remains the lowest-cost configuration, while the impact of infrastructure limitations is concentrated in the no-sharing case. As a result, the relative advantage of higher sharing levels appears to increase under tighter electrification constraints in the tested settings. By reducing the number of trips and increasing utilization per trip, shared-load operations may require fewer energy-intensive movements and less frequent access to swap infrastructure. However, since not all $S1$ and $S2$ instances are solved to optimality, these differences should be treated with caution.

Table 3. Computational performance across all experiments. Values report runtime (minutes) and optimality gap (%) for each sharing configuration. Exp 1 values are averaged over three spatial structures. Experiment 3 includes EV parameters, where "cap" denotes battery capacity and "lim"/"NoLim" denote limited and unrestricted swap infrastructure.

Exp	N	TW	EV (cap, swap)	Runtime (S1|S2|S4)	Gap% (S1|S2|S4)
1	25	Hard	—	90.0 | 2.8 | 0.0	34 | 0 | 0
1	25	Soft	—	90.0 | 30.4 | 0.0	40 | 2 | 0
1	50	Hard	—	180.0 | 180.0 | 1.0	51 | 23 | 0
1	50	Soft	—	180.0 | 180.0 | 3.2	51 | 31 | 0
1	100	Hard	—	240.0 | 240.0 | 88.8	67 | 51 | 4
1	100	Soft	—	240.0 | 240.0 | 160.2	67 | 53 | 16
2	25	W-Hard	—	90.0 | 8.4 | 0.0	30 | 0 | 0
2	25	W-Soft	—	90.0 | 19.8 | 0.0	33 | 0 | 0
2	50	W-Hard	—	180.0 | 180.0 | 32.0	44 | 31 | 0
2	50	W-Soft	—	180.0 | 180.0 | 180.0	48 | 47 | 22
3	25	Hard	(0.6, NoLim)	60.0 | 3.0 | 0.0	26 | 0 | 0
3	25	Hard	(0.8, NoLim)	90.0 | 8.4 | 0.0	28 | 0 | 0
3	25	Hard	(1.0, NoLim)	90.0 | 9.3 | 0.0	35 | 0 | 0
3	25	Hard	(0.6, lim)	60.0 | 0.5 | 0.0	9 | 0 | 0
3	25	Hard	(0.8, lim)	90.0 | 1.7 | 0.0	25 | 0 | 0
3	25	Hard	(1.0, lim)	90.0 | 2.9 | 0.0	39 | 0 | 0
3	50	Hard	(0.6, NoLim)	180.0 | 180.0 | 2.1	52 | 22 | 0
3	50	Hard	(0.8, NoLim)	180.0 | 180.0 | 1.2	48 | 13 | 0
3	50	Hard	(1.0, NoLim)	180.0 | 180.0 | 0.7	51 | 22 | 0
3	50	Hard	(0.6, lim)	180.0 | 180.0 | 0.4	46 | 19 | 0
3	50	Hard	(0.8, lim)	180.0 | 180.0 | 1.3	55 | 20 | 0
3	50	Hard	(1.0, lim)	180.0 | 180.0 | 1.3	53 | 27 | 0

3.4 Computational Remarks

Table 3 shows that $S4$ is typically solved to near optimality, while $S1$ and, to a lesser extent, $S2$ exhibit increasing gaps as instance difficulty grows. The reported results, therefore, represent best-found solutions within the time limits and should be interpreted as indicative rather than definitive. Despite this, the relative performance is consistent across experiments, with $S4$ always best, $S2$ intermediate, and $S1$ most sensitive, suggesting that the observed trends are largely structural rather than gap-driven. Future work should use the present formulation as a benchmark and source of insights, but develop tailored heuristic and matheuristic methods to improve scalability and reduce optimality gaps.

4 Conclusion and Future Research

Inspired by new online booking platforms for less-then-container transport, this paper proposes a shared-load container drayage problem, in which multiple customers are served within a single sealed container. The problem is formulated as a mixed-integer program with clustered service, delivery–then-pickup routing, time windows, and EV-related constraints. To our knowledge, this is the first study that models drayage routing under a shared-load container structure.

The computational study shows that shared-load drayage can generate significant savings relative to traditional operations. These gains are most pronounced under full sharing ($S4$), which consistently performs best across all tested settings, while partial sharing ($S2$) becomes beneficial only in larger or more flexible instances. The improvements are primarily driven by reductions in fleet usage, with smaller contributions from travel costs, and limited impact from lateness. Under electrification constraints, the cost impact is concentrated in the no-sharing case, whereas shared configurations remain largely unaffected, indicating that sharing can mitigate infrastructure limitations. Overall, these results suggest that the value of sharing lies in reducing the number of required trips and improving resource utilization, while also enhancing robustness under tighter operational conditions.

Future research can extend this work in several directions. First, testing in more diverse spatial settings could improve practical relevance. Second, richer operational features such as heterogeneous fleets, charging decisions, and stochastic elements could be incorporated. Finally, the computational difficulty of larger instances motivates the development of tailored metaheuristics to exploit the problem's clustered and multi-trip structure. Variable, Large, or Adaptive Neighborhood Search methods could provide flexible frameworks for integrating specialized operators that target different decision levels: sequencing customers within clusters, ordering clusters within trips, or assigning multiple trips to a single route.

References

1. APM Terminals: Automated priority service for electric trucks (2025). https://www.apmterminals.com/en/gothenburg/about/news-and-updates/2025/250926-fully-automated-priority-for-electric-trucks. Accessed 30 Mar 2026
2. Chen, R., Meng, Q., Jia, P.: Container port drayage operations and management: past and future. Transp. Res. Part E: Logist. Transp. Rev. **159**, 102633 (2022)
3. Fazi, S., Choudhary, S.K., Dong, J.X.: The multi-trip container drayage problem with synchronization for efficient empty containers re-usage. Eur. J. Oper. Res. **310**(1), 343–359 (2023)
4. Imai, A., Nishimura, E., Current, J.: A Lagrangian relaxation-based heuristic for the vehicle routing with full container load. Eur. J. Oper. Res. **176**(1), 87–105 (2007)
5. Maersk: Less-than-container load (LCL) services (2025). https://www.maersk.com/transportation-services/lcl. Accessed 30 Mar 2026

6. Matusiewicz, M.: Logistics of the future–physical internet and its practicality. Transp. J. **59**(2), 200–214 (2020)
7. Moghaddam, M., Pearce, R.H., Mokhtar, H., Prato, C.G.: A generalised model for container drayage operations with heterogeneous fleet, multi-container sizes and two modes of operation. Transp. Res. Part E: Logist. Transp. Rev. **139**, 101973 (2020)
8. Schulte, F., Lalla-Ruiz, E., González-Ramírez, R.G., Voß, S.: Reducing port-related empty truck emissions: a mathematical approach for truck appointments with collaboration. Transp. Res. Part E: Logist. Transp. Rev. **105**, 195–212 (2017)
9. Smilowitz, K.: Multi-resource routing with flexible tasks: an application in drayage operations. IIE Trans. **38**(7), 577–590 (2006)
10. Sterzik, S., Kopfer, H., Yun, W.Y.: Reducing hinterland transportation costs through container sharing. Flex. Serv. Manuf. J. **27**(2–3), 382–402 (2015)
11. Xiao, L., Chen, L., Sun, P., Laporte, G., Baldacci, R.: The container drayage problem for electric trucks with charging resource constraints. Transp. Res. Part C: Emerg. Technol. **174**, 105100 (2025)

A Matheuristic Approach for a Special Case of Train Unloading Planning Problem

Daniela Ambrosino[1,2](✉), Costanza Chiesa[3], and Khawar Bashir[1,3](✉)

[1] Department of Economics and Business Studies and CIELI, University of Genoa, Genoa, Italy
daniela.ambrosino@unige.it, khawar.bashir@edu.unige.it
[2] OPTIMeasy – University of Genoa Spin Off, Genova, Italy
[3] Circle Group SpA Genova, Genoa, Italy

Abstract. This paper addresses the Train Unloading Planning Problem with fixed zones, a structured variant of the Train Unloading Planning Problem (TUPP) introduced in [4], arising in non-automated maritime container terminals. The distinguishing assumption is that each reach stacker is assigned to a designated zone of the export yard. This fixed-zone constraint removes the reach stacker allocation degree of freedom from the optimization. A matheuristic approach is proposed to solve real size instances of this problem; it is derived from the Iterated Local Search proposed in [4]. The derived approach extends and modifies the Iterated Local Search by introducing four complementary seed strategies and a new Greedy Bay-location Re-routing subroutine (GBR) that, embedded within every neighbourhood evaluation, ensures each candidate sequence is assessed under bay-location-optimal conditions. Computational experiments show that no single seed dominates across all instance sizes, confirming the value of the multi-start design. Averaged across instances with up to 70 containers, the matheuristic achieves a mean improvement of 25.5% over time-limited MILP solutions with computation times below 65 s.

Keywords: train unloading · maritime container terminal · iterated local search

1 Introduction and a Brief Literature Review

The steady growth of global containerized trade has intensified pressure on maritime container terminals, key nodes connecting sea transport with inland modes, to improve the efficiency of all operational subsystems. Effective coordination of handling equipment such as gantry cranes, reach stackers, and automated guided vehicles is widely recognized as a critical determinant of terminal throughput and service reliability [1,2]. Among the various terminal subsystems, rail-side operations play a strategic role in hinterland connectivity, yet their operational

J. de Armas and E. Lalla Ruiz (Eds.): LOGMS 2026, LNCS 16679, pp. 194–205, 2027.
https://doi.org/10.1007/978-3-032-30795-8_17

planning remains significantly underexplored relative to quayside and gate processes [3].

Equipment coordination in container terminals has been extensively studied in automated environments integrating rail-mounted gantry cranes, automated stacking cranes, and automated guided vehicles [6,8], while non-automated terminals, which remain the dominant operational model worldwide, have received comparatively less attention. The present study focuses on a non-automated maritime container terminal.

Among rail-side operations, we address the train unloading process, which proceeds as follows. A single gantry crane (GC) lifts containers one at a time from the stationary train and places them on tow tags for yard transfer. The export yard is served by a set of reach stackers (RSs), each responsible for receiving containers from the tow tags and storing them in compatible bay-locations within the yard. The yard is organized into zones, each zone containing multiple bay-locations serving containers of different destinations.

The problem of jointly determining the crane unloading sequence, the assignment of containers to bay-locations, and the RS operations was introduced as the Train Unloading Planning Problem (TUPP) in [4]. The joint determination of the crane service sequence, the assignment of containers to yard bay-location, and the RS operations are strongly coupled decisions: a poor unloading sequence forces unnecessary crane horizontal travel and frequent spreader length adjustments, while a suboptimal bay-location allocation increases RS displacement and may interfere with vessel loading efficiency.

Related work on rail-side unloading includes [7], which sequences reach stacker operations in an inland railway terminal to minimise makespan, and [5], which coordinates gantry cranes and straddle carriers for train unloading at the terminal landside. In automated sea-rail terminals, [6] addresses cooperative multi-equipment scheduling involving rail-mounted gantry cranes and AGVs, while [8] investigates flexible yard crane scheduling under mixed railway and road flows. To the authors knowledge, no studies, apart from [4], jointly optimises the crane unloading sequence, RS operations, and bay-location assignment in a non-automated maritime terminal, which is the specific contribution of the present work.

[4] introduced the TUPP and proposed a Mixed-Integer Linear Programming formulation that achieves proven optimality only for small instances, leaving substantial optimality gaps for medium and large ones. To address larger instances, an Iterated Local Search was developed, initialized from a single MILP warm-start solution obtained within a fixed time limit. For the detailed description of the operational setting, the mathematical formulation, and the solution framework the reader can refer to [4].

The present paper introduces a new assumption for the TUPP and proposes a new solution method. The new assumption concerns the assignment of reach stackers to yard zones. In some non-automated maritime container terminals, the export yard is partitioned into contiguous zones, each one served exclusively by a designated reach stacker. Each zone contains multiple bay-locations and is used to store containers to be shipped to a given vessel, having different size, weight and specific destinations. Under this assumption, the reach stacker responsible for a given zone is fixed, while in the original TUPP [4] the RS-to-container assignment was itself a decision variable. This specialized variant of TUPP is referred here as the TUPP with Fixed Zones, TUPP(fz).

The new assumption simplifies the mathematical model by removing the RS-to-container assignment degree of freedom, thereby reducing the number of binary variables and tightening the LP relaxation. However, this reduction does not ensure that the model can handle real-sized instances, in terms of both the number of containers to be unloaded and the size of the export yard (i.e., the number of bay-locations), even when used to compute the initial solution of the matheuristic approach proposed in [4].

For this reason, a new solution method is proposed: the ILS matheuristic introduced in [4] is enhanced with four complementary seeding strategies, namely MILP, Greedy, Nearest, and Random. Moreover, a Greedy Bay-location Re-routing subroutine (GBR) is embedded within each neighbourhood evaluation, ensuring that sequence modifications are always assessed under bay-location optimal conditions. This remains computationally affordable due to the fixed zone assignment: for any given unloading sequence, the within-zone bay allocation can be efficiently improved via a greedy nearest-bay-location procedure applied independently to each zone.

The multi-start design is the core methodological novelty of the paper. Research on multi-start matheuristic has shown that evaluating a diverse set of starting solutions consistently improves solution quality over a single deterministic start [9,10].

The paper is organised as follows. Section 2 presents the problem in more detail and outlines the main aspects of the mathematical formulation proposed in [4]. Section 3 describes the matheuristic solution approach. Section 4 reports and discusses the computational results. Section 5 concludes.

2 Problem Definition

The problem under investigation TUPP(fz) is a TUPP with reach stackers pre-assigned to specific areas in the export yard and it can be defined as follows. Given:

- a set of containers $\mathcal{C}$ to be unloaded from a single stationary train, each container $i \in \mathcal{C}$ is characterized by a size ($\lambda_i \in \{20\,\text{ft}, 40\,\text{ft}\}$), a weight class ($\phi_i$), a destination ($d_i$), and a wagon position (θ_i) along the train;
- a set $\mathcal{R}$ of reach stackers available in the export yard and pre-assigned to specific zones for storing containers in $\mathcal{C}$;
- a set of bay-locations $\mathcal{B}$ of the export yard partitioned into different subsets $\mathcal{B}_r \subseteq \mathcal{B}$ of bay-locations, each one served by a RS r, such that $\mathcal{B} = \bigcup_{r\in\mathcal{R}} \mathcal{B}_r$ and $\mathcal{B}_r \cap \mathcal{B}_{r'} = \emptyset$ for all $r \neq r'$.

- a set D_r of port of destination assigned to the yard zone served by reach stacker r, such that $D_r \subseteq D$, $D = \bigcup_{r \in \mathcal{R}} D_r$ and $D_r \cap D_{r'} = \emptyset$ for all $r \neq r'$, (with set D of the destination of containers managed by the terminal);
- each bay-location $b \in \mathcal{B}_r$ characterized by a designated size (Δ_b), a weight class (k_b), a destination among those in set D_r (σ_b), a maximum capacity and current occupancy (q_b, e_b);

The problem consists in determining: (i) the sequence in which the gantry crane lifts containers from the train; (ii) the bay-location b to which each container i is delivered by the pre-assigned reach stacker r; (iii) the resulting sequence of operations of each reach stacker within its bay-location $\mathcal{B}_r$, with the main aims of minimizing the total distance travelled by both the GC and the RSs, and the number of crane-spreader length changes. The following operational assumptions are adopted: the train is stationary and parked parallel to the gantry crane rail; the crane starts at the first wagon position; all container attributes and the initial yard configuration are known at the start of the planning horizon; no equipment failures or concurrent rail operations occur during the unloading horizon.

To solve this problem we can adopt the Mixed-Integer Linear Programming formulation proposed in [4]. The main difference regards the pre-assignment of RSs to the bay-locations in the yard, permitting us to know in advance which RS will store a container in accordance with its destination, that enable us to reduce the size of the model and its complexity. The interested reader can refer to [4] for a detailed description of the model. Here we briefly describe the main characteristics of the formulation. Starting from the decision variables, the main decisions define, for each unloading operation t, the assignment of a container i to a bay-location b operated by the reach stacker r; these binary variables $x_{i,b,t,r}$, $\forall i \in \mathcal{C}$, $t \in \mathcal{T}$, $r \in \mathcal{R}$, $b \in \mathcal{B}_r$ are defined only if container i is compatible with the bay-location b (i.e., $\phi_i = k_b$, $\lambda_i = \Delta_b$, and $d_i = \sigma_b$). Other binary variables are used to compute the handling equipment movement that have to be minimized; in particular, these variables permit to verify the activity of the GC, in terms of distance traveled (thanks to s_t) and changes of the spreader length (z_t), and the activity of reach stackers ($u_{r,t}$) and their position in the yard ($p_{r,b,t}$), useful for computing the total distance traveled by RSs ($y_{j,l,t,r}$). The constraints can be distinguished in three groups. The first group governs unloading logic and verifies the correctness of operations (i.e., in each operation, exactly one container is assigned to a yard bay-location, each container is unloaded exactly once, bay-location capacity is respected). The second group tracks RSs state and movement (i.e., an idle indicator is defined together with a position indicator). The third group computes crane travel and spreader changes.

3 Solution Approach

Due to the combinatorial complexity of the TUPP(fz), a matheuristic solution approach is proposed. The approach follows the Iterated Local Search (ILS) framework introduced in [4] for the original TUPP, and the interested reader is referred to that work for a full and detailed description of the approach. This section presents the modifications introduced by the fixed zone assumption on each neighbourhood operator in the local search, and the multi-start extension that constitutes the core methodological novelty of this paper.

The ILS schema follows [4], even if each cycle is different and applies two operators (Swap and Repositioning) sequentially that incorporate the new Algorithm 1 (GBR), together with a 3-swap perturbation between cycles. A global elitist incumbent is maintained. $N_{\text{cycles}} = 4$. Figure 1 illustrates the schema, with in orange the novelties.

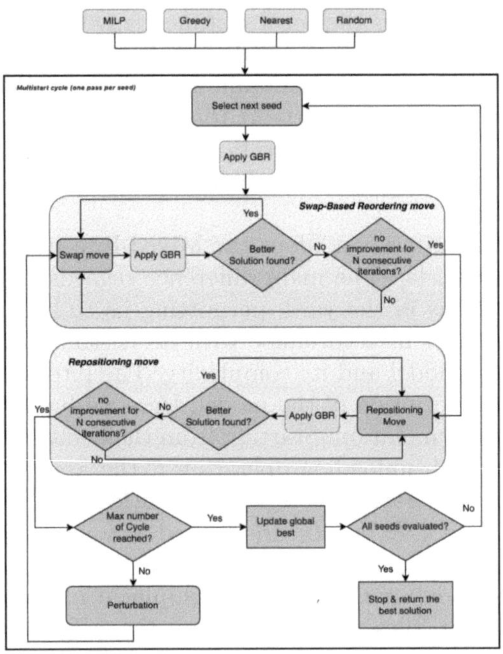

Fig. 1. Multi-Start ILS schema with four seed strategies and embedded GBR. Diversification is achieved via a 3-swap perturbation.

The core novelty is the multi-start strategy: four structurally diverse seeds each launch an independent ILS run, and the best solution is retained. Unlike [4], which used a single MILP warm-start, this design reduces the risk of converging to poor local optima [9,10].

Following [4], a solution is represented as an ordered sequence of unloading operations $S = (o_1, o_2, \ldots, o_{|\mathcal{C}|})$. Each operation o_t specifies: (i) the index $i_t \in \mathcal{C}$ of the container to be unloaded at step t, and (ii) the bay-location $b_t \in \mathcal{B}_r$ within the pre-assigned zone of container i_t where it is stored. Formally,

$$o_t = (i_t, b_t), \quad t \in \mathcal{T} = \{1, \ldots, |\mathcal{C}|\}.$$

Algorithm 1: Greedy Bay-location Re-routing (GBR)

Input: Sequence $(i_1, \ldots, i_n)$; zones $\{\mathcal{B}_r\}$; RS positions $\{p_0^r\}$; bay-location occupancies $\{\eta_b\}$

Output: bay-location assignment $(b_1^*, \ldots, b_n^*)$; RS travel D

for $r \in \mathcal{R}$ **do**
  $\text{pos}[r] \leftarrow p_0^r$
$D \leftarrow 0$
for $t = 1$ **to** $|\mathcal{C}|$ **do**
  $r \leftarrow r(i_t)$
  $\mathcal{F} \leftarrow \{b \in \mathcal{B}_r \mid \phi_{i_t} = k_b,\ \lambda_{i_t} = \Delta_b,\ d_{i_t} = \sigma_b,\ \eta_b < q_b\}$
  $b_t^* \leftarrow \arg\min_{b \in \mathcal{F}}\ \delta(\text{pos}[r], b)$
  $D \mathrel{+}= \delta(\text{pos}[r], b_t^*);\quad \text{pos}[r] \leftarrow b_t^*;\quad \eta_{b_t^*} \mathrel{+}= 1$
return $(b_1^*, \ldots, b_n^*)$,
D

The sequence order determines the crane position and spreader configuration at each operation: the crane resides at wagon position θ_i after operation t, and the spreader is set to size λ_i. Because zones are fixed, the reach stacker responsible for operation t is uniquely identified as r_t; its position within zone $\mathcal{B}_r$ is updated to b_t after each assignment. If reach stacker r is idle at step t (i.e. $r \neq r_t$), it remains at its last active bay-location.

The objective $f(S)$ evaluates the weighted sum of total RS travel distance, total crane horizontal displacement, and the number of spreader length changes, with weight configuration $(\alpha_1, \alpha_2, \alpha_3)$ as defined in [4].

The fixed zone assumption introduces a key modification to every operator used in the local search. Under the TUPP(fz) assumption, the RS responsible for each container is determined by its zone, and only the bay-location within that zone needs to be assigned. This makes it possible to embed a GBR within every neighbourhood move, ensuring that every candidate sequence is always evaluated on bay-location-optimal terms. For a fixed unloading sequence, the subroutine performs a greedy forward pass over all operations. At each operation t, the target reach stacker is uniquely identified by the zone of container i_t; the stacker selects the nearest compatible bay-location within its zone from its current position, and its position is updated accordingly. This pass runs in $O(|\mathcal{C}| \cdot |\mathcal{B}_r|)$ time. Algorithm 1 formalises this procedure.

The local search uses the same two operators as [4]. The *Swap* operator exchanges the position of o_{t_1} and o_{t_2} in the current sequence. The *Repositioning* operator extracts one position from its current position and reinserts it at a different position, shifting all intermediate operations. After every candidate move of either operator, Algorithm 1 is invoked before objective evaluation. Both operators use randomized first improvement and terminate after $N_{\max} = 1000$ consecutive non-improving iterations; Swap runs to convergence first and its output feeds Repositioning.

The complete procedure is referred to as Multi-Start ILS and operates as illustrated in Fig. 1. For each seed in turn, GBR is first applied to the initial sequence to establish a consistent bay-location assignment. The two operators are then applied sequentially to convergence. If the maximum number of cycles $N_{\mathsf{cycles}} = 4$ has not yet been reached, a 3-swap perturbation is applied to escape the current local optimum and the next cycle begins with Swap again. Upon completing all cycles, the best solution of that run updates the global incumbent. It terminates when all four seeds have been processed, returning the best solution found across all seeds and all cycles.

3.1 Seed Strategies

Four seed strategies are proposed, each producing a complete feasible initial unloading sequence. For each seed, Algorithm 1 is applied once to establish the initial bay-location assignment before the first ILS cycle begins. The strategies differ in the criterion used to select the initial bay-location assignment and to order the container sequence, as detailed below.

MILP-Based Initialization. The MILP model is solved by Gurobi with a 300-second time limit. The best feasible incumbent found is used as the starting sequence for the Multi-Start ILS. Algorithm 2 formalizes this procedure.

Algorithm 2: MILP-based Initialization

Input: TUPP(fz) instance; seed time limit $T_{\mathsf{seed}} = 300\,\mathrm{s}$
Output: Initial sequence S_0
Solve TUPP(fz) model with Gurobi within T_{seed}
$S_0 \leftarrow$ best feasible incumbent found
return S_0

Greedy Bay-Location Selection. Containers are processed in their index order within set $\mathcal{C}$ (i.e., the order in which they appear in the input). At each operation, the container is assigned to the lexicographically first compatible bay-location within its pre-assigned zone. Algorithm 3 formalizes this procedure.

Algorithm 3: Greedy Bay-location Selection

Input: Container list $\mathcal{C}$ in input (index) order; zones $\{\mathcal{B}_r\}$
Output: Initial sequence S_0
for $i \in \mathcal{C}$ *in input order* **do**
  $r \leftarrow r(i)$
  $b \leftarrow$ first compatible bay-location in $\mathcal{B}_r$
  Append (i, b) to S_0
return S_0

Nearest Bay-Location Selection. Containers are processed in index order within set $\mathcal{C}$. At each operation, the compatible bay-location that minimizes RS travel from the stacker's current position within its zone is selected. Algorithm 4 formalizes this procedure.

Algorithm 4: Nearest Bay-location Selection

Input: Container list $\mathcal{C}$ in input order; zones $\{\mathcal{B}_r\}$; RS positions $\{p_0^r\}$
Output: Initial sequence S_0
for $r \in \mathcal{R}$ **do**
  $\text{pos}[r] \leftarrow p_0^r$
for $i \in \mathcal{C}$ *in input order* **do**
  $r \leftarrow r(i)$
  $b \leftarrow \arg\min_{b' \in \mathcal{F}(i,r)} \delta(\text{pos}[r], b')$
  Append (i, b) to S_0; $\text{pos}[r] \leftarrow b$
return S_0

Random Bay-Location Selection. Containers are processed in index order within set $\mathcal{C}$. At each operation, a compatible bay-location is drawn uniformly at random from the available options within the container's pre-assigned zone. Algorithm 5 formalises this procedure.

Algorithm 5: Random Bay-location Selection

Input: Container list $\mathcal{C}$ in input order; zones $\{\mathcal{B}_r\}$
Output: Initial sequence S_0
for $i \in \mathcal{C}$ *in input order* **do**
  $r \leftarrow r(i)$
  $b \leftarrow$ uniformly random compatible bay-location in $\mathcal{B}_r$
  Append (i, b) to S_0
return S_0

4 Computational Results

The solution approach has been implemented in Python 3.11 and the MILP component solved using Gurobi 12.0. All experiments were conducted on a desktop PC with a 12th-Gen Intel Core i5-1235U processor (1.30 GHz, 8 GB RAM) running Windows 11. The standalone MILP benchmark (Table 1) was run with a 3600-second time limit. When used as the MILP seed inside the matheuristic, Gurobi is given a separate, shorter limit of $T_{\text{seed}} = 300$ s (Algorithm 2); the two limits serve different purposes and are not interchangeable. All experiments use weight configuration $(\alpha_1, \alpha_2, \alpha_3) = (0.5, 0.3, 0.2)$. These weights reflect the relative operational costs at the reference terminal [4]: reach stacker travel ($\alpha_1 = 0.5$) is dominant because RSs operate continuously throughout the unloading horizon; crane horizontal displacement ($\alpha_2 = 0.3$) is secondary since the GC travels between wagon positions along the train; spreader length changes ($\alpha_3 = 0.2$) incur the smallest penalty as they are infrequent and mechanically fast. This configuration corresponds to W1 in [4], where sensitivity to alternative weight settings is also examined.

To test the proposed approach two benchmark yard configurations are considered, and instances with a number of containers to unload ranging from 10 to 70 have been generated. The 12-bay-location configuration ($|\mathcal{B}| = 12$, $|\mathcal{B}_r| = 6$ bay-locations per zone) is consistent with the instances used in [4] and serves as the reference for comparing exact solver performance under the new zone assumption. The 108-bay-location configuration ($|\mathcal{B}| = 108$, $|\mathcal{B}_r| = 54$ bay-locations per zone) reflects a full-scale operational yard, where each zone contains multiple bay-locations serving containers of different destinations. For each configuration and each container volume, three independently generated instances were used; reported result values are averages over these instances.

Table 1. MILP performance; averages over all instances per size. TL: time limit reached (3600 s). OOM: all instances exhausted RAM.

$\|\mathcal{C}\|$	12-bay-location ($\|\mathcal{B}_r\| = 6$)				108-bay-location ($\|\mathcal{B}_r\| = 54$)			
	Status	Obj.	Gap (%)	CPU (s)	Status	Obj.	Gap (%)	CPU (s)
10	Optimal	16.72	0.00	4.4	Near-opt.	39.55	5.27	1914.4
15	Optimal	24.55	0.00	768.4	TL	54.00	56.34	3601.1
20	TL	28.33	25.43	3600.4	TL	69.75	77.18	3601.2
30	TL	48.52	67.54	3600.4	TL	128.38	86.13	3600.9
40	TL	69.95	82.42	3600.9	TL	166.60	90.19	3600.8
50	TL	97.67	85.90	3600.9	TL	250.02	93.38	3600.4
60	TL	123.42	88.02	3600.5	TL†	320.60	95.94	3600.7
70	TL	146.53	88.83	3601.0	OOM			

† Only 2 of 3 instances solved; the third exhausted available RAM.

4.1 Performance of the MILP Model

Table 1 reports MILP performance for both configurations. By eliminating the RS-to-container assignment degree of freedom, the fixed-zone assumption tightens the LP relaxation, extending proven optimality from 10 containers [4] to 15 in the 12-bay-location setting and halving the gap at 20 containers from 52–55% to 25.4%. The 108-bay-location configuration is qualitatively harder: the 54-bay-locations per-zone model size forces even the smallest instance ($|\mathcal{C}| = 10$) to spend 1914 s for a 5.3% gap, the time limit is exhausted from $|\mathcal{C}| = 20$ onward (gap >77%), and at $|\mathcal{C}| = 70$ all instances exhaust RAM before the LP relaxation completes ($\sim 10^6$ constraints), yielding no feasible solution.

4.2 ILS Performance and Comparison with the MILP

Table 2 reports the best ILS final objective across the four seed strategies for each instance group and compares it with the MILP upper bound. The improvement is defined as $(f_{\text{MILP}} - f_{\text{ILS}})/f_{\text{MILP}} \times 100$, where positive values indicate that the ILS found a better solution than the time-limited MILP. The speedup is computed relative to the 3600-second MILP time limit. The best seed column identifies which starting strategy produced the lowest final objective for each instance group.

Table 2. ILS best objective versus MILP upper bound. Impr. = $(f_{\text{MILP}} - f_{\text{ILS}})/f_{\text{MILP}} \times 100$. For 108-bay-location $|\mathcal{C}|$=70: MILP failed (OOM); ILS result stands alone. GBS: Greedy; NBS: Nearest; RBS: Random bay-location Selection.

$\lvert\mathcal{C}\rvert$	12-bay-location ($\lvert\mathcal{B}_r\rvert = 6$)					108-bay-location ($\lvert\mathcal{B}_r\rvert = 54$)				
	MILP	ILS	Impr. (%)	CPU† (s)	Best seed	MILP	ILS	Impr. (%)	CPU† (s)	Best seed
10	16.72	16.72	0.0	1.8	GBS	39.55	39.55	0.0	3.8	GBS
15	24.55	24.55	0.0	3.2	MILP	54.00	51.75	4.2	5.7	MILP
20	28.33	27.90	1.5	4.8	MILP	69.75	61.35	12.0	7.4	RBS
30	48.52	43.45	10.4	8.9	NBS	128.38	100.40	21.8	12.4	MILP
40	69.95	53.93	22.9	12.0	GBS	166.60	114.72	31.1	16.4	RBS
50	97.67	72.30	26.0	9.0	GBS	250.02	159.85	36.1	23.7	NBS
60	123.42	86.63	29.8	13.1	GBS	320.60	168.20	47.5	34.4	GBS
70	146.53	93.10	36.5	17.0	GBS	OOM	217.20		62.1	GBS
Avg. ($\lvert\mathcal{C}\rvert \geq 15$)			18.2	9.3				25.5	20.8	

† CPU times cover the ILS phase only and exclude the 300 s MILP seed initialisation (Algorithm 2). When the MILP seed yields the best result, total wall-clock time is at most $300 + \text{CPU}_{\text{ILS}}$ s. Instances where a non-MILP seed dominates incur no additional solver overhead.

The ILS exactly recovers the MILP solution for the smallest instances in both configurations, confirming that the local search does not degrade near-optimal starting points. For medium and large instances the advantage grows progressively: in the 12-bay-location configuration the improvement is 10.4% at 30 containers and reaches 36.5% at 70 containers; in the 108-bay-location configuration it is 21.8% at 30 containers and reaches 47.5% at 50 containers. Where the MILP is most severely time-constrained, the ILS advantage becomes dominant. In particular, for $|\mathcal{C}| = 70$ in the 108-bay-location configuration, the ILS delivers the only available feasible solution (217.20), since the solver fails to produce any incumbent within the memory budget.

4.3 Analysis of Seed Strategy Performance

Table 3 and Fig. 2 jointly confirm that no single seed dominates across all instance sizes, justifying the multi-start design. In the 12-bay-location configuration, three regimes emerge: MILP-based initialisation leads for $|\mathcal{C}| \leq 20$, delivering a near-optimal warm-start within 300 s; NBS wins at $|\mathcal{C}| = 30$; and GBS dominates for $|\mathcal{C}| \geq 40$, where processing containers in index order produces a crane-travel-efficient sequence that the local search exploits effectively. RBS, never individually dominant in this configuration, incurs the largest penalty, reaching 25.6% above the best at $|\mathcal{C}| = 70$. In the 108-bay-location configuration the winning seed shifts more frequently: MILP for $|\mathcal{C}| \in \{15, 30\}$, RBS for $|\mathcal{C}| \in \{20, 40\}$

where stochastic diversity compensates for poor solver warm-starts, NBS at $|\mathcal{C}| = 50$, and GBS for $|\mathcal{C}| \in \{60, 70\}$. ILS runtimes are reported in Table 2; in the 108-bay-location configuration they average 20.8 s, confirming compatibility with real-time terminal replanning.

Table 3. ILS final objective by seed; averages over 3 instances. Shaded: best seed per row per configuration.

	12-bay-location ($\|\mathcal{B}_r\| = 6$)				108-bay-location ($\|\mathcal{B}_r\| = 54$)			
$\|\mathcal{C}\|$	MILP	GBS	NBS	RBS	MILP	GBS	NBS	RBS
10	16.72	16.72	16.72	16.72	39.55	39.55	39.55	39.62
15	24.55	25.08	25.65	25.27	51.75	52.75	52.90	53.20
20	27.90	28.77	28.93	30.87	62.22	63.80	62.85	61.35
30	49.58	44.55	43.45	46.03	100.40	102.38	101.87	101.63
40	59.23	53.93	54.70	62.98	120.52	129.72	129.33	114.72
50	85.17	72.30	73.90	83.78	170.75	162.32	159.85	163.80
60	104.28	86.63	87.92	101.10	173.47	168.20	173.87	189.38
70	111.40	93.10	94.10	116.90	238.45	217.20	233.92	237.48

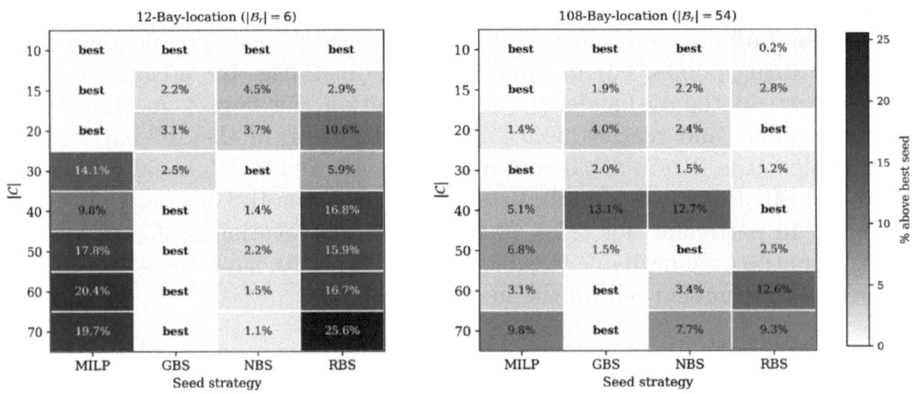

Fig. 2. Percentage gap of each seed above the best for the 12- (left) and 108-bay location (right) configurations.

5 Conclusions

This paper focuses on a special case of the Train Unloading Planning Problem introduced in [4], assuming to have RSs operating in pre-assigned zones of the export yard, and proposes a new solution method based on a multi-start Iterated Local Search. The new assumption removes the RS-to-container assignment degree of freedom, reducing the complexity of the MILP model used to solve it. The new solution method equips the ILS with four complementary seed strategies and embeds a GBR within every neighbourhood evaluation. No single seed dominates across all instance sizes, confirming the value of the multi-start design. Averaged across all instances with $|\mathcal{C}| \geq 15$, the ILS achieves 25.5% mean improvement over time-limited MILP bounds in the 108-bay-location configuration within 65 s. Future research will consider multiple trains and successively the simultaneous loading and unloading operations with one and more trains.

References

1. Weerasinghe, B., Perera, H., Bai, X.: Optimizing container terminal operations: a systematic review of operations research applications. Marit. Econ. Logist. **26**, 307–341 (2024)
2. Abu-Aisha, T., Audy, J., Ouhimmou, M.: Toward an efficient sea-rail intermodal transportation system: a systematic literature review. J. Shipp. Trade. **9**, 23 (2024)
3. Ambrosino, D., Asta, V., Crainic, T.: Optimization challenges and literature overview in the intermodal rail-sea terminal. Transp. Res. Procedia **52**, 163–170 (2021). https://www.sciencedirect.com/science/article/pii/S2352146521001423, 23rd EURO Working Group on Transportation Meeting, EWGT: 16–18 September 2020. Paphos, Cyprus (2020)
4. Ambrosino, D., Asta, V., Bashir, K., Chiesa, C.: Optimizing the train unloading operations in a maritime container terminal. Logistics (2026, submitted)
5. Gharehgozli, A., Roy, D., Saini, S., Ommeren, J.: Loading and unloading trains at the landside of container terminals. Marit. Econ. Logist. (2023)
6. Yang, Y., et al.: Research on the multi-equipment cooperative scheduling method of sea-rail automated container terminals under the loading and unloading mode. J. Mar. Sci. Eng. **11** (2023). https://www.mdpi.com/2077-1312/11/10/1975
7. Kouismi, S., Benabbou, L., Sbihi, N., Penz, B.: Scheduling unloading operations in a railway terminal. In: 2016 11th International Conference on Intelligent Systems: Theories and Applications (SITA), pp. 1–6 (2016)
8. Liu, W., Zhu, X., Wang, L., Li, S.: Flexible yard crane scheduling for mixed railway and road container operations in sea-rail intermodal ports with the sharing storage yard. Transp. Res. Part E Logist. Transp. Rev. **190**, 103714 (2024). https://www.sciencedirect.com/science/article/pii/S1366554524003053
9. Lourenço, H., Martin, O., Stützle, T.: Iterated local search: framework and applications. International Series in Operations Research & Management Science, pp. 129–168 (2019)
10. Martı, R., Moreno-Vega, J., Duarte, A.: Advanced Multi-start Methods. International Series in Operations Research & Management Science, pp. 265–281 (2010)

Mathematical Formulations for the Multi-station Drone Scheduling Problem in Shore-to-Ship Delivery

Jian Hu and Yantong Li(✉)

School of Maritime Economics and Management, Dalian Maritime University, Dalian 116026, China
{hujian,yantong.li}@dlmu.edu.cn

Abstract. Shore-to-ship replenishment is a fundamental operation in maritime logistics, but conventional tender-boat service often suffers from high operating cost, low response efficiency, and considerable operational risk in congested waterways and uncertain weather conditions. Motivated by the increasing use of unmanned aerial vehicles in nearshore logistics, this paper studies a multi-station drone scheduling problem in shore-to-ship delivery, where drones repeatedly execute station–ship–station sorties to serve moving vessels under endurance limits and vessel time-window constraints. To address the resulting spatial–temporal coupling among station assignment, sortie sequencing, service timing, and return feasibility, we formulate the problem as a mixed-integer second-order cone programming model. Computational experiments on randomly generated instances are conducted to evaluate the solvability and computational behavior of the proposed formulation. The results show that the model solves all small-sized instances to optimality and provides feasible solutions for several medium- and large-sized instances within the prescribed time limit. The results also reveal that directly solving the monolithic MISOCP formulation becomes computationally challenging as the instance size increases. Sensitivity analyses further indicate that ship time-window length and land-supplier transportation cost affect station assignment and sortie sequencing. These findings provide a rigorous modeling framework for dynamic shore-to-ship drone operations.

Keywords: Shore-to-ship drone delivery · Multi-station drone scheduling · Mixed-integer second-order conic programming

1 Introduction

Shore-to-ship replenishment is essential in maritime logistics because vessels near ports frequently request small but urgent supplies. These requests are usually served by tender boats, but this mode is increasingly inefficient in congested waterways and uncertain weather under strict traffic regulations [5]. Repeated small-batch trips increase fuel consumption, labor input, emissions, and interaction risk among vessels, while service operations can force ships to slow down,

J. de Armas and E. Lalla Ruiz (Eds.): LOGMS 2026, LNCS 16679, pp. 206–217, 2027.
https://doi.org/10.1007/978-3-032-30795-8_18

drift, or anchor [1]. These limitations motivate faster, safer, and more sustainable shore-to-ship delivery alternatives.

Unmanned aerial vehicles have emerged as a promising alternative to tender-boat operations [4]. With advances in electric propulsion, autonomous navigation, and logistics coordination, drones can cut response time, cost, labor input, and emissions by using direct flight paths and avoiding docking procedures [6]. This feasibility is supported by routine shore-to-ship drone service on the Yangtze River in Nanjing, where moving vessels are served with payloads up to 40 kg [10]. Figure 1 shows representative real-world cases.

(a) A drone flight base

(b) A drone on delivery missions on the Yangtze River

Fig. 1. Real-world cases of drone-based shore-to-ship delivery.

Despite these advantages, scheduling remains difficult in dynamic maritime environments. In the multi-station drone scheduling problem in shore-to-ship delivery, multiple stations and drones must coordinate repeated sorties to moving ships under endurance and ship time-window constraints, jointly determining station assignment, dispatch timing, sortie sequencing, and return feasibility. This strong space–time coupling motivates the operational example in Fig. 2.

As illustrated in Fig. 2, the MSDSP-SSD considers multiple land-based stations and drones serving moving ships through repeated station–ship–station sorties: each sortie serves one ship, requires synchronization with the ship's motion during service to maintain relative stationarity, and ends with a return for battery swap and reloading. Compared with conventional DSP/VRP settings, this problem jointly couples station assignment, cross-station drone scheduling, and time-feasible service of non-stationary customers, yielding a strongly interdependent space–time decision structure under flight-range and operational constraints.

Existing studies have progressed from static urban settings to dynamic maritime operations: time-window MIP models were introduced in [2], MISOCP formulations were developed in [3], and non-stationary vessels, multi-station coordination, and multi-trip features were incorporated in [7–9]. Nevertheless, few models jointly capture multi-station deployment, repeated sorties, continuous vessel trajectories, and dispatch–service synchronization under the relative-

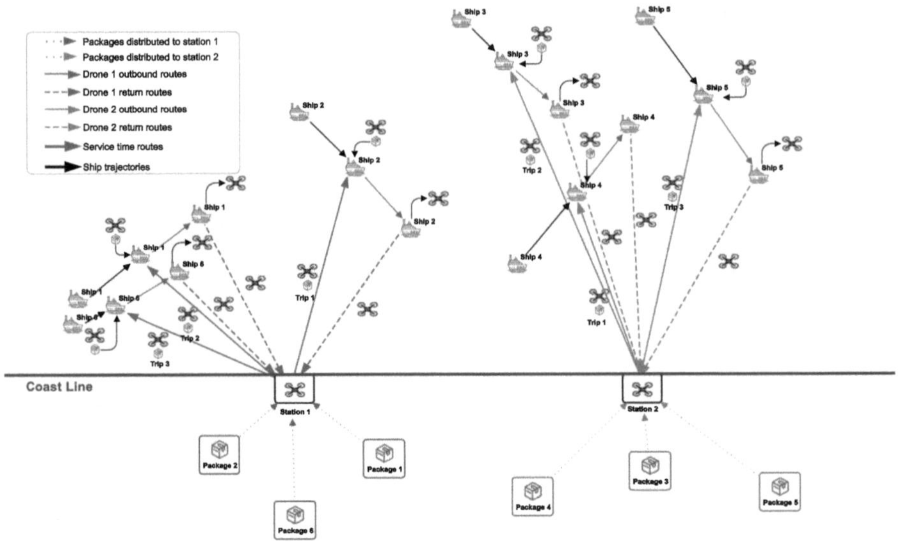

Fig. 2. Illustration of the proposed MSDSP-SSD.

stationary service requirement. This gap motivates the unified MISOCP model developed in this paper.

This paper investigates the MSDSP-SSD. The objective is to jointly optimize station assignment and drone sortie scheduling for moving ships while minimizing the total delivery cost under endurance and ship time-window constraints. To address this problem, we develop a MISOCP formulation that explicitly captures continuous vessel movements, station–ship–station sorties, service synchronization, time windows, and drone endurance constraints. Numerical experiments are conducted on randomly generated instances to examine the solvability and computational behavior of the proposed formulation. The results provide insight into the applicability and limitations of directly solving the monolithic MISOCP model. The remainder of this paper is organized as follows. Section 2 presents the problem description and formulation. Section 3 reports the computational study and result analysis. Section 4 conducts sensitivity analyses on ship time-window length and land-supplier transportation cost. Finally, Sect. 5 concludes the paper and discusses future research directions.

2 Problem Description and Formulation

In this section, we first provide a formal definition of the problem in Sect. 2.1. Subsequently, a symmetric formulation is presented in Sect. 2.2.

2.1 Problem Definition

This study considers the MSDSP-SSD. In this problem, drones perform pickup-and-delivery operations for moving shipborne customers. On land, there are m

drone stations, and each station serves as the departure and recovery location and is equipped with exactly one drone. Offshore, there are n ship demands to be served. Although the base definition assumes one drone per station, the model can still be used to solve scenarios with multiple drones at one station by setting multiple stations to share the same coordinates in the input data.

Each drone departs from its station and sequentially performs pickup–delivery sorties. Each sortie consists of (i) picking up the required item at the station, (ii) delivering it to the associated ship, and (iii) returning to the station. After completing one sortie and returning, the drone starts the next sortie only after a preparation time t^r for reloading and battery swapping.

The ships are moving targets in the two-dimensional Euclidean plane. Ship j starts from an initial position $p_j(0)$ and moves along a straight line at a constant speed V_j^v in a direction forming an angle α_j^v with the land side. Thus, the position of each ship changes continuously over time, and successful delivery requires spatiotemporal synchronization between the drone and the moving ship.

The objective is to jointly optimize drone routing and sortie sequencing, including station assignment, inter-ship visiting order, and service timing for moving ships, so as to minimize the total delivery cost. The objective has two components: drone operation cost and land-supplier transportation cost. The first component is determined by total drone operation time, including outbound flight, synchronized service, and return flight. The second component is determined by the supplier-to-station transport arrangement and increases with the transport distance and assigned transport tasks.

The following assumptions are made:

- Each ship moves at a constant speed along a fixed direction;
- Each drone station is equipped with exactly one drone, and each drone departs from and returns to its own station;
- Each pickup point and its associated ship must be served exactly once;
- The drone cruises at a constant speed V^d during transit, and during service it reduces its speed to the served ship speed V_j^v to maintain relative stationarity; the duration of each pickup–delivery task cannot exceed the endurance limit R.

2.2 Model Formulation

The notation is as follows:

Sets:

N	ships, $N = \{1, \ldots, n\}$.
K	drone stations, $K = \{1, \ldots, m\}$.
N_0	nodes, $N_0 = N \cup \{0, n+1\}$.
Z	integers.

Parameters:

n, m	numbers of ships and land-based drone stations.
R	drone endurance limit.

t^r	reloading and battery-swapping time.
M	sufficiently large constant.
V_j^v	speed of ship j, $j \in N$.
α_j^v	heading angle of ship j, $j \in N$.
s_j	service time of ship j, $j \in N$.
e_j, l_j	earliest start and latest completion times of ship j, $j \in N$.
V^d	drone cruising speed.
p_k^P	coordinates of station k, $k \in K$.
p_j^v	initial coordinates of ship j, $p_j^v = (x_j^v, y_j^v)$, $j \in N$.
p_i^S	coordinates of supplier i, $p_i^S = (x_i^S, y_i^S)$, $i \in N$.
C_d	drone operating cost per unit time.
C_S	supplier transportation cost per unit distance.
C_{ki}	transport cost from supplier i to station k, $C_{ki} = C_S \|p_k^P - p_i^S\|$.

Decision Variables:

x_{kij}	1 if the drone at station k visits node j immediately after node i; 0 otherwise.
y_{ki}	1 if ship i is assigned to station k; 0 otherwise.
t_{kj}	visit time of drone k at node j; t_{k0} and $t_{k,n+1}$ denote departure and return times.
a_{kj}, b_{kj}	start-service and end-service coordinates of drone k for ship j.
u_i	MTZ subtour-elimination variable.
C	total objective cost.

The symmetric formulation is as follows:

$$\min \quad C \tag{1}$$

$$\text{s.t.} \quad C \geq C_d\Big(\sum_{k\in K} t_{k,n+1} - nt_r\Big) + \sum_{k\in K}\sum_{i\in N} C_{ki}y_{ki} \tag{2}$$

$$\sum_{k\in K} y_{ki} = 1, \forall i \in N, \tag{3}$$

$$\sum_{i\in N_0\setminus\{n+1\}} x_{kij} = y_{kj}, \forall j \in N,\ k \in K, \tag{4}$$

$$\sum_{j\in N_0\setminus\{0\}} x_{kij} = y_{ki}, \forall i \in N,\ k \in K, \tag{5}$$

$$\sum_{i\in N\setminus\{0\}} x_{k0i} = \sum_{j\in N_0\setminus\{n+1\}} x_{k,j,n+1} = 1, \forall k \in K, \tag{6}$$

$$x_{kii} = x_{ki0} = x_{k,n+1,i} = 0, \forall k \in K,\ i \in N, \tag{7}$$

$$\sum_{j\in N,\, j\neq i} x_{kij} \leq \sum_{j\in N,\, j\neq i} x_{kji}, \forall k \in K,\ i \in N, \tag{8}$$

$$u_i - u_j + nx_{kij} \leq n - 1, \forall i, j \in N,\ k \in K,\ i \neq j, \tag{9}$$

$$\frac{\|p_k^P - a_{kj}\|}{V^d} \leq t_{kj} - t^r + M(1 - x_{k0j}), \forall k \in K,\ j \in N, \tag{10}$$

$$\frac{\|p_k^P - b_{ki}\| + \|p_k^P - a_{kj}\|}{V^d} \leq t_{kj} - t_{ki} - t^r - s_i + M(1 - x_{kij}),$$
$$\forall k \in K,\ i,j \in N, \tag{11}$$

$$\frac{\|p_k^P - b_{ki}\|}{V^d} \leq t_{k,n+1} - t_{ki} - s_i + M(1 - x_{ki,n+1}), \forall k \in K,\ i \in N, \tag{12}$$

$$\frac{\|p_k^P - a_{ki}\| + \|p_k^P - b_{ki}\|}{V^d} \leq R - s_i, \forall k \in K,\ i \in N, \tag{13}$$

$$a_{ki}^x = p_i^x + \cos\alpha_i^v V_i^v t_{ki}, \forall k \in K,\ i \in N, \tag{14}$$

$$a_{ki}^y = p_i^y + \sin\alpha_i^v V_i^v t_{ki}, \forall k \in K,\ i \in N, \tag{15}$$

$$b_{ki}^x = p_i^x + \cos\alpha_i^v V_i^v (t_{ki} + s_i), \forall k \in K,\ i \in N, \tag{16}$$

$$b_{ki}^y = p_i^y + \sin\alpha_i^v V_i^v (t_{ki} + s_i), \forall k \in K,\ i \in N, \tag{17}$$

$$e_j \leq t_{kj} \leq l_j - s_j, \forall k \in K,\ j \in N, \tag{18}$$

$$x_{kij} \in \{0,1\},\ \forall k \in K,\ i,j \in N_0, \tag{19}$$

$$y_{ki} \in \{0,1\},\ \forall k \in K,\ i \in N, \tag{20}$$

$$t_{kj} \geq 0,\ \forall k \in K,\ j \in N_0, \tag{21}$$

$$1 \leq u_i \leq n,\ u_i \in Z,\ \forall i \in N, \tag{22}$$

$$C \geq 0. \tag{23}$$

The objective function (1) minimizes the total delivery and transportation costs. Constraint (2) provides an epigraph representation of the total cost and ensures that C is no smaller than the sum of drone operating cost and land-supplier transportation cost. Since C is minimized in the objective function, it equals the total cost at optimality. Constraint (3) ensures that each ship is assigned to exactly one drone station. Constraints (4) and (5) represent the flow conservation constraints. Constraint (6) enforces that each drone route starts from the depot and returns to the depot. Constraint (7) eliminates infeasible arcs. Constraint (8) and (9) are the subtour elimination constraints. Constraints (10)–(12) link the binary routing decisions with the continuous timing variables. Specifically, Constraint (10) is activated when ship j is the first ship visited by drone k, and it ensures that the outbound flight time from station k to the service-start point of ship j can be completed before the service starts, after accounting for the preparation time. Constraint (11) is activated when ship j is visited immediately after ship i by drone k. In this case, the drone must finish serving ship i, return from the service-end point of ship i to station k, complete reloading and battery swapping, and then fly from station k to the service-start point of ship j before starting service at ship j. Constraint (12) ensures that, if ship i is the last ship served by drone k, the drone can return from the service-end point of ship i to station k before the route completion time. Constraint (13) imposes the endurance limit on each station–ship–station sortie, including the outbound flight, synchronized service, and return flight.

Constraints (14)–(17) describe the continuous motion of each ship during the service process. Constraints (14) and (15) define the service-start position of ship i at time t_{ki} according to its initial position, speed, and heading angle.

Constraints (16) and (17) define the corresponding service-end position after a service duration of s_i. These constraints ensure that the drone synchronizes with the moving ship throughout the service interval. Constraint (18) enforces ship time windows. Constraints (19)–(23) define the domains of the decision variables.

3 Computational Study

In this section, we examine the solvability and computational behavior of the proposed formulation using 38 randomly generated MSDSP-SSD instances, with the largest instance containing 100 orders and 5 drone stations. The proposed model is coded in C++ and solved by CPLEX 22.1.1.0. The experiments are carried out using a computer equipped with an Intel(R) Core Ultra 9 285H processor running at 2.90 GHz, 64.0 GB of RAM, and a 64-bit Windows 11 operating system. A time limit of 3600 s is imposed for solving the formulation.

It should be noted that the computational study is not intended to claim superiority over existing algorithms. To the best of our knowledge, no public benchmark or directly comparable method is available for the exact MSDSP-SSD setting considered in this paper, which simultaneously involves multiple land-based stations, repeated station–ship–station sorties, continuous vessel movement, endurance limits, ship time windows, and relative-stationary service. Therefore, the experiments are designed to evaluate the solvability, solution behavior, and computational limitations of the proposed MISOCP formulation under controlled randomly generated instances.

3.1 Instance Generation

We generate three groups: 6 small instances with 10–20 orders and 1–4 stations, 12 medium instances with 30–50 orders and 2–5 stations, and 20 large instances with 60–100 orders and 2–5 stations. Stations are evenly placed on the x-axis at 5 km intervals, and vessels move in a two-dimensional plane with $\alpha \in [0°, 180°]$. Vessels are randomly allocated to stations and service sequences are randomly permuted. For each vessel, a feasible visit point and pickup position are sampled, and the post-service departure point is computed from the visit point, vessel speed, service time, and heading. Parameter values are set to $V^d = 80$ km/h, $R = 1$ h, $t^r = 0.03$ h, $V_j^v \in [10, 14]$ km/h, $s_j \in [0.015, 0.030]$ h, $C_d = 20$ CNY/h, and $C_S = 1$ CNY/km. Initial vessel positions are back-calculated from visit points and arrival times. Time windows $[e_j, l_j]$ have fixed width $T = 0.3$ h with $e_j = \max(0, \tau_j - \beta)$, $l_j = e_j + T$, and $\beta \sim U(0, T)$, so that $\tau_j \in [e_j, l_j]$. Although the instances are synthetic, the generation procedure is designed to preserve feasibility and approximate nearshore shore-to-ship settings; validation with real operational data is left for future research.

3.2 Results and Analysis

Table 1 presents the results for small-sized instances, which are the easiest cases in our test set. All six instances are solved to optimality with zero optimality gap.

Table 1. Results of the proposed MISOCP formulation on small-sized instances

n	m	UB	LB	Gap(%)	Time(s)
10	1	177.37	177.37	0.00	0.06
	2	159.76	159.76	0.00	0.80
15	2	239.93	239.93	0.00	3.56
	3	216.60	216.60	0.00	15.80
20	3	335.34	335.34	0.00	54.16
	4	290.68	290.68	0.00	2784.56
Average		236.61	236.61	0.00	476.49

Table 2. Results of the proposed MISOCP formulation on medium-sized instances

n	m	UB	LB	Gap(%)	Time(s)
30	2	356.89	356.89	0.00	2258.61
	3	375.22	366.23	2.40	3600.25
	4	436.44	256.09	41.32	3600.77
	5	379.74	280.84	26.05	3601.00
40	2	509.65	509.21	0.09	3600.52
	3	533.03	467.43	12.31	3600.83
	4	461.64	312.14	32.38	3602.50
	5	560.09	276.03	50.72	3606.88
50	2	629.97	619.69	1.63	3601.11
	3	665.36	450.18	32.34	3603.78
	4	634.45	382.70	39.68	3608.41
	5	671.27	370.55	44.80	3606.44
Average		517.81	387.33	23.64	3490.92

Although the $(20, 4)$ case requires substantially longer runtime than the others, it is still solved to optimality within the time limit. These results indicate that the formulation is tractable for small-sized cases.

Table 2 summarizes the medium-sized instances and shows a clear increase in computational difficulty relative to the small-sized set. For most cases, runtime approaches the 3600 s limit, although one instance terminates much earlier. Nonzero optimality gaps remain prevalent, and the average gap reaches 23.64%. These outcomes suggest that enlarging both the order set and the number of stations weakens bound tightness and makes direct solution of the formulation more difficult.

Table 3 highlights the computational limitation of directly solving the monolithic MISOCP formulation on large-sized instances. Of the 20 tested configurations, only 8 yield feasible UB/LB pairs, while the other 12 terminate without producing a feasible bound pair. Even within the solvable subset, the gap spans

Table 3. Results of the proposed MISOCP formulation on large-sized instances

n	m	UB	LB	Gap(%)	Time(s)
60	2	771.65	659.00	14.60	3605.48
	3	784.62	500.14	36.26	3606.59
	4	766.12	523.49	31.67	3607.22
	5	-	-	-	3610.80
70	2	934.91	763.30	18.36	3603.77
	3	976.14	663.87	31.99	3607.91
	4	916.19	548.63	40.12	3611.66
	5	-	-	-	3618.92
80	2	1040.37	858.41	17.49	3606.88
	3	-	-	-	3612.77
	4	-	-	-	3621.27
	5	-	-	-	3635.36
90	2	-	-	-	3607.53
	3	1167.61	778.75	33.30	3621.30
	4	-	-	-	3635.84
	5	-	-	-	3670.48
100	2	-	-	-	3614.77
	3	-	-	-	3631.34
	4	-	-	-	3670.27
	5	-	-	-	3721.48
Average		-	-	-	-

14.60%–40.12%, with a mean of 27.97%. Although the formulation provides an exact optimization framework, the increasing number of ships and stations leads to substantial branching difficulty and weak lower bounds within the 3600-second time limit. Therefore, the proposed model is more suitable as a rigorous reference formulation for small- and medium-sized instances, while larger-scale MSDSP-SSD instances require decomposition algorithms or tailored heuristics.

4 Sensitivity Analysis

4.1 Time Window Length of Moving Ships

We examine how the ship time-window length T affects routing decisions in the MSDSP-SSD. Figure 3 compares two settings, $T = 0.3$ and $T = 0.5$, with all other parameters fixed. When the time-window length increases from $T = 0.3$ to $T = 0.5$, the total cost decreases from 149.561 to 144.926, corresponding to a reduction of 4.635, or approximately 3.10%. This indicates that a wider service time window provides more scheduling flexibility and helps reduce waiting and detours.

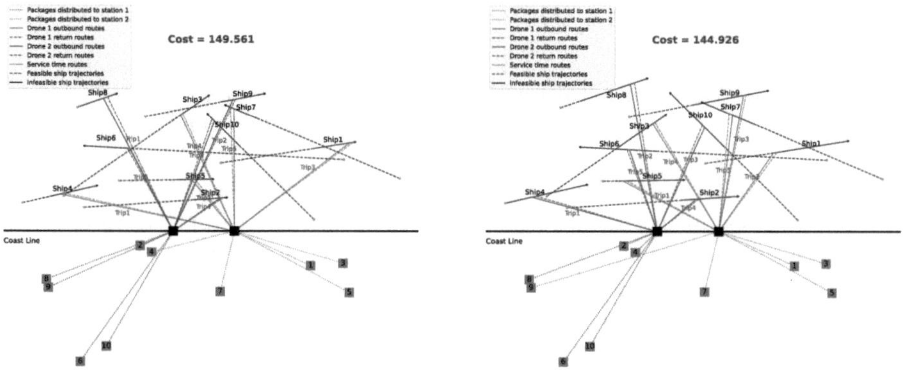

(a) $T = 0\ 3$ (b) $T = 0\ 5$

Fig. 3. Effect of ship time-window length on the MSDSP-SSD schedule

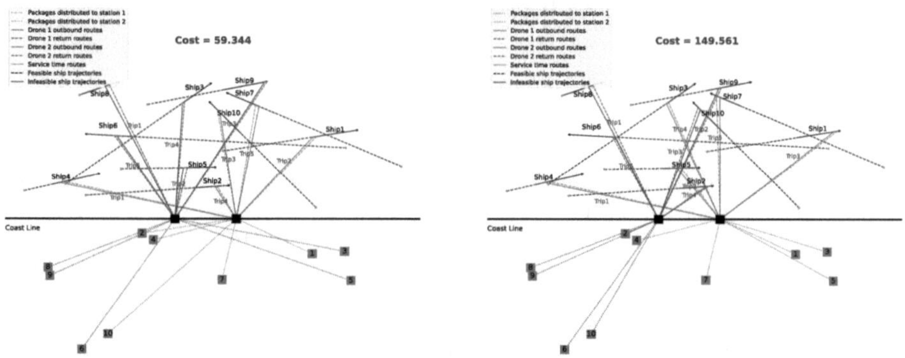

(a) Without land transportation cost (b) With land transportation cost

Fig. 4. Effect of land-supplier transportation cost on the MSDSP-SSD schedule

4.2 Sensitivity to Land-Supplier Transportation Cost

Figure 4 reports a controlled sensitivity analysis in which all parameters are kept unchanged except the land-supplier transportation cost term. Two objective settings are examined in parallel: one excludes this term and the other explicitly incorporates it. The two objective values in Fig. 4 are not directly comparable because the land-supplier transportation cost is excluded in one case and included in the other. The comparison is intended to show that including this cost component changes both station–ship assignment and sortie sequencing, shifting the plan from a drone-operation-dominated solution to a more balanced one that also accounts for supplier-to-station transportation distance.

5 Conclusion

We investigated the multi-station drone scheduling problem in shore-to-ship delivery, in which drones at multiple land-based stations repeatedly perform station–ship–station sorties to serve moving vessels under endurance and ship time-window constraints. The proposed MISOCP formulation solves all small-sized instances to optimality and provides feasible solutions for several medium- and large-sized cases, while also showing that direct solution of the monolithic formulation becomes computationally challenging as the instance size increases. Sensitivity analyses indicate that ship time-window length and land transportation costs affect station assignment and sortie scheduling. Future research will focus on decomposition-based exact algorithms, efficient heuristics, and validation with real-world shore-to-ship delivery data.

Acknowledgments. This study was supported by the National Natural Science Foundation of China (Grant Nos. 72201044 and 72571037).

References

1. Davis, A.R., Broad, A., Gullett, W., Reveley, J., Steele, C., Schofield, C.: Anchors away? The impacts of anchor scour by ocean-going vessels and potential response options. Mar. Policy **73**, 1–7 (2016). https://doi.org/10.1016/j.marpol.2016.07.021
2. Dorling, K., Heinrichs, J., Messier, G.G., Magierowski, S.: Vehicle routing problems for drone delivery. IEEE Trans. Syst. Man Cybern. Syst. **47**(1), 70–85 (2017). https://doi.org/10.1109/TSMC.2016.2582745
3. Gambella, C., Naoum-Sawaya, J., Ghaddar, B.: The vehicle routing problem with floating targets: formulation and solution approaches. INFORMS J. Comput. **30**(3), 554–569 (2018). https://doi.org/10.1287/ijoc.2017.0800
4. Muhammad, B., Gregersen, A.: Maritime drone services ecosystem-potentials and challenges. In: 2022 IEEE International Black Sea Conference on Communications and Networking (BlackSeaCom), pp. 6–13 (2022). https://doi.org/10.1109/BlackSeaCom54372.2022.9858251
5. Nguyen, H.P., et al.: The electric propulsion system as a green solution for management strategy of CO_2 emission in ocean shipping: a comprehensive review. Int. Trans. Electr. Energy Syst. **31**(11) (2021). https://doi.org/10.1002/2050-7038.12580
6. Stolaroff, J.K., Samaras, C., O'Neill, E.R., Lubers, A., Mitchell, A.S., Ceperley, D.: Energy use and life cycle greenhouse gas emissions of drones for commercial package delivery. Nat. Commun. **9**(1), 409 (2018). https://doi.org/10.1038/s41467-017-02411-5
7. Wang, M., Chen, S., Meng, Q.: Drone routing problem for shore-to-ship delivery services considering non-linear energy consumption. Transp. Res. Part B Methodol. **206**, 103410 (2026). https://doi.org/10.1016/j.trb.2026.103410
8. Xia, J., Wang, K., Wang, S.: Drone scheduling to monitor vessels in emission control areas. Transp. Res. Part B Methodol. **119**, 174–196 (2019). https://doi.org/10.1016/j.trb.2018.10.011

9. Yang, Y., Hao, X., Wang, S.: The drone scheduling problem in shore-to-ship delivery: a time discretization-based model with an exact solving approach. Transp. Res. Part B Methodol. **191**, 103117 (2025). https://doi.org/10.1016/j.trb.2024.103117
10. Yao, X.: Revolutionizing river life: Drone delivery brings convenience to yangtze crews (2026), People's Daily Online

A Unmanned Aerial Vehicle Routing Problem with Full Coverage Constraints

Yantong Li[1(✉)], Qi Yang[1], Shanshan Zhou[1], and Shuai Zhang[2]

[1] School of Maritime Economics and Management, Dalian Maritime University, Dalian 116026, China
{yantong.li,yangqi1}@dlmu.edu.cn

[2] School of Business, Operations and Strategy, University of Greenwich, London SE10 9LS, UK
shuai.zhang@greenwich.ac.uk

Abstract. Regularized patrol operations constitute a crucial measure for safeguarding maritime rights, interests, and security. To meet the requirement of round-the-clock coverage across multiple sea areas, this paper proposes a routing method for unmanned aerial vehicles (UAVs) based on discrete time windows, aiming to accomplish 24-hour patrol missions with the minimum number of UAVs. By jointly considering constraints related to endurance, mission continuity, and sea area coverage, we formulate a mixed-integer linear programming model and develop an adaptive large neighborhood search to solve it. Experimental results demonstrate that the proposed method consistently yields high-quality patrol schemes and enables round-the-clock UAV patrols across multiple sea areas, thereby providing effective decision support for unmanned maritime patrol operations.

Keywords: Round-the-clock patrol · UAV routing · Multiple time windows · Adaptive large neighborhood search

1 Introduction

Maritime patrol missions are typically characterized by extensive surveillance areas, spatially dispersed target regions, and long-duration operational requirements. Compared with conventional patrol modes, UAVs offer greater flexibility, mobility, and operational efficiency, and have therefore been increasingly employed in maritime surveillance, target detection, and mission support [1]. This study investigates a round-the-clock UAV patrol routing problem involving multiple target sea areas. Each sea area is required to be visited exactly once within each predefined time window, while two consecutive effective visits to the same sea area must satisfy a prescribed minimum arrival-time interval. In addition, UAV operations are constrained by endurance limits, departure and return requirements, and inter-area travel times. The objective is to minimize the number of deployed UAVs while ensuring continuous patrol coverage over the planning horizon.

J. de Armas and E. Lalla Ruiz (Eds.): LOGMS 2026, LNCS 16679, pp. 218–229, 2027.
https://doi.org/10.1007/978-3-032-30795-8_19

Existing studies have addressed maritime patrol path optimization, UAV scheduling, ship–UAV collaborative routing, and routing problems with time-window or endurance constraints. For instance, Hou et al. developed a multi-UAV scheduling model for long-duration maritime patrol missions [2], Liu et al. investigated multi-trip UAV scheduling for continuous sea-area monitoring [3], Li et al. considered ship–UAV collaborative routing under time-window constraints [4], and He et al. examined robust collaborative planning under uncertain travel times [5]. These studies provide valuable methodological foundations. Nevertheless, limited attention has been devoted to round-the-clock UAV patrol routing that simultaneously incorporates multi-sea-area coverage, repeated time-window service requirements, minimum revisit-interval constraints, and UAV endurance limitations.

To address this research gap, this paper formulates a mixed-integer linear programming (MILP) model for the multi-sea-area round-the-clock UAV patrol routing problem. An adaptive large neighborhood search algorithm is then developed to efficiently solve the resulting routing and scheduling problem. Numerical experiments are conducted to evaluate the proposed method, and the results indicate that it can generate feasible patrol schemes using a limited number of UAVs within reasonable computational time.

2 Problem Description

This study focuses on maritime rights-protection and law-enforcement operations, in which continuous surveillance and operational deterrence are required. The 24-hour planning horizon is discretized into consecutive time windows of equal length, and patrol effectiveness is defined in terms of temporal coverage over each target maritime area. Specifically, a visit by a UAV to a maritime area within a given time window satisfies the corresponding coverage requirement for that period. Additional visits to the same area within the same time window provide limited marginal benefit, because the resulting surveillance information is likely to be highly repetitive while consuming additional UAV endurance and flight resources. Therefore, to avoid redundant resource allocation and maintain balanced coverage across maritime areas, each area–time-window pair is treated as a single patrol task and must be served exactly once.

Figure 1 presents the proposed round-the-clock UAV patrol routing problem through a simplified illustrative example, which involves one airport and three target maritime areas and is intended to explain the basic patrol logic rather than to define the parameter settings used in the computational study. Three UAVs take off from and land at the same airport to maintain continuous 24 h coverage. According to the mission requirements, the 24 h horizon is evenly divided into six time windows, and each maritime area must be visited once by a UAV within each time window. In the figure, different colors distinguish the trajectories of the three UAVs, and the segmented intervals indicate the visit status of each maritime area during each time window. Moreover, to avoid information redundancy and reduced deterrence effectiveness caused by overly dense visits in adjacent time windows for the same maritime area, the visit interval between two consecutive visits to the same maritime area is required to exceed 3 h. For example, the time difference between UAV 1 arriving at maritime area A in time window 2 and UAV 2 arriving at maritime area A in time window 3 must be greater than 3 h.

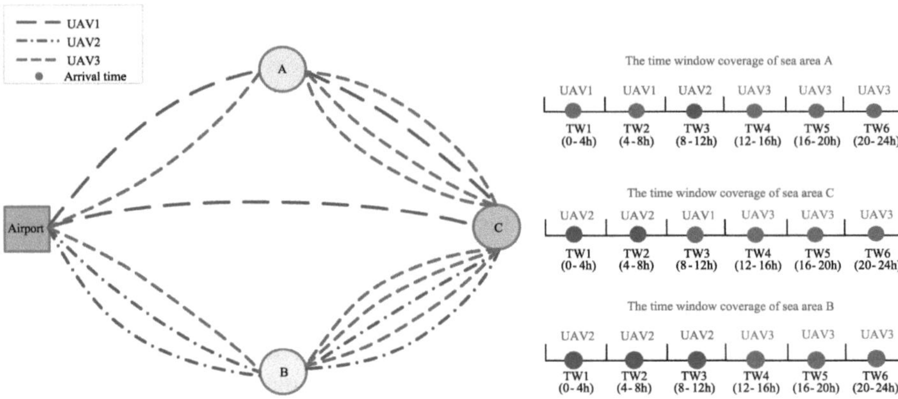

Fig. 1. Illustrative schematic diagram of round-the-clock UAV patrol routing in multiple maritime areas.

Based on the above mission scenario, the problem can be formulated on a directed graph. The node set is defined as $V = N \cup N_0$, where $N = \{1, 2, \ldots, n\}$ is the set of maritime areas, and $N_0 = \{0, N+1\}$ with 0 and $N+1$ representing the airport. The airport time window is defined as $[0, T]$, where $T = 24$ h. For each maritime area i, there are m_i time windows ($m_i \geq 1$), and $[e_i^p, l_i^p]$ denotes the p-th time window of area i. If $[e_i^p, l_i^p]$ is selected to service area i, and UAV k arrives at area i earlier than e_i^p, it must wait until e_i^p; the waiting time is denoted by w_{ip}^k. Arrivals later than l_i^p are not permitted. The travel time between maritime areas i and j is t_{ij}, which satisfies the triangle inequality, i.e., $t_{ij} \leq t_{ik} + t_{kj}$. A fleet of K UAVs is available. Each UAV departs from the airport, visits a subset of maritime areas, and must return to the airport before its endurance is exhausted and no later than T. Without loss of generality, we set $[e_0^p, l_0^p] = [0, T]$, where $p \in \{1, 2, \ldots, m_0\}$, and $t_{0,N+1} = 0$. The objective is to minimize the number of UAVs used while satisfying patrol-quality requirements. Furthermore, to ensure patrol effectiveness, the interval between arrivals in two consecutive time windows for the same maritime area must satisfy a minimum separation requirement, i.e., the interval should be no less than ℓ.

3 Model

3.1 Problem Assumptions

Based on the problem description in Sect. 2, the following assumptions are introduced to facilitate the construction of the MILP model. Accordingly, the model is established under the following assumptions:

- All UAVs depart from the same airport and return to the same airport upon mission completion;
- If a UAV arrives at a target maritime area within any designated time window, the patrol task for that time window is considered completed;
- UAV flight speed is constant, and outbound and return speeds are identical;
- All UAVs are of the same type and share identical performance parameters;
- During the planning horizon, weather conditions, wind speed, and air-traffic flow remain stable and do not affect flight time or route selection;
- For the same target maritime area, the interval between patrol arrival times in two consecutive time windows must be no less than a prescribed threshold ℓ for the patrol to be regarded as effective.

3.2 Definitions of Parameters and Symbols

To formulate the problem, the following notation is defined:

Sets:

V	node set, $V = N \cup N_0$.
N	set of sea areas, $N = \{1, 2, \cdots, n\}$.
N_0	airport node set, $N_0 = \{0, N+1\}$.
K	set of UAVs, $K = \{1, 2, \cdots, k\}$, i.e., the number of available UAVs.
W_i	time window index set of area i, $W_i = \{1, 2, \ldots, m_i\}$, $i \in V$.

Parameters:

n	number of sea areas.
k	number of available UAVs.
b	maximum UAV endurance time.
v	UAV flight speed.
h	length of a unit time window.
ℓ	minimum allowed interval between arrival times in two consecutive time windows of the same sea area.
$[0, T]$	overall patrol planning horizon.
M	sufficiently large positive constant.
m_i	number of time windows of sea area i, $i \in N$.
e_i^p	start time of the p-th time window of sea area i, $i \in N$.
l_i^p	end time of the p-th time window of sea area i, $i \in N$.
t_{ij}	time required for a UAV to traverse arc $(i, j) \in A$, $i, j \in N$.

Decision Variables:

d_k	binary variable, equal to 1 if UAV k is used, and 0 otherwise.
x_{ipjq}^k	binary variable, equal to 1 if UAV k moves from time window p of area i to time window q of area j, and 0 otherwise.
y_{ip}^k	binary variable, equal to 1 if UAV k visits sea area i within time window p, and 0 otherwise.
a_{ip}^k	arrival time of UAV k at time window p of sea area i.
w_{ip}^k	waiting time of UAV k before time window p of sea area i.
Δ_{ip}	difference in UAV arrival times between consecutive time windows $p-1$ and p for sea area i.

The MILP formulation is given as follows:

$$\min\ Z = \sum_{k \in K} d_k \tag{1}$$

$$\sum_{k \in K} y_{ip}^k = 1,\ \forall i \in N,\ p \in W_i \tag{2}$$

$$a_{N+1,p}^k - a_{0p}^k \leq d_k \cdot b,\ \forall k \in K \tag{3}$$

$$a_{ip}^k + w_{ip}^k + t_{ij} \leq M(1 - x_{ipjq}^k) + a_{jq}^k,\ \forall i \in N \cup \{0\},\ j \in N,\ p \in W_i,\ q \in W_j,\ k \in K \tag{4}$$

$$a_{ip}^k + w_{ip}^k + t_{i,N+1} \leq M(1 - x_{ip,N+1,q}^k) + a_{N+1,q}^k,\ \forall i \in N,\ p \in W_i,\ q \in W_{N+1},\ k \in K \tag{5}$$

$$a_{jq}^k \leq M \cdot \sum_{i \in N \cup \{0\}} \sum_{p \in W_i} x_{ipjq}^k,\ \forall j \in N \cup \{N+1\},\ q \in W_j,\ k \in K \tag{6}$$

$$\sum_{p \in W_0} \sum_{j \in N} \sum_{q \in W_j} x_{0pjq}^k = d_k,\ \forall k \in K \tag{7}$$

$$\sum_{i \in N} \sum_{p \in W_i} \sum_{q \in W_0} x_{ip0q}^k = 0,\ \forall k \in K \tag{8}$$

$$\sum_{i \in N} \sum_{p \in W_i} \sum_{q \in W_{N+1}} x_{ip,N+1,q}^k = d_k,\ \forall k \in K \tag{9}$$

$$\sum_{p \in W_{N+1}} \sum_{j \in N} \sum_{q \in W_j} x_{N+1,pjq}^k = 0,\ \forall k \in K \tag{10}$$

$$\sum_{j \in N \cup \{N+1\}} \sum_{q \in W_j} x_{ipjq}^k = \sum_{j \in N \cup \{0\}} \sum_{q \in W_j} x_{jqip}^k = y_{ip}^k,\ \forall i \in N,\ p \in W_i,\ k \in K \tag{11}$$

$$y_{jq}^k \leq \sum_{i \in N \cup \{0\}} \sum_{p \in W_i} x_{ipjq}^k,\ \forall j \in N,\ q \in W_j,\ k \in K \tag{12}$$

$$a_{ip}^k + w_{ip}^k - T(1 - y_{ip}^k) \leq l_i^p \cdot y_{ip}^k,\ \forall i \in N \cup \{0, N+1\},\ p \in W_i,\ k \in K \tag{13}$$

$$a_{ip}^k + w_{ip}^k \geq e_i^p \cdot y_{ip}^k,\ \forall i \in N \cup \{0, N+1\},\ p \in W_i,\ k \in K \tag{14}$$

$$y_{ip}^k \leq d_k,\ \forall i \in N,\ p \in W_i,\ k \in K \tag{15}$$

$$x_{ipip}^k = 0,\ x_{0p,N+1,p}^k = 0,\ x_{N+1,p0p}^k = 0,\ \forall i \in N,\ p \in W_i \tag{16}$$

$$\Delta_{ip} = \sum_{k \in K} a_{ip}^k - \sum_{k \in K} a_{ip-1}^k,\ \forall i \in N,\ p \in \{2, 3, \ldots, m_i\} \tag{17}$$

$$d_k \in \{0, 1\},\ \forall k \in K \tag{18}$$

$$x_{ipjq}^k \in \{0, 1\},\ \forall i, j \in N \cup \{0, N+1\},\ p \in W_i,\ q \in W_j,\ k \in K \tag{19}$$

$$y_{ip}^k \in \{0, 1\},\ \forall i \in N \cup \{0, N+1\},\ p \in W_i,\ k \in K \tag{20}$$

$$\Delta_{ip} \geq \ell,\ \forall i \in N,\ p \in \{2, 3, \ldots, m_i\} \tag{21}$$

The objective function (1) minimizes the total number of deployed UAVs. Constraint (2) ensures that each sea area is visited once within each time window. Constraint (3) limits the mission duration of each UAV to the endurance bound b. Constraints (4) and (5) enforce temporal consistency between consecutive visits. Constraint (6) sets the corresponding arrival-time variable to zero when a node-window is not visited. Constraints (7)–(10) define UAV departure, prohibit invalid starts, mandate return to the airport, and enforce no-relaunch conditions. Constraint (11) enforces flow conservation at each visited sea-area time window. Constraint (12) links visit feasibility to route connectivity. Constraints (13) and (14) define the upper and lower bounds for time-window consistency of service times. Constraint (15) ensures that inactive UAVs cannot be assigned patrol tasks. Constraint (16) eliminates self-loops and prohibits cyclic transitions within the same sea-area time window. Equation (17) defines the arrival-time difference between consecutive windows of the same sea area. Constraints (18)–(20) specify the variable domains. Constraint (21) enforces the minimum inter-window patrol interval threshold ℓ.

4 Algorithm

The multi-sea-area round-the-clock UAV patrol routing problem studied in this paper is an extension of the vehicle routing problem with time windows (VRPTW). Braekers et al. pointed out that VRPTW and its extended variants are NP-hard, and the resulting combinatorial explosion makes it difficult for exact methods to obtain solutions within limited computational time [6]. To address this challenge, an adaptive large neighborhood search (ALNS) algorithm is developed. For clarity, Table 1 summarizes the basic procedure of the proposed ALNS algorithm, and its main components are described as follows:

4.1 Initial Solution

In the proposed ALNS, each patrol task is represented by a node (i, p), where i denotes a target sea area and p denotes a time window. A solution consists of a set of UAV routes, each starting from and returning to the airport. Thus, the number of nonempty routes equals the number of deployed UAVs.

The initial solution is generated by a time-window-clustered greedy insertion procedure. Task nodes are first grouped by sea area and sorted within each group by the starting time of their time windows. The algorithm then scans the groups sequentially and inserts each task node into the feasible position that yields the smallest increase in route duration.

Feasibility is checked with respect to the time-window, endurance, and minimum arrival-interval constraints. If no feasible position exists in the current route, a new route is opened. This process is repeated until all sea-area–time-window tasks are assigned.

4.2 Destroy Operators

At each iteration, the ALNS algorithm partially destroys the current solution by removing a subset of assigned nodes. In this study, seven destroy operators are incorporated to balance diversification and intensification.

- Adaptive random removal. A subset of nodes is randomly removed according to the current solution size, which introduces diversified perturbations and helps the search escape from local optima.

- Worst removal. Nodes with the largest marginal contribution to route cost are preferentially removed. For a node u, its removal utility is evaluated by the change in route travel cost after deleting u, so that poorly positioned nodes are more likely to be selected.
- Shaw removal. Related nodes are removed together according to a composite relatedness measure. In the implemented algorithm, the relatedness between nodes i and j is defined as $RC(i, j) = \phi_1 \bar{d}_{ij} + \phi_2 \bar{t}_{ij} + \phi_3 \bar{r}_{ij}$, where $\bar{d}_{ij}$ denotes the normalized spatial distance, $\bar{t}_{ij}$ denotes the normalized difference between time-window attributes, and $\bar{r}_{ij}$ indicates whether the two nodes belong to the same route. The coefficients ϕ_1, ϕ_2, and ϕ_3 are nonnegative weights. Nodes with smaller relatedness values are considered more similar and are more likely to be removed simultaneously.
- Time-window removal. This operator focuses only on temporal similarity and removes nodes with similar time-window characteristics, thereby intensifying the search in temporally congested regions.
- Distance removal. This operator removes geographically close nodes, which is helpful for restructuring locally compact route segments.
- Route removal. One complete route, typically a route with relatively low utilization, is removed so that its nodes can be redistributed to other routes, thereby creating opportunities for reducing the number of deployed UAVs.
- Minimum-path removal. Nodes are removed from the route containing the fewest distinct target regions, which encourages route consolidation and improves UAV utilization.

4.3 Repair Operators

After the destroy phase, removed nodes are reinserted by repair operators. This study adopts three repair mechanisms.

- Greedy insertion. Each unassigned node is inserted into the feasible position that yields the smallest increase in route duration. If no feasible position exists, a new route is opened.
- Regret-2 insertion. For each unassigned node i, the regret value is defined as regret$(i) = \Delta f_{i2} - \Delta f_{i1}$, where Δf_{i1} and Δf_{i2} are the objective increases associated with the best and second-best feasible insertion positions, respectively. Nodes with larger regret values are inserted first.
- Random insertion. Each removed node is inserted into a randomly selected feasible position to enhance search diversification.

All candidate insertions are checked against the time-window, endurance, and minimum arrival-interval constraints. Therefore, the repair phase reconstructs the solution while restoring feasibility.

4.4 Local Search

To further improve solution quality, two local search operators are embedded in the ALNS framework.

- Intra-route 2-opt optimization. For a single route, all feasible edge-exchange combinations are examined, and the exchange that yields the largest reduction in route flight time is selected.
- Node relocation. A node is moved from one route to another. All feasible relocation positions are enumerated, and the move that provides the greatest improvement in the objective value is selected.

4.5 Adaptive Operator Selection

In the ALNS framework, destroy and repair operators are selected adaptively based on their search performance. All operator weights are initialized to 1, and the search is divided into segments of 30 iterations. At the end of each segment, the weight of operator r is updated by Eq. (22):

$$w_r^{k+1} = (1 - \rho) \cdot w_r^k + \rho \cdot \frac{s_r^k}{t_r^k} \tag{22}$$

where w_r^k is the weight of operator r in segment k, $\rho = 0.15$ is the reaction factor, s_r^k is the accumulated score, and t_r^k is the number of selections.

Operators are scored according to the quality of the generated solution: 50 points for improving the global best solution, 20 points for improving the current solution, a smaller reward for an accepted non-improving solution, and no reward for a rejected solution.

4.6 Solution Acceptance and Rejection

A simulated annealing criterion is used for solution acceptance. The initial and terminal temperatures are set to $T_0 = 1500$ and $T_{\min} = 0.001$, respectively, with a cooling factor of $\alpha = 0.997$. At each iteration, a candidate solution S' is accepted if it improves the current solution S; otherwise, it is accepted with probability $P = \exp(-\Delta C/T)$, where ΔC denotes the increase in the objective value and T is the current temperature.

4.7 Stopping Criteria

To balance search depth and computational effort, a multi-criterion stopping rule is adopted. The algorithm terminates and returns the best solution found when any of the following conditions is satisfied: the number of iterations reaches 2000; the simulated-annealing temperature decreases to the terminal value of 0.001; the CPU time reaches 3600 s; or no improvement in the global best solution is observed for 500 consecutive iterations while the current temperature is below 1% of the initial temperature.

Table 1. Basic Procedure of the ALNS Algorithm

Algorithm 1 Proposed ALNS framework

Require: Task set, travel-time matrix, time windows, endurance limit, minimum interval ℓ
Ensure: Best feasible solution S^{best}
Construct an initial feasible solution S
Set $S^{best} \leftarrow S$ and initialize operator weights
while stopping criterion is not met **do**
    Select destroy and repair operators by roulette-wheel sampling
    Generate S' by destroying and repairing S
    Apply local search to S' if triggered
    if S' is feasible **then**
        if S' improves S^{best} **then**
            $S^{best} \leftarrow S'$, $S \leftarrow S'$
        else if S' improves S or is accepted by simulated annealing **then**
            $S \leftarrow S'$
        end if
        Update operator scores
    end if
    Update temperature and operator weights periodically
end while
return S^{best}

5 Numerical Example

To validate the effectiveness of the proposed model and the ALNS algorithm, this section presents a computational analysis based on generated instances. We first define and describe the instance parameters, and then solve the problem using both direct optimization of the MILP model and the ALNS algorithm for comparison. Both the proposed model and algorithm are implemented in Python via the GUROBI 12.0.1 solver interface. For direct model optimization with GUROBI, the time limit is set to 3600 s, and the computational environment consists of an 11th Gen Intel Core i5-1135G7 @ 2.40 GHz processor with 16 GB of RAM.

5.1 Parameter Settings

In the computational experiments, the performance parameters of the Wing Loong II unmanned aerial vehicle are adopted, with a cruise speed of 370 km/h and a maximum endurance of 20 h. The airport is located at $(0, 0)$, while the target sea areas are randomly sampled without duplicated coordinates from a 300×300 km^2 square region. The travel time between each pair of nodes is computed as the Euclidean distance divided by the UAV cruise speed.

The mission scenario is defined over a 24-hour planning horizon, which is partitioned into eight consecutive 3-hour time windows. All target sea areas share the same set of time windows, and each sea-area–time-window pair is treated as a patrol service task. To assess the scalability of the proposed MILP model and ALNS algorithm, four instance sizes are considered, involving 3, 5, 15, and 30 target sea areas, respectively. For each instance size, five independent instances are generated with different random seeds. The minimum arrival-time interval between two consecutive effective visits to the same sea area is set to $\ell = 1$ hour.

5.2 Computational Results

Table 2 reports the computational results obtained by Gurobi and the proposed ALNS algorithm. In the Gurobi columns, UB and LB represent the incumbent upper bound and the best lower bound returned by the solver, respectively. The ALNS GAP is computed relative to the Gurobi incumbent UB for the same instance, rather than to a certified optimal value. A dash indicates that the

Table 2. Comparison Between Exact Model Solutions and Algorithm Results

n	Instance	Period	GUROBI				ALNS		
			UB	LB	GAP	Time (s)	Best	Time (s)	GAP
3	3–1	24	2	2	0	42.01	2	11.84	0
	3–2	24	2	2	0	67.32	2	9.39	0
	3–3	24	2	2	0	72.5	2	10.41	0
	3–4	24	2	2	0	59.64	2	8.34	0
	3–5	24	2	2	0	41.82	2	7.75	0
5	5–1	24	2	1	1	3600.24	2	53.16	0
	5–2	24	2	2	0	3375.37	2	62.10	0
	5–3	24	2	2	0	1821.91	2	50.19	0
	5–4	24	2	2	0	3054.34	2	54.44	0
	5–5	24	2	2	0	2485.71	2	47.06	0
15	15–1	24	-	1.2	-	3600.03	3	128.69	-
	15–2	24	-	1.2	-	3600.02	4	110.39	-
	15–3	24	-	1.2	-	3600.03	3	101.8	-
	15–4	24	-	1.2	-	3600.08	3	62.17	-
	15–5	24	-	1.2	-	3600.01	3	103.32	-
30	30–1	24	-	2.4	-	3600.11	4	263.35	-
	30–2	24	-	2.4	-	3600.14	4	337.86	-
	30–3	24	-	2.4	-	3600.09	3	396.36	-
	30–4	24	-	2.4	-	3600.08	4	306.33	-
	30–5	24	-	2.4	-	3600.01	4	347.83	-
Average		24	-	1.85	-	2531.07	1.87	20.97	-

corresponding result is unavailable, primarily because Gurobi fails to identify a feasible incumbent within the prescribed time limit.

The results indicate that the proposed ALNS algorithm consistently identifies feasible solutions for all test instances with substantially shorter computation times. For the 3-area instances, Gurobi proves optimality, and ALNS obtains the same objective values. For the 5-area instances, ALNS also attains the best incumbent solutions reported by Gurobi while requiring considerably less computational effort. For the larger 15- and 30-area instances, Gurobi is unable to return feasible incumbents within the 3600 s time limit, whereas ALNS still generates feasible patrol schedules. These observations suggest that the proposed ALNS algorithm is capable of matching exact-solver performance on small-scale instances and remains computationally effective for larger-scale instances where direct exact optimization becomes difficult.

6 Conclusion

In response to the need for round-the-clock UAV patrol planning over multiple maritime areas, this study develops a multi-area UAV patrol routing model and an ALNS algorithm. The proposed model considers time-window requirements, UAV endurance limits, route continuity, and minimum revisit-interval constraints. Computational results show that the ALNS can efficiently generate feasible patrol schedules. For small-scale instances, it obtains solutions comparable to those of the MILP solver, while for larger instances, it remains able to provide feasible solutions when exact optimization becomes computationally difficult. This study provides a preliminary modeling and algorithm framework for the patrol planning of all-weather unmanned aerial vehicles at sea. Future work will refine the model, improve algorithmic efficiency, and conduct sensitivity and comparative analyses under different operational settings.

Acknowledgments. This study was supported by the National Natural Science Foundation of China (Grant Nos. 72201044 and 72571037).

References

1. Shen, L., et al.: Synergistic path planning of multi-UAVs for air pollution detection of ships in ports. Transp. Res. Part E Logist. Transp. Rev. **144**, 102128 (2020). https://doi.org/10.1016/j.tre.2020.102128
2. Hou, B., Yan, W., Zhang, S.: Optimization scheduling for long-term maritime patrol mission with multiple unmanned aerial vehicles. IET Control Theory Appl. **19**(1), e70036 (2025). https://doi.org/10.1049/cth2.70036
3. Liu, Y., Xia, J., Xu, Z.: Drone scheduling optimization for continuous sea area monitoring. Transp. Res. Part E Logist. Transp. Rev. **208**, 104701 (2026). https://doi.org/10.1016/j.tre.2026.104701
4. Li, Y., Wang, S., Sun, H., Zhou, S.: Collaborative vessel-unmanned aerial vehicle routing for time-window-constrained offshore parcel delivery. Transp. Res. Part C Emerg. Technol. **178**, 105189 (2025). https://doi.org/10.1016/j.trc.2025.105189

5. He, Q., Liu, W., Liu, T.L., Tian, Q.: Robust coordinated path planning for unmanned aerial vehicles and unmanned surface vehicles in maritime monitoring with travel time uncertainty. Transp. Res. Part B Methodol. **199**, 103284 (2025). https://doi.org/10.1016/j.trb.2025.103284
6. Braekers, K., Ramaekers, K., Van Nieuwenhuyse, I.: The vehicle routing problem: state of the art classification and review. Comput. Ind. Eng. **99**, 300–313 (2016). https://doi.org/10.1016/j.cie.2015.12.007

A Benders Decomposition Approach for Acoustic-Constrained Maritime Patrol Scheduling

Nirvane Hmid, Mohammad Asghari, and Hamid Afshari(✉)

Dalhousie University, Halifax, NS B3H 4R2, Canada
Hamid.Afshari@dal.ca

Abstract. As maritime traffic increases in the Northwest Atlantic, the conflict between operational security and marine biodiversity conservation intensifies. This paper addresses a strategic allocation and scheduling problem for maritime patrol vessels in Atlantic Canada, with a focus on protecting acoustically sensitive species such as the North Atlantic Right Whale. We propose a Mixed Integer Nonlinear Programming (MINLP) model that maximizes patrolling coverage in mission-critical cells while enforcing strict limits on cumulative underwater radiated noise (URN) in sensitive ecological corridors. To handle the computational complexity of spatiotemporal scheduling under acoustic constraints, a customized Benders Decomposition algorithm is developed for large-scale maritime grids. Computational experiments reveal three key findings: (1) our improved decomposition bypasses the combinatorial explosion inherent in dynamic acoustic tracking, solving multi-vessel instances where standard branch-and-bound solvers exhaust memory, (2) optimal fleet scheduling naturally prevents overlap of transient noise bubbles, ensuring cumulative acoustic energy never breaches behavioral disturbance thresholds, and (3) dynamic spatiotemporal routing enables the fleet to actively manage its acoustic footprint across the time horizon, maintaining high-priority coverage without reducing operational assets. By treating transient acoustic pollution as a strictly constrained mathematical parameter, this framework offers maritime policymakers a scalable, quantitative tool to safeguard search and rescue readiness while enforcing environmental stewardship in sensitive Canadian waters.

Keywords: Maritime Logistics · Maritime Operations Research · Vessel Routing and Scheduling · Underwater Noise · Benders Decomposition

1 Introduction

As global supply chains expand, the Northwest Atlantic is experiencing unprecedented maritime traffic. While this growth strengthens international trade, it introduces severe environmental externalities, most notably underwater radiated

J. de Armas and E. Lalla Ruiz (Eds.): LOGMS 2026, LNCS 16679, pp. 230–242, 2027.
https://doi.org/10.1007/978-3-032-30795-8_20

noise (URN) [1]. Unlike static chemical pollutants governed by strict emission quotas, URN lacks enforceable regulatory thresholds. Maritime authorities have implemented static spatial protections, such as habitat zones restricted from commercial fishing and industrial access, but these do not yet impose limits on acoustic intensity. This regulatory gap largely arises from the absence of real-time monitoring infrastructure capable of measuring vessel-specific sound levels in transit. Consequently, URN remains a transient physical phenomenon that is difficult to regulate without predictive tools. Low-frequency sound from vessel propellers and machinery propagates across vast oceanic distances, disrupting marine mammals' biological frequencies used for navigation, foraging, and communication through *acoustic masking* [2]. Next-generation maritime logistics must therefore extend beyond cost metrics, treating dynamic acoustic footprints as a primary operational constraint.

At the forefront of managing these waterways is the Canadian Coast Guard (CCG), which currently saves an average of 97% of lives at risk each year [3]. This performance relies on proactive maritime patrolling: by maintaining high spatial coverage within dynamic accident cells (geographic zones with fluctuating incident probabilities), vessels are positioned to minimize response times when reactive SAR emergencies occur. Valaei et al. [5] formalized vessel positioning and allocation under spatial uncertainty, highlighting robust prepositioning needs when incident locations are not precisely known. The challenge is therefore to sustain this survival rate without increasing acoustic masking in ecologically sensitive corridors.

Current operations research literature struggles to reconcile these competing objectives. Traditional maritime vehicle routing problems (VRP) and patrol scheduling models prioritize fuel efficiency, route length, or spatial coverage [6]. Although green maritime logistics has advanced, most frameworks focus on greenhouse gas emissions or static speed reduction zones [7], failing to capture dynamic acoustic masking. Conversely, marine biology models accurately describe acoustic propagation and species density but lack optimization frameworks for multi-vessel scheduling. A key methodological gap remains in routing models that dynamically capture transient noise bubbles as vessels move through space and time.

To address this gap, this paper makes three contributions: (i) a novel MINLP formulation for maritime patrol that maximizes dynamic accident cell coverage while enforcing cumulative URN limits in ecological corridors; (ii) integration of dynamic acoustic modeling within routing to compute spatiotemporal noise footprints during vessel transit, treating transient pollution as a constrained parameter; and (iii) a customized Benders Decomposition algorithm [8] that mitigates combinatorial complexity in acoustic tracking and enables exact solutions where standard solvers fail.

The remainder of this paper is organized as follows. Section 2 defines the problem and physical maritime context. Section 3 presents the mathematical formulation. Section 4 describes the Improved Benders Decomposition methodology. Section 5 reports computational results, and Sect. 6 concludes with future research directions.

2 Problem Definition

The core challenge is the strategic routing and scheduling of a maritime fleet within a discretized spatiotemporal grid. The operational area is divided into geographic nodes and a daily planning horizon segmented into uniform time periods. Each vessel navigates this network to observe high-risk maritime zones, aiming to maximize coverage of dynamic accident cells while strictly limiting acoustic energy in protected biological corridors.

Each vessel departs from and returns to a designated home base, navigating the grid over the planning horizon. Cells are either accident cells with time-varying incident probabilities or biological corridors where marine mammals concentrate. The key scheduling tension lies in vessel speed: faster travel increases coverage but expands the acoustic footprint into adjacent corridors. Vessels are restricted to predefined sectors, cannot immediately retrace an arc, and must maintain minimum separation from others at every time step.

Figure 1 illustrates a representative operational scenario, capturing coastal geography and seasonal ice dynamics of the Atlantic Canadian environment alongside patrol vessels operating above a vulnerable marine ecosystem.

As depicted, the fleet must navigate this complex habitat to reach accident cells without overwhelming surrounding biological corridors with acoustic energy. Moving a vessel at high speed to cover a distant high-risk sector generates a large acoustic footprint, creating a fundamental scheduling dilemma.

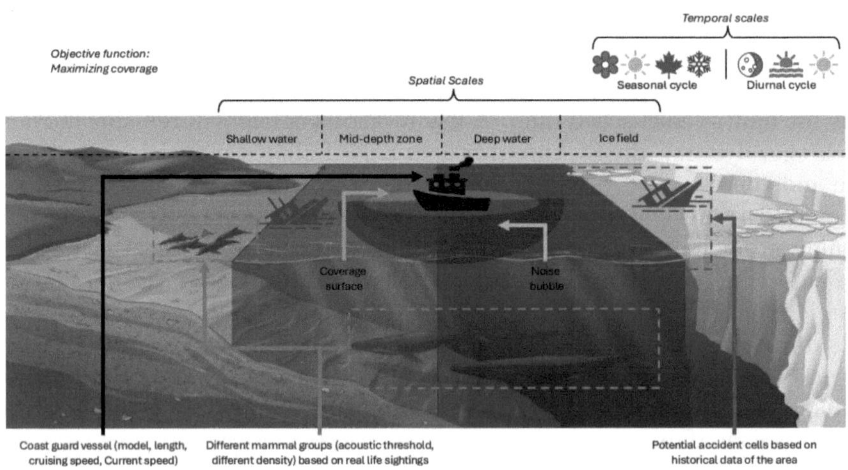

Fig. 1. Overview of the Atlantic Canadian maritime environment and underlying marine ecosystem.

Modeling Assumptions

- **Acoustic Frequency:** The representative frequency is fixed at 100 Hz for all vessels to standardize the calculation of transmission loss and source levels. This captures the range most harmful to baleen whales; broadband spectral modeling is identified as a future extension.
- **Ambient Noise:** Background ocean noise is considered null to isolate and evaluate only the specific acoustic impact generated by the patrol fleet. This conservative assumption ensures any model-feasible schedule remains feasible in practice, where ambient noise partially masks fleet emissions.
- **Time Discretization:** The planning horizon uses discrete time steps. Travel times between nodes are rounded up to the nearest interval to ensure vessels reach grid nodes by the end of each period.
- **Noise Propagation:** Acoustic footprints propagate omnidirectionally. A 360-degree noise bubble is evaluated around each vessel at all times to account for all mammals within the impact radius. Directional models accounting for seabed topology remain a future refinement.
- **Operational Scope:** The framework is restricted to proactive patrolling. In active emergency scenarios, optimized schedules are suspended to allow for unconstrained reactive routing.

3 Mathematical Formulation

This section presents the mathematical formulation for the marine vessel routing and surveillance problem. We define the sets, parameters, and decision variables before specifying the objective function and grouped constraint families.

Sets and Indices

N: Set of available vessels; $n \in N$.
G: Set of marine mammal groups; $g \in G$.
I: Set of grid locations (nodes); $i, i', j \in I$.
T: Set of time periods in the daily patrol horizon; $t \in T$.
S: Set of patrol sectors; $s \in S,\ S \subset I$.
Ω_{nt}: The proximity set (noise bubble) containing impacted nodes; $j \in \Omega_{nt}$.

Parameters

ρ_{jg}: Density of mammal group g at location j.
P_{it}: Risk probability of location i at time t.
σ_n: Operational coverage radius of vessel n.
Ref_n: Baseline acoustic source level of vessel n.
$\mathrm{Loss}(d)$: Acoustic transmission loss over distance d.
$V_n^{\min}, V_n^{\max}$: Minimum and maximum operational speed of vessel n.
d_{ij}: Standard geometric distance between nodes i and j.
$\alpha_{m,g}$: Biological acoustic threshold levels for group g, indexed by m.
Δt: Duration of a single time period (in hours).
R: Acoustic impact radius defining the boundary of Ω_{nt}.

D_{safe}: Minimum safe spatial separation between vessels.
ΔT: Minimum temporal cooling periods before revisiting a node.
$V_S^{\max}$: Maximum number of vessels allowed simultaneously in sector S.
β: Staleness growth weight for location i.
γ: Maximum deviation allowed from the average distance of the fleet.
M: A sufficiently large positive number.
E_{ns}: Binary parameter; 1 if vessel n is assigned to sector s, 0 otherwise.
θ_g: Baseline acoustic disturbance quota for the mammal group g.
β_g: Confidence level for the constraint on acoustic disturbance of group g.

Decision Variables

X_{in0}: Binary; 1 if vessel n starts at location i at $t = 0$, 0 otherwise.
Y_{int}: Binary; 1 if vessel n is at location i at time t, 0 otherwise.
$Z_{ii'nt}$: Binary; 1 if vessel n travels from i to i' at time t, 0 otherwise.
C_{it}: Binary; 1 if location i is covered at time t, 0 otherwise.
$V_{ii'nt}$: Continuous speed of vessel n on edge (i, i') at time t.
S_{it}: Auxiliary variable representing the staleness of location i at time t.

Objective Function

$$\max Z_{cov} = \sum_{t \in T} \sum_{i \in I} P_{it} \cdot S_{it} \cdot C_{it} \tag{1}$$

The objective in Eq. (1) maximizes total surveillance effectiveness by prioritizing the coverage of high-risk accident cells (P_{it}) that have remained unobserved for extended durations, as quantified by the staleness variable S_{it}. A cell with high incident probability that has not been recently visited contributes more to the objective than a recently observed cell with the same risk level, incentivizing the fleet to revisit neglected sectors proactively. The product of staleness and coverage in Eq. (1) is handled by a standard auxiliary-variable substitution, so the formulation remains mixed-integer linear.

Constraints

$$\sum_{i \in I} X_{in0} = 1 \quad \forall n \in N \tag{2}$$

$$Y_{in|T|} = X_{in0} \quad \forall i \in I, n \in N \tag{3}$$

$$Y_{in0} = X_{in0} \quad \forall i \in I, n \in N \tag{4}$$

$$\sum_{i' \in I} Z_{ii'nt} = Y_{in(t-1)} \quad \forall i \in I, n \in N, t \in T \setminus \{0\} \tag{5}$$

$$\sum_{i \in I} Z_{ii'nt} = Y_{i'nt} \quad \forall i' \in I, n \in N, t \in T \setminus \{0\} \tag{6}$$

$$Z_{ii'nt} + Z_{i'in(t+1)} \leq 1 \quad \forall i, i' \in I, i \neq i', n \in N, t \in T \setminus \{|T|\} \tag{7}$$

$$Z_{iint} = 0 \quad \forall i \in I, n \in N, t \in T \tag{8}$$

Equations (2) and (3) enforce mission boundaries, ensuring each vessel departs from and returns to its designated base. Equation (4) synchronizes the initial position variable, while Eqs. (5) and (6) maintain spatiotemporal path continuity between consecutive time steps. Equation (7) prevents a vessel from immediately retracing its prior arc, and Eq. (8) forbids self-loops, requiring movement to a distinct node at every time step.

$$V_n^{\min} \cdot Z_{ii'nt} \leq V_{ii'nt} \leq V_n^{\max} \cdot Z_{ii'nt} \quad \forall i, i' \in I, n \in N, t \in T \tag{9}$$

$$d_{ii'} Z_{ii'nt} \leq V_{ii'nt} \Delta t \quad \forall i, i' \in I, n \in N, t \in T \tag{10}$$

Equation (9) bounds the continuous speed variable $V_{ii'nt}$ relative to the binary routing variable $Z_{ii'nt}$, ensuring valid velocities are assigned only to active transit arcs. Equation (10) links speed, distance, and time, ensuring that the physical distance between two nodes can be covered within a single time period Δt.

$$C_{it} \leq \sum_{n \in N} \sum_{j \in I : d_{ji} \leq \sigma_n} Y_{jnt} \quad \forall i \in I, t \in T \tag{11}$$

$$\sum_{n \in N} \sum_{j \in I : d_{ji} \leq \sigma_n} Y_{jnt} \leq |N| \cdot C_{it} \quad \forall i \in I, t \in T \tag{12}$$

$$S_{it} = \min\left(1, (S_{i(t-1)} + \beta) \cdot (1 - C_{i(t-1)})\right) \quad \forall i \in I, t \in T \setminus \{0\} \tag{13}$$

$$\sum_{i \in s} Y_{int} \leq E_{ns} \quad \forall n \in N, s \in S, t \in T \tag{14}$$

$$\sum_{t \in T} \sum_{i, i' \in I} d_{ii'} Z_{ii'nt} \leq (1 + \gamma) \frac{\sum_{n' \in N} \sum_{t \in T} \sum_{i, i' \in I} d_{ii'} Z_{ii'n't}}{|N|} \quad \forall n \in N \tag{15}$$

Equations (11) and (12) tightly couple the coverage variable to vessel positions, activating coverage only when a node falls within the operational radius σ_n of at least one vessel. Equation (13) models dynamic staleness with a unit cap, continuously accumulating for unobserved nodes and resetting upon coverage; it is applied in its standard linear form (staleness starts at zero, grows by while a node is unobserved, is capped at one, and resets on coverage). Equation (14) restricts each vessel to its assigned geographic sector, and Eq. (15) enforces fleet-wide workload equity by bounding individual distance deviations within a tolerance γ.

$$Y_{int} + Y_{i'n't} \leq 1 \quad \forall t \in T, n \neq n', i, i' \in I \text{ s.t. } d_{ii'} < D_{\text{safe}} \tag{16}$$

Equation (16) enforces a spatial exclusion zone, ensuring a minimum safe separation distance D_{safe} between any two active vessels to prevent collisions and operational interference.

$$R = \max \left\{ d \in \mathbb{R}^+ \;\middle|\; \max_{n \in N}(\text{Ref}_n) - \text{Loss}(d) \geq \min_{g \in G}(\alpha_{m_1, g}) \right\} \tag{17}$$

Equation (17) defines R, the maximum acoustic impact radius, by evaluating the loudest possible vessel source level against the most sensitive biological threshold. Any acoustic energy propagating beyond distance R dissipates safely below behavioral impact levels, establishing the spatial boundary for the fleet's noise proximity set. The empirical acoustic source level for each vessel is derived from its physical profile using the established JOMOPANS framework [4]:

$$\begin{aligned}\mathrm{Ref}_n = K - 20\log(\hat{f}_1) - 10\log\left(\left(1-\frac{\hat{f}}{\hat{f}_1}\right)^2 + D^2\right)\\ + 20\log\left(\frac{L}{l_0}\right) + 10\log(0.231\hat{f})\end{aligned} \tag{18}$$

where K is the baseline acoustic constant, $\hat{f}$ matches the target species' hearing sensitivity, and $\hat{f}_1$ is the vessel's characteristic frequency. D denotes spectral width, L is vessel length scaled by reference l_0, and the final logarithmic term is a bandwidth correction isolating the frequency range responsible for acoustic masking. Acoustic transmission loss over distance d follows the shallow-water geometrical spreading model [9]:

$$\mathrm{Loss}(d) = 15\log_{10}(d) \tag{19}$$

$$\Omega_{nt} = \left\{ j \in I \;\middle|\; \sum_{i,i' \in I} Z_{ii'nt} \cdot \mathbb{1}\{d_{ij} \le R\} \ge 1 \right\} \tag{20}$$

$$L_{ii'njt} = \mathrm{Ref}_n + 60\log_{10}\left(\frac{V_{ii'nt}}{V_n^{\max}}\right) - \mathrm{Loss}(d_{ij}) \tag{21}$$

$$L_{jt}^{\text{total}} = 10\log_{10}\left(\sum_{n: j \in \Omega_{nt}} \sum_{i,i' \in I} 10^{\frac{L_{ii'njt}}{10}} \cdot Z_{ii'nt}\right) \quad \forall j \in I, t \in T \tag{22}$$

$$I_{jtg} = \sum_{m=m_1}^{m_{n-1}} \mathbb{1}\left\{L_{jt}^{\text{total}} > \alpha_{m,g}\right\} \quad \forall j \in I, t \in T, g \in G \tag{23}$$

$$\mathbb{P}\left(\sum_{j \in I}\sum_{t \in T} I_{jtg} \cdot \rho_{jg} \le \theta_g\right) \ge \beta_g \quad \forall g \in G \tag{24}$$

$$L_{jt}^{\text{total}} \le \alpha_{m_n,g} + M \cdot (1 - \mathbb{1}\{\rho_{jg} > 0\}) \quad \forall j \in I, t \in T, g \in G \tag{25}$$

Equation (20) uses radius R to define the proximity set Ω_{nt}, representing the active noise bubble around transiting vessels while excluding distant nodes for efficiency. For nodes within this bubble, Eq. (21) computes acoustic propagation by adjusting baseline source levels for vessel speed and range. Equation (22) aggregates fleet emissions logarithmically to determine total noise at receiver nodes; these acoustic terms are evaluated only on arcs that are actually travelled, where the vessel speed is strictly positive. Equation (23) quantifies behavioral disturbance by flagging exceedances of biological tolerance thresholds. Equation (24) is a chance constraint requiring cumulative acoustic disturbance to remain below quota θ_g with probability at least β_g. The source of uncertainty is mammal density ρ_{jg}, stochastic at planning time due to seasonal whale migration; β_g is a regulatory confidence level (e.g., $\beta_g = 0.90$ requires quota compliance in at least 90% of population scenarios) whose deterministic equivalent requires the quota to hold across a set of seasonal mammal-density scenarios whose combined probability is at least ß$_g$. Finally, Eq. (25) imposes a rigid safety cap to prevent acute physiological injury to marine mammals in populated sectors.

4 Proposed Solution Methodology

The MINLP in Sect. 3 couples binary routing variables $Z_{ii'nt}$ with nonlinear acoustic aggregation in Eq. (22), rendering the problem intractable for standard solvers at realistic grid sizes. Improved Benders Decomposition resolves this by partitioning the problem into two interacting components iteratively.

The **Master Problem (MP)** retains the linear routing, coverage, speed, and fleet coordination constraints (Eqs. 2–16); the probabilistic acoustic quota (Eq. 24) is checked in the Subproblem, which returns a feasibility cut when it is breached, after the product term in the objective is replaced by a standard linear substitution. At each iteration, the MP produces a candidate routing plan $\hat{Z}_{ii'nt}$ and speed assignment $\hat{V}_{ii'nt}$.

The **Subproblem (SP)** receives $(\hat{Z}, \hat{V})$ from the MP and performs an acoustic feasibility check. Given the candidate solution, the SP first computes the active noise bubble for each vessel n and time period t:

$$\hat{\Omega}_{nt} = \left\{ j \in I \;\middle|\; \sum_{i,i' \in I} \hat{Z}_{ii'nt} \cdot \mathbb{1}\{d_{ij} \leq R\} \geq 1 \right\} \tag{26}$$

then evaluates instantaneous noise at each receiver node within the bubble:

$$\hat{L}_{ii'njt} = \text{Ref}_n + 60 \log_{10}\left(\frac{\hat{V}_{ii'nt}}{V_n^{\max}} \right) - \text{Loss}(d_{ij}) \quad \forall j \in \hat{\Omega}_{nt} \tag{27}$$

and logarithmically aggregates fleet emissions at each receiver:

$$\hat{L}_{jt}^{\text{total}} = 10 \log_{10}\left(\sum_{n:\, j \in \hat{\Omega}_{nt}} \sum_{i,i' \in I} 10^{\frac{\hat{L}_{ii'njt}}{10}} \cdot \hat{Z}_{ii'nt} \right) \quad \forall j \in I,\, t \in T \tag{28}$$

The SP then checks the hard physiological injury limit (Eq. 25) at every populated node:

$$\hat{L}_{jt}^{\text{total}} \leq \alpha_{m_n, g} \quad \forall j \in I,\, t \in T,\, g \in G \text{ s.t. } \rho_{jg} > 0 \tag{29}$$

If no violation is detected, the candidate $(\hat{Z}, \hat{V})$ is acoustically feasible and the algorithm terminates. If a violation is detected, the SP first checks whether a slower, acceptable speed exists; if so it adds only the speed cut, and it adds the no-good cut only when no acceptable speed exists. The two are not added together. Each cut eliminates at least one infeasible configuration while preserving all feasible ones, and since the arc-time space $I \times I \times N \times T$ is finite, termination is guaranteed.

The Benders Decomposition framework separates linear routing decisions from nonlinear acoustic physics using four specialized cuts. Let $(\bar{i}, \bar{i}', \bar{n})$ denote the offending arc identified by the SP at a given iteration.

Cut 1 (Global Arc Ban) is applied when the noise violation on arc $(\bar{i}, \bar{i}', \bar{n})$ persists even at minimum speed $V_{\bar{n}}^{\min}$, meaning no feasible speed exists for that arc. It permanently removes the arc from all time periods:

$$\sum_{\tau \in T} Z_{\bar{i}\bar{i}'\bar{n}\tau} = 0 \tag{30}$$

Cut 2 (Speed Bound Tightening) is applied when arc $(\bar{i}, \bar{i}', \bar{n})$ is acoustically feasible at some speed below $V_{\bar{n}}^{\max}$. The SP computes the maximum safe speed $v_{\text{safe}}(\bar{n}, \bar{i}, \bar{i}')$ and injects a tightening of constraint (9):

$$V_{\bar{i}\bar{i}'\bar{n}\tau} \leq v_{\text{safe}}(\bar{n}, \bar{i}, \bar{i}') \cdot Z_{\bar{i}\bar{i}'\bar{n}\tau} \quad \forall \tau \in T \tag{31}$$

Cut 3 (Active Set No-Good Cut) is applied when the violation results from the cumulative interaction of the full candidate configuration $\hat{Z}$ rather than a single arc. It forces the next MP solution to differ from the current candidate by at least one active arc:

$$\sum_{n \in N} \sum_{i \in I} \sum_{i' \in I} \sum_{t \in T} \left(\hat{Z}_{ii'nt} \cdot Z_{ii'nt} \right) \leq \left(\sum_{n \in N} \sum_{i \in I} \sum_{i' \in I} \sum_{t \in T} \hat{Z}_{ii'nt} \right) - 1 \tag{32}$$

Cut 4 (Fractional Pruning Cut) is applied only when an arc breaches the injury limit on its own even at minimum speed, so it can never belong to a valid schedule; otherwise it only guides branching and is switched off in runs that report optimality. Unlike Cut 1, it targets only the specific time period $\bar{t}$ and prunes the branch before it fully develops:

$$Z_{\bar{i}\bar{i}'\bar{n}\bar{t}} = 0 \tag{33}$$

The solution approach follows an improved Benders Decomposition framework where the Master Problem manages spatiotemporal routing, speed assignment, and coverage maximization while satisfying the fleet level acoustic quota defined in Eq. (24). The Subproblem acts as a high-fidelity acoustic filter, verifying proposed routes against the hard physiological injury limits of Eq. (25) by evaluating the logarithmic fleet aggregation in Eq. (22). If a threshold is breached, the framework injects cuts back into the Master Problem: Eq. (30) bans edges found to be acoustically infeasible at any speed; Eq. (31) caps the

Algorithm 1: Improved Active Set Acoustic Callback

```
Input: MP state (MIPSOL or MIPNODE), proposed routing Ẑ, speeds V̂, penalties L̂^pen
Parameters: Injury limits α_{m_n,g}, JOMOPANS baselines Ref_n, transmission loss Loss(d_{ii'})
if Solver State == MIPSOL then
    Identify active arcs: A ← {(i, i', n, t) | Ẑ_{ii'nt} = 1};
    for each time step t ∈ T do
        for each receiver node j ∈ I do
            Calculate fleet aggregate noise L̂_{jt}^total via Eqs. (26)–(28);
            if L̂_{jt}^total > α_{m_n,g} for any g s.t. ρ_{jg} > 0 then
                Identify offending arc (ī, ī', n̄);
                if Violation persists at V_n̄^min for all vessels then
                    Inject Cut 1 (Global Arc Ban) via Eq. (30) ∀τ ∈ T;
                else
                    Calculate v_safe(n̄, ī, ī') for offending arc;
                    Inject Cut 2 (Speed Bound Tightening) via Eq. (31);
                    Inject Cut 3 (Active Set No-Good) via Eq. (32);
                break;
if Solver State == MIPNODE then
    if Node LP relaxation is Optimal then
        Extract fractional arcs: Φ ← {(i, i', n, t) | Ẑ_{ii'nt} > 0.2};
        for each (ī, ī', n̄, t̄) ∈ Φ do
            Evaluate projected noise and inject Cut 4 (Fractional Pruning) via Eq. (33) if
            thresholds are breached;
```

speed variable on specific arcs to a safe maximum v_{safe}; Eq. (32) invalidates the specific proposed routing configuration $\hat{Z}_{ii'nt}$; and Eq. (33) provides early pruning at fractional nodes.

This iterative loop allows the Master Problem to propose maximum coverage schedules while the Subproblem systematically prunes routing configurations that violate ecological safety. The algorithm terminates when a schedule passes all acoustic checks. The callback fires at integer-feasible nodes (MIPSOL) to certify acoustic safety before recording a solution, and at fractional nodes (MIPNODE) to prune subtrees already guaranteed infeasible.

5 Results and Discussion

The framework's performance is evaluated via spatial visualization and computational benchmarking. Figure 2 displays optimal maritime routing in Atlantic Canada, where vessel spacing prevents acoustic overlap between noise signatures. The model maximizes patrol coverage in accident-prone areas while avoiding protected biological corridors.

Table 1 demonstrates scale-dependent computational efficiency. While the direct Gurobi solver is faster at small scales due to low overhead, performance converges at medium scales (845–2,056 nodes). The Improved Benders Decomposition (IBD) excels at large scales: for the 4,428-node, 2-vessel instance, it outperforms the direct solver three-fold. Notably, for the 4,428-node, 4-vessel

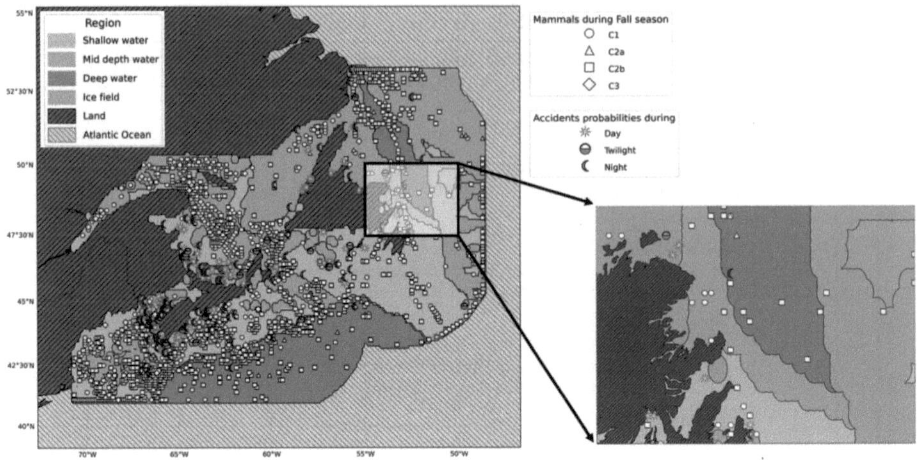

Fig. 2. Operational Study Area in Atlantic Canada.

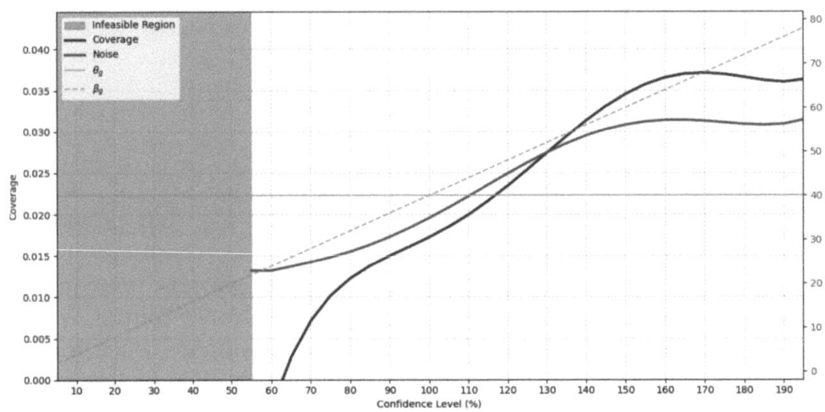

Fig. 3. Trade-off between coverage objective function and noise.

instance, only the proposed method reached a globally optimal, acoustically feasible schedule; Gurobi ran out of memory and standard Benders timed out with a 24.18% gap.

Figure 3 illustrates the sensitivity of the coverage objective (Z_{cov}) to probabilistic confidence levels (β_g).

The model is infeasible below 55% of the quota, as strict acoustic limits preclude valid routing. Above this threshold, increasing the acoustic budget increases spatial coverage and aggregate noise. This provides a quantitative tool for policymakers to balance mission readiness against regulatory limits (θ_g, β_g).

Table 1. Computational Performance of Solution Methods.

Vessels ($\|N\|$)	Nodes ($\|I\|$)	Gurobi Solver (s)	Benders Decomp. (s)	Improved Benders (s)
1	110	20.60	57.80	59.22
2	110	882.29	3,112.75	3,054.14
4	110	26,423.32	11,118.20	17,350.60
1	845	55.40	132.50	135.12
2	845	2,150.81	5,120.23	4,950.80
1	2,056	142.60	315.40	290.85
2	2,056	12,450.22	11,840.55	8,920.40
1	4,428	385.20	810.50	640.35
2	4,428	48,520.80	31,240.60	17,540.25
4	4,428	OOM	86,400.00*	38,650.40

OOM: Out of Memory error recorded during root relaxation.
** Time limit reached with a 24.18% optimality gap.*

6 Conclusion

This research develops a high-performance framework that jointly manages mission timing and ecological safety. Maritime patrols are time-critical, so solver speed is as important as route accuracy. By separating linear spatiotemporal routing from nonlinear acoustic propagation, the Improved Benders Decomposition offers strong computational gains for large-scale multi-vessel instances in our case where standard solvers exhaust memory or fail to close the optimality gap; at smaller scales the direct solver remains competitive. This ensures that for large maritime grids, optimal schedules are generated within operational windows rather than days, enabling responsive and reliable fleet deployment. The trade-off between spatial coverage and acoustic limits provides a decision-support tool for balancing mission readiness and habitat preservation. This study offers a scalable solution for sustainable management of Canadian waters, reconciling human safety missions and environmental stewardship. Future work will explore broadband acoustic models and stochastic mammal density distributions to improve ecological realism.

References

1. DFO. Action Plan for the North Atlantic Right Whale in Canada. Species at Risk Act Action Plan Series, Ottawa (2021)
2. Clear Seas Centre: How Canada is Mitigating Underwater Radiated Noise (2024). https://clearseas.org/insights/canada-mitigate-urn/
3. Canadian Coast Guard: MSAR in Canada (2024). https://www.canada.ca/en/canadian-coast-guard/corporate/publications/maritime-search-rescue.html. Accessed 23 Mar 2026
4. Kinneging, N.: Joint monitoring programme of ambient noise North Sea (Jomopans): opinion paper on continuous noise pollution. J. Sea Res. **195**, 102414 (2023). https://doi.org/10.1016/j.seares.2023.102414
5. Valaei, M., Saif, A., Sarhadi, H., Afshari, H.: Robust prepositioning and allocation of maritime search and rescue vessels with incident location uncertainty. Transp. Res. Part E **209**, 104693 (2026). https://doi.org/10.1016/j.tre.2026.104693
6. Chen, X., Wu, S., Liu, Y., Wu, W., Wang, S.: A patrol routing problem for maritime crime-fighting. Transp. Res. Part E **168**, 102940 (2022). https://doi.org/10.1016/j.tre.2022.102940
7. Asghari, M., Afshari, H., Jaber, M.Y., Searcy, C.: Weather-aware maritime patrolling with dynamic covering and emission control. Appl. Math. Model. **149**, 116276 (2026). https://doi.org/10.1016/j.apm.2025.116276
8. Adulyasak, Y., Cordeau, J.F., Jans, R.: Benders decomposition for production routing under demand uncertainty. Oper. Res. **63**(4), 851–867 (2015). https://doi.org/10.1287/opre.2015.1401
9. Urick, R.J.: Principles of Underwater Sound. McGraw-Hill, New York (1983)

Maritime Intelligence and Data Analytics

A Tutorial on Reinforcement Learning for Maritime Logistics

Fabian Akkerman(✉), Eduardo Lalla-Ruiz, and Martijn Mes

University of Twente, Enschede, The Netherlands
f.r.akkerman@utwente.nl

Abstract. Reinforcement Learning (RL) provides a suitable framework for sequential decision-making under uncertainty. However, its practical adoption in operations research (OR) contexts is often hindered by implementation complexity and the lack of a structured method to evaluate, upfront, whether RL adds value over established heuristics. This creates a clear need for a guiding methodology. This paper presents a tutorial on an incremental stepwise approach to implementing RL for OR problems, aimed at researchers and practitioners with limited prior exposure to machine learning or Markov decision processes. The framework begins with problem formulation and simulation, progresses through supervised machine learning as a structured intermediate step, and ends with a full reinforcement learning model with hyperparameter tuning, ablation, and policy analysis. Each step is motivated by a concrete rationale and linked to the next step, reducing implementation risk and providing natural checkpoints at which progress can be evaluated. The approach is illustrated using a dynamic dispatching problem in which a barge operator must allocate cargo to a vessel or truck across multiple destinations under stochastic demand. All code is publicly available at https://github.com/frakkerman/rl_tutorial.

Keywords: Machine learning · Reinforcement learning · Sequential decisions · Markov Decision Processes · Tutorial

1 Introduction

Sequential decision problems frequently arise in real-world settings, particularly within the planning challenges encountered in operations management practice. In such contexts, decisions must be made over time as new information becomes available. A typical example is dynamically adapting a vehicle's route in response to incoming requests during execution. Because of this evolving information, a single upfront-made plan is insufficient, and decisions should be made, or solutions must be adjusted, in a dynamic manner. Although the information to which we must adapt is unknown in advance, we typically have some belief about its stochastic distribution and can incorporate that into our decision-making through anticipation. Furthermore, these problems are often operational

J. de Armas and E. Lalla Ruiz (Eds.): LOGMS 2026, LNCS 16679, pp. 245–261, 2027.
https://doi.org/10.1007/978-3-032-30795-8_21

in nature, meaning decisions must be made within seconds or minutes, leaving no time to compute an optimal solution. Although fast (meta)heuristics can produce good decisions quickly, they often lack the ability to account for future stochastic dynamics, although some complex frameworks do try to incorporate anticipation, e.g., using simheuristics [7]. Machine learning (ML) methods become valuable when anticipation is required, as they can be fitted to historical patterns and learn a meaningful policy that incorporates anticipation. ML is an umbrella term for three main classes of methods: (i) supervised ML, (ii) unsupervised ML, and (iii) reinforcement learning (RL). RL frames decision-making as an actor that learns through interaction with an environment, optimizing a long-term reward signal in a way that naturally accounts for the sequential and stochastic nature of the problem [11,14]. We observe an increasing interest in RL methods within maritime logistics research; for an overview, we refer to the reviews by [3] and [4].

The remainder of this tutorial paper is structured as follows. In Sect. 2, we present a modeling framework that structures the process of implementing machine learning policies for sequential decision-making problems. In Sect. 3, we follow the framework and apply it to a case on a multi-modal dispatching problem. We end with conclusions in Sect. 4.

2 An Incremental Modeling Approach

Implementing RL methods for sequential decision problems is a complex and time-consuming task. Furthermore, it is often difficult to determine upfront what RL methods would be most suitable and whether they will outperform more traditional OR methods, e.g., exact or rule-based methods suitable for dynamic, stochastic problems. For both researchers and practitioners, it is beneficial to take a stepwise and incremental approach. To support this, we present a guiding framework inspired by [1].

Our framework does not directly assume the use of RL nor any specific ML methodology. Instead, it starts with a data-driven approach, in which a supervised ML model is trained to estimate the value of states under a given heuristic. Supervised ML refers to learning a mapping from inputs to outputs from labeled examples [5]. In our framework, we collect these labeled examples by performing simulations with the given heuristic, where the encountered states form the input and the resulting long-term costs of the decisions made in these states (or the decisions themselves) form the output. This step is valuable because it tests whether the problem has sufficient *structure* for ML-based modeling, without yet requiring the additional complexity of a learning loop. Only once this is confirmed does the framework consider an approach in which an ML model is iteratively updated during simulation to improve the policy. This is the essence of reinforcement learning (RL), in which we learn by trial and error through repeated interaction with an environment [14]. In Fig. 1, we illustrate the artifacts a user builds when using our stepwise approach. First, the user needs to build a simulation model and implement a heuristic to make decisions during simulation. With the simulation model, data is collected, which is used to train a supervised ML model. This supervised ML model is an intermediate step to assess whether we can learn patterns from the simulation data. Only when this step is successful, we move to RL. Importantly, our framework is not strictly linear: it may be necessary to revisit earlier steps as the study progresses, and model validation should be treated as an ongoing activity throughout. See Fig. 2 for a depiction of the framework.

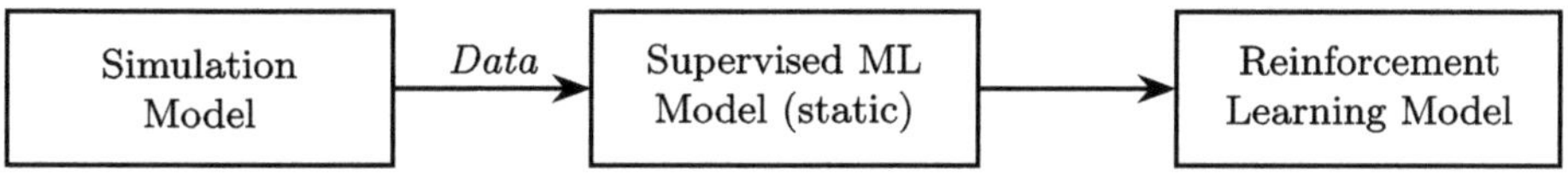

Fig. 1. Artifacts created by the user when following the framework.

Step 1: Formulate the sequential decision problem and define model requirements. The starting point is a clear, non-technical description of the problem and a specification of the intended capabilities of the ML model, e.g., for a container stacking problem, we could state: "The decision-making policy needs to anticipate future container arrivals and container extractions based on historic data, such that we require the least number of reshuffles. The policy needs to be able to find a decision within 10 s of computational time".

With this foundation, it is possible to determine which methods are appropriate and to evaluate whether subsequent steps are successful. This step therefore sets the criteria against which all subsequent steps are evaluated. At this step, it should at least be clear (i) what decisions the policy should make, (ii) to what stochasticity the policy should adapt, (iii) what costs we try to minimize, and (iv) how much time we have to compute a decision.

Step 2: Define states, decisions, costs, and stochastic events. With the solution method requirements and problem definition established, the next step is to translate them into a more formal structure. We identify the core components of a Markov decision process (MDP): states, decisions, costs (or rewards), and stochastic events [12]. For the sake of brevity, we refer to [11] for definitions and more background. An MDP provides a formal language for sequential decision problems in which outcomes depend on both current decisions and uncertain future events. To limit early implementation risk, it is advisable to begin with a deliberately simplified version of the problem, omitting complex constraints that can be added later in Step 6.

Step 3: Implement a simulation model and baseline policy. The MDP formulation from Step 2 is now translated into a working simulation model. The goal of the simulation model is to generate states, apply decisions, observe resulting costs (e.g., travel time) and obtain data that can subsequently be used to train an ML model. Furthermore, we model the stochasticity in our problem, i.e., we determine from what distribution we will sample randomness. For instance, when our stochasticity is a new request arriving from three possible destinations, we could model this using a uniform distribution with probabilities $\{0.5, 0.3, 0.2\}$. During simulation, we will sample from this distribution. Alongside the simulation, a policy, e.g., a rule-based or random policy, is implemented to serve as a baseline. This baseline is essential: it provides the data for Step 4, a performance benchmark for Step 5, and a debugging reference throughout. The simulation loop proceeds as follows:

1. Start from a (random) initial state of the problem.
2. Make a decision and update the state accordingly.
3. Sample a stochastic event and update the state again.
4. Record the states, decisions and resulting costs.
5. Repeat from step (2) until the termination criterion is met.

Step 4: Fit a supervised ML model on static data. Before introducing a learning loop, it is worth asking whether the problem has sufficient structure for ML-based modeling at all, i.e., can a ML model fit to predict costs based on states. With "costs" we refer to the so-called *cost-to-go* [2], which are the costs summed up from the current state until the end of the horizon, or in case of an infinite horizon problem, until a fixed number of steps into the horizon. To test the predictive capability of the ML model, we use the data we collected in Step 3, i.e., states, decisions, and costs. A supervised ML model, such as linear regression or a decision tree [5], is then trained using states as inputs and costs (regression task) or decisions (classification task) as prediction labels. This is analogous to the concepts of "value-based" and "policy-based" RL, see [11]. Value-based RL predicts the value of states or state-decision pairs, and takes the decision that results in the lowest expected costs, whereas policy-based RL directly prescribes decisions based on the state. There is no clear guideline to choose between predicting costs or decisions at this moment, but in general we advise starting with predicting costs, as these can be better interpreted. If the ML model fails to capture costs or decisions adequately, i.e., has a high prediction error on the testing data, this signals that the state representation or problem scope from Step 2 needs refinement before moving to Step 5.

Step 5: Integrate the ML model into the simulation and compare against the baseline. Having confirmed in Step 4 that the problem supports ML-based modeling, the supervised model from Step 4 is now embedded in the simulation to actively guide decisions. The model is queried at each decision moment: in case of a classification model, the decision resulting from the ML model will be used; in case of a regression model, we evaluate all feasible decisions and take the one that results in the lowest expected costs, known as a one-step lookahead policy [11]. Performance is compared against the baseline from Step 3. If the supervised ML model cannot match the baseline, there is little reason to expect RL to succeed, and earlier steps should be revisited before moving to Step 6.

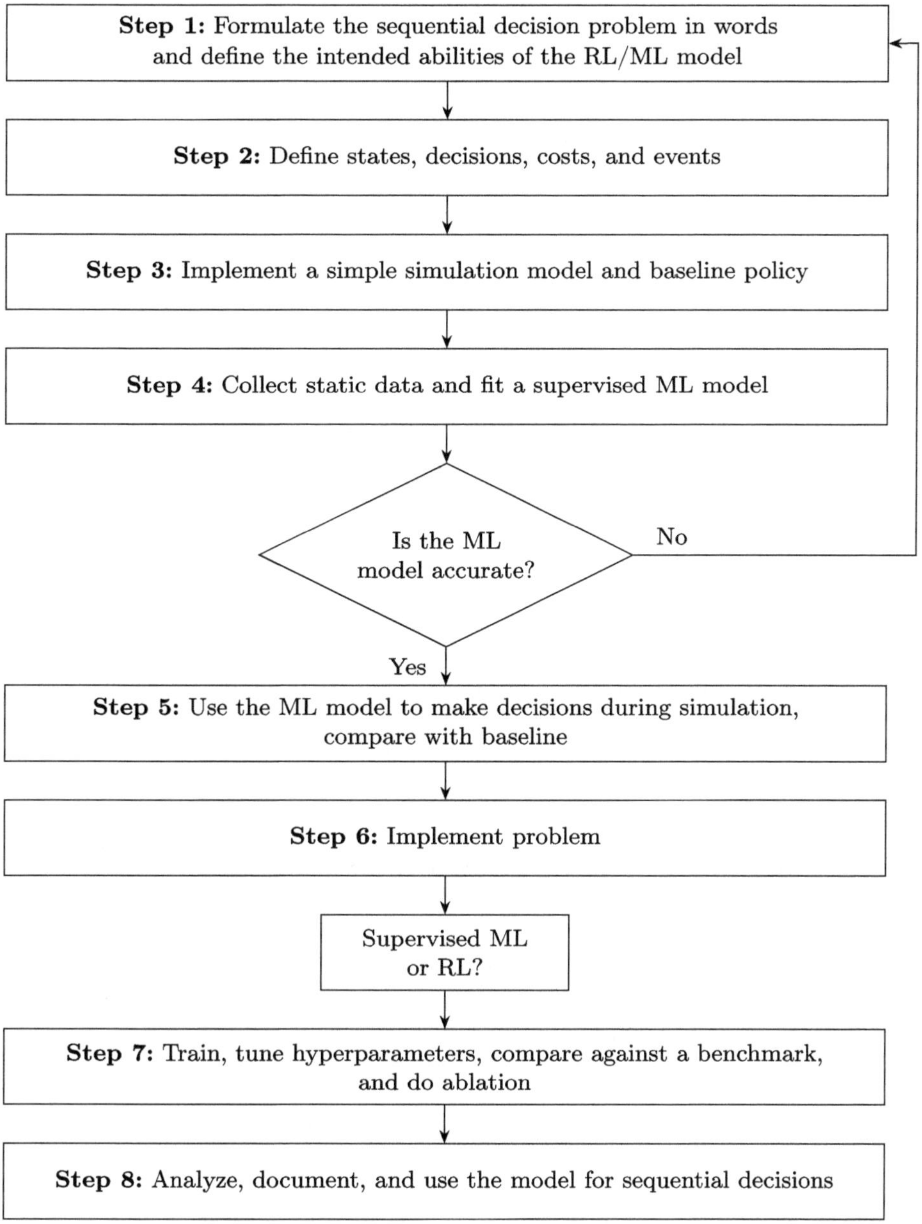

Fig. 2. Steps for implementing RL/ML for sequential decision problems.

Step 6: Implement the problem and decide on RL. Before, we implemented a simplified simulation model, e.g., not having all constraints or relying on generated data instead of real-world data. With a working ML-in-simulation pipeline validated on the simplified problem, the simulation is now expanded to capture all requirements from Step 1, incorporating real-world data where available. At this point, a decision is made on the appropriate ML methodology. If the goal is to replicate or slightly improve upon an existing policy, a supervised ML model may suffice. If the goal is to discover a genuinely better policy, reinforcement learning is warranted: we now learn by interacting with the full simulation rather than imitating a fixed baseline, enabling to improve beyond what the baseline data contain.

Step 7: Training, Tuning, Evaluation, and Ablation. With the decision-making model in place, the focus shifts to robustness. Hyperparameters are tuned, and features are selected to improve performance. Multiple training runs over different random seeds are conducted to assess sensitivity to initialization [6]. Where possible, an ablation study is carried out. Ablation is the systematic removal of individual components of a methodology to identify its contribution and potentially simplify the model, e.g., remove redundant features, which will make the computation of decisions faster. The model is also validated on held-out data to assess generalization beyond the training setting.

Step 8: Analyze and Document. In the final step, the decisions produced by the model are examined against the benchmark to understand not just whether performance has improved, but why. Identifying patterns in the learned policy may suggest further simplifications or reveal structure that could inform future work. Results are visualized and communicated clearly, the code and assumptions are documented, and limitations and directions for future research are indicated.

3 Application of the Framework to a Maritime Logistics Problem

In this section, we illustrate the use of the proposed framework by studying the use of RL for maritime logistics. More specifically, we consider a multimodal dispatching problem in which we need to decide on the prioritization and dispatching of freight containers, and to assign them either to trucks or barges.

Step 1: Formulate the sequential decision problem and define model requirements. We consider the delivery dispatching problem (DDP), as studied in [9,10]. Here, a logistics service provider (LSP) needs to decide on the dispatching of shipping containers. Each day, new containers arrive, characterized by a destination, a release time, and a shipping time window. Containers must be dispatched within the time window but cannot be shipped before they are released. The LSP can choose between two transport modalities for each container: an unlimited fleet of trucks, each with a capacity of a single container, and a single barge per day that can carry multiple containers. For the barge, we pay a fixed cost for the combination of destinations we have to visit and variable costs depending on the number of containers per destination visited. This way, it is more economical to ship containers with the same destination by barge. For the truck, we pay variable costs for each shipment, depending on the destination. In general, economies of scale apply to the barge, as there is a fixed cost component, but the variable costs per container are lower than for the truck. We assume that the dock has infinite capacity for holding containers.

Figure 3 illustrates the problem. The {red, green, blue} colors indicate container destinations. The number inside a container indicates the remaining time window length, i.e., a "1" indicates that a container needs to be shipped today, a "2" tomorrow, etc. On the dock, we have two types of container stacks: released (left) and non-released (right). A decision-maker, therefore, can take into account the future releases of containers when deciding on today's shipment. For this day, the LSP decided to ship two green and two blue containers by barge, and one red container by truck. This means that two blue containers that need to be shipped remain on the dock. For our problem, we assume the non-shipment of containers with due-date "1" is an implicit decision to ship these containers by the more costly truck modality. We consider a finite decision-making horizon, where we have to pay cleanup costs for freight remaining at the end of the horizon, which approximates the costs to dispatch the remaining containers.

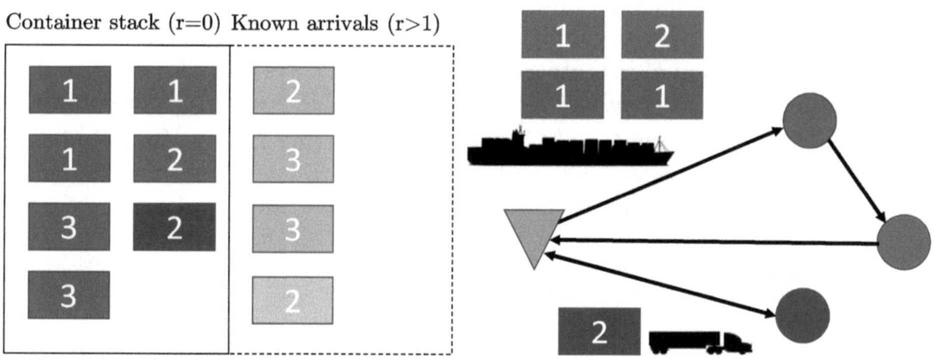

Fig. 3. Problem illustration, derived from [8]. (Color figure online)

Step 2: Define states, decisions, costs, and stochastic events. Next, we provide a formal definition of the problem, i.e., the MDP formulation. We model the DDP as a MDP over a planning horizon of T days, with dispatching decisions made at each $t \in \mathcal{T} = \{0, \dots, T-1\}$. Each container is characterized by a destination $d \in \mathcal{D}$, a release day $r \in \mathcal{R} = \{0, \dots, R^{\max}\}$ relative to t, and a time window length $k \in \mathcal{K} = \{0, \dots, K^{\max}\}$ relative to r. Containers with $r > 0$ are deterministically known but unavailable for dispatch until $r = 0$, at which point they must be dispatched within k days. Each unique (d, r, k)-combination constitutes a *container type*, and the state $S_t \in \mathcal{S}$ counts the number of containers of each type:

$$S_t = [S_{t,d,r,k}]_{\forall [d,r,k] \in \mathcal{D} \times \mathcal{R} \times \mathcal{K}}. \tag{1}$$

Containers are dispatched by one of two modalities $m \in \mathcal{M}$: trucks ($m = 0$) or barge ($m = 1$), each with capacity Q^m. The decision a_t specifies how many containers of each available type are assigned to each modality:

$$a_t = [a_{t,m,d,k}]_{\forall [m,d,k] \in \mathcal{M} \times \mathcal{D} \times \mathcal{K}}, \tag{2}$$

subject to:

$$a_{t,m,d,k} \leq S_{t,d,0,k} \qquad \forall\, [m,d,k] \in \mathcal{M} \times \mathcal{D} \times \mathcal{K}, \tag{3}$$

$$\sum_{m \in \mathcal{M}} a_{t,m,d,0} = S_{t,d,0,0} \qquad \forall\, d \in \mathcal{D}, \tag{4}$$

$$\sum_{[d,k] \in \mathcal{D} \times \mathcal{K}} a_{t,m,d,k} \leq Q^m \qquad \forall\, m \in \mathcal{M}, \tag{5}$$

$$a_{t,m,d,k} \in \mathbb{N} \qquad \forall\, [m,d,k] \in \mathcal{M} \times \mathcal{D} \times \mathcal{K}. \tag{6}$$

Constraint (3) limits dispatch to available released containers; Constraint (4) enforces that all containers with $k = 0$ are dispatched on the day they expire; Constraint (5) enforces modality capacities. Trucks are a special case here, as we, to guarantee feasibility, assume an infinite fleet with unit capacity, which we model as a single truck with infinite capacity ($Q_0 = \infty$).

The cost of decision a_t in state S_t comprises fixed costs $c^f_{m,\mathcal{D}'}$ for each modality m visiting destination subset $\mathcal{D}' \subseteq \mathcal{D}$, and variable costs $c^v_{m,d}$ per container shipped to d by m. For trucks, $c^f_{m,\mathcal{D}'} = 0$ always. Letting $I_{m,\mathcal{D}'} \in \{0,1\}$ indicate whether subset $\mathcal{D}'$ is visited by modality m (note $\mathcal{D}' = 1$ only for the exact subset of destinations visited by modality m), the cost function is:

$$C(S_t, a_t) = \sum_{m \in \mathcal{M}} \left(\sum_{\mathcal{D}' \subseteq \mathcal{D}} I_{m,\mathcal{D}'} \cdot c^f_{m,\mathcal{D}'} \right) + \sum_{[m,d,k] \in \mathcal{M} \times \mathcal{D} \times \mathcal{K}} c^v_{m,d} \cdot a_{t,m,d,k} + I_t\, C^T(S_t, a_t), \tag{7}$$

where $I_t \in \{0,1\}$ activates the cleanup cost function C^T only at $t = T$.

The goal is to find a policy $\pi^* : \mathcal{S} \to \mathcal{X}$ minimizing total expected costs over the horizon, obtained by solving the Bellman optimality equations [11]:

$$V_t^{\pi^*}(S_t) = \min_{a_t \in \mathcal{X}(S_t)} \left(C(S_t, a_t) + \sum_{S_{t+1} \in \mathcal{S}} \mathbb{P}(S_{t+1} \mid S_t, a_t) \cdot V_{t+1}^{\pi^*}(S_{t+1}) \right) \quad \forall\, S_t \in \mathcal{S}. \tag{8}$$

Here, $\mathcal{X}(S_t)$ denotes the feasible action set at state S_t, i.e., all decisions a_t satisfying constraints (3)–(6).

Step 3: Implement a simulation model and baseline policy. We implemented a simulation model in Python building on the `gymnasium` framework. Our Python notebook can be downloaded from https://github.com/frakkerman/rl_tutorial.

Algorithm 1. Simple heuristic

for All destinations $d \in \mathcal{D}$ **do**
  If there are containers with $k = 0$, load on barge, if allowed by barge capacity
end for
for All destinations $d \in \mathcal{D}$ **do**
  If the destination d is already on the barge, load the $k > 0$ containers (earliest due date first) on the barge, if allowed by barge capacity
end for

Apart from the simulation model, we implemented two decision-making policies: a random policy and a simple heuristic, which is detailed in Algorithm 1.

Note that we order $\mathcal{D}$ such that we start with the container destination that has the highest variable truck costs $c^v_{0,d}$. In our implementation, we consider three possible destinations $\mathcal{D} \in \{\text{R, G, B}\}$, analogous to Fig. 3.

Step 4: Fit a supervised ML model on static data. We simulate 1,000 episodes, i.e., complete decision horizons from the initial state to the terminal state, under the heuristic policy and record, at each decision moment $t \in \mathcal{T}$, the state S_t together with the cost-to-go $y_t = \sum_{\tau \geq t} C(S_\tau, a_\tau)$, yielding 7,000 labelled samples. The cost-to-go is a smoother regression target than the single-step cost $C(S_t, a_t)$, as it averages over future stochasticity and reflects the longer-term costs of a decision.

For each destination $d \in \mathcal{D}$ we extract three inventory counts from S_t: the number of must-go containers $n^{mg}_{t,d} = S_{t,d,0,0}$ (containers with $r = 0$, $k = 0$, which must be dispatched today), the number of may-go containers $n^{my}_{t,d} = \sum_{k>0} S_{t,d,0,k}$ (released but not yet urgent), and the number of unreleased containers $n^{ur}_{t,d} = \sum_{r>0} \sum_k S_{t,d,r,k}$ (not yet available for dispatch). From these counts we derive indicator flags $\mathbf{1}^{mg}_{t,d} = \mathbf{1}[n^{mg}_{t,d} > 0]$, which indicate whether the fixed barge cost $c^f_{1,\mathcal{D}'}$ is incurred for destination d, urgency ratios $u_{t,d} = n^{mg}_{t,d} \,/\, (n^{mg}_{t,d} + n^{my}_{t,d})$, and pairwise interaction terms $\iota_{t,dd'} = \mathbf{1}^{mg}_{t,d} \cdot \mathbf{1}^{mg}_{t,d'}$ for all $d \neq d' \in \mathcal{D}$, capturing whether the fixed barge cost is shared across multiple destinations. We further include the total dock inventory $n^{tot}_t = \sum_{d,r,k} S_{t,d,r,k}$ as a proxy for future cost, and the time features t and $T - t$. This yields a 22-dimensional feature vector, denoted by $\phi(S_t, t)$.

We train a Ridge regression and a Random Forest regressor, both with standardized inputs, on an 80/20 train-test split. Table 1 reports performance. A regression of y_t on t alone achieves $R^2 = 0.617$, which serves as a natural baseline since the cost-to-go decreases with t as fewer steps remain. Both models improve substantially: the Random Forest reaches $R^2 = 0.742$ and Ridge $R^2 = 0.733$ on the test set, with the small gap between the two suggesting the remaining signal is largely linear in $\phi(S_t, t)$.

Figure 4a shows the residual curve (prediction vs. actual values), we observe no clear trend in the residuals. Figure 4b shows that t and $T - t$ together account for 71% of the Random Forest feature importance scores, with total dock inventory n^{tot}_t contributing a further 16%: a fuller dock at a given t implies more

Table 1. Cost-to-go regression results. Sample statistics: mean = 18,992, std = 4,235, range [6,900, 34,600] (7,000 samples, $T = 7$).

Model	Train R^2	Test R^2	MAE	RMSE
t-only baseline	0.617	0.617	–	–
Ridge	0.754	0.733	1,717	2,186
Random Forest	0.864	0.742	1,666	2,149

containers to dispatch over the remaining steps and therefore higher expected costs. The remaining 13% is spread across per-destination features, with unreleased and may-go counts at destination G ranking highest among these, consistent with G carrying the largest truck cost ($c^v_{0,G} = 1{,}000$).

Must-go counts and interaction terms $\iota_{t,dd'}$ together account for only 2.4% of RF importance. The Ridge coefficients, see Fig. 4c, however, show that the indicators $\mathbf{1}^{mg}_{t,d}$ carry large negative coefficients while the pairwise interactions carry large positive ones, reflecting the fixed barge cost $c^f_{1,\mathcal{D}'}$: adding a destination to an existing barge route is cheaper than dispatching it separately.

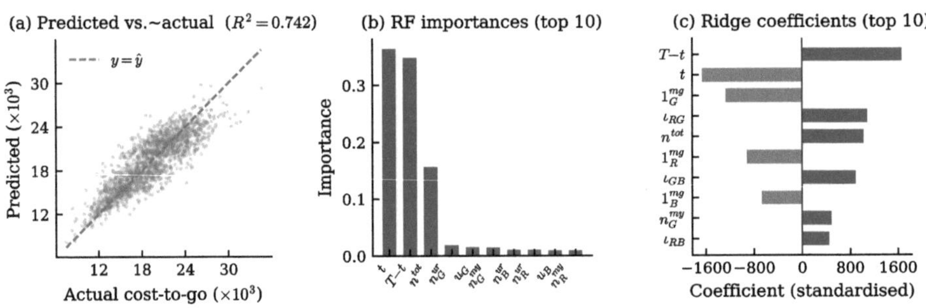

Fig. 4. Diagnostic plots for the cost-to-go regression. *Left:* predicted against actual values for the Random Forest ($R^2 = 0.742$). *Centre:* feature importances. *Right:* standardized Ridge coefficients (top 10); blue bars increase predicted cost-to-go, red bars decrease it. (Color figure online)

Step 5: Integrate the ML model into the simulation and compare against the baseline. We integrate $\hat{V}(S_t, t)$, which is the approximated value function, see Eq. 8, into the simulation via a one-step lookahead policy. The decision space is reduced by noting that, given a per-destination count vector (n_R, n_G, n_B) with $\sum_d n_d \leq Q^1$, the optimal allocation within each destination loads the most urgent containers first (lowest k first). It therefore suffices to enumerate all feasible count vectors

$$\mathcal{N}(S_t) = \left\{ (n_d)_{d \in \mathcal{D}} \,\middle|\, \sum_d n_d \leq Q^1,\ n_d \leq \sum_k S_{t,d,0,k}\ \forall\, d \right\}, \tag{9}$$

convert each to a full decision via the urgency-first loading rule, and score it by

$$a_t^* = \arg\min_{a \in \mathcal{N}(S_t)} \left[C(S_t, a) + \hat{V}(S_t^a, t+1) \right], \tag{10}$$

where S_t^a is the state after applying a.

Table 2 and Fig. 5 report results over 500 episodes. The random policy incurs a mean cost of 32,399, 33% above the heuristic baseline of 24,383. The Supervised ML-guided policy achieves a mean cost of 24,554, within 0.7% of the heuristic, while reducing the standard deviation from 2,554 to 1,442, a reduction of 44%. The lower variance indicates that the lookahead avoids high-cost outlier trajectories: by penalizing states with high $\hat{V}$, the policy hedges against future truck costs even when no containers are immediately urgent.

That the supervised ML policy does not improve on the heuristic is expected at this stage. The value function was estimated from trajectories generated by the heuristic, so $\hat{V}$ approximates the cost-to-go under heuristic behaviour rather than under a better policy. Closing this gap requires iterating the data collection and model fitting, which is the subject of the next step.

Table 2. Policy comparison over 500 episodes ($T = 7$). Costs are total episode costs $\sum_{t=0}^{T} C(S_t, a_t)$.

Policy	Mean	Std	Min	Max	vs. Heuristic
Random	32,399	2,814	25,950	38,950	+32.9%
Heuristic	24,383	2,554	18,350	29,500	—
Supervised ML	24,554	1,442	21,000	27,300	+0.7%

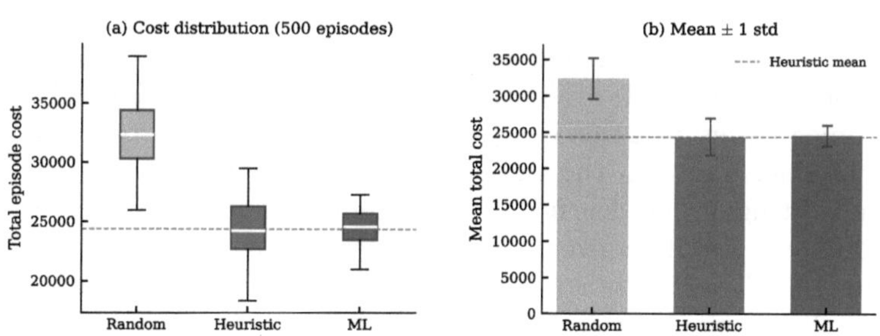

Fig. 5. Cost distributions over 500 episodes. *Left:* box plots; dashed line indicates the heuristic mean. *Right:* mean ± one standard deviation. The Supervised ML-policy matches the heuristic in mean cost while reducing variance.

Step 6: Implement the Problem and Decide on RL. The supervised learning results demonstrate that an ML model can effectively replicate the heuristic policy, confirming that the state–decision mapping is learnable, or at least, that we can learn a pattern in the cost-to-go of states. However, since the supervised model is trained on data generated while using the heuristic, its performance is fundamentally bounded by it: the model cannot discover decisions better than those observed in its training data. This ceiling motivates a reinforcement learning approach, in which we learn a policy by interacting directly with the environment and receiving scalar reward signals [14]. As a practical guideline, we recommend proceeding to RL when the supervised ML policy in Step 5 matches or approaches the heuristic; if it substantially underperforms, the state representation or problem scope should be revisited before investing in a full RL pipeline. Through a cyclical loop of simulation, reward collection, and policy updates, an RL policy can, in principle, surpass any fixed heuristic by discovering structure in the decision problem that the heuristic does not exploit.

We implement two RL policies of contrasting complexity. The first is REINFORCE [15], a Monte Carlo policy gradient method that estimates the gradient of expected returns by rolling out complete episodes and weighting log-probabilities of decisions by their discounted return. REINFORCE is conceptually transparent and straightforward to implement, but suffers from high variance in its gradient estimates and slow convergence, making it a natural baseline rather than a competitive solver. The second is Proximal Policy Optimization (PPO) [13], a state-of-the-art actor–critic algorithm that stabilizes training by constraining each policy update to remain within a trust region, clipping the probability ratio between the new and old policy to prevent destructively large updates. PPO uses a learned value function as a baseline to reduce gradient variance, and processes experience in mini-batches, making it significantly more sample-efficient than REINFORCE. Both algorithms operate on a continuous decision space exposed by the simulation environment, with decisions clipped and rounded to feasible integer decisions at each step.

Step 7: Training, Tuning, Evaluation, and Ablation. Fig. 6 (c and d) report mean episode cost over 500 evaluation episodes for each policy. PPO achieves the lowest mean cost of 21,555, representing an 8.6% improvement over the heuristic baseline, and also the tightest interquartile range among all learned policies, suggesting it has learned a consistent and robust dispatch strategy. REINFORCE, despite its convergence as shown in Fig. 6(a), underperforms the heuristic by 10.4%, which is consistent with the limitations of a linear policy discussed in the previous section. All algorithms are trained on a single compute node with 16 threads (2.4GHz) and 32GB of RAM. PPO trains for 90 min and REINFORCE for 30 min.

Both RL policies were trained across multiple random seeds to assess sensitivity to initialization. Practitioners should be aware of two common pitfalls: RL typically requires orders of magnitude more data than supervised learning, and training instability, particularly with policy gradient methods such as REINFORCE, can mask whether poor performance reflects a bad policy or simply

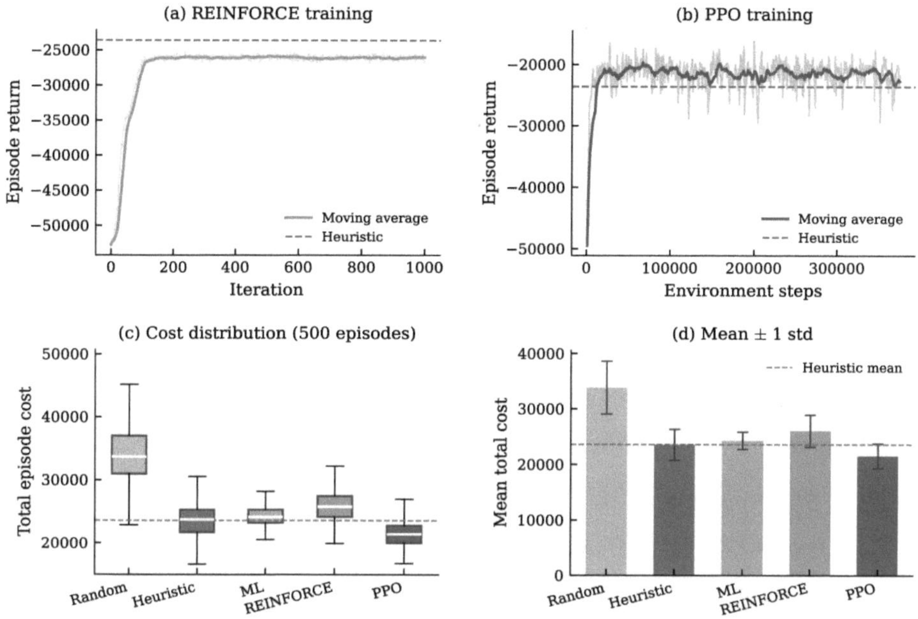

Fig. 6. Training results for REINFORCE and PPO.

insufficient training. PPO showed low variance across seeds, while REINFORCE exhibited greater instability in early training before converging to a similar plateau, consistent with the high-variance gradient estimates characteristic of Monte Carlo policy gradient methods [15]. Learning rates were tuned manually: the final configuration used $\alpha = 5 \times 10^{-3}$ for REINFORCE and $\alpha = 3 \times 10^{-4}$ for PPO, the latter found to be relatively robust to the learning rate.

To assess the contribution of each feature, we retrain PPO seven times, each time zeroing out one group of features while keeping all others intact. Results are summarized in Fig. 7. The most critical feature by a large margin is *time*, whose removal causes mean episode cost to more than double (+135%). Without knowledge of the current period and remaining horizon, the policy cannot reason about urgency relative to time, rendering its policy little better than random. The second most impactful group are the counts of may-go containers, where removal increases cost by 12%, suggesting that non-urgent but dispatchable containers are important context for allocation decisions. Removing unreleased containers causes a moderate increase of 5.6%, consistent with it providing useful forward-looking demand information.

In contrast, removing the counts of must-go containers, urgency fractions, or interaction terms has negligible effect, with cost changes of less than 1% relative to the full model. This suggests that the urgency is already sufficiently captured by the may-go and time features, and that the interaction terms provide no marginal benefit at this problem scale. The model could therefore be simplified by dropping these four feature groups without meaningful loss of performance, reducing the observation vector from 22 to 7 features.

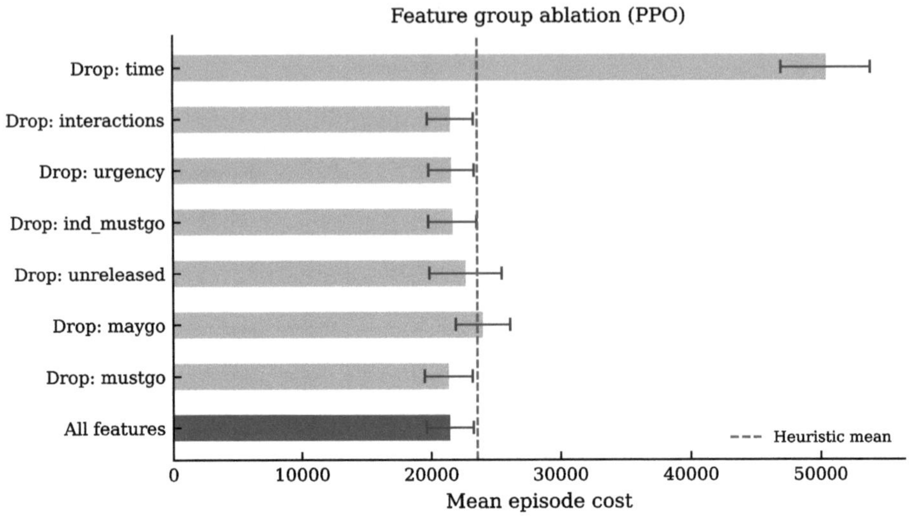

Fig. 7. Ablation study for PPO with different feature sets left out.

Step 8: Analyze and Document. Figure 8 presents a detailed comparison of PPO and heuristic decisions across six diagnostic plots. As shown in Fig. 8a, both policies incur low, stable costs during periods $t = 0$–6, after which costs rise sharply as end-of-horizon penalties accumulate for undelivered must-go cargo. PPO's late-period spike is smaller (reaching approximately 8,000 at $t = 7$) compared to the heuristic (13,000), indicating that PPO better anticipates and mitigates end-of-horizon costs. Note that a myopic policy tends to postpone shipments. This is not straightforward to learn for an RL policy, and Fig. 8a indicates further improvements would be possible. This is consistent with Fig. 8b, which shows that PPO consistently loads more units per period throughout the episode, averaging approximately 10–13 units compared to 6–9 for the heuristic. This suggests PPO adopts a more aggressive front-loading strategy, exploiting available barge capacity earlier to avoid costly end-of-horizon backlogs.

Figure 8c reveals systematic differences in how the two policies allocate capacity across destinations. PPO loads substantially more cargo to destination G throughout most of the horizon, while modestly under-loading R relative to the heuristic. This pattern is economically rational given the cost structure: G carries the highest truck cost (1,000 per unit) compared to R (500) and B (700), so the marginal value of barge capacity is greatest for G cargo. By prioritizing G, PPO effectively maximizes the cost saving per unit loaded, the saving from substituting barge for truck is 900 for G versus 400 and 600 for R and B, respectively. Furthermore, since G accounts for 50% of arrivals by destination probability, it accumulates containers the fastest, making early and sustained dispatch to G particularly valuable. The heuristic, which does not explicitly encode destination-level cost heterogeneity in its dispatch rule, appears to spread capacity more uniformly across destinations and thereby foregoes a portion of the available cost saving.

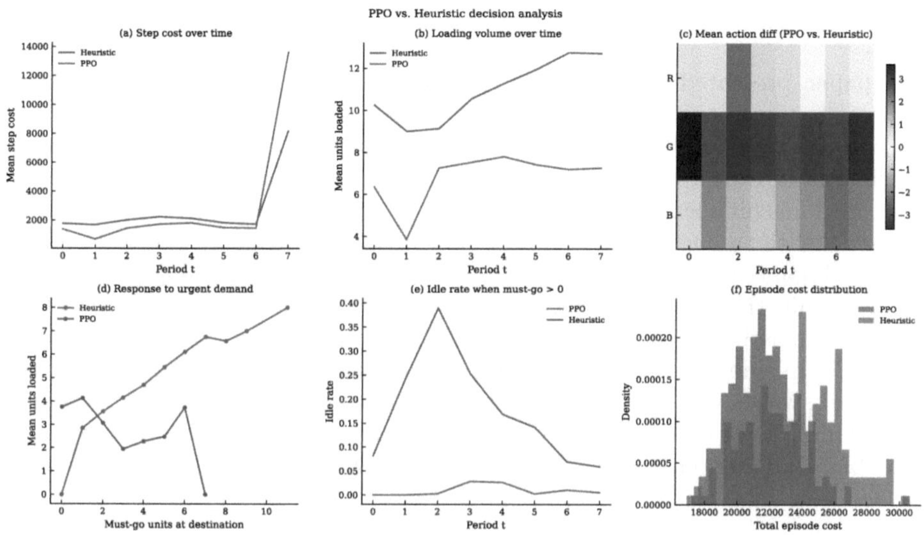

Fig. 8. Decision-making analysis of PPO vs. the heuristic.

Figure 8d examines how each policy responds to urgent demand. When there are no must-go containers, the heuristic still loads around four units on average, whereas PPO loads close to zero, suggesting PPO is more selective and avoids loading non-urgent containers. As must-go inventory grows, both policies increase loading, but the heuristic responds more steeply and linearly. PPO's response is flatter and shows a dip at high urgency levels, possibly reflecting capacity reallocation across competing destinations rather than a simple proportional rule. Figure 8e complements this finding: the heuristic maintains a near-zero idle rate throughout the horizon, meaning it almost never ignores must-go cargo, whereas PPO peaks at an idle rate of approximately 0.38 during $t = 1$–2, meaning it frequently chooses not to load urgent items early in the episode, causing those containers to be shipped by truck automatically. Whether this reflects suboptimal behaviour or a deliberate capacity reservation strategy is ambiguous from these plots alone, though the lower terminal costs in Fig. 8a suggest the latter is at least partially true.

Finally, Fig. 8f shows that PPO's episode cost distribution is shifted approximately 2,000–3,000 to the left relative to the heuristic and exhibits lower variance, with the mode near 20,000 compared to 23,000–24,000 for the heuristic.

The reduced spread suggests PPO has learned a more robust policy that performs consistently across random realizations of demand.

Taken together, these results characterize PPO's advantage as mainly temporal: the RL policy has learned to load more aggressively in early periods and to tolerate short-term idle decisions in exchange for reduced end-of-horizon penalties, a trade-off the hand-crafted heuristic is not designed to make.

4 Conclusion

This paper presented a stepwise framework for implementing reinforcement learning in operations research contexts, aimed at researchers and practitioners who are new to the field. The framework begins with a textual problem description and a formal MDP specification, proceeds through simulation and supervised machine learning as structured intermediate steps, and ends with an RL model with tuning, ablation, and policy analysis. Each step produces a natural checkpoint at which progress can be assessed before moving to the next stage. We illustrated the framework using a multi-modal dispatching problem, in which a logistics service provider must allocate containers to trucks or a barge across multiple destinations under stochastic demand. Following the steps of the framework, we showed that a supervised ML model can replicate a heuristic policy within 0.7% of its mean cost, confirming that the state-decision mapping is learnable. Building on this, a PPO policy achieved an 8.6% cost reduction over the heuristic by learning to front-load barge capacity and prioritize high-cost destinations, a strategy the heuristic does not exploit.

A key contribution of the framework is that it reduces implementation risk: by confirming structure at the supervised learning stage, practitioners avoid investing in a full RL pipeline for problems where ML-based modeling does not add value. At the same time, the framework is not prescriptive about method choice, and the decision between supervised ML and RL remains a deliberate step tied to the goals of the study. Nevertheless, a limitation of the current work is that scalability has not yet been demonstrated on real-world data, and further validation on operational datasets would be needed before drawing broader conclusions about practical performance. Despite this, the framework and accompanying code serve as a practical starting point for OR researchers and practitioners considering machine learning for sequential decision problems.

References

1. Akkerman, F.: Machine learning for sequential decisions in logistics. Ph.D. thesis, University of Twente, Netherlands (2025). https://doi.org/10.3990/1.9789036565349
2. Bertsekas, D.: Reinforcement Learning and Optimal Control. Athena Scientific Optimization and Computation Series. Athena Scientific, Belmont, MA, USA (2019)
3. Çolak, M., Heilig, L., Voß, S.: Reinforcement learning in the context of container terminals. Flex. Serv. Manuf. J. (2025)

4. Dornemann, J., Rückert, N., Fischer, K., Taraz, A.: Artificial intelligence and operations research in maritime logistics. In: Jahn, C., Kersten, W., Ringle, C.M. (eds.) Data Science in Maritime and City Logistics: Data-Driven Solutions for Logistics and Sustainability. Proceedings of the Hamburg International Conference of Logistics (HICL), vol. 30 (2020)
5. Hastie, T., Tibshirani, R., Friedman, J.: The Elements of Statistical Learning, 2nd edn. Springer, New York (2009)
6. Henderson, P., Islam, R., Bachman, P., Pineau, J., Precup, D., Meger, D.: Deep reinforcement learning that matters. In: Proceedings of the AAAI Conference on Artificial Intelligence, vol. 32 (2018)
7. Juan, A.A., Ammouriova, M., Faulin, J., Panadero, J., Ferone, D.: Simheuristics. Springer, Cham (2025)
8. Mes, M., van Heeswijk, W.: Comparison of manual and automated decision-making with a logistics serious game. In: Lalla-Ruiz, E., Mes, M., Voß, S. (eds.) ICCL 2020. LNCS, vol. 12433, pp. 698–714. Springer, Cham (2020). https://doi.org/10.1007/978-3-030-59747-4_45
9. Rivera, A.P., Mes, M.: Dynamic multi-period freight consolidation. In: Corman, F., Voß, S., Negenborn, R.R. (eds.) ICCL 2015. LNCS, vol. 9335, pp. 370–385. Springer, Cham (2015). https://doi.org/10.1007/978-3-319-24264-4_26
10. Pérez Rivera, A.E., Mes, M.R.K.: Anticipatory freight selection in intermodal long-haul round-trips. Transp. Res. Part E Logist. Transp. Rev. **105**, 176–194 (2017)
11. Powell, W.B.: Reinforcement Learning and Stochastic Optimization. Wiley, Hoboken (2022)
12. Puterman, M.L.: Markov Decision Processes: Discrete Stochastic Dynamic Programming. Wiley, New York (1994)
13. Schulman, J., Wolski, F., Dhariwal, P., Radford, A., Klimov, O.: Proximal policy optimization algorithms. arXiv preprint arXiv:1707.06347 (2017)
14. Sutton, R.S., Barto, A.G.: Reinforcement Learning: An Introduction, 2nd edn. MIT Press, Cambridge (2018)
15. Williams, R.J.: Simple statistical gradient-following algorithms for connectionist reinforcement learning. Mach. Learn. **8**(3–4), 229–256 (1992)

Data Platforms in the Maritime Domain: Challenges and Opportunities

Olaf Rendel and Anisa Rizvanolli(✉)

Fraunhofer Center for Maritime Logistics and Services (CML), Blohmstraße 32, 21079 Hamburg, Germany
{olaf.rendel,anisa.rizvanolli}@cml.fraunhofer.de
https://www.cml.fraunhofer.de/

Abstract. The maritime world is characterized by the complex cooperation of multiple actors along the supply chain. With the rise of digitization, the exchange of information between these actors has shifted from manual to a more automatic process. However, digital communication in this industry often remains at a peer-to-peer level and lacks interoperability or experiences media breaks. Various existing digital solutions, such as data platforms or port community systems, have evolved over time, but fall short in terms of standardization or broad adoption.

This article aims to shed light on the current challenges of such solutions, which have not been extensively addressed by the research community. It also presents a case study of a data platform implemented in the maritime domain, based on open standards like OpenID Connect for authentication and OpenAPI for interface specification. The study provides an overview and discussion of the available technologies and standards and compares recent developments, for example the industry standards from the DCSA, efforts of TIC4.0 Association or the platform specification MCP consortium. Additionally, we assess the governance structures that guide the use of these standards, identify their shortcomings and explore the commercial viability and challenges associated with implementing these open standards in a real-world environment. By analyzing the solutions, the article aims to provide insights into the effectiveness of open standards, interoperability, governance structures, while also highlighting potential areas for improvement.

Keywords: data platforms · IT Systems · seamless information sharing · supply chain information sharing · maritime data and information exchange · open standards

1 Introduction

The maritime world is characterized by the complex cooperation of multiple actors along the supply chain. In this context the standardization and optimization of information exchange is one of the current challenges in this sector. With

J. de Armas and E. Lalla Ruiz (Eds.): LOGMS 2026, LNCS 16679, pp. 262–274, 2027.
https://doi.org/10.1007/978-3-032-30795-8_22

the rise of the digitization more and more application programming interfaces (APIs) are being developed to facilitate the data exchange between two specific actors. However, due to the large number of actors, this process is costly and is in need to be optimized. Data platforms are considered as a solution to face this challenge. These are software systems or frameworks that enable organizations to store, manage, process and analyze data from several sources. Additionally data platforms [17] provide a central and secure environment for the integration of new data sources. Additional features are data ingestion, data transformation, data governance, and data visualization. Whereas the exact implementation of the data platform may exclude some specific features, the general advantages of data platforms are the following:

+ **Centralized data storage or management:** Data platforms provide a centralized repository for storing and managing large volumes of data from diverse sources. This promotes a single source of truth and data consistency, accuracy, and integrity.
+ **Data integration and transformation:** Data platforms enable the integration of data from different systems, databases and formats. They may provide tools and capabilities to transform and cleanse data, ensuring its quality before analysis and decision-making.
+ **Scalability and performance:** Data platforms are designed to handle the ever-increasing volume and variety of data. They offer scalability and promote performance and responsiveness.
+ **Advanced analytics and insights:** Data platforms may provide tools and capabilities for advanced analytics, such as data mining, machine learning and predictive modeling.
+ **Data governance and security:** Data platforms may offer features for data governance, including access controls, data lineage, and auditing.They promote data security, protecting sensitive information and mitigating data breaches.
+ **Collaboration:** Data platforms often provide collaboration features, allowing multiple users to work together, share data, and collaborate on data analysis projects. They may also offer self-service capabilities, empowering business users to access and analyze data without extensive IT involvement.

While data platforms offer significant benefits, they also face certain challenges. Some of the current challenges for data platforms include:

- **Data quality:** Ensuring data quality continues to be a challenge. Data platforms need to implement robust mechanisms for data validation, cleansing. Establishing proper data governance practices and policies can be complex, especially with number of involved actors.
- **Data security and privacy:** With the rising concerns regarding data breaches and privacy regulations, safeguarding sensitive data, implementing access controls, encryption, and monitoring mechanisms are critical. This requires a high degree of trust in the provider.

- **Data integration:** Integrating data from various sources is a complex task. Data platforms need to support seamless integration and data transformation, dealing with different formats, schemas and data quality issues.
- **Skill gap and talent shortage:** Data platforms require skilled and specialized professionals who can design, implement, and manage them effectively. However, there is a shortage of software and data engineers, data scientists and other skilled personnel with expertise in data platforms.
- **Cost:** Implementing and maintaining data platforms can involve significant costs, including hardware, software, licensing and personnel. Financing a platform can be challenging, especially for smaller organizations or communities. Optimizing costs and demonstrating the value of data platforms in driving business outcomes is crucial.

However, despite these challenges, the advantages outweigh the shortcomings. In fact this central element for collaboration can lessen the overall expenses for developing new interfaces between the actors of the maritime world and promote standardization of the exchanged data. In the last years several maritime data platforms have been developed and are currently active in the industry. Here are a few examples with a focus on ship and ship-to-shore operations:

1. **Veracity** [15] is a data platform developed by DNV (Det Norske Veritas). It is designed to enable secure digital collaboration across maritime industries with a marketplace for data, analytics and digital services.
2. **Windward** [16] is a maritime data platform that is specialized in maritime analytics and risk assessment. It uses artificial intelligence and big data analytics to analyze vessel behaviors, identify anomalies and assess risks related to maritime trade, security and compliance.
3. The **Maritime National Single Window Systems** is a concept that aims to enhance efficiency in shipping by digitizing the clearance process of ships and all related communications among various actors, e.g., port authorities and by reducing the related administrative burden. Since January 1st 2024 the implementation of such system is mandatory [7]. Since 2015 the national maritime single window concept has found its way toward implemented data platforms [20] at least on country level. The various single windows platforms enable the digital exchange of the required information between ships, ports and government agencies.
4. **Navelink** [9] is a non-profit industry consortium, providing an open infrastructure for secure digital information exchange within the maritime sector. It is owned by two major marine system manufactures Kongsberg and Wärtsilä. It is an operational instance of the Maritime Connectivity Platform (MCP) and as such it provides an identity registry for secure identification and a service registry where the partners can publish and consume digital maritime services. Moreover, Navelink fosters its community, connecting actors from across the maritime domain.
5. The **Global Shipping Business Network (GSBN)** [4] is a neutral, not-for-profit consortium enabling paperless, accessible and sustainable global

trade. The members include mainly carrier and terminals, but also other actors like banks and insurance companies.

These are just a few examples of active maritime data platforms. The maritime industry is evolving, and new platforms and technologies are continually emerging to address the growing need for data-driven insights. Out of this development emerges the discussion of standardization. Mostly, since it is apparent that more and more platforms with similar but inconsistent APIs emerge. This is especially true for the port community systems and the administrative processes, hence the early standardization efforts leading to the Maritime Single Window.

The critics claim that the implementations of the Maritime Single Window are not really standardized, such that shipping companies have to deal with a large bunch of different systems for reporting the same data. Hence, the European union provides the European Maritime Single Window environment (EMSWe) [2] as a concept and platform toward harmonized rules for the provision of the information that is required for port calls, in particular by ensuring that the same data sets can be reported to each Maritime National Single Window in the same way. In the meantime, users and providers of port community systems got together to standardize their industry.

However, some cooperation see the advantages for data platforms but shy away from the initial investment. Pushing a solution, which aims to be used also by your competitors or business partners, requires a lot of trust to be adopted and offers little return on investment. Therefore, consortia emerge that aim to just standardize their use case before anything is implement.

Overall some examples of such efforts include:

1. Maritime Connectivity Consortium (MCC) [6] is the governing body of the Maritime Connectivity Platform, a decentralized platform specification that facilitates secure and reliable information exchange within the maritime domain. It contains a few number of host members, which are all non-profit organizations. The consortium arose out of the EU co-funded EfficienSea project focusing on e-navigation.
2. International Taskforce Port Call Optimization (ITPCO) [5] is a neutral coalition of maritime organizations dedicated to reducing and optimizing vessel berth time at ports, The aim is to standardize the relevant data exchange between ship and shore where all solutions can work effectively and unambiguously alongside one another.
3. Digital Container Shipping Association (DCSA) [1] establishes standards for a common technology foundation that enables global collaboration to improve container transportation services. Founded by MSC, Maersk, CMA CGM, Hapag-Lloyd, ONE, Evergreen, Yang Ming, HMM and ZIM this association has the view point of carrier, but also incorporates the needs other key players in the industry like freight forwarders, banks, ports, terminals and insurers.
4. Terminal Industry Committee 4.0 (TIC 4.0) [13] aims to promote, define and adopt standards that will improve cargo handling. The Committee defines and agrees on common process semantics, language, and operational definitions, makes technical publications accessible, promotes operational proof of

concepts for subsystem interoperability and foster the adoption of the developed standards. It consists mainly of terminal operators and port solution providers. However, other interested parties are also allowed to join and contribute in the working groups.

5. FEDeRATED [3] was an EU project for decentralized data collaboration in logistics. The project was driven by the idea of the Digital Transport and Logistics Forum of the European Commission (DTLF) to develop a federative network of platforms. The project has developed an operational framework and open source software prototypes implementing the framework. The aim was the foundations for stakeholders to structure their IT systems as a node and to start data sharing. The consortium had 15 partners from various actors along the supply chain and the concepts were validated in 23 Living Labs.

We aim to shed light on the current challenges and opportunities of data platforms, which have not been extensively addressed by the research community. For this we use and analyze the findings from the research project "MISSION" [19] in which a data platform inspired by the developments in the Sea Traffic Validation Project and the Maritime Connectivity Platform was implemented. We showcase the available technologies and standards and compare recent developments. Additionally, we assess operational aspects and operating concepts to explore the commercial viability and challenges associated with implementing these open standards in a real-world environment.

2 Use Case Port of Lübeck

As many ports, the port of Lübeck also aims to enhance port operations through improved information exchange. The research project MISSION [19], funded by the German Federal Ministry for Digital an Transportation, was initiated to tackle this problem with the prototypical implementation of a data platform. The project partners jointly focused on the identification of the current challenges specially in information and data exchange in such a huge logistic hub as the port. Particular attention was paid to the IT systems and the information exchange between the actors. The Fig. 1 shows an example of the multimodal transport of a trailer from Italy via the port of Lübeck to Finland, including the IT systems involved and the communication flow. It indicates the large amount of peer-to-peer communication and the media breaks over the various communication systems.

One of the major aims of this project was to design and validate a data platform that enables cross-system information exchange, which is referred to here as MISSION infrastructure. The harmonization of information flow within the port without violating the information property rights of the involved actors was one of the main objectives. The infrastructure aimed to enable a secure access of the right stakeholder to the right data, a seamless information exchange and a low entry barrier for all actors. The project was focused on the propagation of open standards and the implementation of requirements that ensure interoperability and extensibility.

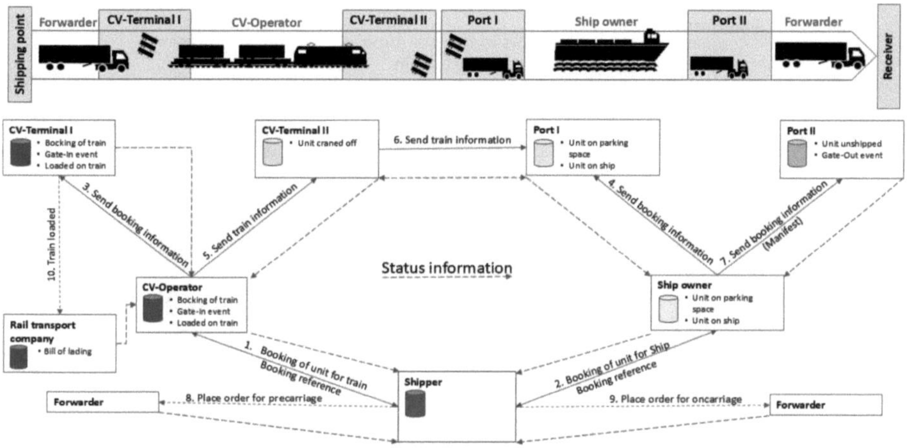

Fig. 1. Multimodal transport of a trailer from Italy to Finland

The MISSION infrastructure was designed to use interface management, authentication and service management as core services to regulate secure access within the system to the same data and an efficient exchange of information between the involved actors. These main services and components as represented in Fig. 2 are intended to facilitate the standard-compliant flow of information and data, lower the barrier to entry for new participants and ensure interoperability. For the validation of the developed concepts and component and for the evaluation in terms of their feasibility and effectiveness, prototypes of selected port services have been implemented and tested including cargo and ETA related data exchange with trucks and yard management. In general, MISSION was aimed to pursue similar goals as the MCP and validate their concepts for ports, but adopted to fit the specific needs of port actors.

For the further assessment we will only look at the core services of the implementation to compare the technologies to other platforms. However we like to remark, that from the planned services it was hard to obtain enough data for sophisticated analysis of the platform usage. The focus of some applications had to be shifted during the project due to the lack of machine readable data. In our opinion this stems from the lack of digitization of smaller actors in the supply chain. The burden to provide a machine readable interface seems to be still an issue, if no particular business interests are associated with it. In our opinion this is one major challenge concerning the broad adoption.

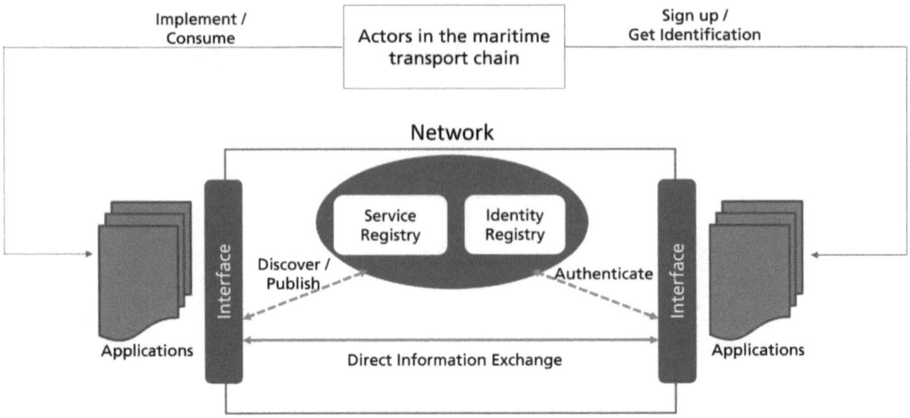

Fig. 2. Interaction of the infrastructure components in MISSION

3 Designing a Data Platform

For designing a data platform we have to consider three main aspects: Data storage, interfaces, access control, and trust. For each of these aspects there exists several solutions, each with its advantages and drawbacks. In the following parts we list the solutions and motivate our choices. With the special focus to fit the needs of the maritime domain, some of the selections may differ from other domains.

3.1 Data Storage

For the data storage two concepts were considered: data lake and federated data storage.

Data Lakes. are centralized repositories that stores large volumes of raw, unstructured, semi-structured, and structured data. Data lakes provide a scalable and cost-effective solution for storing diverse data types from various sources. Moreover, they offer flexibility and agility in data exploration and analysis. Users can explore and analyze data from various perspectives without the need for upfront data modeling or schema design. They eliminate the need for costly data transformations and schema design upfront, reducing data preparation costs.

However, data lakes have a set of disadvantages. Data lakes can become susceptible to poor data quality if not managed properly. The absence of predefined schemas and data transformations may lead to data inconsistency, duplication or inaccuracies. Lack of integration and standardized data models can hinder data accessibility and understanding.

The main disadvantages for using a data lake as a platform solution are data security, privacy and accessibility concerns. If not adequately protected centralizing large volumes of data in a single repository increases the potential impact of a data breach. Hence, a large amount of trust in the provider is needed.

Federated Data Storages. represent a set of independent providers of data storage solutions. In practice this will be a system where everyone offers his own data from its own infrastructure or contracts a service provider that offers storage solutions for specific domains or groups of actors.

Main advantages of federated data storages are improved scalability and data sovereignty. Actors with a large amounts of data usually know how to handle it. Hence the storage space is not an issue for the network. Furthermore, federated data storages enable organizations to maintain control over their data by implementing their custom access control mechanisms.

Federated data storages also have their disadvantages. Managing a federated data storage system can be more complex compared to a centralized approach, requiring additional coordination and synchronization mechanisms. Setting up and maintaining multiple servers for data storage can be more expensive compared to a single centralized storage system. Furthermore, imposing common data structures is a non-trivial task for the governance of such a system.

Conclusion. Ports are logistic hubs in physical and virtual spaces, where various stakeholders with competing business objectives need to share information. Setting up and running a data lake would requires a neutral and trustworthy entity. To address the issue of privacy we selected a federated data storage approach in MISSION. However, data quality and data governance remain a challenge for this approach, since the data is not stored in a central repository. An additional examples for this approach is Navelink, following the MCP specification. The majority of commercial platforms use data lakes, e.g., Veracity.

3.2 Interfaces

A data platform needs interfaces to enable interaction between the system and its users, as well as to facilitate communication between different services. Since the development is driven by the community of the platform, the specification of APIs should be standardized. The hope of the standardization is to counter the skill gap and talent shortage, since developers can easily understand and implement the APIs. There are several technologies available for implementing APIs. Some popular technologies and patterns include RESTful APIs, GraphQL, gRPC ,and SOAP. In principle all could be used and most often the use case favors a specific kind. However, it is crucial that the APIs are well documented an developer friendly. Hence the documentation tools and possibilities should be emphasized.

In MISSION we enforced every API to use the OpenAPI Specifications [10], which defines a standard, language-agnostic interface to document HTTP APIs. But since most organizations are accustomed to dealing with the security issues of allowing HTTP traffic on ports 80 and 443, public APIs and many private distributed APIs use HTTP as the transport. Furthermore, OpenAPI offers a common language and structure for API documentation, making it easier for developers to understand and work with different APIs since they can generate client libraries, code snippets, and SDKs automatically based on the specification. Moreover, OpenAPI Specifications can be utilized for API testing and validation. While other platforms use a less restrictive approach, OpenAPI Specifications remain a commonly used way for documenting APIs, as Veracity, the DCSA, and FEDeRATED are using this way to describe their interfaces or specify their standards.

It is possible to develop an own standard as it was done in context of the Maritime Connectivity Platform [18]. In our opinion this approach obstructs the adoption of the solution, since a developer needs to read and understand the document. On the other hand, the development of a new specialized standard may lessen the burden for the governance body to facilitate harmonization of APIs. However, one should keep in mind that the adoption is the most critical part. If restriction on the documentation are imposed, be sure that the community is able to implement those.

3.3 Access Control and Identity

Access control mechanisms ensure that only authorized users or systems can access certain resources or data within a platform. This helps to protect sensitive information, maintain data integrity, and comply with legal and regulatory requirements. It lessens the burden of data security and privacy issues for the actors and stakeholders, since broken access control remains one of the top web application security risks [12].

In MISSION, the platform included the identity provider, but allowing federation and other identity provider as well. We used OpenID Connect [11], an open standard for providing digital identities. Other platform also favor OpenID Connect like Veracity, Windward and Maritime Connectivity Platform.

This approach benefits from the issues addressed by the standard, including Single Sign-On, secure transmission of credentials, user profile information, federation, and interoperability.

3.4 Trust

As we discussed, a data platform needs trust from the community to be adopted. Trust can be facilitated through the following key factors:

1. Transparency actions, processes, and communication.
2. Implement robust security measures to protect data from unauthorized access, breaches, or misuse.
3. Respect user privacy by adhering to privacy regulations and best practices. Obtain proper consent for data collection and clear communication of how information will be used.

4. Establish strong data governance practices to ensure the responsible handling of data. Ensure compliance with internal policies and external regulations.
5. Consistently provide high-quality products, services, and support.
6. Listen to the feedback and concerns of the community. Provide channels for users to report issues or seek support regarding data privacy and security.

These small items seem reasonable, but are hard to implement properly. In order to uphold all of these points complex business processes have to be implemented. Therefore, the provider of the platform should be an established cooperation. Transparency is delicate topic. If there is an intrinsic conflict in interests for the cooperation, the provider may be incentivised to withhold information. The incentive alone may be enough to lessen the trust in the provider despite best intentions. A common case of this is the provision of the platform from a competitor.

In our opinion, trust is a serious challenge for platforms. In order to know and support the use cases for the community, one must be part of it, thus being a competitor is likely. This may be avoided by forming a consortium and establish a new cooperation or a formal association. However, it is hard to balance expertise against independence. Examples of this approach are Navelink and GSBN.

On the other hand, there exist some neutral actors in the industry which have experience in providing services based on trust. A prominent example for this is a classification society like DNV. This may be the reason why Veracity is one of oldest platform other than port community systems.

4 Operation of the Infrastructure

Operating the infrastructure of a platform is a complex task and comes with certain technical and non-technical issues. This applies above all to the operation of the server infrastructure, monitoring, support, governance, and the further development of individual components to support other and future standards.

In our opinion, the work that needs to be done can be divided into three parts: infrastructure operation, further development, and supervision of a technical working group. Note that these points result from our experience in the MISSION project and the provided platform was designed to provide a minimal set of features to reduce the costs.

For infrastructure operation the heavy lifting is done by cloud or infrastructure-as-a-service providers.

The further development of the existing infrastructure services as well as the development and implementation of new infrastructure services is needed to ensure the long-term viability of the platform. There are also constantly new features and extensions in the used protocols and standards. In order to utilize the benefits of these improvements, adjustments may be necessary. The developments should take place with the consent of the users. A key point here is backwards compatibility. This allows the operation of software or specifications that are based on an older version of the infrastructure. It must therefore be ensured that changes to the infrastructure do not have any corresponding incompatibilities. In particular small providers can not afford constant adjustment of their services. This can lead to rejections of the platform.

Supervision of the infrastructure is also important to ensure the smooth operation and to address any technical issues that may arise. A technical working group consisting of experts and users of API technologies and applications should be set up and supervised for the lively exchange and the mutual expansion of the infrastructure.

Also worth mentioning is the governance, i.e. the legal administration of the infrastructure, as well as public relations and advertising, for which corresponding strategies must exist. However, these strategies are strongly based on the operator concept and are therefore described in the next chapter.

5 Operating Concepts

Various concepts are suitable for covering the costs of the operation. Based on the experience gained in the MISSION project and looking at similar platforms and networks, there are four possible operator concepts. In the following, these are explained, examples are introduced and advantages and disadvantages are discussed, as well as an assessment of the suitability of the corresponding concepts for the further operation.

1. A project consortium can easily fund the initial operation that is required to handle the tasks of the infrastructure. The advantages of this concept are the relatively high sums that can be accumulated as contributions, subsidies or investments with low associated risks. The governance is usually coordinated by the project partners. However, it is important that it is defined how other participants can participate in the network and, if necessary, be reflected in the cost structure. A major disadvantage of the concept is the lead time to agree on the project goals, win over the partners and negotiate the type and amount of the contribution. Due to the usually limited project duration, it is uncertain what will happen afterwards. A project consortium is not suitable for continuous operation.
2. Another option is to set up an association to operate the infrastructure. The coordination effort at the beginning is similar to that of the project consortium. Operating costs are covered by membership fees. The budget allows planning and, with a larger number of members, adequate scaling of the infrastructure. However, the start of such an association requires the support of financially strong members, since membership fees do not necessarily cover the upfront development costs.
3. Such a network can also be managed by a public provider. An example of this is the Mobilithek [8], which is provided by the German Federal Ministry of Transport and Digital Infrastructure. It is free of charge and some publicly funded projects even require contributions to the platform. In general, these public platforms are mostly used to exchange official data and are mandatory due to regulation. Hence, the platforms usually follow a specific political agenda and are not very flexible when it comes to changes.

4. A provision of the platform by a cooperation with a commercial interest is always a possibility. A prominent example is Veracity. The advantage of this is the flexible pricing and uninhibited implementation. However, governance issues can be decided by the operator alone. This can deter customers fearing high costs for lock-in effects and the need for additional implementation or adaptation in later stages. Furthermore, the cooperation needs trust from the community. This excludes basically all competitors.

6 Conclusion

In general, the technical challenges of data platforms in the maritime domain are well understood and there exist enough industry standards to ensure a future proof implementation. There are some technologies that are favored by specific use cases, but in general it is possible to combine these. With the FEDeRATED project and the Maritime Connectivity Platform we have basically blueprints for the implementation. Git repositories even showcase the source code of reference implementations.

However, there are still challenges concerning provision and governance as the needed trust in the platform remains an issue. Also the responsibility of the platforms are debated. It is still unclear if the industry tends towards one platform for all or to use case oriented platforms. Furthermore, standardization processes are still ongoing. With associations like the DCSA and the TIC 4.0 we have different groups of stakeholders working on standardization on similar issues. To harmonize the standards still needs some time.

Another often overlooked point is the commercial viability. Adopting or providing a platform needs specialized software and its development, which is very costly. Hence, the provision of a platform requires a critical starting mass or start-up capital, excluding the individual cost for developing and adapting the API and services. This is in contrast to the commercial value gained by such a platform, which is often hard or impossible to assess. Moreover, one cannot guarantee that the solution will be successful, as even platform solution TradeLens [14] of Maersk and IBM announced the discontinuation. Actors, who want to avoid uncertain investment, may hesitate in the adoption of a platform and thus driving the upfront investments of a platform.

The question of governance type that should be used to facilitate the further development of the platform is a relevant and not easy to answer. Either we have a single actor as provider with full dependency or we have association, in which in term are usually driven by the actors with the most contribution, financial or other. Either way, the use cases of smaller cooperation may not be addressed thus preventing the adoption of the platform by those actors.

Fortunately, from personal communication of the authors with relevant stakeholders in the maritime community, the providers of platforms are aware of those issues and discussion in the standardization bodies are also targeted to solve these issues. In the end, if a platform fails to be adopted by its targeted community, it will die regardless how properly it was implemented.

References

1. DCSA. https://dcsa.org/about-us. Accessed 02 June 2024
2. European Maritime Single Window environment. https://www.emsa.europa.eu/emsw.html. Accessed 03 June 2024
3. FEDeRATED. https://federatedplatforms.eu/. Accessed 02 June 2024
4. Global Shipping Business Network. https://www.gsbn.trade/about-gsbn. Accessed 02 June 2024
5. International Taskforce for Port Call Optimization. https://portcalloptimization.org/. Accessed 02 June 2024
6. Maritime Connectivity Consortium (MCC). https://maritimeconnectivity.net/consortium/. Accessed 02 June 2024
7. Maritime national single window. https://www.imo.org/en/OurWork/Facilitation/Pages/MaritimeSingleWindow-default.aspx. Accessed 02 June 2024
8. Mobilithek. https://mobilithek.info/. Accessed 04 June 2024
9. Navelink. https://www.navelink.org/. Accessed 02 June 2024
10. OpenAPI Specification. https://spec.openapis.org/oas/latest.html. Accessed 04 June 2024
11. OpenID Connect. https://openid.net/. Accessed 04 June 2024
12. OWASP Top Ten. https://owasp.org/www-project-top-ten/. Accessed 03 June 2024
13. TIC 4.0. https://tic40.org/. Accessed 02 June 2024
14. TradeLens. https://www.tradelens.com/. Accessed 04 June 2024
15. Veracity by DNV. https://www.veracity.com/. Accessed 04 June 2024
16. Windward. https://windward.ai/. Accessed 04 June 2024
17. Bonina, C., Koskinen, K., Eaton, B., Gawer, A.: Digital platforms for development: foundations and research agenda. Inf. Syst. J. **31**(6), 869–902 (2021)
18. ENAV: The specification of e-navigation technical services (2021). https://www.iala-aism.org/product/g1128/
19. Lohse, T., Österreich, T.P.: Ihatec mission: Gesamtabschlussbericht (2021)
20. Tijan, E., Agatić, A., Jović, M., Aksentijević, S.: Maritime national single window—a prerequisite for sustainable seaport business. Sustainability **11**(17), 4570 (2019)

Defining and Detecting Waiting Time in Maritime Traffic: An AIS Approach

Jonas Hedegaard and Julia Pahl(✉)

University of Southern Denmark, Campusvej 55, 5230 Odense, Denmark
{jhed,julp}@iti.sdu.dk

Abstract. Reducing vessel waiting times near port areas offers potential for lowering fuel consumption and emissions in maritime operations. The application of just-in-time (JIT) port call optimization (PCO) strategies requires accurate identification of waiting behaviour, which is a challenge when only automatic identification system (AIS) data is available. This study develops and compares two data-driven approaches for detecting vessel waiting times at the Port of Valencia (ESVLC) using one year of AIS data. The first approach is a speed-mode classification method proposed by University Maritime Advisory Services (UMAS) [7], which follows international maritime organization (IMO)-aligned definitions and interprets anchoring-related vessel states as waiting. The second approach introduces spatio temporal waiting behavior (STWB), a novel movement-pattern method that identifies waiting through spatial and kinematic signatures, including low speed over ground (SOG), trajectory compactness, minimal directional progress, and proximity to port before entry, inferring waiting behaviour directly from position and speed using geometric and straightness criteria to distinguish loitering from slow navigation. Bootstrap analysis is employed to compare the two methods across vessel categories and destination terminals, revealing significant differences in estimated waiting times. The UMAS method generally yields higher mean waiting times compared to STWB, particularly for certain vessel categories and terminals.

Keywords: Just-in-Time · Port Call Optimisation · Vessel Waiting Time · AIS Data · Spatio-temporal Analysis

1 Introduction

PCO and JIT arrival are increasingly emphasised as near-term operational means to reduce waiting times, fuel consumption, and emissions by aligning vessel arrival with berth and service availability [2,3]. A persistent inefficiency is the "sail-fast-then-wait" practice, where vessels proceed at service speed and then idle at anchor or low speed near port due to insufficient readiness or coordination on the port side [3,7]. While JIT concepts presume earlier and more reliable readiness information exchange, such information are rarely available in research

J. de Armas and E. Lalla Ruiz (Eds.): LOGMS 2026, LNCS 16679, pp. 275–285, 2027.
https://doi.org/10.1007/978-3-032-30795-8_23

datasets. AIS-only approaches that infer congestion from observed traffic patterns are therefore valuable for benchmarking and decision-support. JIT arrival strategies aim to synchronise vessel arrivals with berth availability, reducing unnecessary waiting and associated emissions [6]. Effective JIT implementation requires accurate predictions of vessel arrival times and port readiness, which can be challenging due to uncertainties in vessel operations and port logistics.

Ports are complex systems where multiple stakeholders interact under varying operational constraints, regulations, and incentives. Understanding and optimising port calls require integrating different data sources and perspectives, including vessel operations, port logistics, environmental factors, and economic considerations. This complexity motivates robust, data-driven methods to characterise and predict vessel behaviour around ports. AIS data, which provide high-resolution spatio-temporal vessel movement information, is available as a key resource for analysing maritime traffic patterns, including waiting and anchorage behaviour [5]. However, AIS data is often noisy and incomplete, necessitating careful preprocessing and robust definitions of operational states such as waiting, berthing, and sailing [4]. Thereby, a major challenge is the variability in vessel behaviour and operational contexts across different ports and regions as well as its stochastic nature is influenced by a wide range of factors. This variability complicates the development of generalisable definitions and models for waiting and congestion, as patterns observed in one context may not hold in another. For example, some vessels may choose to wait at anchor while others may loiter near the port or even enter the port and wait at berth, depending on factors such as vessel type, cargo, operational constraints, and port policies.

This paper proposes and evaluates two AIS-based definitions of waiting for arrivals to the ESVLC. First, we implement a widely used baseline aligned with IMO guidance and operationalised in prior work (hereafter "UMAS"), which classifies vessel movement into speed modes and interprets anchoring-related modes as waiting. Second, we introduce a movement-pattern definition STWB, that identifies waiting as *loitering*: sustained low-speed behaviour that is spatially compact and directionally non-progressive, occurring within a defined proximity of the port and terminating before port entry. Rather than relying on self-reported AIS fields like navigational status, STWB is sensor-first: it infers waiting primarily from position and SOG, and uses geometric constraints, e.g., anchorage/near-region membership, run compactness, combined with a track straightness criterion to separate loitering from slow, purposeful navigation.

2 Related Work

AIS-based studies have developed methods to detect waiting and/or anchorage behaviour and construct port performance indicators, often noting that navigational status is manually entered and may be unreliable, which motivates sensor-based definitions using speed and location [5]. In addition, estimated time of arrival (ETA) prediction and port-call analytics have been proposed as enablers of port call optimisation and improved planning.

Chen et al. (2023) [1] explore the use of AIS data for identifying and characterizing vessel waiting behavior in port environments. They propose a method that integrates speed, position, and temporal information to detect and classify different types of waiting activities, contributing to a better understanding of port operations and potential optimization opportunities.

Ship behavioral analysis using AIS ranges from simple rule-based methods using speed and position, aligned with Davenport-style "speed too slow" and "loitering" patterns to more advanced clustering and neural approaches that capture non-procedural detection of abnormal ship behavior (DASB) is provided by [8]. In most abnormal-behavior work, "abnormal" is defined relative to a baseline of normal operations. Waiting outside a port can be operationally normal, but it is distinct from sea passage or slow steaming.

Across the AIS-based literature, pre-arrival waiting for berth is commonly split into two types: (i) waiting at anchor in designated anchorage areas and (ii) low-speed loitering in the port approaches. Definitions vary, but many studies converge to three criteria: low speed, spatial confinement in port-specific "waiting waters," and a minimum duration. For example, the authors in [4] derive vessel-type-specific low-speed thresholds from the speed distribution, e.g., considering the saddle point, and label waiting when a vessel remains below the threshold inside a defined waiting area for longer than a minimum time. Related stop-detection and port-performance studies use similar methods; speed, dwell time, and spatial compactness, often enriched with geographic semantics, e.g., fairways, berth/anchorage locations, coastline, depth, to extract stop events and distinguish berth versus anchorage stops. Loitering studies further add trajectory-shape descriptors, e.g., heading variance, turning angles, radius around a centroid, to separate meandering or circling from transit; "stationary areas" can also be detected as clusters of slow positions in a small region. In anchoring-specific work, anchoring appears as dense clusters of near-zero-speed points largely confined within charted anchorage polygons, with limited spatial spread over time [9].

Because waiting is inherently location-dependent, polygon-based geo-fencing is widely used to delineate port approach zones, waiting waters, and anchorages, enabling rule-based classification and supporting DASB workflows [10]. Recent work combines geo-fencing with machine learning to improve efficiency and robustness in behavior classification and anomaly detection. More generally, vessel behavior is often represented as a set of discrete states, e.g., normal navigation, maneuvering, stopping, which provides a practical framework for separating transit from pre-arrival waiting in port-centric analyses.

3 Case Study and Data

We analyse arrival voyages at the Port of Valencia, Spain (ESVLC), using: (i) AIS position reports containing timestamp, latitude/longitude, SOG, and vessel identifiers; (ii) arrival metadata containing `voyage_id`, arrival timestamp, and destination information; and (iii) a port-boundary file with polygons for terminals, port areas, and anchorage zones. AIS and metadata are linked by `voyage_id`. The observation period spans 1 January 2024 to 31 December 2024, based on recorded arrival times for Valencia-bound voyages. We restrict the analysis to pre-arrival behaviour, as JIT interventions primarily target the approach and anchorage phases before port entry. The raw arrivals dataset contains 3,311,442 AIS records and 43,352 arrival voyages. After restricting to Valencia arrivals, removing observations after recorded arrival time, applying spatial and vessel-type filters, and excluding sparse or short trajectories (fewer than 36 points or less than 2 h), the cleaned sample contains 4,705 voyages and 545,687 AIS observations.[1]

4 Methodology

The analysis uses two distinct definitions of waiting time, the first used by [7] in the "Port congestion, Waiting times and Operational Efficiency", based on IMO guidelines, i.e., UMAS, and the second method is the STWB method. The UMAS method defines waiting time based on vessel speed and location relative to the port and coast, while the STWB method defines waiting time based on vessel movement patterns derived from AIS data. Both methods are applied to the same dataset of vessel arrivals at ESVLC to compare their estimates of waiting time and identify any discrepancies or insights.

4.1 UMAS Waiting Time Definition

The UMAS method defines waiting time based on vessel speed and location relative to the port and coast. The method categorizes vessel movements into five speed modes: 1) at berth, 2) at anchor, 3) maneuvering, 4) slow steaming, and 5) at sea. Each speed mode is defined by specific speed ranges and additional conditions such as distance to port or coast and main engine load. Waiting time is identified when a vessel is in Speed Mode 2 (at anchor) within the anchorage area or near-region before port entry.

4.2 STWB Waiting Time Definition

The STWB method defines waiting time based on vessel movement patterns derived from AIS data. The method identifies periods when a vessel is stationary or moving below a certain speed threshold within a defined anchorage area. To detect if a vessel is defined as loitering prior to a port call, consecutive AIS data points p are grouped into runs R of run k.

$$R_k = \{p_i, p_{i+1}, ..., p_j\} \quad \text{where} \quad p_n \text{ is consecutive to } p_{n-1} \quad \forall n \in [i+1, j]$$

[1] The datasets used in this study are proprietary and were obtained under non-disclosure agreements and cannot be shared publicly. The processing steps and model parameterization are documented to support reproducibility with comparable AIS data.

Run R_k is classified as loitering if it meets the following conditions to be included in the set of candidate loitering runs L, where $v(p)$ is the vessels speed and v_{wait} is the low-speed threshold for a waiting vessel. $\tau_{\min}$ is the minimum duration of a waiting run:

$$L = \{R_k | v(p_n) < v_{wait} \quad \forall p_n \in R_k \quad \text{and} \quad \Delta t(R_k) = t_j - t_i \geq \tau_{\min}\}$$

The candidate loitering runs L are then filtered based on geometric and temporal criteria to identify valid waiting periods prior to port calls. The run must occur within a defined proximity area of the port, and must end before the vessel enters the port boundary. The geometric filtering ensures that only relevant loitering behavior near the port is considered, while the temporal filtering ensures that the waiting period is directly related to the subsequent port call. A centroid of the loitering run is calculated to determine if the run is within the defined proximity area of the port. Each run is checked for spatial compactness by calculating the centroid of the run and ensuring that all points in the run are within a defined radius r_{max} from the centroid. The centroid is defined as:

$$\hat{p} = \frac{1}{K} \sum_{l=i}^{j} p_l$$

where K is the number of points in the run and p_l are the individual points in the run.

$$K = |R_k| = j - i + 1$$

The spatial compactness condition, which ensures that all points in the run are within the defined radius r_{max} from the centroid, is expressed as:

$$d(p_l, \hat{p}) \leq r_{max} \quad \forall p_l \in R_k$$

where $d(p_l, \hat{p})$ is the distance between point p_l and the centroid $\hat{p}$.

To distinguish loitering from normal navigation, we also impose a straightness condition on the run. The straightness $S(R_k)$ of the run is defined as the ratio of the direct distance between the start and end points of the run to the total distance traveled during the run:

$$S(R_k) = \frac{d(p_i, p_j)}{\sum_{l=i}^{j-1} d(p_l, p_{l+1})}$$

For a perfectly straight track, $S \approx 1$, while for highly circuitous movement, the sum in the denominator becomes large and S decreases. Runs are treated as waiting if $S(R_k)$ is below a chosen threshold σ_{max}, indicating that the vessel is moving within a small area without making directional progress. Candidate runs that satisfy the speed, duration, radius and straightness criteria are labeled waiting runs.

Table 1 summarizes the key parameters used in the STWB waiting time definition.

Table 1. Key parameters used in the STWB waiting time definition.

Parameter	Value
v_{wait} (knots)	3.5
$\tau_{\min}$ (hours)	0.2
$\tau_{\max}$ (hours)	168.0
r_{max} (nautical miles)	5.4
σ_{max}	0.90

4.3 Bootstrap Resampling

Waiting times are heavily right-skewed, i.e., bounded at 0, but some ships wait for days. Because the mean is sensitive to extreme values, we quantify uncertainty using a non-parametric bootstrap. This approach allows us to construct confidence intervals for the mean waiting times and their differences without assuming a specific distributional form, which is appropriate given the skewness of the data. By resampling voyages with replacement, we can assess the variability in our estimates and provide a more robust measure of uncertainty around the mean waiting times for both methods.

Bootstrap provides a powerful method for estimating confidence intervals and other measures of uncertainty. In our case, since we are interested in statistics like mean waiting times, limits of agreement, percentiles, and the mean gap of heavily skewed data, the bootstrap is a more flexible and reliable method for quantifying uncertainty than parametric approaches that may not fit the data well. The bootstrap allows us to empirically derive confidence intervals and other statistics directly from the observed data. This allows for a comparison of the two methods, and an assessment of the variability in the estimates, which is crucial for understanding the reliability of our findings given the skewed nature of waiting time data.

5 Comparison Results of the Two Methods

5.1 Vessel Type Results

The distribution of waiting times by vessel category shows that bulk carriers have the longest median waiting time (UMAS: 13.26 h; STWB: 9.96 h) and the highest mean waiting time (UMAS: 35.97 h; STWB: 33.26 h), while roll-on roll-off vessels have the shortest median waiting time (0.00 h for both methods) and the lowest mean waiting time (UMAS: 4.72 h; STWB: 1.68 h); see Table 2. Container ships, which represent the largest category in terms of sample size, have a median waiting time of 1.50 h under UMAS and 0.68 h under STWB, with mean waiting times of 10.22 h and 9.30 h, respectively. The "Unspecified" category also shows a high median waiting time (4.71 h under UMAS and 4.15 h under STWB) and mean waiting time (16.03 h under UMAS and 15.51 h under STWB), which may

Table 2. Summary statistics for waiting time (hours) by vessel category. Q_1 and Q_3 denote the first and third quartiles; W_L and W_U the lower and upper whiskers ($\pm 1.5 \times$ IQR).

Vessel Category	n	UMAS				STWB			
		Q_1	Mdn	Q_3	Mean	Q_1	Mdn	Q_3	Mean
Container Ship	2595	0.28	1.50	11.56	10.22	0.00	0.68	10.26	9.30
Unspecified	125	0.68	4.71	22.30	16.03	0.00	4.15	21.26	15.51
Roll-on Roll-off	208	0.00	0.00	0.00	4.72	0.00	0.00	0.00	1.68
Chemical Tanker	173	0.00	0.49	11.56	10.38	0.00	0.00	11.31	10.27
Tanker	76	0.00	0.70	12.89	9.76	0.00	0.46	13.85	10.46
Pure Car Carrier	218	0.00	0.00	0.39	1.79	0.00	0.00	0.00	1.43
General Dry Cargo	155	0.26	5.27	25.61	16.95	0.00	5.02	24.98	16.59
Bulk Carrier	70	0.55	13.26	57.72	35.97	0.21	9.96	53.03	33.26
Vehicle/Passenger	20	0.00	0.72	19.15	14.21	0.00	0.48	19.08	13.96

reflect a heterogeneous mix of vessel types or operational contexts that are not captured by the available classification.

Overall, the distribution of waiting times is highly skewed across all vessel categories, with many voyages having zero waiting time and a long tail of higher values. The STWB method tends to detect slightly lower median waiting times for most categories compared to UMAS, which may suggest that the geometric criteria used in STWB are more selective in identifying waiting behavior, particularly for categories like container ships and general dry cargo vessels. However, the mean waiting times are generally similar between the two methods, indicating that they capture comparable aggregate waiting durations across vessel categories. The results can be seen in Table 2, which provides summary statistics for waiting times by vessel category under both methods.

The high proportion of voyages with zero waiting time, as indicated by the first quartile Q_1 being zero for most categories, suggests that many vessels are able to arrive and berth without significant pre-arrival waiting, which could be due to efficient port operations, low congestion levels, or effective scheduling. The long tail of higher waiting times indicates that while most vessels experience little to no waiting, a subset of voyages encounter significant delays, which could be attributed to factors such as port congestion, operational issues, or specific vessel characteristics. The median (Mdn) provides a measure of central tendency that is less sensitive to extreme values than the mean, and the fact that many categories have a median of zero further emphasizes that the majority of voyages do not experience waiting, while the mean captures the influence of the few voyages with long waiting times. This highlights the importance of considering both median and mean statistics when analyzing skewed data, as they provide complementary insights into the distribution of waiting times across vessel categories.

5.2 Destination Terminal Results

Table 3 shows that Terminal 01 (Container) has the highest median waiting time under UMAS (5.39 h) and a high mean waiting time (15.29 h), while Terminal 03 (General/Bulk) has the lowest median waiting time (0.00 h) and mean waiting time (0.60 h). Terminal 04 (Container) also has a relatively high median waiting time (1.76 h) and mean waiting time (6.96 h). The STWB method generally shows lower median waiting times across terminals compared to UMAS, with Terminal 01 having a median of 0.60 h and a mean of 13.04 h, while Terminal 03 has a median of 0.00 h and a mean of 0.59 h. The results suggest that certain terminals, particularly those handling container traffic and bulk cargo, may experience longer pre-arrival waiting times, which could be due to factors such as higher congestion levels, operational practices, or specific vessel characteristics associated with those terminals.

Table 3. Summary statistics for pre-entry waiting time (hours) attributed to the anonymised destination terminal ultimately served by the voyage. Q_1 and Q_3 denote the first and third quartiles.

Destination Terminal	n	UMAS				STWB			
		Q_1	Mdn	Q_3	Mean	Q_1	Mdn	Q_3	Mean
T02 (Multipurpose/Container)	603	0.00	0.34	4.03	5.03	0.00	0.00	1.09	4.41
Unknown/Unattributed	822	0.50	1.26	10.02	9.68	0.00	0.00	5.91	8.13
T03 (General/Bulk)	32	0.00	0.00	0.00	0.60	0.00	0.00	0.00	0.59
T04 (Container)	377	0.36	1.76	7.68	6.96	0.00	0.00	1.79	4.48
T01 (Container)	1163	0.27	5.39	21.75	15.29	0.00	0.60	20.05	13.04
T07 (Specialised Terminal)	129	0.00	3.66	20.45	13.26	0.00	1.92	20.17	12.88
T05 (Ro-Ro/Vehicle)	333	0.00	0.00	0.20	4.11	0.00	0.00	0.00	1.92
T06 (Bulk)	97	0.26	7.51	47.46	29.65	0.00	7.22	47.21	28.83
T09 (Ro-Ro/Vehicle)	83	0.00	0.00	1.66	5.07	0.00	0.00	0.00	4.50

5.3 Bootstrap Results

The bootsrap analysis provides estimates of mean waiting times and their confidence intervals for each method, as well as the mean difference between methods, stratified by terminal and vessel category. From Table 4, we see that container ships have a significantly higher mean waiting time under UMAS compared to STWB, with a mean difference of −1.86 h (95% CI: −2.17 to −1.59). Chemical tankers and tankers show a significant increase in mean waiting time under STWB compared to UMAS, with mean differences of 4.26 h (95% CI: 3.02 to 5.60) and 4.19 h (95% CI: 1.21 to 9.44), respectively. Since the confidence intervals for the mean differences in other vessel categories do not include zero, we can infer that there are statistically significant differences between methods for those categories as well, with UMAS generally yielding higher mean waiting times than STWB for most categories except for chemical tankers and tankers.

Table 4. Bootstrap waiting-time estimates by vessel category. Mean waiting times are reported in hours with percentile 95% confidence intervals in brackets. The mean difference is defined as $\Delta = \bar{W}_S - \bar{W}_U$.

Vessel category	n	UMAS mean [95% CI]	STWB mean [95% CI]	Δ mean [95% CI]
Container Ship	2595	10.22 [9.49, 10.96]	8.36 [7.67, 9.05]	−1.86 [−2.17, −1.59]
Vehicle/Passenger	20	14.21 [6.03, 24.00]	12.68 [4.63, 22.49]	−1.53 [−3.18, −0.14]
Chemical Tanker	173	10.38 [7.73, 13.33]	10.14 [7.47, 13.09]	−0.24 [−0.36, −0.15]
Roll-on Roll-off	208	4.72 [1.33, 9.73]	1.58 [0.67, 2.72]	−3.14 [−8.10, −0.13]
Bulk Carrier	70	35.97 [25.90, 46.92]	33.15 [23.96, 43.26]	−2.83 [−7.97, −0.20]
Pure Car Carrier	218	1.79 [0.96, 2.77]	1.31 [0.58, 2.20]	−0.47 [−0.86, −0.18]
General Dry Cargo	155	16.95 [13.04, 21.32]	16.30 [12.51, 20.52]	−0.65 [−1.28, −0.22]
Tanker	76	9.76 [6.18, 14.07]	10.21 [6.29, 14.79]	0.45 [−0.81, 2.59]
Unspecified	125	16.03 [12.16, 20.21]	14.50 [10.57, 18.75]	−1.53 [−2.22, −0.95]

From Table 5, we observe that Terminal 01 (Container) has a significantly higher mean waiting time under UMAS compared to STWB, with a mean difference of −2.25 h (95% CI: −2.90 to −1.72). Terminal 04 (Container) also shows a significant increase in mean waiting time under UMAS compared to STWB, with a mean difference of −2.48 h (95% CI: −3.07 to −1.97). Since the confidence intervals for the mean differences in other terminals do not include zero, we can infer that there are statistically significant differences between methods for those terminals as well, with UMAS generally yielding higher mean waiting times than STWB for most terminals except for Terminal 03 (General/Bulk) and Terminal 08 (Passenger/Ferry), where the mean differences are not statistically significant. The results suggest that the choice of waiting time definition can lead to significant differences in estimated waiting times for certain terminals.

Table 5. Bootstrap estimates of pre-entry waiting time by anonymised destination terminal. Mean waiting times are reported in hours with percentile 95% confidence intervals in brackets. The mean difference is defined as $\Delta = \bar{W}_S - \bar{W}_U$.

Terminal	n	UMAS mean [95% CI]	STWB mean [95% CI]	Δ mean [95% CI]
T02 (Multipurpose/Container)	603	5.03 [4.11, 6.09]	4.41 [3.50, 5.46]	−0.62 [−0.78, −0.48]
Unknown/Unattributed	822	9.69 [8.40, 11.12]	8.13 [6.87, 9.53]	−1.56 [−2.14, −1.11]
T03 (General/Bulk)	32	0.61 [0.02, 1.37]	0.59 [0.00, 1.35]	−0.01 [−0.05, 0.00]
T04 (Container)	377	6.97 [5.78, 8.20]	4.49 [3.37, 5.68]	−2.48 [−3.07, −1.97]
T01 (Container)	1163	15.30 [14.00, 16.63]	13.05 [11.83, 14.29]	−2.25 [−2.90, −1.72]
T07 (Specialised Terminal)	129	13.26 [10.10, 16.76]	12.88 [9.73, 16.37]	−0.38 [−0.62, −0.19]
T05 (Ro-Ro/Vehicle)	333	4.12 [1.83, 7.34]	1.92 [1.07, 2.93]	−2.20 [−5.30, −0.25]
T06 (Bulk)	97	29.65 [21.88, 38.08]	28.83 [21.18, 37.08]	−0.82 [−1.78, −0.17]
T09 (Ro-Ro/Vehicle)	83	5.08 [2.26, 8.73]	4.50 [1.70, 8.15]	−0.58 [−1.06, −0.20]
T08 (Passenger/Ferry)	1	48.08 [48.08, 48.08]	48.11 [48.11, 48.11]	0.04 [0.04, 0.04]

Overall, the bootstrap analysis indicates that there are statistically significant differences in mean waiting times between the UMAS and STWB methods across various vessel categories and destination terminals. The UMAS method tends to yield higher mean waiting times compared to STWB for most categories and terminals, which may reflect differences in how each method classifies waiting behavior based on their respective criteria. These findings highlight the importance of carefully considering the choice of method when estimating pre-arrival waiting times, as it can have significant implications for operational decision-making and performance assessment in maritime logistics.

6 Learnings and Future Work

Since there is no ground truth such as labeled data classifying waiting time, the complexity of the underlying operational concept, an avenue for future work is to conduct a more detailed validation of the two methods against expert-labeled data. This could involve an inter-rater reliability study where multiple maritime experts independently label waiting periods for a sample of voyages, and then comparing those labels to the classifications produced by UMAS and STWB. Such an analysis would provide insights into the extent to which each method captures the operational concept of waiting as understood by practitioners, and as a benchmark for further method development.

An in-depth sensitivity analysis can further be conducted to explore the impact of varying the speed thresholds and spatial criteria used in both methods. For instance, systematically varying the low-speed threshold in STWB and the mode boundaries in UMAS across a wider range of values could help identify whether there are specific parameter settings that yield better agreement with expert labels or with each other. Additionally, exploring alternative geometric criteria for defining loitering behavior in STWB, such as incorporating measures of track curvature or spatial deviation, could enhance the method's ability to distinguish between purposeful navigation and waiting. Some of the conditions for the UMAS buckets 4–5 ("Slow steaming" and "At Sea") also include a main engine load criterion, which we did not implement in the present analysis because it is not available in our AIS data. Future work could explore how to incorporate engine load information into STWB. Main engine load could be a valuable additional signal for distinguishing between slow steaming and waiting, as vessels may reduce speed but maintain engine load during slow steaming.

7 Conclusions

This study compared two methods for defining and measuring waiting time in maritime port arrivals: the established UMAS method, which is based on vessel speed modes and spatial criteria, and the proposed STWB method, which uses geometric criteria to identify loitering and drifting behavior. The results indicate that the choice of method can lead to significant differences in estimated waiting times, with UMAS generally yielding higher mean waiting times compared to STWB across various vessel categories and destination terminals. The bootstrap analysis revealed statistically significant differences in mean waiting times between the two methods for specific vessel categories and terminals, suggesting that the operational context plays a crucial role in determining which method may be more appropriate for capturing waiting behavior. These findings underscore the importance of carefully selecting a waiting time definition that aligns with the specific operational characteristics of the maritime traffic being analyzed, as it can have significant implications for performance assessment and decision-making in port operations.

Acknowledgements. This research was funded by the European Union's Horizon Europe research and innovation programme under grant agreement No. 101138583, the MISSION project. The authors would like to thank the project partners for their support and collaboration.

References

1. Chen, W., et al.: Monitoring and evaluation of ship operation congestion status at container ports based on ais data. Ocean Coast. Manage. **245**, 106836 (2023). https://doi.org/10.1016/J.OCECOAMAN.2023.106836
2. GIA: Just in time arrival guide – barriers and potential solutions (2020). https://portcalloptimization.org/images/JIT%20Guide%20Final.pdf. Accessed 06 Jan 2026
3. Global Maritime Forum: Port call optimisation: a pathway to reducing waiting times and emissions (2025). https://globalmaritimeforum.org/report/port-call-optimisation-a-pathway-to-reducing-waiting-times-and-emissions/. Accessed 06 Jan 2026
4. Ma, J., Zhou, Y., Zhu, Z.: Identification and analysis of ship waiting behavior outside the port based on ais data. Sci. Rep. (2023). https://doi.org/10.1038/s41598-023-38080-2
5. Martinčič, T., Štepec, D., Costa, J.P., Čagran, K., Chaldeakis, A.: Vessel and port efficiency metrics through validated ais data. arXiv preprint (2021), https://arxiv.org/pdf/2105.00063
6. Pahl, J.: Just-in-time port call optimization: challenges and IT-systems. iopscience.iop.org **2867**, 12009 (2024). https://doi.org/10.1088/1742-6596/2867/1/012009/META
7. Smith, T., Francis, H.: Port congestion, waiting times and operational efficiency. Technical report, UCL Energy Institute and UMAS (2024). https://safety4sea.com/wp-content/uploads/2024/12/UCL-UMAS-Port-Congestion-Report-2024_12.pdf
8. Wang, Y., Liu, J., Liu, R.W., Liu, Y., Yuan, Z.: Data-driven methods for detection of abnormal ship behavior: progress and trends. Ocean Eng. **271**, 113673 (2023). https://doi.org/10.1016/J.OCEANENG.2023.113673
9. Wijaya, W.M., Nakamura, Y.: Loitering behavior detection by spatiotemporal characteristics quantification based on the dynamic features of automatic identification system (AIS) messages. PeerJ Comput. Sci. **9**, e1572 (2023). https://doi.org/10.7717/PEERJ-CS.1572/SUPP-6
10. Yun, U., etal.: Improved ship emission model considering load factor-based power and hull shape: implication in a Chinese port cluster. JGRD **130**, 2024JD042005 (2025). https://doi.org/10.1029/2024JD042005

Delineating Port Nautical Infrastructure Areas and Characterising Their Usage Based on AIS Data

Lisette Võlu[1(✉)], Nadia Pourmohammad-Zia[1], Floor P. Bakker[1], Alex Kirichek[1], and Mark van Koningsveld[1,2]

[1] Department of Hydraulic Engineering, Delft University of Technology, Delft, The Netherlands
L.Volu@tudelft.nl

[2] Van Oord Dredging and Marine Contractors, 3068 NH Rotterdam, The Netherlands

Abstract. This paper presents a framework for delineating port nautical infrastructure areas and analysing their usage patterns based on AIS data. Using heuristics, DBSCAN and K-means clustering, three key functional areas are identified (berths, anchorages, and tug-assisted turning areas), and relevant time-based indicators based on area geometries and vessel trajectory sequences are derived. The presented method, though simple and open to further development, can give detailed and comparable insights into port performance and support more effective port planning, traffic management, and operational decision-making.

1 Introduction

In recent years, the maritime sector has experienced significant volatility and uncertainty, with disruptions along major shipping routes, consequent shifts in trade flows, and evolving maritime policies, standards, and practices. At the port level, these dynamics are reflected in larger vessels, congestion, and strain on the ports' infrastructure and services, limiting their capacity and efficiency, and impacting safety and sustainability. Consequently, research and industry initiatives increasingly focus on monitoring ports' functional areas and activities, often using indicators such as turnaround time, vessel waiting time, number of port calls, or some composite congestion metrics. These indicators enable performance evaluation and strategic decision-making in traffic management and port planning, while also supporting specific downstream tasks, like trajectory prediction, anomaly detection, or berth planning [5]. However, such metrics are rather difficult to acquire from individual ports [8], limiting their comparability. This has driven interest in extracting performance information from alternative sources, particularly vessel movement data, which can be standardised and directly reveal behavioural patterns such as prolonged waiting in anchorage areas.

Knowledge of port infrastructure areas constitutes a fundamental component in these operational evaluations, yet port layouts are typically delineated

J. de Armas and E. Lalla Ruiz (Eds.): LOGMS 2026, LNCS 16679, pp. 286–296, 2027.
https://doi.org/10.1007/978-3-032-30795-8_24

manually, either by port authority, related hydrographic services, or open source contributors. These maps are not always publicly available, can be outdated, vary in accuracy, and do not reflect infrastructure usage. This has prompted Automatic Identification Systems (AIS) based approaches for functional port area detection and localisation, both as a stand-alone research topic [3,5], as well as an integrated part of broader performance assessment [1,4]. For example, Bai et al. [1] and Peng et al. [4] use delineated areas to develop congestion metrics. Wijaya and Nakamura [8] derive port boundaries alongside berthing and anchoring locations to construct several performance indicators based on berthing, anchoring and manoeuvring durations. At the same time, port functional area mapping is increasingly treated as an independent research topic, such as in Qiang et al. [5] who propose an unsupervised data mining framework to delineate port zones without manual annotations. The scope of port area identification also varies across studies: some focus on berth detection [3], others on broader stationary areas encompassing both berth and anchorages [1,4], and some extend the analysis to include approach channels [5] or broader port boundaries.

Port functional areas are often inferred from distinct behavioural characteristics that vessels exhibit in and around different areas. For example, around berths, quays and anchorages, ships have higher stop density; manoeuvring areas display changes in heading, while vessels in approach channels usually show consistent speed and direction. However, most studies focus on a single behavioural pattern of interest, most commonly stopping behaviour to identify berths and anchorages. For instance, Hadjipieris et al. [3] employ Density-Based Spatial Clustering of Applications with Noise (DBSCAN) as a pre-processing step to cluster trajectory points based on their (lack of) movement, and use Gaussian Mixture Model (GMM) to localise berths. Peng et al. [4] identify stopping segments with speed thresholds, and use DBSCAN to cluster the trajectory points. Similarly, Bai et al. [1] first detect stopping segments and propose an iterative, multi-attribute DBSCAN (IMA-DBSCAN) to identify anchorage areas and individual berths. In contrast, other areas have received considerably less attention. Despite their high safety risk and relevance, turning and manoeuvring areas remain comparatively under-explored in the literature [7], and vessel activity within these is seldom analysed in a systematic way. Furthermore, studies that simultaneously consider multiple functional areas within a unified framework are also scarce, and when they do exist, they typically stop at spatial identification rather than explicitly linking area-level activity patterns to operational insights. Thus, understanding how vessel behaviour can effectively inform usage and performance monitoring across various functional areas remains largely under-researched.

Current paper addresses this gap by proposing an approach that jointly delineates multiple nautical infrastructure areas and analyses their activity patterns. Building on prior research, as well as exploring the under-analysed domains, the methodology integrates multiple behavioural indicators to delineate three key functional areas (berths, anchorages, and tug-assisted turning areas) and derives time-based indicators using delineated geometries and vessel trajectory data. Applied to Port of Los Angeles AIS data, the results offer granular insight into port activities and could be relevant for operational traffic management, safety analysis, congestion monitoring, and infrastructure investment decisions. By combining multiple usage-based functional areas and quantifying their utilisation within a single framework, this paper advances existing research, which predominantly addresses these topics in isolation, and supports more holistic performance assessment, improved port planning and standardised cross-port benchmarking.

2 Methodological Approach

The methodological approach considers two main stages: functional area detection and descriptive analytics of detected areas, preceded by data pre-processing, as outlined in Fig. 1. The method uses publicly available AIS data from August 2024, spatially filtered to 33.60–33.85° N latitude and 118.45–118.15° W longitude, roughly capturing the port of Los Angeles area. Analysed data fields include: latitude, longitude, speed over ground (SOG), course over ground (COG), heading, timestamp, vessel type, length and width. The data are filtered to include only cargo, tanker and tug vessels.

First, duplicate and missing values are removed, data grouped by MMSI, and points temporally sorted. Given that in the span of a month, vessels might call at a port multiple times, the trajectories are further divided into separate port calls if the duration between consecutive AIS messages is greater than 12 h [1]. Since AIS data are susceptible to various errors, including data gaps, trajectories are further separated into distinct time-based segments if the gap between two consecutive AIS messages exceeds five minutes, aiming to separate short-term irregularities from true discontinuities. Short gaps ($\leq$5 min) are resampled with a forward fill to a 1 min resolution. This is mainly motivated by the need for consistent derivation of kinematic features, including changes in SOG, COG, heading, and rates of change in COG and SOG for each vessel trajectory. Additionally, mean, maximum and 80th percentile of these features were computed over a rolling five-minute window. In future, the pre-processing workflow could be further enhanced with more elaborate trajectory reconstruction.

2.1 Functional Area Delineation

After pre-processing, area delineation workflow involves behaviour type identification and subsequent clustering. In research, behavioural segmentation is approached with either geometry/shape-based or behaviour-based methods, using either preset thresholds or unsupervised segmentation methods [9]. Since trajectory segmentation is not the core focus of this study, behavioural states (stationary, direct course, and tug-assisted turning) are determined with a rule-based approach to accommodate simplicity, computational efficiency and robustness. Similar to previous research [1,4], this involves setting several thresholds;

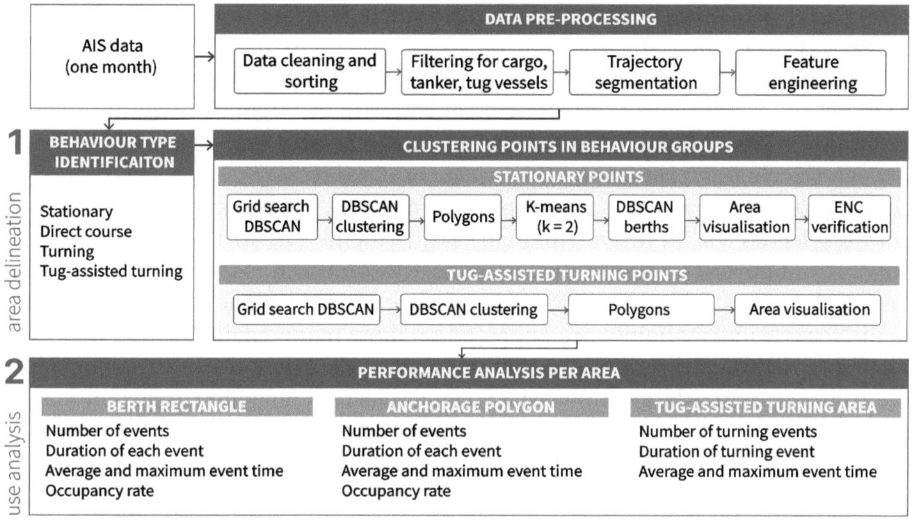

Fig. 1. Methodological workflow of port functional area delineation and performance analysis

however, threshold values reported in literature vary: for example, a point has been considered stationary if its SOG is less than three knots [3], but also more conservatively if it is below 0.5 knots [8]. Several configurations were thus evaluated, and the final thresholds aim to reflect plausible behaviour over a five-minute window: stationary points have consistently low speeds (both maximum and 80th percentile SOG < 0.5 knots), straight movement combines low directional variability (80th percentile turning $\leq 10°$) with relatively high speeds (mean SOG ≥ 5 knots), and turning behaviour is identified by sustained directional change (mean and 80th percentile turning $\geq 15°$) at lower speeds ($0.5 <$ mean SOG < 4 knots). Since turning behaviour can occur sporadically, the method filters out minor manoeuvres by small vessels and focuses on tug-assisted turning areas. Potential tug-assisted interactions were identified when a cargo/tanker was within 300 m of a tug, with only continuous events of at least six minutes retained. While the selected thresholds are informed by prior literature and domain knowledge, and yield plausible results, they remain heuristic in nature and may not capture the full variability of vessel behaviour. As such, future work could refine these criteria or adopt alternative trajectory segmentation methods, like matheuristics [9] or clustering to further enhance behavioural differentiation.

After behaviour type determination, area delineation included stationary and tug-assisted turning point clustering. Density-based algorithms, like DBSCAN, OPTICS, and DBCLASD, are often used in the case of the noisy and arbitrarily shaped low-dimensional spatial data [2], like the latitude and longitude of the behavioural category points. The algorithms mainly differ in their handling of cluster densities, parameter requirements/sensitivity and computational efficiency. This study adopted DBSCAN due to its relative computational efficiency and its prevalence in similar studies, however it is to be noted that algorithms like OPTICS, though slower, may be more robust to parameter setting. This also reflects on the choices and trade-offs that decision-makers must make in the selection of appropriate analytical tools. DBSCAN requires two parameters: minimum points (MinPts) required to form the cluster and epsilon (Eps) value between the clusters. Bai et al. [1] use a generalised iterative approach to identify the appropriate parameters based on intermediate variables. Parameters could also be selected via iterative (manual) adjustments [4]. In this study, Eps and MinPts configurations are evaluated over a grid search, assessing the resulting clusters in terms of noise ratio, cluster size, variance, and density. Plausible results for stationary points are expected to show many small clusters for berths and fewer, larger clusters for anchorages, whereas a low noise ratio may indicate that Eps is too large. However, cluster selection currently relies on manual inspection rather than a fully reproducible criterion. This is a limitation that should be addressed, either through a more robust scoring framework, iterative parameter selection as in Bai et al. [1] or alternative clustering methods. This becomes especially important when applying the workflow to different ports.

Stationary clusters are then represented as geometric polygons using convex hull, as also demonstrated by Hadjipieris et al. [3] and Peng et al. [4]. Anchorage and berth polygons are distinguished using K-means clustering (k = 2) based on polygon-level features, including density, size, distance to land (open-source Natural Earth data), and vessel heading alignment of the polygon. Heading alignment was quantified using cosine similarity, reflecting the fact that vessels at berth typically exhibit consistent or opposing headings, whereas anchorage headings are more disorganised due to wind and wave variations [1]. As a sanity check, berth polygons are post-processed to identify potential misclassification as anchorages. Each berth polygon's centroid is compared with its three nearest cluster centroids; if all correspond to anchorage clusters, the polygon is relabelled accordingly. This assumes that true berths are typically located near other berth clusters, whereas isolated polygons surrounded by anchorages are likely misclassifications. Berth polygon points are then re-clustered using DBSCAN to remove noise and identify smaller berth sub-clusters that may have been missed in the initial clustering. Polygons are reconstructed for each sub-cluster and converted into minimum bounding rectangles oriented along the dominant vessel heading and sized to accommodate the longest and widest vessels observed.

Tug-assisted turning areas are delineated using a similar DBSCAN-based approach, followed by convex hull polygonisation. For each tug-assisted turning cluster, a turning circle is generated by computing the cluster centroid and defining the radius as the maximum distance from the centroid to any cluster point, producing circular polygons enclosing all associated turning trajectories. These areas do not necessarily indicate completion of full turn for all vessel, rather, they represent areas where vessels typically slow down and manoeuvre with tug assistance.

Directly verifying the detected areas is complicated due to the general unavailability of complete ground truth data. Nevertheless, some berth and anchorage information is available in Electronic Navigational Charts (ENCs). ENC anchorage zones are broadly defined, exceeding the operational areas inferred from AIS clustering. Thus, the precision of detected anchorage polygons is calculated as the number of detected polygons that fall entirely within ENC anchorage regions divided by the total number of detected anchorage polygons. For berths, it is checked whether ENC berth points fall within close proximity of detected polygons. Berth precision is calculated as the number of correctly detected berths divided by the total detected berths. Missed detections are computed as the number of correctly detected berth polygons divided by the total number of ENC berths. However, since ENC datasets include a wider range of berth types than those considered in this study (e.g., beyond cargo and tanker vessels), this metric is less informative and therefore interpreted with caution. Misclassifications are calculated whenever detected area corresponds to another ENC element. For tug-assisted turning areas, which might also correspond to turning basins, no external datasets were found for direct validation. Instead, these areas are identified using consistent behavioural patterns in AIS data, characterised by low-speed manoeuvring and tug interactions, which are strongly associated with turning operations. Their spatial consistency across multiple vessel calls and location within wider parts of the harbour basins provide supporting evidence for their validity. While not a formal ground truth validation, this behaviour-based approach offers a plausible representation of turning areas, with further validation left for future work. Given the validation limitations, the subsequent performance metrics ought to be interpreted with caution, as they primarily reflect activity-based indicators rather than providing definitive evidence of performance within particular area.

2.2 Calculating Case-Specific Performance Metrics

UN Trade and Development (UNCTAD) [6] has previously discussed various indicators of port performance, including number of port calls, turnaround times, port waiting times, cargo handling, and liner connectivity, which are primarily used for global performance comparison. Analysing individual functional areas could further deepen the insights and facilitate reasoned decision-making. Therefore, in this study, descriptive statistics are computed for each derived area based on individual vessel trajectories. Each trajectory point is mapped to berth rectangles, anchorage polygons, or tug-assisted turning circles, and metrics computed based on time spent within these areas. The calculated area-level indicators are seen in Fig. 1. Area-level metrics are summarised across all polygons of the same type (e.g., average dwell time across all berths) to generate both port-level indicators, as elaborated in Sect. 3, and enable global comparisons between ports in the future.

3 Results

The initial dataset for August 2024 in port of Los Angeles consisted of 4,056,967 total rows, of which, after data cleaning, 510,161, 182,371, and 998,281 points corresponded to cargo, tanker, and tug/tow vessels, respectively. Following vessel behaviour determination, first stage DBSCAN clustering was performed with parameter configuration of Eps = 140 and MinPts = 40. Clusters were then converted into geometric polygons representing functional areas, presented in Fig. 2. Out of the detected 92 berth rectangles, 65 lie in close proximity of the ENC points, while ENC chart itself provides total of 254 berth point references for the area. The excess of ENC points is likely due to current study only focusing on cargo and tanker vessels. The method detects 9 tug-assisted turning areas, whereas two of them lie in the ENC-defined anchorage zone while others are closer to the berths. The validation results are presented in Table 1.

Table 1. Functional area delineation validation results

Validation metric	2024 August
Berths Detected	92
Anchorages Detected	32
Tug-assisted Turning Areas Detected	9
Berth Precision (Manual Check)	70.65%
Berth Recall (Manual Check)	25.59%
Anchorage Precision	90.63%
Berth Misclassified As Anchorage	1 (out of 92)
Anchorage Misclassified As Berth	0 (out of 32)

Analysing individual vessel trajectories within these polygons enables describing the time between vessel's entry and exit from the area (an event) and the calculation of a set of descriptive intra-port indicators shown in Table 2. Importantly, however, since the events are sensitive to area delineation results which could not be fully validated, the indicators only reflect illustrative case-specific observations rather than broader empirical evidence of the port's performance. Thus, terms like "berth dwell time" only describe the time spent in the method-defined berth-like areas, which might not always represent actual berths.

Furthermore, automated reproducibility of the method is limited as case-specific post-processing was required: since several berth sub-cluster rectangles overlapped, a trajectory point could simultaneously appear in two areas. Although these sub-clusters mostly do refer to separate berths, as corroborated by the respective individual ENC reference points, they were merged in this case, resulting in 66 merged rectangles used for clearer analysis. Initially, the method identified 2,577 events within merged berth areas, 1,014 events in anchorage areas, and 580 events in tug-assisted turning areas. For both berths and anchorages, events were occasionally fragmented, possibly due to AIS reporting inconsistencies or marginal movements near polygon boundaries. Treating such instances as separate events is not reflective of true operational events

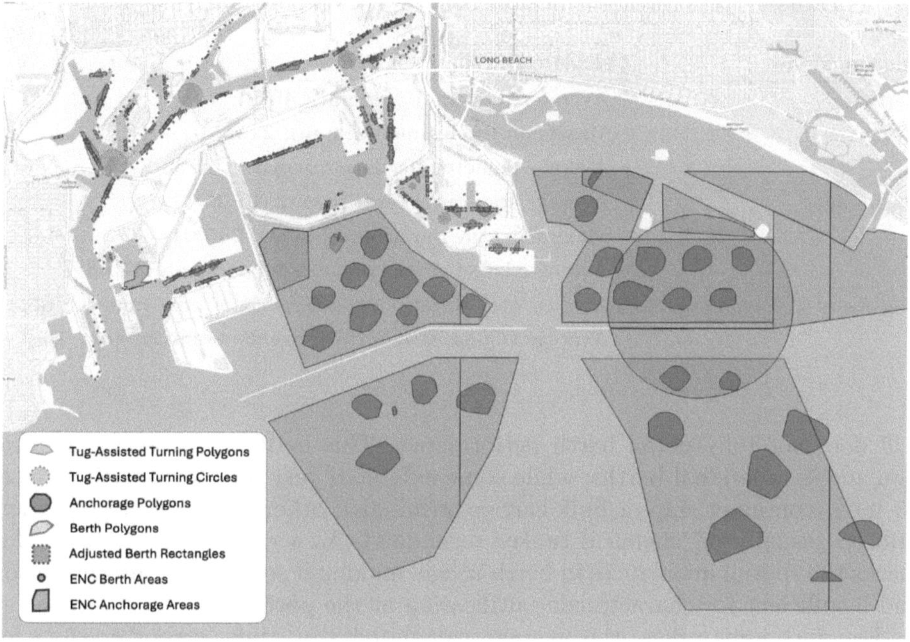

Fig. 2. Visualisation of the area delineation results for port of Los Angeles in August 2024.

and can bias the duration-based performance indicators. Therefore, temporally proximate events, defined as those separated by gaps up to ten minutes within the same area, were merged, resulting in 426 berthing and 222 anchoring events. Particular caution is required in cases where different area types overlap (e.g., anchorage and turning area), leading to apparent "jumps" in AIS messages between the areas. As such occurrences were relatively infrequent, they were excluded from the analysis. Distinct events shorter than 10 min for berths and anchorages were excluded from performance analysis, as they reflect more of moving vessels that arbitrarily touch the geometric boundary. Additionally, some berthing events lasted for 2–4 weeks, indicating an extended port stay, which potentially includes vessel repairs or other operations unrelated to standard loading/unloading activities. These limitations and manual adjustments illustrate the persisting shortcomings of the current area delineation method, necessitating further improvement and fully reproducible research.

After post-processing and excluding extended stays, the longest berth stays tended to be around 6 days, while the berth with highest average dwell time was a bulk carrier terminal that accommodated 5 vessels in the month of August, with an average dwell time of 136 h and 24 min. Shorter dwell times were seen at berths which accommodated smaller vessels. The berth occupancy rate calculations were biased by the rectangle merging procedure; after adjusting for these changes, the average berth occupancy rate of 30.22% (excluding extended stays)

Table 2. Performance indicators of the detected port functional areas

Functional area	Calculated evaluation metrics
Berths	– Average dwell time (hh:mm): **49:01** – Maximum dwell time (hh:mm): **216:23** – Average detected berth occupancy rate: **30.22%**
Anchorages	– Average stay duration (hh:mm): **40:25** – Maximum stay duration (hh:mm): **245:01** – Average detected anchorage occupancy rate **37.68%**:
Tug-Assisted Turning Areas	– Average stay duration, tug-assisted turning (mm:ss): **05:11** – Average tug-assisted turning events within an area: **10**

still does not fully detail berth performance. This is due to substantial variation across individual berths; while some exhibited very high utilisation rates of 70–90% (container ship or bulk carrier terminals), others were relatively underutilised (usually oil/chemical tanker terminals). As a result, the average value masks the spatial imbalances in berth usage, making it sensitive to interpretation and insufficient for characterising utilisation at the port level.

For anchorage areas, the average calculated stay time is shorter than for berths. This could be due to the method differentiating between separate subareas in the broader ENC-defined anchorage zone. Hence, when a vessel moves from one anchorage polygon to another, these are considered separate events, despite both contributing to the total stay at anchor. Anchorage stays lasting longer than three days were quite common, with 40 recorded events. However, several vessels showed anchorage shifting, meaning the total of longer anchorage stays may be even higher. For tug-assisted turning areas, initial analysis encompassed all trajectory events, both passing and turning, whereas the former proved more cumbersome than expected, due to some circles overlapping with berth or anchorage zones. Thus, to ensure meaningful interpretation, the analysis focused on tug-assisted turning behaviour in these areas, showing 95 events, and average event duration of 05:11 (Minutes:Seconds). In future studies, however, in-depth analysis of turning versus passing through events in such areas could prove valuable.

The method can also be applied for individual vessel analysis to support detailed follow-up analysis, for example in investigating anchorage waiting times. For instance, a crude oil tanker entered an anchorage area on 12/08/2024 06:52, shifted to a closer anchorage on 22/08/2024 12:45, staying there until an assumed tug operations commenced on 25/08/2024 23:17. Then, a berth visit was recorded at 25/08/2024 23:52 for ensuing 28 h. After the berth visit ended on 27/08/2024 04:13, another 6-minute tug-assisted manoeuvre occurred in the nearby turning area. Thus, even though the berthing event lasted one day, the vessel spent 13 days at anchor prior. Similar prolonged anchorage patterns were observed for several other crude oil tankers, potentially reflecting the vessel type's port call behaviour, and potential commercial or operational strategies (like waiting for better oil prices).

4 Discussion

The presented workflow demonstrates how trajectory point clustering and polygonisation can facilitate granular analysis of port nautical infrastructure areas and their usage patterns. However, the results must be appropriately interpreted. Since the functional areas are derived from the trajectories themselves, the resulting performance metrics only reflect the time spent *within those* trajectory-defined operational regions, which is not necessarily reflective of the area's definitive performance. A meaningful performance inference depends on the accuracy of area delineation relative to external ground truth. Additionally, AIS-based zones may change over time due to inherent variations in traffic density, which affects the robustness and consistency of delineation results. Temporal robustness could be evaluated by deriving polygons across multiple time periods and comparing them using spatial overlap metrics such as Intersection-over-Union. Combining polygons from multiple observation windows may improve the reliability of the area estimations. At the same time, the temporal sensitivity could be considered advantageous as it enables detecting changes in nautical infrastructure use that may not otherwise be apparent from static maps. This makes it potentially valuable in contexts where official geometries are unavailable or where detailed operational insights across multiple areas are required.

5 Conclusion

This paper demonstrates a method to delineate three port nautical infrastructure areas (berths, anchorages, and tug-assisted turning), followed by constructing descriptive usage indicators within these areas. First, AIS data are analysed to reveal behavioural patterns pertaining to direct course, stopping or tug-assisted turning. Two latter behavioural categories are clustered using DBSCAN, and polygonised using convex hull algorithm, whereas the stationary polygons are further clustered with K-means to differentiate between anchorage and berth areas. Berth and anchorage areas are validated with ENCs. Performance indicators are calculated with individual trajectory-based analysis. The workflow combines the domain of port area delineation with multi-indicator usage analysis, and could support decisions related to congestion monitoring, berth planning, nautical infrastructure utilisation, safety analysis, and capacity expansion. In future studies, the workflow's methodological limitations should be addressed: behaviour segmentation could be improved through clustering or matheuristics approaches; clustering stage needs more systematic parameter selection or alternative density-based methods; area validation should be strengthened, potentially through the integration of satellite imagery for quay and berth detection; and post-processing and event analysis should be expanded with full reproducibility ensured across different time and spatial characteristics.

Acknowledgments. This research is financially supported by SmartPort, which is a collaboration between the Port of Rotterdam, Universities, Institutes, and Companies in the Dutch Inland Waterway Transport (IWT)-sector.

Disclosure of Interests. The authors have no competing interests to declare that are relevant to the content of this article.

References

1. Bai, X., Ma, Z., Hou, Y., Li, Y., Yang, D.: A data-driven iterative multi-attribute clustering algorithm and its application in port congestion estimation. IEEE Trans. Intell. Transp. Syst. **24**(11), 12026–12037 (2023). https://doi.org/10.1109/TITS.2023.3286477
2. Berkhin, P.: A survey of clustering data mining techniques. In: Kogan, J., Nicholas, C., Teboulle, M. (eds.) Grouping Multidimensional Data: Recent Advances in Clustering, pp. 25–71. Springer, Heidelberg (2006). https://doi.org/10.1007/3-540-28349-8_2
3. Hadjipieris, A., Dimitriou, N., Arandjelović, O.: Unsupervised port berth localization from automatic identification system data. Sensors **25**(22), 6845 (2025). https://doi.org/10.3390/s25226845
4. Peng, W., Bai, X., Yang, D., Yuen, K.F., Wu, J.: A deep learning approach for port congestion estimation and prediction. Maritime Policy Manage. **50**(7), 835–860 (2023). https://doi.org/10.1080/03088839.2022.2057608
5. Qiang, H., Niu, W., Peng, X., Li, H., Yang, Z.: PortMiner: unsupervised data mining for functional areas extraction in port areas. Transp. Res. Part E **209**, 104715 (2026). https://doi.org/10.1016/j.tre.2026.104715
6. United Nations Conference on Trade and Development: Review of maritime transport 2022. https://unctad.org/system/files/official-document/rmt2022ch4_en.pdf. Accessed 10 Apr 2026
7. Wei, Z., Meng, X., Li, X., Zhang, X., Gao, Y.: Vessel manoeuvring hot zone recognition and traffic analysis with AIS data. Ocean Eng. **266**, 112858 (2022). https://doi.org/10.1016/j.oceaneng.2022.112858
8. Wijaya, W.M., Nakamura, Y.: Port performance indicators construction based on AIS-generated trajectory segmentation and classification. Int. J. Data Sci. Anal. **20**(3), 2473–2492 (2025). https://doi.org/10.1007/s41060-024-00614-w
9. Wu, F., Liu, Y., Li, R., Voß, S.: A matheuristic framework for behavioral segmentation and mobility analysis of AIS trajectories using multiple movement features. J. Marine Sci. Eng. **13**(12) (2025). https://doi.org/10.3390/jmse13122393

AI-Based Delay Estimation for Freight Trains

Chhandosee Bhattacharya(✉), Anisa Rizvanolli, Maximilian Reimann, and Ole John

Fraunhofer Center for Maritime Logistics and Services (CML), Blohmstraße 32, 21079 Hamburg, Germany
{chhandosee.bhattacharya,anisa.rizvanolli,maximilian.reimann, ole.john}@cml.fraunhofer.de
https://www.cml.fraunhofer.de/

Abstract. Train transportation plays a crucial role in supporting the operations of maritime industry. They provide an efficient, cost-effective and environment friendly transportation between seaports and inland distribution centres shipping large volumes of cargo over long distances quickly. With scheduled services and dedicated rail networks, rail transport provides a higher level of reliability and predictability.

Managing train arrivals is an important challenge for inland terminals. Terminals typically operate within strict time constraints leaving little room for delays or disruptions. Delay in freight trains can disrupt terminal processes and lead to inefficient resource planning and customer dissatisfaction. Therefore, it is imperative to have early information about changes in expected time of arrival (ETA) of cargo trains such that logistic processes and resource allocation can be coordinated accordingly.

In recent years, multiple studies were conducted to forecast train delays and determine factors affecting it. They provided a comprehensive knowledge about performance of various algorithms ranging from regression to gradient boost and artificial neural networks. However, most studies were focused on passenger trains and research related to freight trains were very limited. This paper focuses on delay estimation for German national freight trains bound for a selected destination. Additionally, it tackles the issue of constantly changing intermediate stations for running trains and for journeys on the same route.

The aim of this study is to predict arrival delay of freight trains arriving at destination considering factors like historical delay, calendar data, geographical and meteorological parameters. The task was designed as a sequence prediction problem, and a multi-step multi-variate LSTM model was used to achieve the goal. The chosen model offered an advantage of capturing spatial and temporal dependencies and handle non-linear relationships in a multi-variate setting.

With this study, it was possible to observe the busiest routes to the destination, distribution of delays across different states of Germany, patterns of lateness in freight trains throughout the day/week and achieve a realistic estimation compared to existing baseline methods. The LSTM model achieved an MAE of 49.5 min and an RMSE of 76 min,

J. de Armas and E. Lalla Ruiz (Eds.): LOGMS 2026, LNCS 16679, pp. 297–307, 2027.
https://doi.org/10.1007/978-3-032-30795-8_25

outperforming the baseline, particularly when the train is far from its destination, indicating potential to enhance terminal efficiency and customer satisfaction.

Keywords: eta prediction · maritime logistics · data-driven models · LSTM

1 Introduction

Freight trains are vital in supply chain logistics, offering a reliable, cost-efficient and environment friendly alternative for transporting goods between seaports and dry port terminals. They reduce greenhouse gas emissions [7] and overall logistics costs by minimizing truck transportation distances and leveraging large cargo capacities [5]. Despite its benefits, rail freight accounted for only 19% of Germany's inland transport in 2021 [8], significantly lower than the 73.6% share held by road transport [6]. This gap highlights the need for research to make rail transport more appealing to stakeholders.

Freight train transportation in Germany involves various stakeholders operating through peer-to-peer contracts and information exchanges, all of whom must coordinate their actions to ensure timely arrivals. The primary actors include:

- **Railway Transport Companies:** These companies are chiefly responsible for transporting the freight.
- **Wagon Owners:** These entities own the wagons, though often the railway transport companies themselves also own the wagons.
- **Railway Infrastructure Companies:** They maintain and operate the infrastructure and allocate slots, such as those in port terminals, for the freight trains of transport companies.
- **Shunting (Switching) Service Providers:** These providers handle the movement of rail vehicles, excluding train movements. Their tasks include forming, breaking up, and reconfiguring trains, as well as operating points of use or additional facilities like port terminals. Their services encompass moving groups of wagons or individual vehicles to different station tracks or repositioning locomotives at terminals.

The interaction among these services, and their coordination with terminals, is complex and significantly affects the propagation of delay information. Often, the lack of a robust contractual framework prevents terminal operators from requesting and receiving real-time ETA information promptly. These challenges highlight the necessity for tools that provide more reliable data.

Handling cargo trains is one of the important terminal operations as it involves meticulous planning and allocation of resources such as equipment, personnel, tracks, and storage space. Delays in train arrivals can lead to customer dissatisfaction and compromised service quality, particularly affecting truckers who collect or drop off containers, may face prolonged wait times resulting in congestion near gates. Knowledge of train arrivals can greatly assist terminal operators to optimize logistic processes and ensure a smooth transition to hinterland transport.

The objective of this paper is to develop a forecasting model to estimate train arrival times at Nürnberg Hafen starting from the train's departure point. The presented model incorporates historical delays, geographical factors, meteorological conditions and influence of weekdays/weekends and peak/off-peak hours. Additionally, it addresses the challenge of changing intermediate stations during an on-going journey. Our research seeks to answer the following questions:

1. How beneficial will our research be for optimizing terminal activities at Nürnberg Hafen?
2. Does our method provide significant improvement over the chosen baseline method?

The scope of the study is limited to German national freight trains traveling to Nürnberg Hafen and based on data collected from April 2022 to December 2023.

The rest of this paper is organized as follows: Sect. 2 reviews existing research on freight transport, highlighting the unique aspects of our experiment. Section 3 details the study's workflow, including data collection, data cleaning and the proposed forecasting methodology. This is followed by an evaluation of the model's performance in Sect. 4. Finally, Sect. 5 presents our concluding remarks, discusses existing challenges, and offers recommendations for further improvements in this field.

2 Literature Review

In recent years, machine learning, simulation and optimization techniques have been investigated to analyse and predict arrival time of trains. With the advancement in data-driven approaches and availability of train delay data, it makes sense to attempt to mitigate this problem. In this paper, the focus is mainly on research that used machine learning to addresses the problem of train delays.

A variety of machine learning models have been tried out in the past along with an analysis about factors affecting train delay. The related work helps to get an insight about performance of different models, and railway situation in different countries.

Oneto et al. (2018) [3] developed a data driven Train Delay Prediction System (TDPS) for large scale railway networks, leveraging in-memory data processing for enhanced efficiency. Laifa et al. (2021) [2] examined the prediction of arrival delays in Tunisian passenger trains, comparing LightGBM with other widely used models. Zhang et al. (2022) [9] focused on train delay prediction at high-speed railway stations in China, incorporating spatiotemporal characteristics of train operation data and external influences. Pineda-Jaramillo et al. (2023) [4] explored data-driven approaches for forecasting short-term arrival delays in freight rail operations, identifying key factors such as departure delay, trip distance and train composition. Barbour et al. (2018) [1] aimed to estimate freight train arrival times in the United States by considering train characteristics, network conditions and potential traffic conflicts.

Most of the work mentioned here address the problem of passenger train delay and there is very limited work done for freight trains. Our paper contributes to this area by trying to predict arrival times of freight trains that originate within Germany and arrive at Nürnberg terminal.

3 Research Process and Methodology

This section outlines the systematic process flow of our study with a visual illustration in Fig. 1. It starts with a description of input data along with their respective sources and further details handling of missing data and unnecessary information. Subsequently, an exploratory analysis shows hidden patterns and provide more insights into the data. The final section explains the selected modelling approach and rationale for its selection. The next steps are designed as follows:

3.1 Data Collection
3.2 Preprocessing & Feature Engineering
3.3 Exploratory Analysis
3.4 Model Training

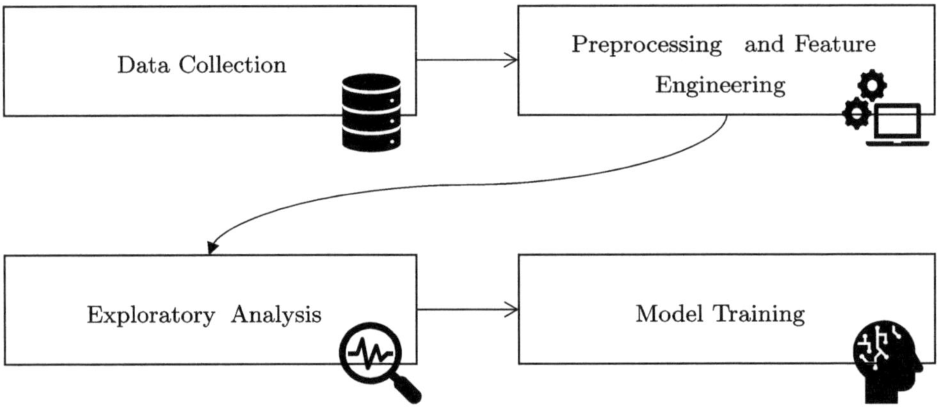

Fig. 1. Process flow of conducted research work.

3.1 Data Collection

The methodology outlined in this paper utilized various features to predict Estimated Time of Arrival (ETA) for freight trains. A concise overview of input data is provided in Table 1. Historical delay data for cargo trains originating within Germany and bound for Nürnberg Hafen was sourced from RNE's (Rail Net Europe) TIS portal (Train Information System). TIS is an online platform offering real-time information on the operation of national and international passenger and freight trains. Weather information was gathered on an hourly basis from Meteostat, a provider of open weather and climate data sourced from reputable entities such as the National Oceanic and Atmospheric Administration (NOAA) and Germany's national meteorological service (DWD). Meteostat provides both historical observations & future estimations and is conveniently accessible via a Python library. Calendar and route-related parameters were derived from existing data. The study is based on data collected from April 6, 2022 to December 12, 2023.

Table 1. Summary of employed input features.

Parameters	Attributes
Historical delay	Delay in previous stations
Route	Station names, distance to destination, route identifier
Calendar	Hour, weekday, season
Weather	Air temperature, dew point, relative humidity, precipitation, snow depth, average wind speed, average sea-level air pressure

3.2 Preprocessing and Feature Engineering

In this section, we detail the process of handling missing data and imputing values to ensure the completeness and accuracy of our dataset. Not all journeys could be included in our study as there were some which had no delay information throughout their entire run. As mentioned earlier, trains do not always follow their planned routes, which can be identified by checking the actual arrival times. If the actual arrival time is missing for a station, it means the train did not pass through that station, and those records can be deleted. After this, there were 1.4% missing data for station delays, which were fully imputed. Delays were calculated where both planned and actual arrival times were available. For the rest, average delay values from the previous and next stations on each journey were used. For the weather data, we checked the five nearest weather stations and used the closest one with available information. Any remaining missing values were imputed with the average values for the regions the train passed through during its journey. The calendar parameters were calculated from actual arrival times at each station. Several other parameters were present in the collected dataset; however, they were excluded from consideration either due to their irrelevance to train delays or high proportion of missing values.

3.3 Exploratory Analysis

The data was analysed to observe significant trends, anomalies, and dependencies within the dataset, thereby laying the groundwork for subsequent modelling and predictive analysis. The collected data consisted of historical delay information for 2875 unique train runs to Nürnberg Hafen originating from 30 different stations within Germany. The analysis provided insights into distribution of count of trains handled per day and delays at Nürnberg Hafen over the period of 1.5 years. Additionally, it was interesting to observe how train operations varied between weekdays and weekends, as well as during peak and off-peak hours.

Figure 2 illustrates the distribution of freight trains to Nürnberg Hafen from various German states (left) alongside their average delay (in minutes) upon arrival (right). Among 2875 train runs, 45% trains commenced from Hamburg, followed by 25% from Niedersachsen, 19% from Bremen, 7% from Bavaria, 3% from North Rhein Westphalia and remaining 1% from other states. Trains originating from Hamburg and Bremen exhibit very high average delay of 110 and 74 min respectively and Bavarian-origin trains demonstrate a lower mean delay of 52 min, attributed to their distance from Nürnberg. Despite a smaller number of departures, trains from North Rhein Westphalia incur a relatively higher mean delay of 89 min while Niedersachsen-origin trains display the least mean lateness of 30 min reflecting distinct operational dynamics.

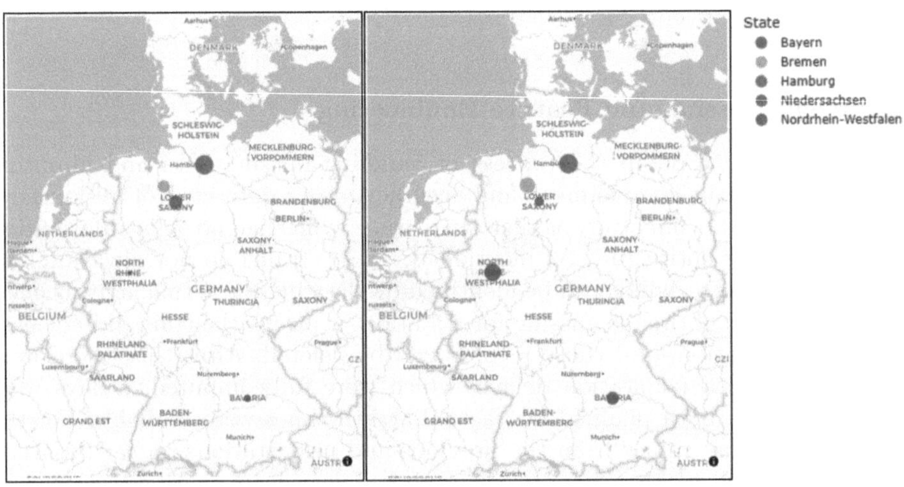

Fig. 2. Total count of Nürnberg Hafen bound freight trains originating from different German states (left). Average arrival delay (minutes) at Nürnberg Hafen for trains originating from German states (right).

Figure 3 illustrates the average arrival delay of cargo trains (top) and the number of trains (bottom) arriving at Nürnberg Hafen during peak/off-peak hours daily. Delays peak midweek from Wednesday to Friday with lowest delay observed on Sunday, likely influenced by corresponding train frequency. Interestingly, Tuesday exhibits relatively low mean delay despite high train volumes. Rush hour periods (06:00–10:00 & 15:00–19:00) significantly impact train delays, particularly for cargo trains which face priority challenges against passenger trains. Trains arriving between 15:00–19:00 experience the highest mean delay despite lower train volumes, whereas trains during 19:00–05:00 encounter lesser delay despite higher volumes.

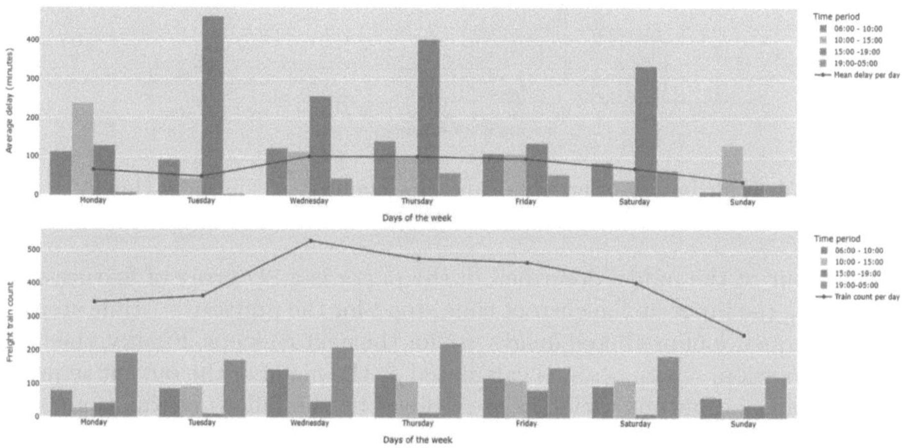

Fig. 3. Average arrival delay (in minutes) at Nürnberg Hafen during peak/off-peak hours daily (top). Total count of freight trains arriving at Nürnberg Hafen during peak/off-peak hours daily (bottom).

Figure 4 depicts the distribution of arrival delays (in minutes) at Nürnberg Hafen. Approximately 30% of trains arrived 1.5 h late while another 30% arrived 1.5 h early. Around 13% of trains experienced delays ranging from 1.5 to 3 h, and 10% were delayed by 3 to 6 h. Moreover, approximately 8% of trains encountered very high delays spanning from 6 to 20 h.

3.4 Model Training

This study used a multi-step, multivariate Long Short-Term Memory (LSTM) model. LSTMs are a type of recurrent neural network (RNN) designed to recognize underlying patterns in sequential data, capture spatial and temporal relationships, retain long-term dependencies, and handle non-linear relationships in a multivariate setting. These advantages made it a suitable choice for our task.

An LSTM model consisting of four layers was employed, including an input layer, two hidden LSTM layers with sigmoid activation functions, and an output layer with a linear activation function. The model was trained using the Adam optimizer with mean squared error (MSE) as the loss function. For each train journey, 85% of the data was used for training and the remaining 15% for testing.

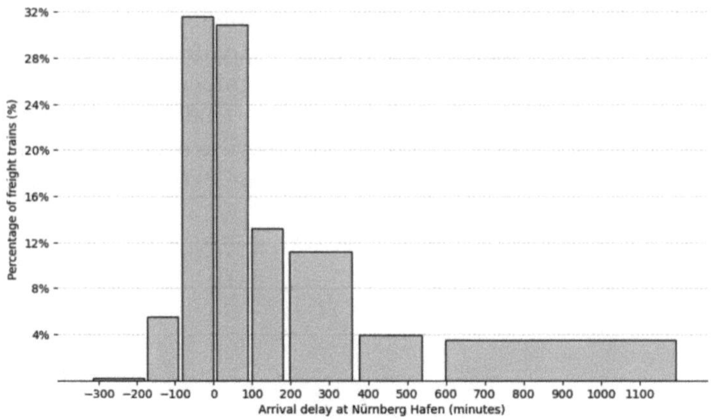

Fig. 4. Distribution of arrival delays (in minutes) at Nürnberg Hafen.

The input to the model described in the paper is a 2D array of features, X_t, representing the input at the current time step t for the previous n_1 time steps. It returns a sequence of predicted delays, $\hat{y}_t$, for the next n_2 steps. Finally, the delay at the destination, $\hat{\delta}_{t,\text{destination}}$, is calculated as the mean of the output sequence $\hat{y}_t$. The input and output variables are defined by the following equation:

$$\mathbf{X}_t = \begin{bmatrix} \delta_{t-n_1+1} & \cdot & \cdot & \cdot & \cdot & \cdot & \cdot & \cdot & \cdot & \cdot & \cdot & \cdot & \cdot & \rho_{t-n_1+1} \\ \vdots & \vdots & \vdots & \vdots & \vdots & \vdots & \vdots & \vdots & \vdots & \vdots & \vdots & \vdots & \vdots & \vdots \\ \delta_t & S_t & O_t & D_t & h_t & w_t & s_t & Te_t & Td_t & RH_t & Pr_t & Sn_t & Ws_t & \rho_t \end{bmatrix} \tag{1}$$

$$\hat{\mathbf{y}}_t = \left[\hat{\delta}_{t+1}\ \hat{\delta}_{t+2} \cdots \hat{\delta}_{t+n_2}\right] \tag{2}$$

$$\hat{\delta}_{t,\text{destination}} = \frac{1}{n_2}\sum_{i=1}^{n_2} \hat{\delta}_{t+i} \tag{3}$$

4 Model Evaluation

The model was evaluated using a set of train journeys, $T = \{T_1, T_2, \ldots, T_m\}$, where each T_i traversed n stations, $S_i = \{S_{i1}, S_{i2}, \ldots, S_{in}\}$ for $i \in [1, 416]$. The deviation (in minutes) was estimated at Nürnberg Hafen for each T_i at each passing station S_{ij}. The deviation was calculated as the absolute value of the difference between actual delay and predicted delay at the destination, $d_{ij} = \delta_{i,\text{destination}} - \hat{\delta}_{ij,\text{destination}}$ for $j \in [1, n-1]$. Each journey T_i had a range of predictions throughout its journey, yielding a minimum, mean, and maximum value for deviation, $d_{i,\min} = \min_{1 \leq j < n} d_{ij}$, $d_{i,\text{mean}} = \frac{1}{n-1} \sum_{j=1}^{n-1} d_{ij}$, $d_{i,\max} = \max_{1 \leq j < n} d_{ij}$, respectively. These values were used as the basis for performance evaluation of the model.

A common method of estimating delays is equating the delay at the destination to the delay at the most recently known station. This method was used as the baseline for comparison with our model. Predictions on the test dataset were made using this approach. In this method, $\hat{\delta}_{ij,\text{destination}} = \delta_{ij}$ for $j \in [1, n-1]$. The minimum, mean, and maximum values for deviation (in minutes) at the destination were calculated using the same formula as above, and those values were used for comparison.

Table 2 summarizes the distribution of journey-level prediction errors for the LSTM and baseline models. For the LSTM model, the average deviations were 40 and 60 min for 50% and 75% of cases respectively, while maximum deviations reached about 1.5 and 2.5 h for the same percentiles. Both models exhibited similar average performance but LSTM showed improved robustness in worst-case scenarios, with lower maximum deviations compared to the baseline.

In addition to the standard baseline, a LightGBM model was included for comparison. Considering overall model performance, LSTM achieved the best results, with MAE 49.5, RMSE 76, and R^2 0.83. LightGBM model showed slightly lower accuracy, with MAE 52.6, RMSE 80.2, and R^2 0.77. The baseline performed worst, with MAE 52.7, RMSE 89.3, and R^2 0.76. All MAE and RMSE values are expressed in minutes (Table 3).

Table 2. Performance statistics of LSTM and baseline methods.

Statistics	Deviation in prediction (in minutes)			
	Average Prediction (Mean)		Worst Prediction (Maximum)	
	Baseline	LSTM	Baseline	LSTM
Max	512	521	1431	1276
Upper Fence	119	121	250	255
Q3 (75%)	64	65	136	138
Median (50%)	37	37	90	92
Q1 (25%)	23	24	58	59
Lower Fence	7	8	19	8
Min	7	8	19	8

Table 3. Summary of mathematical notations used

Symbol	Description
t	Current timestamp
n_1	Number of input timesteps
n_2	Number of output timesteps
X_t	Input matrix at tth time-step
$\hat{y}_t$	Predicted output matrix at tth time-step
T	Set of train journeys
S_i	Set of stations for ith train journey
S_t	Station at tth time-step
O_t	Train identifier number at tth time-step
D_t	Distance to destination at tth time-step
h_t	Hour of the day at tth time-step
w_t	Day of the week at tth time-step
s_t	Season at tth time-step
Te_t	Air temperature at tth time-step (°C)
Td_t	Dew point temperature at tth time-step (°C)
RH_t	Relative humidity at tth time-step (%)
Pr_t	Precipitation at tth time-step (mm)
Sn_t	Snow depth at tth time-step (mm)
Ws_t	Average wind speed at tth time-step (km/h)
ρ_t	Average sea-level air pressure at tth time-step (hPa)
δ_t	Actual delay at tth time-step (minutes)
$\hat{\delta}_t$	Predicted delay at tth time-step (minutes)
$\hat{\delta}_{\text{destination}}$	Predicted delay at destination (minutes)
$\delta_{\text{destination}}$	Actual delay at destination (minutes)
d	Deviation, difference between actual and predicted delay (minutes)

5 Conclusion and Outlook

The freight train under consideration currently experiences delays exceeding 3 h in 18% of cases, and its ETA estimation is based solely on the delay at last known station without accounting for the influencing factors considered in this study. The proposed model, which outperforms the standard baseline in overall performance, demonstrates potential to improve resource scheduling, reduce bottlenecks, and enhance operational efficiency at terminals. Furthermore, its lower error in extreme cases makes it more reliable for long-horizon predictions when the train is still far from its destination, thereby reducing uncertainty.

In our research, we faced several challenges. Firstly, intermediate stations varied for the same routes (OTNs), leading to inconsistency in data patterns. Secondly, deviations from planned schedules made it challenging to factor in the number of stations and stoppages for predictive analysis, which could have offered valuable insights. Lastly, unplanned stoppages along the route, with varying durations, added complexity to the modelling process. Despite these challenges, addressing these factors could enhance the accuracy and reliability of future predictive models.

For future work, factors like presence of other passenger trains, construction activities, halt signals, unplanned stoppages, and speed limitations could be considered. Although these elements significantly impact delays, obtaining such data is challenging. Incorporating these factors as inputs could enhance the accuracy of delay predictions.

References

1. Barbour, W., Mori, J.C.M., Kuppa, S., Work, D.B.: Prediction of arrival times of freight traffic on us railroads using support vector regression. Transp. Res. Part C: Emerg. Technol. **93**, 211–227 (2018). https://doi.org/10.1016/j.trc.2018.05.019
2. Laifa, H., Ghezalaa, H.H.B.: Train delay prediction in Tunisian railway through LightGBM model. Procedia Comput. Sci. **192**, 981–990 (2021). https://doi.org/10.1016/j.procs.2021.08.101
3. Oneto, L., et al.: Train delay prediction systems: a big data analytics perspective. Big Data Res. **11**, 54–64 (2018). https://doi.org/10.1016/j.bdr.2017.05.002
4. Pineda-Jaramillo, J., Bigi, F., Bosi, T., Viti, F., D'ariano, A.: Short-term arrival delay time prediction in freight rail operations using data-driven models. IEEE Access **11**, 46966–46978 (2023). https://doi.org/10.1109/ACCESS.2023.3275022
5. RSI Logistics: Comparing the costs of rail shipping vs truck (2024). https://www.rsilogistics.com/blog/comparing-the-costs-of-rail-shipping-vs-truck/. Accessed 15 May 2024
6. Statista Research Department: Road freight transport as a percentage of total inland freight transport in Germany from 2008 to 2021 [infographic] (2023). https://www.statista.com/statistics/1069118/germany-road-freight-share-of-inland-transport/. Accessed 15 May 2024
7. Statista Research Department: Amount of greenhouse gas emissions in german freight transport by mode of transport in 2019 and 2021 [infographic] (2024). https://de.statista.com/statistik/daten/studie/881600/umfrage/co2-emissionen-im-deutschen-gueterverkehr-nach-verkehrsmitteln/. Accessed 15 May 2024
8. Statista Research Department: Rail freight transport as a percentage of total inland freight transport in germany from 2007 to 2021 [infographic] (2024). https://www.statista.com/statistics/693223/germany-rail-freight-share-of-inland-transport/. Accessed 15 May 2024
9. Zhang, D., Xu, Y., Peng, Y., Zhang, Y., Wu, D., Wang, H., Liu, J., Mohammed, S., Calvi, A.: Prediction of train station delay based on multiattention graph convolution network. J. Adv. Transp. **2022**(1), 7580267 (2022). https://doi.org/10.1155/2022/7580267

Author Index

J. de Armas and E. Lalla Ruiz (Eds.): LOGMS 2026, LNCS 16679, pp. 309–310, 2027.
https://doi.org/10.1007/978-3-032-30795-8

MIX
Papier aus verantwortungsvollen Quellen
Paper from responsible sources
FSC® C105338

If you have any concerns about our products,
you can contact us on
ProductSafety@springernature.com

In case Publisher is established outside the EU,
the EU authorized representative is:
Springer Nature Customer Service Center GmbH
Europaplatz 3, 69115 Heidelberg, Germany

Printed by Libri Plureos GmbH
in Hamburg, Germany